UNIPRESS

United Press International
Covering the 20th Century

Richard M. Harnett AND Billy G. Ferguson

Fulcrum Publishing
Golden, Colorado

Library of Congress Cataloging-in-Publication Data

Harnett, Richard M. & Billy G. Ferguson
  Unipress : covering the 20th century / by Richard M. Harnett & Billy
G. Ferguson.
      p. cm.
Includes bibliographical references and index.
  ISBN 1-55591-481-0 (pbk. : alk. paper)
  1. United Press International—History. I. Ferguson, Billy G. II.
Title.
PN4841.U66 H37 2001
070.4'35—dc21

                              2002151742

Printed in the United States of America
0 9 8 7 6 5 4 3 2 1

Fulcrum Publishing
16100 Table Mountain Parkway, Suite 300
Golden, Colorado 80403
(800) 992-2908 • (303) 277-1623
www.fulcrum-books.com

This book is dedicated to the late Dick Harnett,
who was determined that UPI's legacy should outlive those who created it.

Contents

Foreword

THE SEEDS OF UNITED PRESS INTERNATIONAL WERE PLANTED IN TWO sprawling California estates early in the 20th century.

Publishers E.W. Scripps and William Randolph Hearst were as different in most ways as were the two lavish retreats they built to memorialize their success: Scripps' dusty Miromar Ranch in the desert near San Diego and Hearst's gaudy palace at San Simeon.

But the two men shared a vision of the power that the written word would wield in the 20th century. They also shared a common problem: the Associated Press' refusal to serve their newspapers.

In 1907, Scripps launched United Press to compete with the monopolistic Associated Press, and just two years later, Hearst formed International News Service to compete with AP and UP. It was the beginning of competition at the motherlode of the news industry

The story of how UP and INS battled the AP and each other until they joined forces in 1959, is also a story of the men and women who wrote the running history of the 20th century.

UNIPRESS, the biography of UPI, details the triumphs and travesties of the individuals who brought competition and independence to American journalism and made it the best in the world.

UPI White House Correspondent Merriman Smith was riding in the front seat of the press car just four limousines behind President Kennedy on November 22, 1963, when he heard three shots. In a split second, he grabbed the car's only mobile phone. Then, as he watched the president's convertible speed away from the motorcade, he dialed the UPI bureau in Dallas and dictated the first words that alerted the world to the assassination of America's thirty-fifth president.

"Smitty" held on with a grip of steel as his competition, AP's Jack Bell riding in the rear seat of the press car, tried to get the phone away and alert his office. But "Smitty," a fierce competitor, clung to the phone, dictating details, even as Bell frantically beat on his back.

It was the start of what has been called the greatest reporting job in America's journalism history. It was a high-water mark for United Press International.

That competitive fire that drove Merriman Smith and the rest of UPI was the legacy of a turn-of-the-century dandy who helped start the never-ending war between AP and UPI.

Diminutive Roy Howard forged United Press in his own intense image as he guided both United Press and the Scripps-Howard newspaper empire.

Like Merriman Smith, Howard lived to beat the AP and he was willing to take a chance. His dramatic "beat" on the end of World War I touched off celebrations around the world, but it stained forever his reputation and the credibility of United Press.

Howard's "beat" was based on an official telegram announcing an armistice sent to the commander of the American Navy in the French port of Brest. But the telegram was premature and Howard's flash was two days ahead of the actual end of the war.

But the history of UPI is not just the big stories and the big names, it's the achievement of people not famous, on stories long forgotten, against huge odds and their strange addiction to working endless hours for little money, even less fame, with flimsy resources and always against the clock.

It's a story also of the incredible changes of the 20th century, from the dispatches on the Lindbergh kidnapping tapped out on Morse keys and Prince Albert tobacco cans to the huge volumes of 1988 election copy collected in computers and relayed by satellites to clients at 5,600 words a minute.

Those changes played a large role in the rise and fall of the proud news agency, from its start in 1907 until 1999 when its beleaguered managers announced that UPI was leaving the wire service business and would seek new systems and new markets.

The name "UNIPRESS" was born of UP's never-ending quest to save pennies as well as to chase news. In the early days of the 20th century, telegraph and cable rates were based on so-much per word. So, United Press became Unipress in all of its transmissions and UP staffers became Unipressers.

"UNIPRESS" traces the fortunes of the world's first independent news service from 1907 when E.W. Scripps launched the United Press with what he called "a bag of wind" to the hurly-burly days of the 1960s when United Press International successfully competed head-to-head with the older and bigger Associated Press. And it examines the painful fall of UPI from the heydays of the 1970s when nearly 7,000 newspapers and broadcast clients subscribed to UPI services.

But the numbers don't tell the real story of UPI. Only those who became "Unipressers" during the ninety-two years that UPI served journalism can do that.

This history lets those men and women tell the story.

The history tells how the world-wide news wholesaler operated, in intimate detail provided by many of the 10,000 to 15,000 people who toiled for the company at some time in their careers and are still proud of being "Unipressers." It was, they usually say, the most memorable time of their working days.

The many voices are needed to tell the real story of United Press International, of why so many were willing to do so much with so little and for so little.

There was glamour and glory, but there was drudgery and disquiet. UPI's people were eager for the glory and adept at the drudgery. They loved nothing more than the big story, but they were always ready to take the daily livestock market.

In the May 1933 issue of *Fortune* magazine, the author Stephen Vincent Benet wrote:

> "UP is neither a charity nor a philanthropy. It is a business concern and its members work for profit. But there is another motive that drives them quite as strongly. You can call it pride of profession or professional zest or enthusiasm or self-hypnosis. But, whatever you call it, it is as common to the stockholding executives to the lunch-money copy boy—it is indeed the strongest of bonds that holds UP together. And what it boils down to, when the sentiment and the wisecracks are both skimmed off, is an actual and genuine love of the game."

E.W. Scripps, the founder of United Press, built his newspaper empire from a shoestring. He started UP with, he said, a few dollars and "a bag of wind." Yet, he said, it was the best thing he ever did.

Scripps is generally pictured as a maverick publisher, a political liberal and friend of labor. This history discloses that he was, in reality, a cunning, conservative businessman who happened to understand that most newspaper readers were not capitalists.

E.W. advocated infanticide to limit the population, he demeaned women and was a racial and religious bigot.

The dark side of E.W. Scripps has been overlooked by subsidized biographers. It is not overlooked in *Unipress.*

E.W., who rarely left his ranch at Miromar, was proud of the fact that he had no hands-on relationships with his newspaper or UP. But he knew how to get the most from others.

Scripps' business plan was simple. He gave underlings a stake in what he called the "concern"—always a minority stake—which would have no value until they paid for the shares with dividends they earned for themselves and for him.

William Randolph Hearst, who founded the International News Service, was the antitheses of the reclusive Scripps. He was born to immense wealth, inherited his first newspaper, the *San Francisco Examiner,* and became totally involved in running the paper. "Citizen" Hearst pioneered sensational news coverage, later called "yellow journalism." One-sided reports in Hearst's newspapers of Spanish atrocities in Cuba are generally credited with starting the Spanish-American war.

The soul of United Press at the start was Roy Howard, the diminutive dynamo who was the first general manager of the news agency. Given almost no resources, Howard scratched like a cornered bobcat to get news and sell it. He traveled the world, signing on clients in Europe, South America and Asia, where all other new agencies were handcuffed by the cartel that Reuters dominated.

Howard was always personally out in front, interviewing world leaders, covering a boxing match, pleading with a publisher to buy the UP wire. His enthusiasm and enterprise, even his frugality, were infectious.

Unipress provides intimate looks at those who followed Howard at the helm of UP and later UPI.

The first was Karl Bickel, a dapper, well-bred gentleman who started his journalism career by walking 35 miles to San Francisco to help cover the great earthquake of 1906. He was president from 1922 to 1935. It was Bickel's vision that saw the infant broadcasting industry as a vehicle for news as well as entertainment.

After Bickel came Hugh Baillie, a formidable, crewcut, Marine-like battle tank. The one-time gun-toting crime reporter kept a bayonet as a paper weight on his desk and directed United Press into what author Reynolds Packard called "whambo-zambo" journalism, putting life and drama into news coverage.

Frank Bartholomew (1955–1962) was the last of UPI's reporter-presidents. He was an occasional correspondent at the front in World War II and Korea. When he took over the presidency he had one burning obsession. He wanted to get International News Service, Hearst's wire, and bring it into United Press. He succeeded and UP became UPI in the spring of 1958.

After Bartholomew, UPI turned to the business side for its leadership, spurred by a growing flow of red ink. First it was Mims Thomason and then Rod Beaton, but neither could stop UPI's losses.

In 1982, Scripps Howard gave up on UPI and sold it for one dollar to two men who called themselves "entrepreneurs," but had little experience as managers and none in the business of producing and selling news.

Bill Geissler and Doug Ruhe picked Bill Small as their president, but the former network news chief, shared their lack of knowledge in news wholesales and soon the turnstile to the top of UPI was spinning as fast as UPI was plummeting toward oblivion. UPI had thirteen chief executives in the seventeen years after UPI was sold.

UNIPRESS charts the influence of these men with the news events that made the history of the 20th century. More importantly, it digs deeply into the workings, the people and soul of UPI.

Acknowledgments

UNITED PRESS INTERNATIONAL'S MUSCLE WAS THE ROUNDUP, WHERE reporters and editors around the world dug up, distilled and delivered timely information for statewide, nationwide and worldwide summaries of significant and compelling news.

This history, too, is a roundup of information gathered by thousands of men and women who shared the believe that UPI was more than just a job and deserved a legacy.

Some whose contributions were so vital to this history must be named: H. L. Stevenson, long-time editor of UPI, started collecting materials for this book but wrote only an introduction before his death; Al Webb, who circled the globe as a UPI reporter and editor; Peter S. Willett, a working executive who wore all the hats at UPI; Tom Foty, the reporter-editor and unofficial historian of UPI Audio; Carl Lundquist, the onetime master of big league baseball roundups; Preston McGraw, the gifted writer and dogged reporter who hefted the coffin of presidential assassin Lee Harvey Oswald when others would not.

New York News editor Donald Mullen and Wesley Pippert, whose career ranged from the plains of South Dakota to the United States Senate, provided vital information as did former Financial Editor Dorthea Brooks and Lillian O'Connell of Special Services, Michael Freedman, who directed UPI's audio network, and Lonnie Falk, who helped cover the civil rights movement in the South.

Other major contributions came from Martin Murphy and Jack Warner, who worked the Atlanta news desk; Larry Lorenz, a former news editor on the National Broadcast desk in Chicago; Al Kaff and Pat Killen, whose beats ranged from New York and Washington to Asia; Al Kuettner, who directed UPI's civil rights coverage from Atlanta, and Mike Rabin, the reporter-sportwriter, who was locked in a garage at the Dallas police station after witnessing the assassination of Lee Harvey Oswald.

Two earlier UPI histories were extremely helpful, *Deadline Every Minute* by the late Joe Alex Morris, and *Down to the Wire* by Gregory Gordon and Ronald Cohen

Four former top executives, President Roderick Beaton; Vice President-General Manager Frank Tremaine, Vice President and General Manager Robert E. Page and Vice President and Sales Manager Wayne Sargent gave us never-before published correspondence and recollections. UP Australia Manager George McCadden; sales executive Robert Bennhoff; and war correspondent and manager Robert C. Miller helped document UPI's Asian operations.

Many, many more helped with research, editing, ideas and unflagging support. However, none helped with these vital chores more than Joyce Harnett and Betty Ferguson.

Introduction

By H. L. Stevenson

THE EYEWITNESS HAS BEEN THE CORNERSTONE OF HISTORY.

Without someone to observe, to tell others, to record for posterity, there would be no history, nothing to trace the development of humankind, the rise and fall of civilization.

From the scribes of ancient Egypt, putting down their observations on the flattened and dried leaves of a plant called papyrus, to the battlefield images relayed instantly from the sand dunes of the Persian Gulf by satellite, man has depended on surrogates to enlighten, entertain and educate.

In the process, most will agree, two witnesses have always been better than one.

Two sets of eyes. Two sets of ears. Two brains distilling and organizing the details observed by someone who was fortunate enough to be standing close by, within earshot, within sight, of history, major and minor, as it was made.

In the 20th century, much of the task of eyewitnessing history fell to men and women who called themselves reporters. They were the paid, poorly by most comparisons, representatives of newspapers, magazines, radio and television stations, speaking and writing in a hundred tongues.

A special breed of eyewitness emerged, the men and women of the news services. Two, in particular, United Press International and The Associated Press, often were the sole surrogates for everyone else.

As the population of the world swelled, war and famine and floods ravaged every part of the planet, and man learned to fly, eventually deeper into the heavens, the news services became the primary witnesses to everything of significance, as well as lesser events, in every part of the globe.

Historians have an advantage in that they go to work after the roar of the cannon, the rush of the water, the end of the conflict. They can interview, review, reconstruct, and record the facts from those who took part, or were fortunate enough to emerge alive from a cataclysmic upheaval.

The UPI and the AP, also known as wire services or news agencies, wrote history as it occurred.

"A UPI Man Is at the Scene," read the promotional blurbs, later changed to read, "A UPI Reporter Is at the Scene," because so many of the agency's reporters were women.

With the growing need for pictorial, as well as written, history, photographers were there, too, and the list of war casualties, dead and wounded, included a score or more of shooters and scribblers.

UPI began as United Press in 1907, to challenge the already-entrenched AP. It became United Press International when it swallowed up a lesser, but vigorous, competitor, International News Service.

It closed the gap in size and resources but fell far short of true parity with the larger Associated Press, a goal that drove the UPI for most of its existence.

For well over three-quarters of the 20th century, the two news services were fierce competitors, with correspondents and photographers stationed throughout the world, the heaviest concentration in the United States.

In addition to two major world wars, they reported in daily detail on scores of regional conflagrations, hundreds of natural disasters, hundreds of human conflicts, and thousands of personal stories of bravery, success, failure and daring do.

"What do the wires say?" was often the first question editors all over the world asked as they debated whether they could provide their own coverage, or rely on the news agencies to inform their audience. Most often, they relied on the wires.

UPI and AP served as the early alert force, the fire bell ringing in the night, the sentry firing a signal shot or two from a distant outpost, the weathervane pointing the direction of the gale, the messenger riding hard in the night bearing news of a battle won or lost.

This is a history of UPI's role in the brawling, bare-knuckled, toe to toe fight with the AP, the battles won and lost, the UPI people who fought them, and finally the agonizing demise of United Press International in the last few years of the century.

It is written as the smaller agency clung to life with forces a fraction the size of the wealthier and still growing Associated Press.

Some will ask, was the competition necessary?

The answer is still to come, but there is a mountain of evidence that it propelled the news gathering capability of the United States media, and much of the world's, to its loftiest heights.

The readers of daily newspapers, those who listened to radio, and the many millions who came to depend on the tube for information were the real beneficiaries.

Now AP survives alone as a wire service, despite efforts by various owners to keep UPI alive. Without the competition of old to keep it on its toes, its job is a vastly tougher challenge.

The UPI's ranks were filled with reporters who went on to fame, to writing history at a more leisurely pace, to success running large newspapers and networks, to places of distinction in the academic, business and legal world. A few even became men of God.

Their reflections of their UP and UPI careers offer partial answers to the reason for the competition, and for the information it furnished a waiting world.

From that flow of knowledge, history is written.

J. Wallace Carroll was one of the pioneers, a reporter for UP in London and Europe before World War II, later a distinguished Washington bureau chief for *The New York Times*, then a prominent publisher of the dailies in Winston-Salem, North Carolina.

He recalled that as rumors of war swept Europe as Adolf Hitler rose to power, the UP's man in Berlin, Fred Oechsner, wrote story after story reflecting skepticism of the public statements about peace from Hitler. The UP man was ostracized by the Nazi Party, put at the tail end of motorcades, shunned and bullied.

AP's correspondent, Louis Lochner, at the same time, was reporting the Fuhrer's pronouncements of nonaggression with the solemnity of a church warden reading from a bishop's manifesto.

Carroll, harking to those dark days of 1939, remembered the September weekend when UP's dispatch from Berlin hinted that war, starting with a surprise invasion, seemed imminent, while the AP was downplaying the possibility and relaying Hitler's renewed promise of peace.

Within hours, Nazi troops occupied Poland.

The news did not surprise readers of the UP's dispatches. Some papers, Carroll recalled, printed both the UP and AP stories in their Sunday editions, leaving it for the reader to mull the possibilities.

The war in Vietnam came to an end in 1975, after more than 20 years of fighting, with the forces of North Vietnam advancing on the capital of the southern half of the country, Saigon.

Thousands of American troops and terrified Vietnamese were being airlifted to safety, including most of the large Western press corps.

AP's Peter Arnett, a tough New Zealander who had spent more time covering combat in Vietnam than any other reporter, let it be known he intended to remain to record the arrival of the conquering North Vietnamese.

He reasoned why leave after all those months in the rice paddies, watching Americans and Vietnamese and their allies die in what by now was widely acknowledged as a futile engagement?

Leon Daniel, an equally tough combat reporter for UPI from the hills of Tennessee, himself a veteran of combat in Korea, said the words that Arnett was saying made his own decision easy.

"We stay," he said, and he did, along with colleague Alan Dawson.

For several weeks, the outside world relied on every word, even if sparing, filed by two reliable sources in Saigon, until the victorious Communists ushered Daniel, Arnett and a few of their colleagues to the airport, having decided they had stayed long enough. Dawson stayed even then and was the last American correspondent in Vietnam.

While the world was still in shock following the assassination of President John F. Kennedy in Dallas, the man who pulled the rifle trigger that killed the youthful president himself was assassinated in the basement of the jail where he was being held.

Kennedy's body was flown almost immediately to Washington on the day he died, November 22, 1963.

Lee Harvey Oswald was gunned down the following day by a Dallas nightclub owner named Jack Ruby, who stepped from a crowd in the basement of the jail, as Oswald was being ushered to a vehicle that would take him elsewhere.

Oswald's body lay unclaimed and police tried to recruit pallbearers for his funeral from among local reporters. Preston McGraw volunteered. He was UPI bureau manager in Dallas and considered one of the best writers in the Southwest.

His boss, Jack Fallon, the division news editor, had quarterbacked the coverage from the moment shots rang out, mobilizing off-duty reporters, shaping every bit of detail that could be offered by the staff. Merriman Smith, the UPI White House correspondent, was a couple of hundred feet behind Kennedy, and instantly seized the car phone, dictating the first word and tying up the phone with other details while his AP competitor pounded him on the back trying to wrest the instrument for his own initial report. Smith won the Pulitzer prize for his coverage.

McGraw, nine years later, offered some thoughts about the art of pulling together and writing the big stories he had covered or written.

In the October 14, 1972, UPI Log, an internal publication for staff members, he said:

> "Every chance you get, be a reporter. Visit the police, the sheriff's office, city hall, the courts, look at a wreck, or where a storm has passed or a body in the morgue.
>
> A person who writes about things he has never seen is going to wind up writing about things as he thinks they ought to be, and that is bad."

It was more than sufficient explanation for his volunteering to be a pallbearer for the slain assassin of John F. Kennedy.

It could serve as the credo for thousands of reporters who toiled during nearly a century for UP and UPI, then moved on to other things. They wore proudly their badges of service and talked fondly, even reverently, of the days and nights they were pitched into combat with the AP, serving as eyewitnesses to history.

1

National Tragedy and UPI at Its Best

AIR FORCE ONE LEVELED OFF AT 41,000 FEET AND HEADED NORTHEAST, out of Texas toward Washington, D.C.

In the rear compartment, Jacqueline Kennedy sat quietly in a chair next to the coffin of her husband, John F. Kennedy. Only three hours earlier she had been sitting beside the president in the sunshine as they toured, smiling and waving, through crowds in downtown Dallas.

In a forward section of the plane, President Lyndon Baines Johnson struggled to find exactly the right words to convey his feelings about the assassination that had propelled him into the highest office in America.

It was Friday, November 22, 1963, a time embedded in history.

For United Press International White House Correspondent Merriman Smith it was a time to put the tragic, unbelievable events of the last three hours into order and perspective.

Merriman Smith was a tough veteran of twenty-two years covering America's presidents. He was in Warm Springs, Georgia, when President Franklin D. Roosevelt died. He was aboard another, older presidential airliner with President Harry S. Truman when Hiroshima was destroyed by an atomic bomb.

But this trip aboard Air Force One was unrivaled. He had witnessed the assassination of an American president and met the task of reporting the tragic event quickly and accurately.

Merriman Smith, known throughout UPI and the Washington press corps as "Smitty," now had just over two hours during the flight to Washington to write a complete account that would chronicle for newspapers around the world the violent death of John F. Kennedy and the hurried elevation of Lyndon B. Johnson to the highest office in the land.

Secret Service agents, concerned that Kennedy's assassination could be part of a wider conspiracy against the United States, stepped up security around Johnson and rushed to have the vice president sworn in and returned to Washington as quickly as possible. The swearing-in ceremony was held aboard *Air Force One* with U.S. District Judge Sara T. Hughes of Dallas, a long-time friend of Johnson, administering the oath of office.

Smith barely got aboard the silver and blue 707 before the swearing-in began. He counted twenty-seven people crammed into the main compartment of the plane. The ceremony was delayed briefly while Jacqueline composed herself in a small bedroom. When she finally stepped next to Johnson and his wife, Lady Bird, she was dry-eyed and still wearing the bright pink suit she wore in the motorcade, now caked with her husband's blood.

The ceremony ended at 2:38 P.M., Central Standard Time, and Johnson, the thirty-sixth American president, said firmly, "Now, let's get airborne."

Smith's portable typewriter had been misplaced in the rush to load *Air Force One* for its flight to Andrews Air Force Base. However, he was given the electric typewriter that had been used by Kennedy's personal secretary, Mrs. Evelyn Lincoln.

"Smitty" had barely started his story when President Johnson came to the table where he was working along with Charles Roberts of *Newsweek* magazine. Smith and Roberts were the "pool" reporters who flew aboard Air Force One with the responsibility to share their notes with other White House reporters, who were aboard *Air Force Two*[1]

The president told the two newsmen that he would make a short, public statement aboard *Air Force One* and repeat it when he was on the ground at Andrews.

Johnson's first official words as president were brief and moving.

"This is a sad time for all people. We have suffered a loss that cannot be weighed. For me it is a deep personal tragedy. I know the world shares the sorrow that Mrs. Kennedy and her family bear. I will do my best. That is all I can do. I ask for your help, and God's."

"Smitty" returned to his notes and tried to think back to the motorcade as it moved toward an expressway through a grass-covered park in downtown Dallas.

Merriman Smith was riding in the front seat of the press pool car, wedged between the driver and Malcolm Kilduff, acting White House press secretary for the Texas tour. The back seat was crowded with three other pool reporters, including Smith's chief rival, Associated Press White House Reporter Jack Bell.

The presidential motorcade had moved through huge crowds of Texans, who lined Dallas' Main Street despite unseasonably hot, muggy weather. The bubble top had been removed from the president's limousine, which now was approaching a labyrinth of underpasses that led to the Stemmons Expressway.

Three shots rang out. Smith recalled that the first shot sounded as if it might be a firecracker, but said the next two were unmistakably gunfire.

The press car was the fourth behind the limousine carrying President Kennedy, Jacqueline, Texas Governor John B. Connally and his wife, Nellie. Still, the reporters could see a flurry of activity by Secret Service agents as the chief executive's car slowed momentarily and then started speeding away.

"Smitty" had to make a desperate decision in a matter of seconds. Were those really gunshots and did those shots disrupt the presidential motorcade? Smith was a gun buff who often took target practice with the uniformed White House guards, and he was sure that what he heard was gunfire and that something had happened in the president's limousine.

Smith grabbed the mobile radio-telephone from its cradle in the front of the pool car and called the UPI Dallas bureau. He held in his hand the only phone in the car.

Wilborn "Bill" Hampton, a rookie newsmen who was just about to leave the bureau for the day, answered the phone and nearly froze at his typewriter when Smith shouted that he had a bulletin and that three shots had been fired at the motorcade. It seemed like the world's longest minute to the young reporter before he finally composed himself enough to write a "precede," a brief bulletin capsule that newspapers use to update a story sent earlier and already in print.

Hampton gave the bulletin to Jack Fallon, Southwest Division news editor, who quickly checked the copy, then handed it to Jim Tolbert, a veteran operator with a reputation for accuracy. Tolbert hit the "break" key on the teletypewriter to interrupt the Minneapolis bureau in the middle of a story on a murder trial. He then belled the Kennedy story onto the A-Wire, the main circuit serving UPI's newspaper clients.

PRECEDE KENNEDY
DALLAS, NOV. 22 (UPI)—THREE SHOTS WERE FIRED AT PRESIDENT KENNEDY'S MOTORCADE TODAY IN DOWNTOWN DALLAS.
JT1234PCS

Smith's words were already on their way to hundreds of newspapers, but he asked Fallon, who now had the phone, to carefully read back the copy to make sure there were no errors. Smith was taking his time and AP's Jack Bell was frantic to get the phone. Bell started pounding Smith on the back and trying to grab the phone, but "Smitty," a fierce competitor, clung doggedly to his only link to the world, methodically double-checking every word.

At the urging of the four reporters, the driver pulled the press pool car out of the line and sped in pursuit of the president's car. It was heading for Parkland Hospital.

As the pool car skidded to a stop, Smith jumped out and ran to the side of the president's limousine. The scene was overwhelming. The president was lying face down on the back seat, his head cradled by Jacqueline, who was bent over and seemed to be whispering to him. Smith could not see Kennedy's wounds, but he saw blood splattered around the seat where he had been sitting and he saw a dark stain spreading down the president's dark gray suit.

Governor Connally was on his back on the floor and his wife was holding his head and shoulders in her arms, sobbing without tears. Blood oozed from the front of his suit.

Clint Hill, a Secret Service agent assigned to Mrs. Kennedy, was leaning into the car.

"How badly was he hit, Clint?" Smitty asked.

"He's dead," Hill replied.

Smith had abandoned the pool car and its single phone. Now he searched desperately for another. As agents screamed for someone in the hospital to load the wounded onto gurneys, Smith rushed inside where he found a phone in a small cage-like office. He told a hospital worker that the president had been shot and he needed to make an emergency call. The man slid the phone to "Smitty" and told him to dial nine first. It took Merriman two tries but he reached the Dallas bureau and once again had Fallon on the horn.

Smith dictated and Fallon rolled out a flash on the A-Wire. A flash was the highest possible priority on UPI's newswires and it carried ten bells to alert news editors in papers around the world to an extremely important dispatch.

FLASH
KENNEDY SERIOUSLY WOUNDED PERHAPS FATALLY
BY ASSASSIN'S BULLET.
JT1230PCS

As he dictated the flash, litters carrying the president and the governor rolled by, behind his back. He saw the litters disappear behind two swinging doors to the emergency room.

Smith kept dictating details as he tried to sort out the confused panorama in the hospital corridor. Kilduff of the White House staff rushed back and forth, and two police captains shouted for everyone to clear the area.

Secret Service agents escorted two priests into the emergency room and they were soon followed by a police lieutenant carrying a large carton of blood for transfusions.

Fallon and veteran desker Don Smith were taking reports from Merriman Smith and other staffers who rushed to the hospital and rolled the breaking copy onto the A-Wire. The control bureau in New York had ordered all other UPI bureaus to stay off the wire so that the Dallas copy could move without delay.

Don Smith recalled that New York also ordered all bureaus to stay off the B-Wire, a second telegraph circuit used for secondary and regional news. "It kind of scared me when I realized that Jack (Fallon) and I had taken over all of UPI's news wires."

Fallon and Smith hadn't actually taken over all of UPI's wires. Just a few feet from where the two men were rushing copy onto the wire, Jud Dixon, the veteran Texas broadcast editor, was rewriting the copy "for the ear" and sending it to Texas radio and TV stations.

At Parkland, the two priests came out of the emergency room and said that Kennedy had received the last rites. They said he was alive but unconscious.

Smith hung onto his phone, even though it limited his mobility, he saw no other phones in the hospital corridor.

He was forced to move quickly when Kilduff and Wayne Hawks of the White House told reporters that Kilduff would make a statement shortly in the nurses' room on the floor above the emergency room.

"Smitty" raced up the flight of stairs, but then had to hurry to the other end of the hospital to the nurses' room. He found two other UPI reporters already there, Hampton, the rookie who took his original phone call, and Preston "Mac" McGraw, a veteran editor and reporter well known to Merriman Smith.

The three barely had time to plot their strategy before Kilduff, fighting to keep his emotions under control, announced: "President John Fitzgerald Kennedy died at approximately one o'clock."

Smith dashed to a nearby office and grabbed a phone, but the hospital switchboard was tied up and ringing busy. He raced back into the corridor where he spotted Virginia Payette, a veteran reporter and the wife of William Payette, UPI's Southwest Division manager. Smith told her to try to find a pay phone on the floor above and "Smitty" tried again to use the office phone but the switchboard was hopelessly snarled. He appealed for help to a nurse who led him through a maze of corridors to a pay phone on another floor.

When he finally reached the Dallas bureau, he was relieved to find that the young reporter Hampton and Virginia Payette had both beaten him to the punch. The flash had cleared at 1:35.

FLASH
PRESIDENT KENNEDY DEAD.
JT135PCS

Hampton had an ace in the hole when he crowded into the nurses' room for the announcement. Just before he got there, he found a pay phone, called the Dallas bureau and got UPI reporter Don Smith on the line. Hampton had Smith call him back at the pay phone and this put a lock on the line for UPI. As long as the UPI office kept the line open on its end, no one else on the other end could use it. This gave Hampton a chance to leave the phone and head for the news conference without surrendering this vital link to the bureau.

When Hampton raced from the nurses' room back to the phone, he found another reporter trying to figure out why the phone wouldn't work. Hampton told him the line belonged to UPI, grabbed the phone and dictated the flash to Don Smith.[2]

After he phoned the DA bureau and found that the flash had cleared, "Smitty" ran back to the nurses' conference room for more information from the White House. He had barely reached the room when Jiggs Fauvere, of the White House transportation staff, grabbed his arm. He said that Kilduff wanted three pool reporters to immediately fly back to Washington on *Air Force One*.

"He wants you downstairs, and he wants you right now," Fauvere said.

"Smitty" raced back downstairs and out the doors where he had first entered the hospital, only to learn that Kilduff had just pulled away in the press pool car.

Smith, Charles Roberts of *Newsweek* and Sid Davis of *Westinghouse Broadcasting* persuaded a Dallas policeman to take them to Love Field in a squad car. The reporters made it to the airport with just minutes to spare.

AP's Jack Bell had been left at the gate and had trouble catching up. He did not fly back to Washington with the presidential party, choosing instead to stay in Dallas to gather more material on the assassination.

AP's first word of the shooting came from AP staff photographer James Altgens who was assigned to cover a section of the motorcade's route. He called AP Dallas Bureau Chief Robert Johnson and said that Kennedy had been shot and that he saw blood streaming down the president's head as the dark blue Lincoln convertible rushed past him.

Johnson pounded out a bulletin that cleared AP's trunk wire at 12:40, a full ten minutes behind the UPI flash that Kennedy had been wounded, maybe fatally. AP's flash that Kennedy was dead was timed off at 1:37 P.M., just two minutes behind UPI.

It read:

FLASH
PRESIDENT KENNEDY DIED AT 1 P.M. (CST).

Even though AP was right on UPI's heels with the flash, UPI was actually pulling further ahead on the strength of Smith's fast, accurate and detailed dictation, along with a stream of material from Hampton and McGraw at the hospital.

AP's assassination story was also hobbled by two false reports, one that a Secret Service agent had been shot and another that Vice President Johnson had been wounded. Johnson had been seen sitting on a gurney in a treatment room at Parkland. Secret Service agents had taken the vice president there because the room could be secured and he could await word on the president.

"Smitty" managed one more phone call at Love Field before he boarded Air Force One. It was just two hours since he heard those three shots and worked flawlessly with other UPI staffers to make those shots heard around the world.

The first television network on the air with the UPI flash when the mortally wounded president reached Parkland was the American Broadcasting Company. At 12:36 P.M. Don Gardiner of ABC broke into daytime programming to broadcast that three shots had been fired at the president's motocade. Four minutes later, CBS broke into "When the World Turns" and Walter Cronkite, himself a former UP staffer, was on the air with the UPI bulletin.

William Manchester said in his book, *The Death of a President*, that administration officials back in Washington, including FBI Director J. Edgar Hoover, got the first word from UPI teletypes in their departments six minutes before Secret Service head-quarters heard from Roy Kellerman, the agent in charge of the Texas trip.

UPI staffers in Washington, New York and Chicago had pitched in with Dallas to turn this incredible reporting into the finest day ever for the news service that publisher E.W. Scripps incorporated in 1907 as United Press Associations with hardly any capital and what he called "a bag of wind."

The Chicago UPI bureau housed the National Broadcast Department which tailored the news of the world for 3,500 radio and television stations.

Before the shots rang out across the park that became known as the so-called grassy knoll, a UPI staffer's designation that stuck, it had been a relatively slow news day. John Pelletreau, the National Broadcast news editor, relinquished his normal spot on the "first desk" where he would have been the editor in charge. He chose to serve instead as one of the two writers who converted newspaper wire copy into copy written for the ear and formatted for broadcast. As a writer on a slow day, Pelletreau figured he could take care of some overdue paper work. John decided to entrust the responsibilities of the "first desk" to Larry Lorenz, a young "comer" who had won the respect of veteran editors with a quick, bawdy wit and an ability to write solid broadcast copy.

At 12:30 P.M., Teletype operator Henry Renwald hit a series of switches that converted the national broadcast wire from its web-like national configuration to a series of independent spokes. The routine was that for 20 minutes of every hour, the national broadcast wire was split into scores of state wires that other bureaus used to merge their local broadcast copy with the national file. Lorenz recalled that he was just about to leave for lunch and that Pelletreau had moved to a back office when he heard five bells on the A-wire.

Bill Roberts, another relative newcomer on the broadcast "second desk," stripped the bulletin from the A-wire and yelled, "Hey, look at this." The bulletin said three shots had been fired at President Kennedy's motorcade in Dallas. Lorenz hurried back to the "first desk" and told Renwald to take back control of the broadcast wire. Renwald battled with many bureaus trying to send their state copy as Lorenz typed his bulletin. It read:

BULLETIN
DALLAS—AN UNKNOWN SNIPER FIRED THREE SHOTS AT PRESIDENT KENNEDY'S MOTORCADE IN DALLAS.

Renwald tried to send the bulletin, but other bureaus kept breaking in causing the copy to garble. Renwald ordered the bureaus to stay off the wire, but it did little good. He was still trying to send the bulletin when ten bells sounded on the A-wire. Lorenz tore off the flash that Kennedy had been wounded, perhaps fatally. He told Renwald to forget trying to send the bulletin while he dashed off a shorter flash for the broadcasters. Renwald managed to get this flash on the wire without garble.

FLASH
KENNEDY SERIOUSLY WOUNDED.

Pelletreau was back at the news desk by this time and he decided to leave Lorenz and Roberts on the desk. He would write the "subs" on the Kennedy story.

Pelletreau was a veteran broadcast writer who had moved from New York to Chicago when UPI switched its broadcast headquarters to the Windy City in 1957. He was a Catholic, a life-long democrat and a romantic. He idolized the "First Family" and the promise of Camelot. Yet, he was able to choke back his emotions and write clear, concise broadcast summaries hour after hour as the bizarre story unfolded. Lorenz said Pelletreau later told him that he was saying Hail Marys as he wrote.

Lorenz' problem was to keep up with the fast-breaking developments while Renwald battled at the teletype to keep other bureaus from breaking onto the wire to send local copy. Renwald won the war and was moving developments onto the wire play-by-play.

Lorenz considered putting out a bulletin with "Smitty's" report that Secret Service Agent Clint Hill had told him Kennedy was dead. However, Larry conferred with Pelletreau who told him to wait, that Hill could not have possibly made such a determination.

Alice Guenther took over the teletype duties from Renwald at 1:30 P.M. as scheduled and was still battling to hold off bureaus trying to clean up state copy when Lorenz got the word that Kennedy was dead. He had already written a flash and had it on his desk, but Pelletreau waved it away and turned to the operator. "Alice," he said, "type 'flash President Dead.'" The young woman immediately took her hands from the keyboard, covered her face and cried "Oh my God!" Another operator saw that she had frozen and moved quickly into action.

Lorenz recalled that Jim Darr, the short and stocky chief operator, gently lifted Guenther from the chair, sat her on the floor, then leaned over the keyboard and punched the broadcast flash.[3]

FLASH
PRESIDENT DEAD
(garble) JD135pcs

UPI's headquarters was located on the twelfth floor of the *New York Daily News* Building, the stone-faced skyscraper used by Clark Kent and other reporters in the Superman movies. UPI's editorial brain trust was working behind two large, wooden, flat-top desks that lined the north wall of a cavernous general newsroom. No need for an outside view, they sat with their backs to a line of windows that looked out onto 42nd Street so they could watch the men and women who kept the UPI news machines running.

Roger Tatarian, thoughtful and intellectual, was UPI's executive editor and the man in charge. Fran Leary, crafty and politic, was managing editor. The initial bulletin from Dallas galvanized Tatarian, along with everyone else in the bureau, into action. Everyone, it seemed, except Leary.

Bryce Miller, who would later fly to Dallas to help cover the story, was in the New York bureau and recalled the puzzling actions of Leary.

"He was sitting at his desk, calm as could be," Miller recalled, "and I remember thinking, what the hell, the president has been shot and Leary's looking like he's trying to decide whether to have macaroni or pork chops for lunch."

It wasn't until later that Miller found out what Leary was thinking. He was thinking communications for covering this mushrooming story.

In Dallas, Fallon was grinding out running takes from Smitty at the hospital in machine-gun fashion.

In New York, like magic, a delivery man wheeled an extra teletype into the bureau. It was hooked up. Someone punched out "HELLO DALLAS," and immediately the wire clattered back "HELLO NEW YORK."

It was just seventeen minutes since Kennedy was shot by an unseen sniper and Leary had already set up a new communications link to the Dallas bureau. Leary realized Dallas was going to need help. He quickly ordered AT&T to set up a private circuit that Dallas could use to send the assassination material to New York where the well-staffed general desk could handle the editing. At Leary's forceful urging, AT&T rushed a teletype through Manhattan traffic from the Western Electric shop on Hudson Street about one mile to UPI's newsroom in the *Daily News* Building at 220 East 42nd Street. The new line to Dallas was ordered, installed and operational before doctors at Parkland Hospital gave up their futile efforts and pronounced President John F. Kennedy dead at 1:00 P.M.

United Press International Chicago Bureau, 1976. Known identities, from back left, Jim Pecora's forehead. Chris Graham (glasses), unidentified woman with hair hiding face, Tom McGann (glasses, background), Weber Trout (foreground), Sharon Baker, Pamela Reeves, Don McKay, Greg Gordon (white shirt).

In Dallas, Jack Fallon was still knee-deep in breaking assassination developments while *Air Force One* was in the air on its way back to Washington. Fallon was one of UPI's best writers. He began at United Press as a writer on the national radio desk in New York. He had learned how to make every word count by packing the action and color of national and international news stories into broadcast summaries of fifty words or less.

On the Dallas general desk, Fallon was in charge. He was the distiller of information, taking disjointed notes from scattered reporters, verifying, prioritizing, organizing and crafting the information into a running story of the tragic events. The individual takes he rushed onto the newswire had to provide a quick, chronological account of the assassination and, at the same time, fit together into a comprehensive story that newspaper editors could, at any time, put into print.

He was writing running copy onto the A-wire from the hospital reports of McGraw and Hampton when he got word that a Dallas policeman had been shot and killed. Another Dallas staffer, Terry McGarry, was sent to the police station and soon reported that a 24-year-old man named Lee Harvey Oswald had been charged with the fatal shooting of the policeman, J.D. Tippit, and that Oswald was also a suspect in the Kennedy assassination.

Oswald worked at the Texas School Book Depository, located on Elm Street at the spot where the president was shot. Secret Service agents swarmed into that building soon after the shooting and found a rifle and scope on the sixth floor. They learned that an employee, Lee Harvey Oswald, was missing. An all-points bulletin was put out for a young, white male, 150 pounds with dark hair. Based on that description, Tippit had spotted Oswald walking down a street two miles from the grassy knoll. When Tippit approached, Oswald drew a .38 caliber pistol and fatally wounded the veteran patrolman. Oswald fled into the nearby Texas Theater. Witnesses alerted police. Other officers flooded the theater and when they turned on the lights, they found Oswald hiding behind some seats. Oswald tried to shoot another policeman, but the officer jammed his finger into the revolver's trigger guard and prevented Oswald from getting off a shot.

After his arrest, Dallas police were releasing few details about the suspected assassin. Fallon thought he could use the world-wide staff of UPI reporters to turn up more information on Oswald. He put out a page to all UPI bureaus, foreign and domestic, for any information they could dig up. The query hit gold. Aline Mosby, a veteran UPI reporter, cabled from the Paris bureau that she had run into Oswald when she was in the UPI bureau in Moscow. She said that Oswald had tried to defect to Russia while he was serving in the U.S. Marine Corps but had been rebuffed by Soviet officials. A UPI staffer in Moscow, Robert "Bud" Korengold had interviewed Oswald several times in Moscow's National Hotel on Red Square when there were questions as to whether Oswald was a genuine defector.

The story was building, and Fallon would not escape from the dingy UPI Dallas bureau for three more days. Preston McGraw recalled that "Jack's son brought him a clean shirt every night." *Air Force One* was on the ground at Andrews Air Force Base, and Oswald was in a cell at the Dallas police headquarters by night time.

Merriman Smith had finished writing a long story on the assassination for afternoon newspapers and had retired to the National Press Club bar with several UPI staffers, including Pat Sloyan, who recalled that "Smitty" complained about a pain in his back. Sloyan said when Smith lifted his shirt, it revealed numerous red marks he received from the pounding in the press car. Sloyan said it looked like he had been hit with a club.[4]

Merriman Smith won the Pulitzer Prize for his quick and sure coverage of the assassination. A picture of "Smitty" and Jacqueline Kennedy with others crowded into the main cabin of *Air Force One* is displayed at the LBJ Museum in Austin, Texas. It was taken just after Lyndon Baines Johnson had been sworn in as president. Smith is seen biting the temple of his glasses with his eyes focused on the blood-splattered former First Lady.

The shots from Oswald's mail-order rifle had set off the most intensive battle ever between Associated Press and United Press International. UPI had clearly won.

2

From Pigeons
to Satellites

AN EARLY VERSION OF THE ASSOCIATED PRESS WAS ESTABLISHED IN MAY 1848, in New York, at a time when news agencies were using carrier pigeons and rowboats to move copy. Six New York City newspapers were the founders. They were: the *Evening Express*, the *Journal of Commerce*, the *Sun*, the *Tribune*, The *Herald* and the *World*.[1]

Six is a bad number for an organization—you need a tie-breaker. Soon after the wire agency's founding, the *New York Times* came in as the seventh member.

The organization, incorporated on January 11 the next year, was not incorporated as Associated Press but as the "Harbor News Association." A few years later it began calling itself the Telegraphic and General News Association. It was in the 1860s that it began calling itself the New York City Associated Press.

Samuel F. B. Morse had invented the telegraph in 1844 and it was quickly used by newspapers and was the essential backbone of the news services, the "wire" services. On May 24, 1844, a telegraphed news item was sent from Washington to New York: "One o'clock—There has just been made a motion in the House on the Oregon question. Rejected—ayes 79, nays 86." From then on, news from Washington was pooled for telegraphing and identical copy began turning up in several New York newspapers.

The need for newspapers to get dispatches from other parts of the nation and the world had become obvious. People spreading out across America wanted to know what was going on in their old countries and in the big cities of their new country.

Publishers of those seven New York papers, including James Gordon Bennett of the *Herald*, Horace Greeley of the *Tribune* and David Hale of the *Journal of Commerce*, were bitter and intense competitors for New York's growing newspaper reading population. They were all interested in one thing, profit. They saw pooling the news gathering operation as a way to cut down on costs and make more profit.

One hundred and fifty years later, the same motivation disposed publishers, whose ranks had been decimated by other media, to abandon the United Press International in the 1980s. Why have two news agencies covering the same stories?

The Associated Press's first staffer-executive was Alex Jones, a medical doctor turned journalist. To run the news operation, he was paid $20 a week. He had a small office in the upstairs of a building at Broadway and Liberty Streets, New York. He had one assistant. In various cities, AP hired correspondents that they called "agents." These agents were usually reporters, editors, telegraphers or printers who worked for newspapers and sent AP the news they found in their local papers, mostly by mail.

What kinds of things did they cover?

There was a story about the wedding of a young army lieutenant, Ulysses S. Grant. Another item reported that a fellow named James A. Garfield had gotten himself a job as a mule driver. There were stories about gold in California. News might be months old, coming around the Horn on ship, but it was news all the same.

The New York AP soon started selling its news to other papers in the city that were not among the original seven and to publications outside New York City. This helped cover the cost of collecting the news. Those new customers were not "members" and hence did not share in any way in control of the news service.

Various groups of newspapers in other regions began to set up similar "Associated Press" organizations. They all looked to the New York AP for news from outside their own region. The New York AP became the news "broker"[2] for all the other Associated Press organizations, gathering news from them and exchanging it across regional borders.

The New York AP in the 1850s, 1860s and 1870s had an exclusive contract with Reuters, the English-language member of the world's news cartel, or "ring" as it was called. Reuters was established by Julius Paul Reuters in London in 1851 as an outgrowth of his commercial information service, which had been exchanging commercial reports on shipping and finances in Europe. New York AP also controlled the news from the nation's capital, Washington, D.C., and the market quotes from Wall Street.

Reuters was to become known as "Rand" to its Unipress competitors throughout Europe. This was a reference to its financial services involving the Krugerrand, the South African monetary unit heavily involved in the currency markets.

On October. 21, 1856, the seven New York AP members had a meeting. They decided on some rules, aimed particularly at protecting their own interests. They were all morning newspapers, so the rules did not provide for an afternoon news report, although some of their "outside" customers were afternoon sheets.

One of the rules prohibited any newspaper receiving AP from having any other news service on its premises or providing news to any other service. The Associated Press enforced this rule, discontinuing service to Scripps newspapers that exchanged news among themselves.[3]

The first cable across the Atlantic from Europe to North America was completed in 1858. The AP was on hand to pick up the first message, from Queen Victoria to President Buchanan.

The Civil War came and AP reported it, with no competition. If AP missed the right angle for the lead, everybody missed it. At Gettysburg in November 1863, the story was about a long speech given by Edward Everett, who had been billed as the main orator of the day. You had to read the AP story to the very end to learn that President Abraham Lincoln also spoke…"Four score…etc."

Near the end of the Civil War, AP was the victim of a hoax. A boy dashed around to all the newspapers in New York with a story marked "for the Associated Press." It said 400,000 more Union troops were being called up by Lincoln. It was a hoax, eventually traced to an editor named Joseph Howard, of the New York *Daily Star*. He was helping a Wall Street speculator who hoped to cash in on news of an expanded war.

In 1863, another newspaper group was formed—the Western Associated Press. "Western" meant anything outside the state of New York. Newspapers in Pittsburgh, Cleveland and Detroit, were among the members of the Western Associated Press, which was based in Chicago, where Joseph Medill, the instigator of the association, had established the *Chicago Tribune*. Western AP linked a large number of papers in that part of the country to exchange news among themselves.

Another purpose of the Western AP was to gain some leverage against the New York AP, which took everyone's money but listened only to the wishes of the seven New York City member papers.

Soon there were a dozen "Associated Press" organizations around the country, all independent of each other. Besides the New York City Associated Press and the Western Associated Press there were the Baltimore Associated Press, Philadelphia Associated Press, Texas Associated Press, California Associated Press, Northwest Associated Press, Kansas and Missouri Associated Press, Northern Associated Press, Colorado Associated Press, New England Associated Press and the New York State Associated Press. They were all combinations of newspapers sharing news among each other and with the other Associated Presses through the New York AP.

Four of the seven owners of New York City AP had the votes to make the rules. These were not necessarily the four strongest papers. The majority was usually the *Times, Express, Journal of Commerce* and *Sun*.

Competition in burgeoning, bustling New York City was getting stiff with one dozen newspapers. Within the New York AP there was bitter dissension, particularly over the self-serving rules imposed by the majority four publishers.

One of the brazenly monopolistic by-laws required every member to give its telegraph news to the other six before publishing it. This meant, for example, that when James Gordon Bennett sent a reporter to Europe or Cuba for a story, he could not publish it in his own *Herald* until he had given it to his competitor, the *Times*, the only cost to the latter being a share of the tolls.

Besides monopolizing news sources, the AP was partner in a common-law marriage with Western Union, then fighting to dominate telegraph service in the United States.

In the 1870s, Congress called Associated Press and Western Union to task for monopoly practices. AP news reports about the case and the rapidly expanding telegraph business were heavily biased in favor of Western Union. One of AP's rules forbade any newspaper, whether member or subscriber, from doing business with any other telegraph company than Western Union.

Nevertheless the AP reported most of the general news of the nation as fairly as it could. Among the big stories of the time were the Republic's centenary in 1876, the 1881 Chicago fire caused by Mrs. O'Leary's cow, the Johnstown flood of May 1889 in which 2,000 people died, and Washington politics. When General George Armstrong Custer set out to the Dakotas to punish Sitting Bull, AP correspondent Mark Kellogg was riding with him, and died with him.

Toward the end of the century, America was growing mainly outside of New York. Strong newspapers were published in Chicago and other cities. They demanded a voice with New York newspapers in running the national wire service. Disagreements among newspaper publishers involved news content, morning vs. evening papers, urban vs. rural, republican vs. democrat, conservative vs. liberal, staid vs. sensational. These differences eventually led, early in the new century, to competing national general news agencies, United Press Associations, the International News Service and a new and more inclusive version of Associated Press.

One complaint against the AP operation was that news was being written in one city and transmitted under the dateline of another city. New York wrote news stories under Washington datelines. Some editors were concerned about this but the practice continued through the history of all the major wire services, with debatable justification.

In 1883, leaders of the New York and Western AP's decided to form a five-member Joint Executive Committee to run the service. Power on the committee still was tilted heavily in favor of the New York AP, which had three members to two from Western AP. Charles Dana of the New York *Sun* was chairman of the joint committee. The Western AP was represented by Walter N. Haldeman of the *Louisville Courier-Journal* and Richard Smith of the *Cincinnati Gazette*.

William Henry Smith (no relative of Cincinnati's Richard Smith), was chosen to manage the joint service. He had his own conflict of interest, holding, at the same time, the lucrative political post of "collector" for the Port of Chicago.

Improvements were being made in telegraphy, and thousands of miles of wire were being strung across the country. Linotypes and rotary presses came into use by newspapers. These were the biggest innovations in printing since Gutenberg.

The Associated Press had monopolistic rules prohibiting any AP member from using another news service. A Chicago newspaper, the *Inter-Ocean*, took the Laffan news service, a small agency owned by the New York *Sun*. AP tried to expel the newspaper even though the *Inter-Ocean* had been an AP member since 1866. The newspaper sued and Illinois courts stunned the AP by ruling in favor of *Inter-Ocean*, saying the Associated Press was a public service and must be accessible to anyone who could pay for it.

The Western Associated Press decided to move, lock stock and barrel, from Illinois to a more friendly state. They would merge with the New York AP and make it a stock company. In developing this plan, the AP publishers offered E. W. Scripps a 25 percent stake in the news service. Some aides urged him to take it. He declined. He said later he considered the AP publishers "old fossils." The Associated Press group decided to become a cooperative. It was incorporated May 23, 1900, in New York State as a cooperative membership organization. This is the Associated Press that still exists.

Years later, when Joseph Pulitizer's estate was in court, the judge asked Don C. Seitz, business manager of the *New York World*, if the Associated Press was a corporation.

Seitz answered: "The Associated Press is a fish and game club. That is, it is organized under the New York law providing for the organization of fish and game clubs."

The young United Press could not let that pass. Its newsletter, the *Hellbox*, commented: "Ye gods, how the name fits! A fish and game club is an organization of amateurs who have leisurely occupations, long imaginations and incurable credulity."

Control of the Associated Press cooperative did not rest with the majority of members, who had one vote each. It was structured so that the fifteen original publishers were each permitted to buy up to $150,000 worth of bonds. They were entitled to one vote for each $25 bond investment up to $1,000. Thus these fifteen publishers commanded 6,000 votes while the rest of the members all together controlled only 1,200 votes.

In 1907, Scripps established the United Press Associations. A third important American news service, the International News Service, was launched by publisher William Randolph Hearst in 1909. In 1958, the INS was merged with UP to form United Press International. Hearst was given five percent equity, which he later relinquished.

3

Eddie Makes Good

E.W. SCRIPPS WAS THE FIFTH CHILD OF THE THIRD WIFE OF HIS FATHER, James Mogg Scripps, a farmer in Rushville, Illinois. He was born June 18, 1854. Not much good at farm work, Eddie was considered the "laziest boy in the county."[1] When his brothers left the farm and his dad got sick, Eddie, in his early teens, needed to help keep the farm going. He began to show his initiative.

A farmhand could have been hired for $1 a day, but instead Eddie offered several boys from town 25 cents a day to do the chores. They were glad to get the money.[2] When they showed up at the Scripps place outside Rushville, Eddie set them to hoeing and weeding while he sat on the fence and supervised.

Eyeing one little fellow who was faster than the others, he taunted the laggards to compete with the pace-setting youngster, and promised a nickel extra to whoever did the most hoeing.

Many years later Eddie's mother said her son spent most of his time sitting on the fence, and she wondered if his newspapers were being run the same way. They were. He seldom visited them but encouraged aggressive managers like Roy Howard, to compete at the hoeing.

Physically, E.W. was "tall, lanky, blotchy-faced, copper-headed, had a cast in one eye and a deadly quiet look in the other—a natural for the role of pirate if properly made up."[3]

The Scrippses were from England. The name was originally spelled Cripps. William Scripps, E.W.'s great grandfather, immigrated to America in 1791 and was an early settler of Morgantown, Pennsylvania. His son, William Armiger Scripps, E.W.'s grandfather, stayed in England and was publisher of the *London Daily Sun* and the *Literary Gazette*.

William Armiger's son, James Mogg Scripps, E.W.'s father, was a London bookbinder. His business was not good and he migrated to the United States in 1844. He had three wives, not at the same time of course, who gave him thirteen children. The youngest was Edward Wyllis. Sometimes it was spelled "Willis." E.W. didn't care how his name was spelled as long as everyone knew that "E.W." was the boss.[4]

When James Mogg Scripps, the London bookbinder, settled at Rushville, some of his relatives were already well-established in the newspaper business in the Midwest. The *Rushville Telegraph* had been founded by Benjamin Franklin Scripps and was published by the Reverend John Scripps. They were among the progeny of E.W.'s great-great-grandfather, who had nineteen children. Others in that part of the family included John Locke Scripps, a founder and editor of the *Chicago Tribune*, and George Washington Scripps, who founded the *Schuyler Citizen*.

There was little, if any, demand for bookbinding services in the farm town of Rushville, in the middle of the 1800s. James Mogg Scripps tried tannery, brick-making and lumber planing businesses as well as farming, with little success.

His oldest son, born to Ellen Mary, his second wife, was James E. Scripps, who left Rushville for Chicago in 1857 to take a job with the *Chicago Press and Tribune*, of which James Locke Scripps, a relative, was part owner. Two years later James E. moved to Detroit and joined the staff of the *Daily Advertiser*. He advanced quickly to become the paper's news editor and in 1861 he bought a half interest in it.

James merged the *Daily Advertiser* with a couple other small papers. In 1863, he was both business manager and managing editor. In 1865, he brought in Hiram Walker, the whiskey maker, as a partner. James eventually sold his interest in the *Tribune-Advertiser* to Walker and launched his own paper, the *Evening News*, selling it for two cents on the street. It quickly became Detroit's largest circulation newspaper.

James bought the *Detroit Tribune* in 1891, combined his two Detroit papers and cut the street price to one cent. The "penny press" was where all of the Scripps newspaper people thought—correctly—the circulation was.

Eddie, 19 years younger than James, was sent by his family to Detroit to work for another relative who was opening a drugstore. He was glad to get away from Rushville, but he definitely did not want to be a druggist. For one thing, he didn't like selling the alcohol-based nostrums that in those days the less affluent imbibing class used to gargle themselves into a pleasant stupor. After a week or two in the drugstore, E.W. quit. He went to see his older half-brother, James, publisher of the *Detroit News*.

E.W. once made an assertion that he had $80 sewn in his coat when he went to Detroit for his first job. True, but that was not his entire fortune. He was not a poor farm boy starting from scratch to build a newspaper empire. His family was not poor. He just did not like farming.

When young Eddie showed up looking for a job, James was not very enthusiastic about his half-brother but gave him a job doing odd chores around the paper for $3 a week. Eddie did errands and swept up the shop. However, he was not satisfied with those menial tasks and thought the pay his brother gave him was an insult. He quit after a few weeks and got a job in the commercial print shop next door, which was affiliated with the *News*.

James soon took him back to the *News* at double the earlier wage. That happened because their sister, Ellen, put in a good word for him. She had been a mother to her young half-brother since the death of his own mother.

E.W. decided he was going to make his fortune in newspapers. He eventually did, becoming the most successful person in the family and one of the most powerful figures in the American press. At one time he controlled thirty-five newspapers and the United Press Associations news service.

Most of his capital, when he was starting his newspaper empire, came from his brothers and sister. He insisted on holding the majority stock in every newspaper he owned and quickly became personally rich. He built for himself a large ranch near San Diego. He called it Miramar. From there, he ran his operations, once a year making a swing via private railroad car around the country to visit his newspaper properties.

His parsimonious character, which marked Scripps' news enterprises throughout their history, may have begun in 1884 when E. W. wrote to James saying there was no need for "lavish expenditure" for telegraph news or $35-a-week writers.[5]

E.W. Scripps was a deliberate eccentric. He was also ungraceful, unsociable, a physical clod, even a slob, and he bragged about it. None of his biographies say that anyone liked him or enjoyed his company except, perhaps, his sister, Ellen. E.W. said very often that he didn't give a damn about having people like him.

Toward people he considered below him—including everyone female, all racial minorities, Jews and Catholics—Scripps' attitude bordered on contempt. It was contempt.

When he needed a crew for his winter cruise in 1925, he published a "help wanted" ad that brought bushels of mail. His aide, Harry Smithton, was at a table sorting the applications. Scripps wagged a finger at the pile and said, "First throw out all the Jews, then the Catholics."[6]

He thought women were worth very little, dividing them into "nice" and "not nice." He paid "not nice" girls for certain physical favors, but when he decided he needed a wife, he wanted one of the "nice" girls. Four or five of them turned him down before he got Nackie Holtsinger Benson, the daughter of a preacher. She married him October 17, 1885. They had six children. E.W. didn't much like any of them either, quarrelling with and even suing several of them.

In 1898, although very wealthy, Scripps got into a snit with Nackie and kicked her parents off the family farm.[7]

He never went to a ball game, never went to the theater, never went into a church. He was an avowed atheist and hated religion. When he learned that one of his lawyers was giving substantially to a church, Scripps tied up most of the man's pay in a trust so that it had to accumulate for the man's heirs.[8]

E.W. drank heavily when he was young, claiming later to have ingested enough whiskey to float a ship. But he was nobody's "drinking buddy." He enjoyed the physical feeling one can get from alcohol even without the social camaraderie that is part of the pleasure for most drinkers.

When he was 47 years old his doctor told him he would go blind and kill himself if he continued the booze, so he slowed down.

When E.W. was 61 he became sick and thought he had cancer. On his doctor's instructions he measured the weight of his bowel movements and the quantity of his urine (average 37 ounces in 24 hours). During the same period of his life he was quarrelling bitterly with his sons and other relatives, all except his sister Ellen. He became a hypochondriac. He cut down to 12 cigars and three ounces of whiskey a day, but he often sneaked an extra shot in the evening.

The entire Scripps family was an unhappy bunch. Brothers and sisters mistrusted each other, quarreled, and even took each other to court. E.W. turned against his sons. James resented Eddie. Eddie resented James. George and John were at odds with their brothers and sisters. Throughout their lives, members of this family used each other, schemed against each other, carried on petty feuds against each other, sued each other, cut each other out of their wills.

The women in the family were on a different and lower level than the men. They were never given any position of power. Even his older sister, Ellen, E.W.'s benefactor and best friend, got no further than being feature editor and columnist for the newspapers.

In 1982, when UPI was dumped by the Scrippses, there was still a running family feud among E.W.'s six surviving grandchildren.

E.W. became the richest and most powerful Scripps because he was best at these family tussles. He recognized the roots of power in business and family matters—the man with the dollars. He always owned at least 51 percent of any enterprise he was involved in. His decisions could and did prevail. He demanded that every unit earn 15 percent annual profit.

E.W., Ellen and George agreed their businesses should borrow only from each other and that they personally would not borrow except from each other.

Scripps said he retired in 1890 at the age of 36. But he kept a close eye on his property and intruded often until his death. When he was 55 years old, he declared himself a "damned old crank" and proud of it.

Scripps claimed he had no interest in political or social affairs. However, when he called together the chiefs of his newspapers every year, there was indeed discussion of the political issues of the day and how their newspapers and the UP news service should stand on political matters. E.W. did not hesitate to bulge his political muscle for President Wilson and others. He claimed he was "two percent responsible for all that is good or ill in the management of this great nation."

When World War I broke out, all Scripps papers were ordered to publish Newspaper Enterprise Association (NEA) and UP dispatches that aroused readers to the war danger. From Miramar, E.W. issued a letter telling his editors he had come out of retirement and was taking away their independence because of the war. This caused some confusion and in-fighting because his son, James, had taken charge after E.W.'s "retirement" and had been giving the orders.

While Scripps was enthusiastic about U.S. participation in the war, he didn't want his own family to get shot at. He pulled strings to get son Robert exempted from the draft.

Scripps backed a third party movement with Theodore Roosevelt as its presidential candidate. He ordered his twenty-four daily newspapers, the NEA, and in a less blatant way, the United Press, to carry stories supporting the Roosevelt candidacy. The UP was less politicized than the newspapers because it had many clients who were not owned by Scripps and not necessarily similarly minded.

"I have the ear—or perhaps I should say the eye—of more than a million voters in this country....I have learned how effective is the instrument I have in my possession," Scripps wrote to Gifford Pinchot, U.S. Forester, on September 27, 1910.

He also wrote to W. B. Colver, an officer of the NEA, "It is because we have our newspapers, little and big, scattered all over the country, and because through the United Press and the Newspaper Enterprise Association we are able to find our way into the editorial sanctums of many other newspapers, that we are really able to force upon the attention of the whole people every important news fact and very many of our own ideas." With a touch of slyness he told his friend, "We should, for strategic purposes, remain unrecognized as a moving spirit in the body politic."[9]

Journalism historian Richard Kaplan, assessing the Scripps family politics, said, "Not strong political opinions but the profit to be earned by playing one potential candidate against another determined their political advocacy."[10]

Scripps dictated essays—he liked to use a longer word, disquisitions—expounding at length on his asserted love for the common working class. But he also maintained that this class was on a level categorically many rungs below his own.

The great writer Lincoln Steffens was one of the few people who ever publicly praised E.W., if the following can be considered praise: "He was on to himself and the world, played the game and despised it. He was sincere, not cynical. He showed a strength which he took care to keep from becoming refined; he avoided other rich men so as to escape being like them; he knew the danger his riches carried for himself, for his papers and for his seeing. Of rough, almost ruthless force, he was restrained by clear, even shrewd insight; an executive, capable of fierce action, restrained by the observation that a doer must not do too many things himself, but must use his will to make others do them."[11]

Max Eastman, editor of *The Masses*, once visited Scripps, seeking financial help for his left-wing publication. He didn't get the money, but he later wrote a profile in which he quotes Scripps: "I am sure that from the time I was twenty-four, more than half my days have been spent with no conscious thought or attention to business of any sort. The practice of journalism seems to me, even now, to have been an unimportant incident in my life."[12]

Nevertheless, at one of his last face-to-face meetings with his editors, in May 1922, aboard his yacht *Kemah* on the Potomac River, he told them he planned to establish new dailies in New York, Baltimore and Philadelphia and eventually enlarge the chain to 100 newspapers. He said he would expand UP and NEA worldwide. He also wanted to test his theory that newspapers could be published and sold without advertising. He tried this in Chicago and San Francisco. The Chicago experiment, the *Day Book*, was launched in 1912 and survived six years before war shortages of newsprint and other demands caused him to close it down.

He enjoyed being the "commander-in-chief" of the news empire but was not addicted to paying much attention to it other than to look at the checks coming in. He said he averaged about two hours work a day and bragged that he was as rich as most millionaires who spent almost their whole time working.

Scripps "didn't like rich men and couldn't abide poor men," the *New Yorker* magazine said.[13]

On May 22, 1925, about a year before he died, Scripps dictated what he intended to be his intellectual legacy to posterity. It was one of the last of many "disquisitions" he dictated. He did not publish them; instead, he bequeathed them to his grandchildren, not trusting his immediate offspring.

One of his simple, if not simplistic, dictums for getting rich: "Never do anything today that you can put off 'til tomorrow." Also, "Always buy, never sell," and "Never do anything yourself that you can get someone else to do for you."

Another E.W. maxim: "One of the greatest assets any man can secure is a reputation for eccentricity. If you have a reputation for eccentricity, you can do a lot of things, you can even do the things you want to do without attaching to yourself the enmity of others."

One of his axioms was a puzzler: "A man can do anything he wants to do in this world, at least if he wants to do it bad enough. Therefore, I say that any of you who want to become rich can become rich if you live long enough."

Scripps, besides being anti-black, anti-Catholic and anti-Semitic, was an advocate of infanticide and abortion. He had a shocking master race social agenda. In several astonishing disquisitions and letters he said the human race should be controlled as an orchardist controls production of oranges, by destroying much of the production, preferably before birth.[14]

He went on, "It should be society's rule that no adult persons who, for any reason, are suspected of being unable to be parents of sound and healthy offspring should be allowed to be parents." Such inferior citizens, he said, should be sterilized.

"Society should first make a selection of all men and women who are presumably perfectly fit for parenthood and, further, make a classification of these candidates for parenthood according to their qualities and characteristics, so that only a sufficient number of men and women of each group of qualifications should be produced to fill the needs, or the approximate needs, of a given society."

He thought the first and second born children were inferior to later ones. "The first, and possibly even the second, child born of a woman should be destroyed at birth," he said.

"But after birth, in infancy and even in very young childhood, there is room for innumerable accidents which may so cripple a child, physically or mentally, as to make him of doubtful usefulness in the future. Perhaps up to the age of ten or maybe twelve years, children are so incapable of thinking or so little inclined to think, and hence be possessed of fear and dread, that any child could have its life ended without suffering itself. So there would be no cruelty to the child itself in having its life snuffed out."[15]

In E.W.'s weird world of ethics "chastity is a sin against the laws of Nature." He suggested that "inferior" females should be sterilized and set aside as public concubines to enable males between 10 and 24 to freely have sex without danger of becoming fathers.[16]

The way to arrive at his Utopia, he said, was through a dictatorship. Otherwise the white race would decline and "the inferior races" would multiply.

He said the problems of world governance were caused by society having been "too long allowed freedom from the lash of its tyrant or strong man, who alone in all the history of the world have ever been able to compel obedience and order—autocracy in fact—great autocracy, ruling autocracy, not the simulant of autocracy like the late German emperor and the late Czar of Russia.

"As Caesar grasped the imperial crown when the Roman republic had become decadent, as Napoleon seized power in France at a given time, and as Lenin has striven and is still striving to seize and hold power of dictator in Russia, so may we have to depend on some coming strong man to reorganize the family of nations called European to save the white race from destruction either at its own hands or at the hands of some other nations or races submissive to and ruled by some strong man picked from their numbers."[17] He wrote this before Hitler, but it was a remarkable summary of the Nazi philosophy.

"We want famines and more famines, providing that the people who starve to death and are eliminated are the people of inferior qualities in all races, and especially the people of all inferior races," said Scripps. "It is no more painful to die of starvation than it is from any other cause."

E.W. disparaged higher education. He said college "is about the last place in the world where a man should go to learn journalism."[18] When he was hiring somebody he always asked about education. If they said they went to college, he counted that as a negative.

He thought journalism was a low-class occupation anyway. "There are few opportunities for a man to be both a gentleman and a journalist," he said.[19]

Like many rich men, E.W. tried to buy longevity. In his will he bequeathed $50,000 to his nurse if she kept him alive until June 1, 1928. If he died before then she would get only $15,000.

Scripps was still alive when several of his underlings, including Roy Howard, decided that a marble or bronze bust of the founder ought to be put up in every one of the newspapers. E.W. wouldn't go for that, but he agreed reluctantly to sit for a portrait. However, when it was finished he rejected it, saying the picture gave him "a Jew nose."

In an attempt to head off some of the family bickering that he knew would come when he died, he had his lawyer, Tom Sidlow, set up a unique trust that was to control the properties for two generations. It would remain under tight control of Robert and E.W.'s grandchildren born before his death. One of its provisions was that one-third of net income had to be reinvested in newspapers.

When his brother James Scripps died, his widow owned not quite 5 percent of the Detroit paper. E W. held 44.5 percent. Ellen held 19 percent, which she let E.W. vote, giving him more than 63 percent control.

E.W. Scripps died March 12, 1926, on his yacht Ohio off Monrovia, Liberia. He was, according to his own instruction, buried at sea, latitude 6 degrees 14 minutes, 0 seconds north, longitude 11 degrees 8 minutes 0 seconds west.

E. W. was very proud of launching the United Press Associations. He said in one of his disquisitions:

> I believe the most valuable service I have rendered to my country has been that of thwarting the plans of greater, abler and richer men than myself to establish a monopoly of news in the United States, and hence a dominating influence over all the newspapers of the country.
>
> When, if ever, an accounting is made of my life's work, especially my financial contribution to public service, I would require, in fairness to me, that account should be taken, not only of the huge effort, but the great outlay of money that I have made personally to secure freedom of the press in this country.
>
> I am talking about the foundation of the United Press in competition with the Associated Press.[20]

Scripps once wrote a heavily autobiographical but naive novel, *Theory and Practice*. The ending paragraphs were:

> The armistice was signed. Francis boarded his yacht and sailed the South Pacific and returned to America and the "golden boys" three years later. He was then fairly past forty years of age.
>
> But what's Francis Wilton to do now? What is he going to do for the remainder of his life? The author does not know and neither does the reader.

When E. W. died, control of the Scripps empire went to Roy Howard along with F. W. Hawkins and George B. "Deak" Parker.

4

A Bag of Wind Soars

UNITED PRESS STARTED WITH A LOT MORE THAN E.W. SCRIPPS' $500 capital and a "bag of wind."

The fledgling news agency opened with two exceptional players who would steer the initial course for UP and carve an indelible legacy.

Edward Wyllis Scripps and Roy Wilson Howard made an unlikely pair who shared just one thing, a burning desire to succeed: Scripps for profit, Howard for show.

Scripps was a big, broad-shouldered newspaper publisher who liked to spend his time in boots and khakis at his ranch called Miramar in the Southern California desert near San Diego. He had an incredible knack for making money.

Howard was a small, dapper news editor who seemed determined to prove to the world that he was much bigger than five-foot-six. He was infected with non-stop energy.

The two men who would form the foundation of the Scripps-Howard newspaper empire met for the first time in February of 1908 at Miramar. Howard was 24 years old; Scripps 62.

Howard had been the news manager for Scripps-McRae and Publishers Press Association. When Scripps merged them into United Press Associations, Howard became news manager of UP's eastern operations with headquarters in New York. He was on a tour of West Coast operations when he was summoned to visit the big boss at the ranch.

Howard knew it was customary for visitors at Miramar to dress casually, but such garb did not appeal to the spiffy newsman. When he stepped into Scripps' office at the ranch, Howard was wearing a derby, spats, a striped shirt and a tie tightly knotted. He was, however, covered with a light coat of dust from the desert ride to the ranch.

Scripps was not overly cordial, but he did have an admission and some advice for the young man he had chosen to run his news operations.

"I tried to run a press association, but I wasn't much of a success. I was probably too closely associated with my newspapers to know how to do it.

"Now there are only a couple of things that I ask of you…. Always see that the news report is handled objectively as far as it is humanly possible. You must not be biased or take sides in controversies. You won't always succeed in being completely objective but you must always try to tell both sides of any dispute.

"Second, never make a contract to deliver news exclusively to one newspaper in any territory."[1]

Scripps told Howard that he believed there must not be a news monopoly in America and that any newspaper should be able to buy the service of United Press.

At the turn of the century the news wholesaling business was dominated by The Associated Press in the United States and by government-subsidized or government-controlled agencies abroad.

An earlier United Press news agency was established in 1882. Started to serve newspapers shut out by AP, it soon was related to AP in a devious manner.

The "old" United Press was owned by John P. Walsh, publisher of the *Chicago Chronicle*. He was a banker who would end his career and his life in the penitentiary. The manager of the news service was Walter P. Phillips, who is best known for devising the Phillips Code, a system of journalism shorthand for telegraph and cable messages.

Walsh leased a cable line from Europe to start his service and the E.W. Scripps papers were among his first clients. The "old" UP was aggressive and was soon the dominant service in the United States. However, corruption and intrigue in its financial dealings brought down the service at a young age.

Corruption was rampant in the news industry although it seldom came to light, owing, of course, to the fact that publishers controlled publishing.

The "old" UP and AP were secretly conniving to gouge publishers and would-be publishers. When a newspaper signed on with one of the wire services it received an exclusive territorial franchise. No other newspaper could buy the service in the same city without a waiver from the established client. This waiver usually could be purchased for a price—really a bribe, paid to the established newspaper.

E.W. Scripps acknowledged that he received his share of such "swag." For one thing, the old UP was paying all his telegraph costs, which not only covered the cost of the news service but put him ahead by $40 or $50 a week at each of his newspapers.

Phillips quietly sold $300,000 in UP stock to newspapers in New York City, who happened to be also the owners of the Associated press of New York. UP then issued a 100 percent dividend, thus fully paying these publishers for their investment and leaving them in control of both news agencies.

Soon editors noticed that stories on AP looked similar to stories on UP and vice versa. News dispatches were being secretly exchanged between the two agencies and cosmetic rewrites could hardly hide the conspiracy.

The scandals caught up with old United Press and the agency went out of business October 5, 1905. Several other organizations also had used the name United Press. When Scripps incorporated the United Press Associations, his lawyers had to spend the next two years in courts establishing ownership of the name.

Scripps wanted to be free to start newspapers wherever he wished. He felt that under the existing monopoly situation the Associated Press held life-or-death control over newspaper publishers. AP was formed as a co-operative and its rules allowed its publisher members to deny service to any new entrepreneurs who might offer a challenge.

"I do not believe in monopolies," Scripps said, "I believe that monopolists suffer more than their victims in the long run. I do not believe it would be good for journalism in this country that there should be one big news trust such as the founders of the Associated Press fully expected to build up."[2]

But E.W. also had motives not nearly so lofty. He desperately needed a wire service for his afternoon newspapers. He had to have cable news from overseas and a national news report. Unable to break the AP stranglehold on wire news, Scripps decided to start a comprehensive service of his own for afternoon papers. One of his key advisers, John Vandercook, publisher of the *Cincinnati Post*, suggested Scripps buy out the scandal-tainted Publisher's Press Association, which was involved in attempted manipulation of the Stock Exchange.

In 1906 Scripps was running three small news services of his own. One was called the "Adscititious Report" (the word means supplemental), with Robert F. Paine in charge. The others were the Scripps-McRae Service and the Scripps-Blades Service on the West Coast, supervised by Hamilton B. "Ham" Clark.

Scripps considered making a deal with Publishers Press Association to let it serve the East Coast and he would have the rest of the country and they would exchange news. But, when he learned PPA was in serious trouble, he negotiated its purchase for $150,000.[3] He also acquired the Laffan News Agency which was owned by the *New York Sun* and had European cable news. Scripps decided to combine all the telegraph agencies into United Press.

Charles McCabe, who married Scripps' granddaughter, said United Press was born in the bathroom at the Miramar ranch. Scripps "got most of his best ideas while seated on the throne," said McCabe. "One of these ideas, and possibly the best thing that ever happened to American journalism, was the creation of a telegraphic news service that broke the monopoly of the Associated Press." McCabe adds that the bathroom at Miramar was still called the "UP bathroom" even though it was the most expensively decorated room at the estate.[4]

On June 21, 1907, the United Press Associations was incorporated in New York, issuing $400,000 worth of stock. Scripps immediately pulled out half that sum as a "dividend" paid to himself. He thus had $200,000 to pay other bills and still owned 100 percent of the new company.

To meet the requirements of incorporating United Press, E.W. was obliged to set aside $500 as UP's capital. He said later that United Press Associations started with $300,000 liability and "a bag of wind."

Scripps put John Vandercook in charge as president and general manager. Other incorporators were Hamilton Clark, business manager, who became president when Vandercook died unexpectedly, and Clayton D. Lee, an associate of Scripps who became third president of United Press when Clark left for other pursuits. Also in a top UP management post at the start was Max Balthazar, who had been running Scripps' West Coast news service in San Francisco.

Scripps gave Clark 20 percent of the stock, Vandercook 20 percent, and Balthazar 9 percent. They did not have to pay for it at once but from United Press dividends to be earned by the agency. This scheme motivated executives to keep expenses down so that there would be profits and dividends. From its first day, the company made a profit.

Scripps promised that his new wire service would provide 10,000 words of news by Morse telegraph daily to 360 newspapers it served in the United States. The company started with a half dozen bureaus, mostly one or two-man operations. It had only about twenty employees in all.

E.W. was enthusiastic about his news service. He said the United Press "would either have to be a flat failure or a property worth many millions."

Before the company was a year old it had an agreement to provide news to European papers through Exchange Telegraph, a British agency. Cable service to the Japanese Telegraph News Agency began in 1909.

When UP had been operating ten years, Scripps boasted that besides the $200,000 he took out of it at the start, it had paid him $20,000 a year in dividends. He had given associates some shares but the 51 percent he owned himself was worth $500,000. Growth and profit continued. On its 20th anniversary, General Manager Roy Howard said the company was worth $2.5 million. At that time, E.W. noted that his half would be worth $1.25 million, which, even without the dividends he had taken, represented $125,000 annual capital appreciation since its founding. He said he hadn't put a lick of work into it.

However, he observed, there was some doubt of whether United Press Associations could be considered a property at all. "There are practically no capital goods in it, and none are required. A few office desks, a safe, typewriters, chairs, filing cases and such things, represent the total of its tangible possessions."

Scripps did not give his executives and staff any credit for the company's early success. Though saying he had not done any work on it, he attributed the existence of the service entirely to himself. He said the only thing that sustained UP was the belief by its clients that E.W. Scripps could and would personally keep it going.

"I can control this institution. Certain men will do certain things they would not do if I were dead, or if I did not own the controlling stock....These may be the very things on which the life and prosperity of the institution depends," he asserted.

Having control of the United Press also assured Scripps that he could start as many newspapers as he wanted to. If AP was allowed to be a monopoly, serving only one newspaper in a city as its by-laws provided, "we would never be able to start another newspaper," Scripps told associates.

On a number of occasions he expounded on his altruistic goals for United Press. "I believe I have done more good indirectly with the UP than I have done with it directly, since I have made it impossible for the men who control the AP to suppress the truth or successfully disseminate falsehood.

"The mere fact that the United Press can be depended upon to disseminate news that is of value to the public and that is against the interests of the plutocrat band makes it not only not worthwhile but positively dangerous for the Associated Press to withhold any information from the public. If a United Press paper in Cleveland gets a piece of news that the Associated Press client there doesn't get, there is a kick from the Associated Press paper to the management."

The above is recorded in a letter E.W. wrote to Roy Howard from Miramar September 27, 1912. The fact is, however, that little altruism was involved when E.W. established the news service. He had to do it. The AP at that time would not serve two papers in the same city. The Scripps paper was usually the newer one and hence left out in the cold.

That was the origin of United Press Association, which became one of the two largest news organizations in the world, the only worldwide independent service and the only real competitor of the Associated Press as a comprehensive wholesale news provider.

The Newspaper Enterprise Association (NEA) was organized about the same time, as a non-profit editorial service exclusively for Scripps' own newspapers. When outside clients showed an interest in this material, Scripps agreed to sell it to them. He then created the Scripps-Howard Newspaper Alliance (SHNA) to be his "house" agency for editorials and columns.

On July 15, 1907, the first "By United Press" credit line was published in the *Cleveland Press*. Shortly after that the new UP said it had 400 evening and sixty Sunday customers.

Six months after it started, UP had a wire extending from the East Coast to Chicago and St. Louis. The Scripps papers and a few client newspapers on the West Coast were served by a separate wire out of San Francisco. News from the East had to be priced by the word and sent by regular commercial telegram to California. Max Balthazar was the San Francisco United Press chief in charge of the West Coast.

At that time, UP already had a dozen bureaus although they were still mostly one-man operations. Stringers—correspondents paid on a piece-work basis—were commissioned in all major cities. The stringer was usually a newspaperman or telegrapher with some access to news in the community. Throughout its life, the agency had trouble engaging stringers because Associated Press had a rule forbidding its member newspapers from allowing any employees to cooperate with any other news agency.

An important early milestone for the company came in 1912 when United Press rejected a bid to ally itself with Reuters, choosing instead to go it alone with independent foreign coverage.

During its early years, the United Press had few scoops. Associated Press had little to fear. It did not appear that this competitor was much different from a half dozen other news services that had come and gone.

But UP did place an ad in *Editor & Publisher* boasting about a scoop with radio-telegraph coverage of the American Navy's excursion to Panama.[5]

The Scripps service was not strongly capitalized and its managers understood clearly that frugality must be the name of their game. This birthmark, or stigma, remained throughout United Press history. It created a culture that inspired unusual initiatives among its employees. It undoubtedly was partly responsible for the ultimate failure of the service. Frugality was the principal virtue in the eyes of the owners, and every employee, from chairman on down, knew it.

Unipressers in San Francisco learned how to expand a skeletonized 500-word news report from the East by telegraph into a 2,000-word file to move on its West Coast wire for afternoon newspapers.

In l908 the national leased wire ran from 7 A.M. to 3 P.M. and carried 12,000 words a day. Because it was geared to afternoon newspapers, the staff was taught to find a "today" angle on news that had already been in the morning newspapers. United Press desk men, always ready to jump on a breaking story during the day, used their calendars effectively. For events known to be coming up they got ready with background copy prepared in advance. It would be used to expand a brief telegram received when the event occurred.

Roy Howard ordered at least one "human interest" story from every bureau every day. This contrasted with the AP under Melville Stone, who wanted only straight factual accounts.

United Press operated more informally than almost any other news operation. There were few rules, few directives, or at least few that were taken seriously. The company did not have a training program. It was a sink-or-swim process. A new employee might be sent out to cover a story within an hour of his hiring. Managers were not called into headquarters to get indoctrinated. All of this made it much different from the Associated Press, which was tightly organized and supervised.

UP bureaus were indoctrinated with the idea that a request from a client was word from God. Get what they want no matter how difficult or how trivial. This served well throughout UP's history whereas, not having that kind of pressure, Associated Press editors often felt the member newspapers had to take what was handed to them on the wire and not expect more.

Journalistic initiative and freedom became the marks that distinguished the United Press report from Associated Press. AP conformed with the views of the "member" customers and usually had only whatever news that those members contributed. The AP report was considered staid and dull.

In its earliest years, the United Press tried to be different from AP and not to imitate the senior agency. Later generations of United Press editors moved away from that philosophy and began trying to copycat its rival. Some say this made it, in the eyes of newspaper publishers, an unnecessary duplication and expense.

The U.S. Department of Justice in the 1940s brought a case against the AP accusing it of monopoly. The U.S. District Court ruled that the cooperative had to drop the rule that gave a single member in any city the right to bar service to a competitor. The court said dispensing news is a public interest function and those who have news for sale must sell it to all comers. Still, it allowed a 51 percent vote of AP members to reject any application. Memberships had sold for as much as $500,000 according to Clyde H. Knox, Kansas City newspaper broker, in a speech to the Missouri Press Association in November, 1943.

5

Miniature Dynamo

> It was largely his personal pioneering that pushed the outposts of the United Press to the far-flung foreign lands which they have come to occupy.
> — *Victor Rosewater, wire service historian.*

IN THE SPRING OF 1933, MILES "PEG" VAUGHN, UP ASIA MANAGER IN Tokyo, received a cable from New York telling him that Roy Howard, head of the Scripps-Howard newspapers, was planning to come to Asia. Vaughn was told to render the usual "gofer" attention to the boss of the concern that owned United Press.

Vaughn was instructed to line up a tour of the war fronts in China where the Japanese were fighting various warlords and the Chinese Nationalists were fighting the Chinese Communists for control of the vast country.

The final item on Howard's agenda, the cable said, should be an interview in Tokyo with Emperor Hirohito of Japan.

"I had been trying to interview the Emperor for nine years and had made no progress whatever," said Vaughn. But he would try.[1]

Vaughn accompanied Howard to Korea and Manchuria. They flew out of Tokyo in an old, single-motor, Fokker plane. The Japanese had sent word ahead to commanders in the field to be ready for a VIP visitor. A welcoming delegation met Howard at Keijo (Seoul) airport.

Getting from the airport into the city of Seoul they encountered a problem that might have turned an ordinary VIP back. A stream had swollen from heavy rain and flooded the road. The driver of the car plunged ahead into the water. In mid-stream the engine stalled. The driver got out into the cold water and tried to push the vehicle. It went deeper into the mud.

The officer with them, their official host, was unusually tall for a Japanese. He removed his striped formal trousers, laid them down neatly and placed his morning coat and silk hat atop them. Then he waded back to the car and carried Vaughn and Howard piggy-back across the stream, leaving the car in the stream. Another vehicle was sent out from town for them and they made it to the formal dinner waiting for them at the Yamato Hotel.[2]

Howard and Vaughn flew the next day to Hsinking, where the government of Manchuokuo, the Japanese puppet state in China, was situated. They found an elaborate program had been planned for them under instruction from the Japanese.

Howard had a round of interviews with Manchurian officials, including Emperor Pu Yi. "None of the Manchurians had anything of importance to say," Vaughn reported in his memoir.[3]

While in Hsinking, Howard came up with the bright idea that they should cross no-man's land from the Japanese side to the Chinese side to get another view of the war from Peiping. At the time, Chinese forces were holding the mountain passes along the Great Wall, despite ferocious Japanese bombing, artillery and infantry attacks.

When Japanese Army Chief of Staff General Koiso was explaining the battle lines on a wall map at his headquarters, Howard suddenly pointed his finger at a place called Miyuen-hsien. "That town looks as if it is right next to Peiping," Howard said. "Why can't we leave your military plane there, cross through the lines and then go to into Peiping by automobile?"

"That's right in the middle of the war," General Koiso said with a smile. "I might be willing to suspend operations for a few hours to let you through, but unfortunately I doubt if I could persuade the enemy to do so."

Howard was not to be put off. The next day he confronted General Koiso again and persuaded him to grant a safe-conduct pass.

He still needed a pass from the other side of the war, the Chinese. Vaughn sent a telegram to UP's Peiping Bureau Manager, H. R. Ekins, who managed to arrange safe passage for the Howard party. Meanwhile, Jack Howard, Roy's son, had also shown up in China and was on his way to Peiping by rail from Shanghai.

Roy Howard and Vaughn went by rail from Mukden to Chinchow. The next day, they flew through a heavy rain along the treacherous hills near the Great Wall to Miyuen-hsien. They landed in a bean patch where an old Chinese peasant was calmly hoeing his crop within hearing of the artillery from serious warfare nearby.

Meanwhile, Ekins could not find a driver in Peiping who would risk his neck by driving to the Japanese lines to pick up Roy and Vaughn. Finally he drafted his cook, who, under threat of being fired, drove to Miyuen-hsien. They brought along a basket of sandwiches and a dozen bottles of iced beer for Howard and Vaughn.

The two parties met at Miyuen-hsien, had their sandwiches and beer, and set out together for the return trip to Peiping. They drove 40 miles through an army of retreating Chinese soldiers. It was only a day or two before the Chinese surrendered.

Roy was keeping to his hectic schedule. He flew from Peiping to Shanghai, while Vaughn stayed in Peiping to cover truce talks between the Chinese and Japanese.

Back in Tokyo a few days later, Vaughn and Howard learned that an audience with Hirohito had, surprisingly, been approved. No interview would be allowed because the Emperor never is quoted directly except in his Imperial commands. Howard and Vaughn were, instead, to have an interview with Foreign Minister Count Yasukya Uchida. The text would be shown to the Emperor for his approval and so the interview would represent the Japanese government's viewpoint.

Everything went smoothly except for one little problem. Howard had not brought in his baggage for the journey a silk hat and morning coat, requisite dress for an audience with the god-ruler. Vaughn, the loyal, local UP manager, loaned his tails to Howard. Vaughn's hat was too small and the coat too large for the diminutive Howard.[4] He looked a bit like a clown.

On the appointed hour, Howard was accompanied into the imperial presence by Joseph C. Grew, U.S. Ambassador to Japan. When the meeting was over Vaughn, Grew and Howard backed out of the Emperor's sacred presence bowing their heads.

Howard's story, written mainly by Vaughn, had this lead:

BY ROY HOWARD.

JAPANESE-AMERICAN FRIENDSHIP, UNDERSTANDING AND COOPERATION ARE OF THE UTMOST IMPORTANCE TO THE PEACE, NOT ONLY OF THE FAR EAST BUT OF THE WORLD, IN THE OPINION OF HIS MAJESTY, THE EMPEROR HIROHITO. THIS FACT WAS IMPRESSED UP ON ME IN AN UNFORGETTABLE MANNER TODAY WHEN I WAS GRANTED THE FIRST AUDIENCE EVER EXTENDED TO AN AMERICAN NEWSPAPERMAN BY ANY JAPANESE RULER.

"THERE EXISTS TODAY NO QUESTION THAT CAN DISTURB THE GOOD RELATIONS EXISTING BETWEEN JAPAN AND THE UNITED STATES" IN THE OPINION OF FOREIGN MINIS- TER COUNT UCHIDA, TO WHOM I WAS REFERRED FOR AN OUTLINE OF THE GOVERNMENT'S ATTITUDE TOWARD THE PRESENT WORLD SITUATION.

Howard was not only acting as a reporter in these meetings, he intended person- ally to have some influence on relations between the United States and Japan. He thought he had a diplomatic role. The U.S. was then annoyed by Japan's aggression in Manchuria. Howard promised Hirohito he would help the emperor in the cause of peace.

Howard became a good friend of Japan. Later, when war between the United States and Japan was imminent, he tried to persuade President Roosevelt to pursue a conciliatory policy—until Pearl Harbor.

E. W. Scripps, although he put Howard in charge of UP, called him an "upstart," and seldom had anything good to say about him.[5]

"His manner was forceful, and the reverse from modest. Gall was written all over his face. It was in every tone and every word he voiced. There was ambition, self- respect and forcefulness oozing out of every pore of his body," E.W. said of Howard.[6] Scripps liked those qualities.

Howard had started his career with the *Cincinnati Post*. He was news manager of Scripps-McRae and Publishers Press Association when Scripps merged them into United Press. He was made manager of the New York bureau, and general manager of the company when John Vandercook, its first president, died unexpectedly on April 11, 1908. Howard was then 25.

Hamilton Clark was first chairman of the board of United Press. He became its second president when Vandercook died, but he left two years later to undertake a newspaper venture in Philadelphia. When C. D. Lee, an old Scripps associate, succeeded Clark in 1910, Howard was promoted to first vice president as well as general manager.

A Scripps biographer, Jack Casserly, wrote that Scripps "never trusted Howard despite the executive's long tenure with Scripps' organization. E.W. felt that Howard not only made major managerial mistakes in running UP, but played fast and loose as a man."

Scripps said he chose Howard to run UP partly because Howard was the grandson of a tollgate keeper near the Scripps' place in Illinois.

According to another Scripps biographer, Gilson Gardner, Howard had been "as active as a wasp trying to get through a window pane" in his desire for the top UP job.[7]

In 1908 United Press had gone into the black by about $1,200. The company also had moved its headquarters from Park Row to Pulitzer's *New York World* building. At a meeting of the UP board in January 1910, held at the Scripps estate in Miramar, California, Howard was told he must squeeze $12,000 profit out of the company the next year.

Howard became president of United Press in 1913. On becoming president, he was allowed to buy Vandercook's 20 percent of the stock and when Hamilton Clark resigned, he got a share of his equity as well. The wire service was at that time returning huge profits. Roy Howard became personally very wealthy, owning 30 percent of United Press and shares in the closely held parent E. W. Scripps company.

By 1916 Howard was making $32,000 in dividends from the UP plus a $15,000 salary and bonuses of $15,000 a year.[8] The company was then worth a million dollars and Howard's stock had appreciated by $75,000 in a single year.

At one point Howard considered leaving Scripps. He told E.W. he thought he could do better on his own. When he had bought the *Pittsburgh Press* for Scripps, he told E.W. he could have bought it for himself. Scripps told Howard to his face that no way did he have enough talent to make it on his own in the newspaper business.[9]

In managing the United Press, Howard displayed fanatic enthusiasm and initiative. Self-starting enterprise and enthusiasm became the keystone of UP news reporting.

Although understaffed almost everywhere, the UP tried valiantly to present a complete news service. Competition with the Associated Press focused on major news stories which all newspapers would want and which would showcase the UP's high quality coverage. In the early days these kinds of stories usually found Roy Howard on the scene leading the troops. He also wanted UP to do things differently than AP did, with features, bylines and lively writing, while the AP was constrained and dull.

When Wall Street magnate J. P. Morgan was vacationing on the Nile in Egypt, he was rumored to be sick. The stock market was affected. Howard, attacking the story, spent $25 on a person-to-person cable to Morgan asking him to reply by collect cable on the health rumor.

Next day, Howard received a reply, prepaid by Morgan, saying he had been sick but was better and doctors did not consider the ailment serious. When Howard's story moved on the UP wire the stock market revived. The truth was, however, that Morgan was indeed very sick. He died soon afterward.

As news manager, Howard himself covered the 1908 Socialist convention in Chicago at which Eugene Debs was nominated. He also covered the Republican and Democratic conventions later that year.

Howard masterminded play-by-play accounts of the World Series for several years and covered the championship boxing match in Reno, Nevada, July 4, 1910, when Jack Johnson knocked out Jim Jeffries. For that event, UP had wires installed from ringside to San Francisco and Chicago. Two telegraphers were used. The round-by-round narrative was dictated by Howard, assisted by San Francisco bureau manager Max Balthazar.

Physically, Howard was short—5 feet 6 inches. He was quite conscious of his stature. After interviewing Joseph Stalin in Moscow in 1936, he came out of the visit and observed to an associate that Stalin was "a little fellow, not as tall as I am." He usually put his own height at "almost five foot seven."

Another trademark was the gaudy vesture he always wore. As a very young man he had made himself a clotheshorse, wearing striking shirts that spanned the color spectrum, bow ties, and patent leather shoes. He carried a walking stick for appearance, and pince-nez spectacles. When someone took note of the green band on his homburg, Howard proudly reported that it was made from the feathers of a tropical bird and it took 200 birds to produce enough material for one band.

As head of the Scripps-Howard organization, he maintained a stunning Chinese lacquered office in New York that was described as a loud version of an imperial temple. A secretary summoned to his home one day when he was indisposed said she found him in a Marie Antoinette canopied bed with purple and yellow bedding. Howard had on pajamas that matched the sheets.[10]

RWH was wholeheartedly a penny-pincher. His club was the Dutch Treat Club in New York. He liked the house rule that everyone pays for his own meal. A friend once said Roy had "a feminine reluctance to part with money except for clothes."

He complained once that Joseph P. Kennedy, the millionare, had kept him on the phone 45 minutes. Howard was sore because he had initiated the call and paid for it while Kennedy dawdled on the other end. The writer Forest Davis, who profiled Howard in the *Saturday Evening Post*, said Howard would walk around the block to avoid a hat-check tip and that he always figured a waiter's 10 percent tip down to the penny.

Negotiating a deal with Ross Walker to buy the Akron (Ohio) *Times*, Howard and Walker were stuck at a difference of $10,000 on price for the $650,000 property. Roy suggested they flip a coin for the difference. He took a quarter out of his pocket and gave the seller the call. Walker won the toss and picked up the quarter. Howard went white with anger. "Roy," his aide whispered, "you can't get sore. It was your suggestion."

"That's all right," Howard blared, "but the son-of-a-bitch stole my quarter."

A month before he died, he was seen after a board meeting going around turning out the lights in the room.

Howard was not a sociable person and was not graceful at taking a joke. In company, he liked to be the center of attention. When dining at a Chinese restaurant, he proudly gave his fellow diners lessons in how to use chopsticks.

He was well-informed and sometimes smug about it. An associate said of him: "Roy does not believe anything that is not told to him confidentially."

Howard ran the company until August 1, 1920, when he resigned from UP to become general business director of the Scripps-McRae League of newspapers. He was then thirty-seven.

After he moved from UP to the parent organization he maintained close interest in United Press but seldom interfered in the wire service's business. He did call upon its bureau chiefs around the world for such chores as greasing the way in his trips abroad, as Vaughn did in China in 1937. But "Wilmax"—Howard's UP code name—was seldom seen on directives to the wire service. One of the rare occasions was when General Dwight D. Eisenhower was being talked of as a candidate for president in 1951. Howard ordered that a lengthy, favorable and unsigned profile of Ike move on all the wires.

When E.W. Scripps died, control of UP and the E.W. Scripps Co. went to Howard along with F. W. Hawkins and George B. "Deak" Parker.

E.W.'s grandson, Edward "Ted" Scripps, held Howard in professional contempt because of what he conceived as UP's increasingly weak news coverage. Edward finally got so fed up that he canceled the contract between the Scripps League newspapers and the wire service. Howard "was a big man on personal prestige—not on principle," said Ted.[11]

Roy Howard, when he worked under Scripps, was, for his public image at least, pro-labor and liberal, as was E.W. But later, when Scripps was gone, he turned colors and sided with conservative politicians and conservative causes. The Scripps-Howard newspapers became anti-union. Howard personally hated, above all, the American Newspaper Guild, which was organizing newspaper and wire service employees. He said it was Communist influenced.

Howard's ambition, even when he was running UP, was not merely to write and report important news but to influence history. Before the United States entered World War I, he made several trips to England and became an intimate of Lord Northcliffe, who owned the London *Times* and several other newspapers.

The two of them thought that the United States was insufficiently enthusiastic about England's war against Germany. With Northcliffe's help, Howard got an interview with British War Minister David Lloyd George at Whitehall on September 27, 1916. The UP story received worldwide attention. The British minister made a strong attack on efforts in the United States to keep America out of the war.

Some critics said the interview was phony, claiming that a British diplomat would never use "sporting" language such as the reference to a "knockout." However, the story had been shown to Lloyd George before publication and he approved it with a few minor changes.

Lloyd George said later that while "the interview is not verbatim," nevertheless "Mr. Howard has conveyed my message to the United States to a nicety, even though he has partly clothed it in his own language. I only wish I had such facility of expression myself. It is exactly as I should wish it to be."[12]

Journalistically the interview also made history. It came up in the House of Commons, where Lloyd George described it as a "public report of a private conversation."[13] It was "a journalistic event that shook the world," according to a news historian.[14]

Interviews with political leaders were, at the time, almost unknown. The United Press was pioneering the technique. *Editor & Publisher* praised UP for developing and popularizing the "great American institution, the interview."[15]

Karl Bickel, who followed Howard as president of UP, said the Lloyd George interview was "the first great smash exclusive in a fresh, new world of modern journalism."[16]

Howard and Northcliffe continued their efforts to increase American support for Britain through such means as a lengthy, exclusive special article written for United Press under Northcliffe's byline.

Northcliffe and Howard were sometimes called "Napoleons"[17] of journalism. They continued fighting to kill off anti-war sentiment in the U.S. until the decision was made to send American doughboys to France. They also maintained their assault on censorship of war news.

Bickel, in a letter to Howard, said, "Those terrific stories that you boiled up and the men you made who got them on your directions and your orders won the world against the Kaiser…and built the UP."

Roy Howard might have become an English press lord instead of an American newspaper squire. Northcliffe offered him a job in which he would be "second in command over the biggest empire of printers' ink in all Europe."[18] Howard declined.

At the outset of World War II, Howard was still trying to employ his influence on political events. He opposed United States sending lend-lease material to Britain in the early years of the war. He defended Charles A. Lindbergh speaking in favor of the Nazi regime in Germany. He joined senators delaying American mobilization programs such as conscription and he believed that the appeasement at Munich made good business sense. Howard also pleaded for sympathy toward Japan up until the day the emperor's planes bombed Pearl Harbor.

These stands, in addition to Howards' enthusiasm for Wendel Wilkie and Herbert Hoover as presidential candidates, earned him the passionate wrath of President Franklin D. Roosevelt, who was unkind enough to restrict Howard's travel during World War II by denying him a passport or press credentials.

Once the U.S. was in the fighting, Howard strongly supported the war effort. He "was frantically adaptable," observed A. J. Liebling, the *New Yorker's* journalism critic.[19]

Roy Howard died in 1964 after a massive coronary at his office at the age of 81.

6

Picking Up
the Cudgels

THE EARLY YEARS OF UNITED PRESS SAW FOUR SCRIPPS CRONIES ENTER A
revolving door to the office of the president. But things changed in 1912 when Roy
Howard jostled his way to the top. He had been running the wire service for four years
as general manager.

Howard stayed at the helm for a dozen years and set the company on a course
of relative stability that lasted seventy years, with experienced newsmen moving
up into the top job. When the company was sold in 1982, it began churning
CEOs almost yearly.

UP's first president, John Vandercook, a former editor of the *Cincinnati Post*, died
in April 1908, just months after he was elected president. He was on a business trip
to the Chicago bureau when he collapsed with a ruptured appendix and died a
few days later.

Hamilton B. Clark, an associate of Scripps, succeeded Vandercook as president
but he left the infant news agency a short time later, and C. D. Lee, a telegrapher and
an old Scripps friend, was named president. Roy Howard became business manager as
well as news manager. Roy was running the company and campaigning keenly to get
the top spot.

The Republican Party convention in Chicago in 1912 that nominated William
Howard Taft was the noisiest and most boisterous political nomination process to date.
United Press was armed mainly with enterprise and enthusiasm but not enough to
challenge the Associated Press, which boasted a coast-to-coast leased wire.

Howard tried hard. Because UP did not have a leased wire to the West Coast he
provided the San Francisco office in advance with a raft of hold-for-release material
that could be released by a brief telegram from the convention hall. But UP convention
copy was not competitive with AP's spot reports via leased wire.

For the Democratic convention later that year, UP ordered up a leased wire from
Denver to San Francisco. J. H. "Barney" Furay, a former managing editor of the *Cleve-
land Press* and head of UP's pivotal Chicago bureau, was sent to Denver to supervise it.
He stayed there as Rocky Mountain manager for twenty years.

Furay's replacement in Chicago was Edward T. Conkle, who also came from Cleveland.

Conkle was the first in a long line of great teachers of the news business in the Chicago bureau of United Press. It was universally regarded as the best place in the world to learn how to report and write all kinds of news on a break-neck, wholesale basis. Among those whom Conkle trained were Raymond Clapper, Webb Miller, Miles Vaughn, L. B. Mickel, Wilbur Forrest, Westbrook Pegler and scores of others who became distinguished reporters and writers after working under him in Chicago.

Conkle did not use a typewriter, writing everything in longhand. He did not smoke but constantly dangled a stogie in his teeth.

In 1910, the Associated Press was spending $2.7 million a year on collecting news for 800 newspaper members. AP's official view of the United Press was "down the nose," according to Joe Alex Morris, the UP historian. The Scripps agency was considered an upstart. It was proud of the reputation.

In 1910, United Press had 392 afternoon clients, twenty-one bureaus in the United States and permanent offices in London, Paris, Rome, Berlin, Tokyo and Havana. In other cities, UP was represented by stringers.

The organization's financial structure was very flimsy. The Boston UP office had a budget of only $300 a month, including salaries, rent—everything.

Two years later, when Roy Howard was elected chairman of the board, the company had increased its client list to 491 newspapers. It was making money, most of which went into the coffers of E. W. Scripps.

By 1914, UP had 15,000 miles of leased wire and 30,000 miles of part-time telegraph lines. Two hundred newspapers were on the full-time wire and another 300 on the part-time service. Some were receiving only a news summary of 500 words a day by telephone.

United Press bureaus in Europe were staffed by U.S.-trained correspondents. This helped sell the service because Americans were hungry for news from the old country and the AP's foreign report came mainly from the internal agencies in those countries, written for their home readers.

A tactic that proved effective for UP's smaller staff and tighter facilities was advance preparation of detailed, carefully written copy on developing news stories. This material was sent by mail to New York, where it could be put on the wire at the appropriate time. These mailers were often better than spot copy because they were prepared under less pressure.

Associated Press was geared particularly and deliberately toward serving morning newspapers. Even important news breaking during the day was often held for the night or A.M. wire. UP, serving afternoon newspapers, raced to get breaking news out on the streets the day it happened.

Another distinguishing UP practice was filling special requests. Clients were encouraged to call upon the service for anything they wanted, such as the visit of a local dignitary to the Pope or the condition of the grape harvest in France. If a fatal fire occurred in a city and the newspaper editor wanted to have news of other fires around the country, he could ask the local UP office. A request would be sent to all UP bureaus, drawing material for a full roundup of fires.

United Press was recognized as the pioneer in human interest stories, features and interviews. Associated Press shunned everything except stark, colorless reports of "facts." Many editors preferred the AP's staid approach. They thought UP was too breezy, too jaunty and less dependable than the old service under its general manager, Melville Stone, who kept AP true to his name, "rock."

Press critic Silas Bent blamed United Press for leading the AP astray. He wrote:

> The AP has succumbed to what I may call United Pressure. It has bobbed its hair and rouged its cheeks and got out its lipstick in order to keep up with a flapper. It has taken on vaudeville features to meet the showmanship of the rowdy and irrepressible United Press.

AP's later headlong dive into florid prose was laughed at by editors. It gushed tears over President Wilson's death, the death of Rudolph Valentino in 1926 and the story of Floyd Collins, a man trapped in a West Virginia mine. In its dispatch on the accident AP canonized Collins as a hero of great dimensions when he was really a workman fighting for his life.

In the 1920s most publishers sided boldly with conservative political sentiment, were anti-union and pro-capitalist. Many saw the UP as a more liberal news vendor than the AP. Garrison Villard, in the publication *Nation*, said "in ninety-nine cases out of a hundred" Associated Press reports represented the view of the employing class.

AP was also accused of ignoring racially controversial stories. Villard wrote that when several Negroes were murdered for attempting to vote in Florida the AP did not carry the story at all.

Frank B. Kellogg, U.S. senator from Minnesota, accused the AP of carrying only pro-Standard Oil stories during a court dispute in Chicago over the company's practices.[1]

William G. Shepherd arrived from St. Paul, Minnesota to take a job with UP in New York on Saturday, March 25, 1911. He was walking to his hotel when he saw smoke pouring from windows of the Triangle Waist Company garment factory.

Shepherd got to a telephone in a building across the street and called the bureau. Roy Howard was on the desk.

"Thud-dead! Thud-dead! Thud-Dead!" were the first words of the story that moved on the UP wire. Sixty-two persons jumped to their deaths from the burning building. It was a typical United Press kind of lead. In his eye-witness dispatch written when he got back to the bureau, Shepherd wrote: "I learned a new sound—a more horrible sound than description can picture—it was the thud of a speeding, living body on a stone sidewalk…."

That kind of prose was the UP trademark. Shepherd is credited with originating the "Omaha milkman" phrase in United Press lore. He advised young reporters joining the service that the way to tell the news quickly and simply was to write it for the milkman in Omaha.

Reynolds Packard, a Unipresser who learned that lesson, wrote a best-selling novel titled *Kansas City Milkman*, first published by E. P. Dutton in 1950. It became a prized cult fiction version of the intimate conditions of wire service work.

Although it was, of course, fiction, Unipressers enjoyed guessing at the characters. Hugh Baillie, president of the company, recognized himself in the story and it put him in highest dudgeon. He tried through several channels to get the book suppressed, without success. A story is told that a fuming Baillie, heading out to lunch with the company lawyer, Ezra Bryan, and several others executives, said to Bryan, "We're going to sue that sumbitch. What do you think?" Bryan is said to have responded: "Well, Hugh, everyone on this elevator knows who he was talking about. When we file the suit, if you insist, everyone in the goddam world will know. So if you want to go ahead with it, just let us know." There was no suit.

Kansas City Milkman was published in paperback under two other titles, *Dateline Paris* and *Low Down*. When it went out of print, copies became prized memorabilia for ex-Unipressers.

In 1912, one of America's landmark industrial labor strikes occurred in Lawrence, Massachusetts. Textile workers went out on picket lines and there was much violence when police were called to subdue the strikers. Local officials, businessmen and newspapers, played down the violence. Associated Press did not even report it.

Marlen E. Pew, the New England manager of UP, based in Boston, made sure that UP carried objective but complete dispatches from Lawrence. The local Chamber of Commerce wrote to publishers throughout the country, urging them to suppress the story and to boycott United Press. Few did. More of them decided that United Press was a needed competitor for AP.

The Lawrence strike story was discussed at a meeting of newspaper editors held afterwards in Wisconsin and UP's performance was praised. Will Irwin, a distinguished *Harper's Weekly* critic, described the UP's dispatches as accurate and commendable. The *American Magazine* also praised UP in a lengthy article about the strike. "The United Press was true to its responsibility and as a result of its accurate representation of that labor conflict the whole nation was aroused," *American Magazine* editorialized.

The outcome was an investigation in the Senate, which led to a further inquiry by the Department of Labor into the violence by police against the Lawrence strikers.

In 1912[2] Reuters agency of Europe made the first of several attempts, to combine with the UP. At a meeting of the UP board in Chicago in June, the question first arose. Baron Reuter had talked to Roy Howard secretly, offering him a deal to replace Associated Press as the North American outlet for the cartel. Reuter proposed a 10-year contract to exchange news.

Howard was in favor of it, but prudently waited to get other views. He and Scripps had often praised themselves for opposing exclusive ties with foreign news agencies on principle. But UP had similar agreements and, in this case, the company came within a hair's breadth of signing with Reuters, a deal that could have radically altered its future.

United Press then had its own men in London, Paris and Berlin. They were American-trained correspondents who wrote for American newspaper readers. Howard knew that clients in the U.S. liked this but he thought his low-budget European operation might be enhanced by a tie-up with Reuters. UP's American correspondents sometimes had difficulty obtaining European government news. In Germany, for example, it was a penal offense to release a story to any agency before the Wolff agency carried it.

Accountants told the board that the cost of the contract with Reuters would increase UP expenses by about $35,000 a year, an amount equal to the company's entire annual profit.

Some of the Scripps publishers at the board meeting were so enthusiastic about ousting AP from its Reuters connection that they offered to stand a $20,000 annual UP rate increase to meet the cost.

E. W. Scripps was not in attendance at the meeting. He was then semi-retired at his ranch in Miramar. J. C. Harper, the whiskey maker, who was on the Scripps board, wondered aloud what E.W. would think of teaming up with a government news agency. The discussion went nowhere and the group adjourned, deciding to vote the next day. When they resumed their session, held at the LaSalle Hotel, John P. Scripps suggested that E.W. should be consulted.

"I don't think that is necessary," said Hamilton Clark, chairman. John Scripps then said he thought that at least they should consult James Scripps, his brother, who was running the Scripps affairs in San Diego and was the contact between the company and E.W.

A decision was postponed until Clark, then president of UP, went to California to outline the proposition to E.W. at the Miramar ranch. When he did so, there must have been a resounding, "No!" There would be no Reuters-UP deal.

At the same Chicago meeting, Howard and Clark also suggested that the UP change itself into a cooperative like the Associated Press. They argued that this would lower costs and enable them to get more news from clients. Some of the other directors thought Howard and Clark may have been looking for a substantial rise in the value of their own stock. The idea was dropped.

Robert P. Scripps, who headed the parent E.W. Scripps Company, and who was given controlling interest in UP by his father,[3] decided that he would pay closer attention to the wire service. He wrote Howard, April 9, 1913, that he had decided to become chairman of the UP board. "That means everybody steps down a notch," he told Howard whose step down was to president. He was still given a free hand in running the wire service.

An enterprising UP bureau manager in Indianapolis at this time, Kent Cooper, came up with the idea of serving smaller newspapers by telephone. UP quickly began selling what it called a "pony" service to newspapers that could not afford a leased wire.

The term "pony" derived from the phone company's rate structure, which provided a "Public News Transmission" tariff or PNT. Somehow that became "pony." Cooper went to the American Telephone and Telegraph Company and persuaded it to establish this special rate for telephone conference calls to several newspapers at one time. On such a conference call a UP staffer could dictate the news while typists at the newspapers transcribed it. Often the arrangement was for several brief calls during the day, the final one near deadline time. Small newspaper clients loved the pony reports.

UP staffers became good at dictating the ponies, and newspaper typists, some employees of United Press, became good at transcription. Esther Robbins, of Kankakee, Illinois, could transcribe cleanly 625 words in five minutes. A good team could get 1,200 words to newspapers in 15 minutes. Newspapers bought a pony report for as little as $10 or $20 a week. The system continued into the 1940s.

Occasionally there was some back-and-forth between the person dictating the pony and the receiving typist. Westbrook Pegler, who became a big-name columnist, was a pony reader in Chicago with United Press. One day he was dictating a story about the death of the poet, Joaquin Miller, when a literate typist in Joliet, Illinois, stopped him and pointed out that it was not "Joe Quinn" but "Wha-keen."

Almost everyone who started at United Press got the pony reading assignment early in their careers, including Walter Cronkite, whose smooth, pony-reading, diction skills led to a long broadcast career with CBS News.

Cooper left United Press, taking eighteen small Indiana pony clients, and tried to set up a telephone news service of his own. After a year he sold his operation back to UP for $50 and went to work for Scripps again, this time selling the service.

After two years he felt he was working too hard and asked for a raise. Hamilton B. Clark, president of UP, wrote him back saying, "Just remember that you are not on the road for the billion-dollar U.S. Steel Corporation but for an up-and-coming press association, your connection with which some day may make you rich."[4] He did not get a raise and went over to AP.

In 1916, Roy Howard, who had been friends with Cooper since both were reporters in Indianapolis, asked Cooper to come back to UP. Cooper declined and, when Melville Stone retired in 1921, he became assistant general manager of AP, then general manager when Frederick Martin resigned in 1925. Cooper built the cooperative into a progressive worldwide news service, reversing Stone's austere approach to news and imitating UP style writing, features and use of bylines.

At first a byline was only used on a few major stories each day, but gradually they became common. Frequently, however, the bylined correspondent was not the actual author, who was on a desk in the bureau doing "rewrite."

During World War II the war desk in New York used regular bylines for morning and afternoon wires, William B. Dickinson for A.M. and Phil Ault for P.M. At the request of the *New York Daily News*, the bylines were switched because Dickinson's was too long a line.

Newspaper editors often had the mistaken notion that the byline was the actual writer. In another World War II case, the *Los Angeles Times* asked UP to have Virgil Pinkley sign the war story because the paper liked his "style," even though he was seldom the writer.

To help newspapers fill their columns, United Press began publishing the Red Letter, a sheet of background stories, features, shorts and one or two-line "fillers" that were mailed to clients. Editors or printers could use these briefs during makeup to fill holes and help balance their pages. Later the Red Letter sheet was supplemented with pictures in cardboard matrix forms that were used to mold lead images that could be used for printing.

Roy Howard's wife, Margaret, wrote a women's column for the Red Letter called "Margaret Mason Letters." In one of them she wrote that she had "two children and two chins."

The 1916 election pitting President Woodrow Wilson against Republican Charles Evan Hughes, a former governor of New York, was a major news event in which UP tried to showcase its quality coverage. Declaring a winner was the objective for the rival news agencies and counting the votes was labor. It was a close election. Counting continued from Tuesday night until late Thursday evening. AP, UP and INS services were in desperate competition to win election coverage honors. United Press claimed it flashed the Wilson victory in California 10 minutes before Associated Press.

Throughout the years, the wires fought over vote counting honors until they joined forces in the National Election Service in 1964. The NES counted votes for all the participating wire services and broadcast networks. With a common count, the competition became who could first correctly "call" a winner based on the voting trends rather than actual counts. Bureau managers in each state became experts in analyzing the vote in their own areas. The wires remained conservative on these decisions while the broadcast networks sometimes declared a winner on the basis of projections with only a few votes counted.

Technology for the wires was also advancing rapidly during the 1920s. The old clickers used for Morse code, called "bugs," were replaced by teleprinters. Edward E. Kleinschmidt in 1914 invented the teletype, which became the most successful of several machines invented about the same time.

All three agencies, AP, UP and INS, claimed first use of the teletype. Oswald Garrison Villard, a press critic at the time, gave it to United Press.[5]

The network of telegraph wires was stretching into every city and town of the nation. In 1915, United Press had leased wires reaching from New York to New Orleans, Dallas, Denver and the Pacific Coast. The number of newspaper clients was 625.

Ed Conkle, the UP editor who didn't type, moved from Chicago to New York but the on-the-job journalism school he had launched continued in Chicago. Illustrious Unipressers who broke in there included Earl J. Johnson, Herbert Little, Marquis Childs, Edward Derr, Carl V. Little, Hal O'Flaherty, Robert T. Loughran, Harry Heydenberg, Jeremiah L. O'Sullivan, and many others.

All of them had affection for the United Press. Many left because of low pay. When O'Sullivan quit in Kansas City to teach journalism at Marquette University, Karl Bickel asked him by wire, "You sure you want to leave?"

O'Sullivan wired back:

KAB NX (Karl A. Bickel New York)
PAY TOO LOW. HOURS TOO LONG. LIFE TOO SHORT.
JLOS KP (Jeremiah L. O'Sullivan Kansas City)

Striving to produce a complete news report with a limited staff sometimes led wire service editors into the shady practice of news piracy and schemes to thwart their shortcomings. In January 1918, a dispatch moved on the United Press wire with a Petrograd, Russia, dateline about an international meeting going on there. The story included a one line quote attributed to Russian "Under Foreign Secretary Nelotsky."

A few minutes after the story moved on the wire, UP put out a correction eliminating the reference to "Nelotsky," which was a fictitious name. But the trap had sprung. International News Service that day also had a dispatch on the Petrograd meeting, under a London dateline. It mentioned Mr. Nelotsky prominently.

United Press announced, with some glee, that it had caught the INS red-handed in news piracy. The name "Nelotsky" was "Stolen" spelled backward "with the 'ky' thrown in for Russian camouflage."[6]

Hearst's International News Service, smallest of the major news agencies, was frequently caught pirating news. In 1914, the AP suspected its news was being filched. To trap the pirates, AP put a story on its wire going to one New York newspaper where the spy was thought to be lurking. The story said a Russian battleship, the *Fliba*, hit a mine and sank in the Gulf of Finland with a loss of 450 lives.

The news spy, a telegrapher for a small news ticker service in the New York newspaper's office, overheard the AP's Morse message and passed the story along to its own syndicate members, which included INS. The Hearst agency quickly flashed the story to its clients and UP and AP began getting calls to match the *Fliba* story.

UP did not pick up the story but was dragged into the fracas when AP General Manager Melville Stone called reporters in and told them both United Press and INS had stolen the story from the AP.

When calls began coming in, the New York UP bureau cabled London: "OTHERS HAVE REPORT RUSSIAN BATTLESHIP SUNK BY MINE. ANY CONFIRMATION?" UP London was unable to confirm the *Fliba* sinking and UP never carried anything about it.

Stone was forced by an insistent member, the *New York Evening Mail*, to apologize, declaring he "had no thought of saying that the United Press had any part in this incident."

UP, of course, took the opportunity to bash Stone. He had maligned UP "purely by accident, of course, and without the slightest malice," the UP company newsletter Hellbox said, tongue in cheek. It went on to relate that the AP executive had "another think and another say. He admitted what every other man in his organization knew all along, but what he, of course, had no way of knowing, namely that the United Press had never touched a line of the stolen stuff."

The Associated Press claimed that it owned all news collected by member papers. All 80,000 newspaper employees in the country were also AP employees, the cooperative insisted. They were prohibited from giving news to any other organization.

In a federal court suit, INS was accused of lifting news from early editions of the New York newspapers and transmitting it after a little rewrite to INS customers on the West Coast. Telegraph Editor R. E. Cushing of the *Cleveland News* was accused of passing local Cleveland stories as well as international news to INS.

Judge Augustus N. Hand of the U.S. District Court in New York granted AP an injunction against the INS on April 14, 1917. The U.S. Supreme Court upheld the ruling in 1919.[7]

The INS had argued that facts were not property that anyone could own. But Judge Hand said facts were "like fish in the sea," and when someone catches them, he owns them. AP was the lucky fisherman. No one else could publish facts as long as they had commercial value to AP, the court ruled. That meant at least until AP members everywhere in the country had a chance to print the news.[8]

The ruling was applauded by newspapers everywhere. The *New York Times*, in an editorial, called it an "admirable example of legal reasoning."[9]

In the summer of 1915, *Harper's* Magazine published an article in which it was asserted that INS was creating fictitious correspondents as well as filching stories. Byline dispatches were being carried on its wires from a half dozen European correspondents who did not exist. *Harper's* said the dispatches were written at an INS bureau in the United States and carried on the wire with bylines by "Frederick Werner" in Berlin, "Franklin P. Merrick" in Paris, "John C. Foster" and "Lawrence Elston" in London, "Brixton D. Allaire" in Rome and "Herbert Temple," identified as European news manager. *Harper's* said it tried to locate these men by mail and asked other newsmen in the European cities whether they knew these correspondents. It failed to find any of them.[10]

Throughout wire service and newspaper history, there has always been a good deal of "lifting" information from one service by another, sometimes deliberately and sometimes accidentally.

A news item is generated by a UP writer. It appears in a local newspaper without credit to the wire service. The AP bureau in that city picks it up and puts it on the AP wire. An interesting problem could arise if the AP tried to enforce its claim of ownership on everything published by a member newspaper. In the scenario above, AP would become owner of the United Press story.

Wire service desks were under standing instructions to check and verify everything put on the wire. But this was impractical and sometimes impossible. The general practice in both AP and UP was to verify controversial or questionable material before using it. For example, if a local newspaper quoted the police chief on a factual matter, the wire service editors typically did not feel they had to call the chief if they were in a rush to get out a news story. Nevertheless, when something erroneous got on the wire, the editor responsible received a memo from his boss telling him that EVERYTHING must be verified before being put on the wire. Those memos meant little.

UP staffers quickly learned one crucial thing. It was vital to make friends among the ground level people who could help you: Tipsters, business friends, fellow journalists, mechanics, waiters and bellboys. Hundreds of scoops and news leads were obtained from people who liked to be a player and hoped to become one by tipping off their wire service friend.

In 1914, William Shepherd was the UP man in Mexico City. He had taken every opportunity to make friends with telegraph operators whenever he met them. He was on friendly terms with all the Western Union operators in Mexico City. When Shepherd learned that the U.S. fleet was en route to Vera Cruz with troops aboard, he asked the Western Union man if he could get any information from Vera Cruz.

"Sure," said the operator, "my buddy works there." Through an exchange between the two Western Union men, Shepherd was able to get a play-by-play on the arrival of the American fleet, Mexican guns firing at the ships, Marines wading ashore, fighting in the streets and seizure of the port.

The U.S. government denied the action for seven hours and Associated Press advised its members that the UP story was probably a fake. Then Washington announced the invasion.

United Press took every opportunity to promote itself. At the San Francisco Pan American Exposition in 1915, the Underwood Typewriter Company exhibited a mammoth typewriter weighing 14 tons. It typed news bulletins received from UP. On May 7, 1915, visitors to the exposition saw:

BULLETIN BY UNITED PRESS
LIVERPOOL, May 7—The Cunard liner *Lusitania* with a heavy passenger list of Americans, was torpedoed and sunk off the Irish coast this afternoon. Small boats rushed from Queenstown to help save survivors.

One of the very fortunate things for United Press in its early years was that its owner, E. W. Scripps, insisted on absolute freedom for the wire service. He prohibited his own newspapers from dictating to UP editors or using UP wires to exchange their own material.

At a meeting of Scripps editors at San Diego on January 11, 1911, a resolution was passed declaring that "final judgment of all such [editorial] matters should lie with the general news manager of the United Press."[11] The group of editors at that meeting also supported a resolution introduced by Roy Howard declaring that every Scripps newspaper editor was to be held personally responsible for seeing that any news collected by the newspaper be furnished promptly to the nearest UP bureau and that the newspapers should, when requested by UP, try to cover stories the news service wanted. This rule was widely ignored by the Scripps editors.

A problem of "too much news" was already present in 1911. The Scripps papers urged UP to have its reporters write tighter leads.

Scripps newspapers were outspoken in support of labor and liberal causes, but the UP was, like AP, carefully neutral because it had clients on both sides of any fence.

Some liberals felt that "the press" was pro-employer. They got together in 1919 and established a new wire service called Federated Press. It was a cooperative on the order of the AP and quickly signed on 100 newspapers in the U.S. and a few overseas.

Federated Press opened bureaus in the United States and abroad and hired a number of talented journalists, including Carl Sandburg, the Chicago poet; Louis P. Lochner, former AP bureau manager in Berlin; and Frederic Kuh, who had been a top UP correspondent in Europe. Federated Press collapsed after a short life.

Raymond Clapper of UP gained a place in political history books by introducing the phrase "smoke-filled room" on the selection of candidates. In the Republican convention of 1920, four contentious ballots failed to provide a simple majority for any of the candidates. Stymied by the deadlock, the party powers, including Henry Cabot Lodge of Massachusetts, decided to go to a hotel room where they could quietly agree on a nominee.

They chose Warren Harding, a dark horse. Clapper said in his dispatch that the choice was made, not on the convention floor, but in "a smoke filled room" at the Blackstone Hotel. The phrase entered the political lexicon.

Later at the convention, Clapper was at the door of the room when the session broke up. He asked Harding for a statement to use if he were nominated. The next day Harding handed him a note with a comment he could use at the appropriate time. It gave UP an edge when he was named the party's candidate.

Clapper received a $100 bonus from UP and went on to cover the Harding campaign, leading to a distinguished career as UP Washington manager. He resigned in 1913 and was writing for the Scripps-Howard Newspaper Alliance when he was killed February 1, 1944, in a bomber collision in the Marshall Islands over Eniwetok in the Pacific war.

Although understaffed almost everywhere, the UP tried valiantly to present a complete news report. Major news stories usually found Roy Howard himself leading the UP troops.

7

World War Sells News

WORLD WAR I WAS GOOD BUSINESS FOR UNITED PRESS, BUT IT LEFT A permanent, ugly scar on the young news agency.

As the European nations maneuvered for power and security in the face of an impending war, AP found itself shackled by its total dependence for news coverage on the European cartel members, all closely allied with European governments.

United Press was independent and free to pursue the building story with its own reporters in the capitals of Europe and at the battlefronts.

War, like most of the horrors of the world, was "good copy" for American newspaper editors. They wanted more than the propaganda-tinged cartel dispatches, written in the dull, dry manner that was AP's trademark.

The ambitious young reporters of United Press went to Europe with daring exuberance and determination to tell the story for the *Omaha Milkman.*

UP's aggressive and sharp coverage at the onset of the war in 1914 drew worldwide attention to the agency. In one 30-day period, UP signed twenty-two new clients, and in the war's first year, 100 new newspapers came into the fold. There was enough revenue to expand the staff and, at the same time, provide E.W. Scripps, Roy Howard and the other owners a tidy profit. A lucrative contract with *La Nacion* of Buenos Aires for neutral war news had given UP a foothold in South America.

When the first shots were fired, UP rushed in re-enforcements to aid London bureau Manager Edward L. Keen. The new staffers included such distinguished reporters as Carl W. Ackerman, Westbrook Pegler, Lowell Mellett, Frank J. Taylor and Webb Miller.

Even though United Press recognized that the war in Europe was big news, some UP editors still put sex ahead of the politics and intrigue that preceded the heavy shooting.

Archduke Franz Ferdinand, heir to the Austro-Hungarian throne, was shot June 28, 1914, at Sarajevo. This is often called the spark that touched off the war. William Simms, in the Paris bureau, was pouring out wordage about tension on the Continent. It happened that the same day Paris also had the ongoing trial of Madame Caillaux, wife of a former premier, who was accused of shooting to death a French newspaper editor who had published her love letters. American editors, not yet aware that the United States would be involved in the war, were clamoring for more on Madame Caillaux. Simms got a rocket from Fred Ferguson, the managing editor in New York:

PRESS UNIPRESS PARIS
SIMMS DOWNHOLD WARSCARE UPPLAY CAILLAUX
FERGUSON

Americans might be forgiven for not being too excited about the war in Europe. President Wilson's administration had at first vowed to stay out of the conflict and, when he saw the inevitable, he deliberately encouraged the idea that the U.S. would need to make only a modest arms contribution and perhaps send a few troops.

Webb Miller, covering the War Department in Washington for UP, broke a story saying that this country would most likely be required to send a huge expeditionary force and mobilize much of the civilian economy. Newspapers ignored the story. Miller said later he saw only one newspaper that gave it the merited top play, a small daily in Manistee, Michigan.[1]

In 1916, Miller also wrote an exclusive dispatch from the Mexican border which said German emissaries had offered Pancho Villa money and support to resume attacks upon the American border towns. The story originated with the U.S. administration, Miller wrote. The motive, he said, was to stir up enmity in the United States against Germany. President Wilson was about to take the country into that war. Many years later, documents were released which confirmed Miller's story that it was part of a propaganda scheme to get the United States into the European war.

American Mercury Magazine carried an article saying Associated Press war stories were fashioned "like a country editor covering the farm report."

Another advantage United Press had was the time differential between the United States and Europe. When the day's action ended on the war fronts it was around 10 A.M. in the U.S., giving afternoon newspapers the first crack at communiqués on the day's activity. United Press was an afternoon service. The AP was a morning service.

When the new American UP writers arrived in England, they saw how serious the war was. Food, coal and clothing were rationed and often not available. Webb Miller said he lived in an unheated room in a cheap hotel on Norfolk Street, London. He said a breakfast provided by the hostelry usually consisted of a flabby fish called a "bloater," served whole, with tea and dry toast. The fish was so soggy and repulsive that he could not eat it.

In his memoir, *I Found No Peace*, Miller said one day he looked at his breakfast and the fish looked familiar. It was the same one he had been served the previous day and rejected. From then on, Miller said he marked the breakfast fish with his initials every morning so that it wouldn't be offered to him again.[2]

Rationing tickets allowed fresh meat only twice a week per person. Miller and a couple of his press companions managed to outwit the rationing system. They ate at a little restaurant on Fleet Street called the Wellington, where they were supposed to give the waiter a small paper tab from their ration card for each meal. The waiter, named Carlo, had poor vision. Miller discovered that the corner of a two-penny bus ticket was exactly the same size and color as the ration tab and thus he and his friends had meat four or five days a week.

Miller's reporting sometimes called for cunning. He talked to Lord French of Britain when the British leader was a target of Irish rebels. During their conversation French told Miller he did not want to give an interview and should not be quoted. The lead on Miller's story said:

> THIS IS NOT AN INTERVIEW. LORD FRENCH INSISTS THAT HE NEVER GIVES INTERVIEWS. BUT TO THE BEST OF MY KNOWLEDGE AND BELIEF, THIS IS WHAT HE SAID DURING A HALF HOUR'S TALK TODAY AT THE VICE REGAL LODGE. AND LORD FRENCH IS HEREBY RELIEVED OF ANY RESPON-SIBILITY FOR WHATEVER APPEARS IN THIS REPORT OF OUR TALK.

The British leader never denied the interview. Among things he had told Miller was that he was not afraid of riding on his horse around the Irish countryside but would not dare walk.

"I would not dare walk," he said, "but I'm safe on horseback. The Irish are soft-hearted and wouldn't want to chance killing my horse."[3]

British censorship was much stricter than German and this resulted in stories from the German side getting out quicker and in more detail. UP reports from Germany did not have to go through British censorship as the AP/Reuters copy did.

British censors were quite willing to pass stories that put the Germans in a bad light. When William Shepherd filed the first report of poison gas being used by the Germans on the Western Front, his unemotional but stunning eyewitness story from Ypres on April 22, 1915, went through quickly. Others stories became mired in the censorship office.

Shepherd was among Unipressers in the first wave of reporters from the United States flocking to Europe when the war broke out. His first achievement was an exclusive interview on August 30, 1914, with Winston Churchill, then First Lord of the Admiralty. Because of a peculiarity of British censorship, newspapers in England could not use the interview until a day after it appeared in the United States.

The first German zeppelin bombing raid on London occurred September 8, 1915. British censorship rejected all dispatches reporting the attack and so Shepherd needed an evasive tactic again. Instead of a straightforward story on the bombing, he filed an account telling of the heroism of the London population under battle hardships:

"THESE CIVILIANS, NOT PRIVILEGED TO FIGHT AT THE FRONT, HAD PROVED THEIR METTLE NOW THAT THE WAR HAD REACHED THEIR HOME AREA. THEY HAD FOUGHT FIRES, RESCUED WOUNDED, SHRUGGED OFF AN ENTIRELY NEW TYPE OF WARFARE AND PATCHING TOGETHER THEIR HOUSES AND SHOPS HAD CARRIED ON AS USUAL."

The censor found no reason to delete even a word, and every reader easily knew what was going on in London.

Karl H. Von Wiegand, a German-speaking American in the Berlin UP bureau, through great persistence obtained an interview with Crown Prince Wilhelm of the German royal family. It was the first direct statement by any member of the German royalty since the war started.

"Undoubtedly this is the most stupid, senseless and unnecessary war of modern times," the prince told Von Wiegand. "It is a war not wanted by Germany, I can assure you, but it was forced on us, and the fact that we were so effectually prepared to defend ourselves is now being used as an argument to convince the world that we desire conflict."

The interview took place while the prince was with the German forces in France. Von Wiegand sent the copy by courier to The Hague and thence to London where it was cabled to New York. It made front page headlines everywhere.

 UP promoted the scoop aggressively, declaring it to be "the greatest journalistic success of the war." Clients praised it. The La Porte, Indiana, *Herald* commented that UP reporters Von Wiegand and Shepherd "have executed more perfect scores in the great war than all other correspondents combined." The *Milwaukee Sentinel* said the crown prince interview was "one of the finest pieces of American journalistic achievement of the war."

But some people accused United Press of being pro-German for circulating the interview and other news from the German side. UP responded that it had been similarly charged with being under English influences when, earlier in the war, on August 30, 1914, Shepherd had achieved his exclusive interview with Churchill. In the interview Churchill had made a strong case for the Allied side.

In Paris, William Simms customarily had coffee each morning at the Cafe Viennoise on the Boulevard Montmarte. He was sitting there one day when a small German plane flew over at about 1,000 feet. Simms saw the pilot toss a bomb out of the plane. It fell in a courtyard across the boulevard from where he was sitting with coffee cup in hand. The UP correspondent hurried back to his office and wrote an eye-witness dispatch on the first bombing raid against Paris.

A German submarine sank the British liner *Lusitania* on May 17, 1915, with the loss of 1,153 lives, including some Americans. Again, the British government was revealing nothing. Wilbur Forrest, an eager new recruit on the UP staff in London, heard a rumor that a passenger liner had been hit and its survivors were being taken to

Queenstown, Ireland. He immediately hopped a train to the Irish port and spent three days without sleep getting interviews and details from the ship's passengers. He was able to give UP the most detailed account of the incident available.

In September 1916, before the U.S. was in the fighting, Roy Howard showed up in London to personally mastermind war coverage. Always looking for ways to enhance the prestige of his wire service, Howard prevailed upon Lord Northcliffe, publisher of the *London Times*, to help him set up an interview with David Lloyd George, British Secretary of State for War.

In the interview, the British leader expressed a view much more belligerent than other Allied leaders had taken. He said the war should be fought to a "knockout." It was big news in the United States where people still hoped for a quick peace without their country being directly involved.

Howard took his dispatch back to Lloyd George's office for approval. It was okayed with little change and put on the wires in the United States. Again British censorship held the interview for 24 hours before releasing it in England.

BY ROY W. HOWARD
LONDON, SEPTEMBER 28 (U.P.) THERE IS NO END OF THE WAR IN SIGHT. ANY STEPS AT THIS TIME BY THE UNITED STATES, THE VATICAN OR ANY OTHER NEUTRAL IN THE DIRECTION OF WORLD PEACE WOULD BE CONSTRUED BY ENGLAND AS AN UNNEUTRAL, PRO-GERMAN MOVE. THE UNITED PRESS IS ABLE TO MAKE THESE STATEMENTS ON NO LESS AUTHORITY THAN THAT OF THE BRITISH MAN OF THE HOUR, RIGHT HON. DAVID LLOYD GEORGE, SECRETARY OF STATE FOR WAR.

"BRITAIN HAS ONLY BEGUN TO FIGHT," WAS THE WELSH STATESMAN'S SIZE-UP OF THE SITUATION. "THE FIGHT MUST BE TO A FINISH—TO A KNOCKOUT."[4]

United Press, and Howard in particular, felt good about their coverage of the war and the inroads that the service was making against the Associated Press. However, the euphoria was premature. The war was not over. And the daring enterprise that had lifted UP so high would eventually take a huge toll.

Howard's pro-British view contrasted sharply with that of William Randolph Hearst, who owned America's largest newspaper chain at the time. Hearst was violently anti-British, against the war. While Lord Northcliffe ignored his overtures to join in an anti-war crusade, Hearst's writers received special entree in Germany. In fact, some of them were determined later to be German agents.[5]

When President Woodrow Wilson was scheduled to issue a declaration of war on April 6, 1917, Robert J. Bender, UP bureau manager in Washington, assigned a speedy copy boy to grab the first copy of the handout at the president's office and run with it to the White House press room. Bender and several other staffers were there waiting. Bender seized the sheets from the copy boy and frantically paged through them to the crucial words declaring the United States at war.

"Flash," Bender shouted. "PRESIDENT DECLARED UNITED STATES STATE OF WAR WITH GERMANY." The Morse telegrapher tapped out the flash onto the wire. Bender then tore the text apart and gave several pages to different writers. Each of the writers hastily ran through his section, jotting down on slips of paper the most important phrases or sentences and handing them back to Bender.

Bender glanced at the slips, quickly and smoothly put them in order of importance and dictated short, meaty flashes to the telegraph operator. Within a few minutes all the essential points of the president's message were on the wire, clicking into hundreds of newspaper editorial rooms. At the same time, Webb Miller was editing the full text of Wilson's remarks and moving it out on another wire.[6]

When numbers were to be drawn for the first American men to be drafted into the army in 1917, it was again a story of tremendous interest everywhere. Bender assembled a crew of five reporters to cover the event—himself, Carl. D. Groat, Charles McCann, Tony Demma, Robert K. MacCormac, and a telegrapher.

E.W. Scripps often expounded his belief that the UP and the Scripps newspapers were on automatic pilot, not under his domination. However, when World War I broke out, E.W. roused himself out of hibernation at his quiet ranch at Miramar, California, and issued a call-to-arms. He wrote to all Scripps-Howard managers and editors telling them they could no longer run their newspapers as they saw fit themselves. He was taking away their independence because of the urgent crisis facing the country.

Scripps summoned Roy Howard, Harry Rickey, Charles R. Cranes, Walter Rogers, and his son Robert for a war council. At the end of the meeting, he sent a telegram to his troops. "Conclusion: NEA, UP and all papers must take definite stand on war policy. Object: wake up country to real fact of serious situation. First step: immediate big drive on food problem."

E.W. ordered that every Scripps paper publish all NEA and UP dispatches that might arouse readers to war fever. Pro-war stories were to be stamped "must."

There were limits to E.W.'s call to arms. He didn't want his own sons going to war. When it appeared that Robert might be drafted, he pulled strings to have him exempted from service.

During World War I, United Press achieved a standing and respect as the leading American wire service in Europe. Military and political leaders on both sides of the fighting knew that a dispatch from the United Press was more likely to be believed than any from the other national agencies, even the Associated Press, which was boasting that it limited itself to official news from the European capitals. United Press told its customers that official reports put out by the involved parties were "valueless when it comes to real news getting out."

UP's American correspondents in Europe had a distinctly different approach than the writers for the European agencies. In a talk to editors, von Weigand said European journalists were mainly "doctors and professors who want their tea and coffee, and howl like hell if they don't have their meals on time and travel in closed autos."

French authorities permitted William Simms, Paris UP manager, to visit the battle-front headquarters. He was the only American reporter given the clearance. William Shepherd was the only American reporter allowed to accompany Franz Joseph's general staff in Austria.

U.S. troops arrived at the war front in February 1918. Fred Ferguson of UP, who had gone over with the American Expeditionary Force, was with them, filing daily stories on the moves and progress of the war. One of the major battles he covered was the American First Army's conquest of what was thought to be a strong German position at Saint-Mihiel later that year.

U.S. reporters were called in for a briefing September 12, in advance of the attack. A half million American troops were to move the next day on the French town, supposedly strongly held by the Germans. The correspondents were shown maps, given extensive detail and a step-by-step timetable on how the action would be carried out. They received a schedule of artillery bombardments, air sorties, tank advances and infantry assaults.

Ferguson, experienced in the practice of hold-for-release writing, prepared his dispatch in the past tense, using the schedule of plans handed out. Then he persuaded an officer whom he had befriended in the censor's office to take his stack of cables and hold them until each move of the Army had been accomplished, then send them one at a time when official reports came in on the troop operations. He knew the German positions were vulnerable and that the action would, in all likelihood, follow the schedule laid out in the briefing.

The censor's officer did as Ferguson had requested. Next morning the correspondents, including Ferguson and his opposition, the AP reporter, went out with the troops. The plan was that they would write their dispatches after observing the action. Ferguson was in no hurry to get back.

According to *Deadline Every Minute*, the semi-official United Press history by Joe Alex Morris, Ferguson's story was on the UP wire before any other service had it. He received congratulations from New York for "an outstanding beat."

However, George Seldes, an acerbic reporter and media critic who was on the scene in France wrote that there was no fighting at all at Saint-Michiel that day. Seldes, who once worked for UP himself but was with the *Chicago Tribune,* said he and two companions hired a French driver who knew the territory. The American forces ran into impossible traffic on the main highway to the town. The French driver took Seldes and his companion into Saint-Mihiel by a back route. They found no Germans in the town. Seldes says they drove undisturbed through the streets to meet the U.S. army coming by the main road. Seldes took a picture of General Pershing making his "triumphal entry," greeted only by a few Frenchmen and Seldes' party.

Ferguson's pre-written story and those of the other reporters with the U.S. army, written after the engagement, described to the world how the Americans "stormed" the town. Historians to this day tell how "a force of more than 500,000 Americans wiped out the Saint-Mihiel German bastion," Seldes wrote in his memoir many years after the war that a German officer, General Ledebour, told him there were no Germans in the town to oppose the American forces, no artillery fire, no rifle fire, no airplanes. There was nothing.

"We had made the greatest attack of the war against an enemy that had departed at least seven days earlier," Seldes wrote in his autobiography, *Witness to a Century.*[7]

Because United Press was making a splash with its war coverage, Associated Press, for the first time, became a bit worried about competition. AP leaders held meetings to work out a counter-strategy, and they began boasting about their scoops and criticizing United Press for its slip-ups. The war of the wires was on! And UP's darkest day was nearing.

German general headquarters sent a radio message to the allies in Europe at 1 P.M. on November 7, 1918. It announced the Germans were ready to discuss the allies' peace terms. The radio said, "Orders were given to cease fire on the front at 3 o'clock P.M. until further orders." Top German officers were reported coming across the lines to sue for an armistice.

Roy Howard was in the French port city of Brest, waiting for a ship to take him back to New York. A very strong rumor was circulating that the Germans were seeking peace. The same rumor was reported in a half dozen other French cities and in Holland, Belgium and London. When Howard visited Admiral Henry B. Wilson, commander of the American Navy in the French port, the admiral showed him a telegram from the Navy's office in Paris, signed by the U.S. naval attache in the French capital. It said:

"ARMISTICE SIGNED THIS MORNING AT 11. ALL HOSTILITIES CEASED AT 2 P.M. TODAY."

Howard was startled when he read this. Wilson, also elated, sent the news over to Brest's President Wilson Square where a U.S. Navy band happened to be performing a concert. The armistice announcement was read to a cheering crowd.

Howard knew he had a major scoop on his hands. Nothing about the armistice had been reported in the normal news channels from Paris.

He handled the story with the skill, professionalism and speed that had become the marks of a wire service correspondent. He asked Admiral Wilson if he could use the information in the telegram. Wilson said yes, it was an official communication. Howard dashed directly to the cable office nearby. On the way he decided the news was too important to scribble by hand or dictate to a telegraph operator. So he went across the street to the editorial room of *La Depeche*, a French newspaper client of United Press. He asked a telegraph operator to type up his bulletin. He signed the message "HOWARD/SIMMS." William P. Simms was the Paris UP bureau manager.

Howard went back across the street and requested the cable company to send the bulletin urgently. Since it had been typed on a telegraph printer, it looked like a telegram from Paris which would already have been censored, so it was passed without question. It was received in New York six minutes later and put on the UP wire.

The celebrating began.

That evening Howard was also celebrating the war's end at the Brasserie de la Marine restaurant in Brest with a party of friends and officers including First Lieutenant Arthur Hornblow, Jr., a military intelligence officer.

A French orderly came into the restaurant and headed for the table where Hornblow and Howard were dining amidst the singing and dancing patrons. A note handed to Hornblow was in code. He carefully translated it and read the key passage to Howard and the others.

"Armistice report untrue. War Ministry issues absolute denial and declares enemy plenipotentiaries to be still on the way through the lines, cannot meet Foch until evening. Wire full details of local hoax immediately."

Howard's face turned white. He knew he had put out a false story with monumental impact. He immediately tried to cable a correction but the correction was held up in the censorship process and was too late anyway.

The news from UP was enough for a world anxious to end the war. They danced in the streets of New York and everywhere else. Associated Press and other news agencies scrambled frantically to check it out. U.S. officials denied it. For hours UP had an exclusive to beat all exclusives—too exclusive!

Seven hours later, UP was still holding to its guns with the story on the wire. Newspapers were demanding more proof or a correction. W.W. Hawkins, general manager of UP, said the company would stand on Howard's report until it was proven erroneous.

It was without doubt "officially" premature, and according to government officials, it was erroneous. The U.S. State Department issued a release denying that the armistice had been signed at the time the United Press filed its flash.

The official announcement of an armistice issued several days later said fighting ended on the 11th hour of the 11th day of the 11th month. It is doubtful that everybody kept shooting until the official hour, but some military units in the trenches did suffer casualties after the false armistice report.

Howard, reflecting on the incident later, insisted he had done what any good wire service reporter who has a lucky scoop would do. There was an official source. The top U.S. navy officer in France, Admiral Wilson, backed up Roy's explanation. The telegram he received was signed by Commander Jackson, the admiral's aide in Paris. That message was said to have been based on a telephone call from the French Ministry of War. But in the subsequent inquiry, the phone call could not be traced. The French ministry said it had not called Jackson.

Later, pondering his colossal gaffe, Howard came to the conviction that a German spy must have made the undocumented call. This version was endorsed by Hornblow, the naval intelligence chief in Brest. Admiral Wilson accepted responsibility for giving the dubious telegram to UP.

Why would a German spy report the end of the war? Hornblow, in *Century Magazine*, November 1921, wrote that on November 7, 1918, the peace rumor was being circulated in a half dozen other French cities besides Brest, including St. Nazaire, Bordeaux, Marseilles, Nice and Lorent. It was also being spread in London, New York and cities of Holland and Belgium. The UP scoop was the welcomed verification of a widespread rumor.

The reasoning by Howard and Hornblow was that the Germans were finished fighting and in a hurry to win support for a negotiated peace. However, strong sentiment on the part of many allied military leaders was to delay an armistice until their armies, now at peak strength, had completely overrun Germany and eliminated any power it had to bargain. Germany's intelligence service knew that anything to encourage the sentiment for peace would help bring about the quick armistice that Germany needed to save anything. So, the argument went, they made the disputed phone call that was the source of Howard's armistice.

E.W. Scripps, owner of UP, was apparently not greatly upset by Howard's embarrassment and the loss of credibility it brought upon the news agency. But UP was never allowed to forget the goof. Few remember that Reuters, the British news service, also carried the false armistice story, tracing it to the same source as Howard's.[8]

For the rest of the twentieth century many newspaper editors, some who were not even born when Howard ended the war prematurely, would not print a United Press "beat" but would wait for the AP to confirm it.

Vivid writing is what brings a war scene sharply into the mind of the reader. UP's correspondents in World War I were paragons of vivid writing. Here are a few paragraphs from a 25-paragraph dispatch sent by Karl Von Wiegand from the Eastern Front where German and Russian armies confronted each other. He was the first correspondent to report from there.

ON THE FIRING LINE, NEAR WIRBALLEN, RUSSIAN POLAND, OCT. 8 (UNITED PRESS)—AT SUNDOWN TONIGHT, AFTER FOUR DAYS OF CONSTANT FIGHTING, THE GERMAN ARMY HOLDS ITS STRATEGIC AND STRONGLY ENTRENCHED POSITION EAST OF WIRBALLEN.

AS I WRITE THIS IN THE GLARE OF A SCREENED AUTO HEADLIGHT, SEVERAL HUNDRED YARDS BACK FROM THE GERMAN TRENCHES, I CAN CATCH THE OCCASIONAL HIGH NOTES OF A SOLDIER CHORUS. FOR FOUR DAYS THE SINGERS HAVE LAIN CRAMPED IN THOSE MUDDY

DITCHES, UNABLE TO MOVE OR STRETCH EXCEPT UNDER
COVER OF DARKNESS. AND STILL THEY SING. THEY BELIEVE
THEY ARE ON THE EVE OF A GREAT VICTORY.
I REACHED THE BATTLEFIELD OF WIRBALLEN SHORTLY
BEFORE DAYLIGHT, ARMED WITH A PASS ISSUED BY THE
GENERAL STAFF AND ACCOMPANIED BY THREE OFFICERS
ASSIGNED TO CHAPERONE ME AND FURNISH TECHNICAL
INFORMATION.

TODAY I SAW A WAVE OF RUSSIAN FLESH AND BLOOD
DASH AGAINST A WALL OF GERMAN STEEL. THE WALL
STOOD. THE WAVE BROKE, WAS SHATTERED AND HURLED
BACK. RIVULETS OF BLOOD TRICKLED SLOWLY IN ITS
WAKE. BROKEN BLOODY BODIES, WRECKAGE OF THE
WAVE, STREWED THE BREAKERS.

TONIGHT I KNOW WHY CORRESPONDENTS ARE NOT
WANTED ON ANY OF THE BATTLE LINES. DESCRIPTIONS
AND DETAILS OF BATTLES FOUGHT IN THE YEAR OF OUR
LORD 1914 DON'T MAKE NICE READING....

As the war progressed, it became more difficult to get action stories. William Simms, Paris UP manager, tried to join the French armies at the front. When he showed his credentials at a check-point, a French officer took the papers and tore them up, saying "Get out. We don't want you."

In Berlin, Von Wiegand was arrested and briefly held on spying charges. After the war, he left UP and joined the International News Service for higher pay. UP was never known to compete with cash to hold onto even its most talented correspondents.

One of the feisty UP reporters with the American forces in Europe was Westbrook Pegler, who later became a widely syndicated newspaper columnist. He was not with General Pershing's headquarters long before he managed to get on the general's list of painful people.

Pershing was not friendly to any correspondents and was especially indignant when Pegler showed up at his office demanding an interview. A few minutes later, "Peg" was back at press headquarters tapping away at his typewriter. One of the other correspondents was curious to see what luck he had. Pegler pulled the sheet of paper out of the machine and handed it to the competitor. It read: "This correspondent had an interview with General Pershing today. The general said, 'Pegler, get the hell out of my office.'"

A short time later Pegler wrote a dispatch telling about unsanitary and unhealthy conditions in the American camps, detailing poor food, lack of heat and much sickness.

Headquarters would not like this story. To avoid putting it through the censors Pegler handed it to Lowell Mellett of UP's Paris bureau, who happened to be visiting the front. Mellett took it to London and turned it over to Edward L. Keen, European manager, who saw it as a worthy piece and cabled a summary of it from London to Roy Howard in New York. British censors not only intercepted the cable but sent a copy of it back to Pershing.

As a consequence, the general asked United Press to pull Pegler from the front, using the excuse that he was too young. Pegler was twenty-three. UP managers decided his usefulness as a war correspondent was over and brought him home.

Pegler's pugnacious personality had been with him from his childhood and was well known to his UP associates. He was not a man to do any joking. Once he threatened mayhem on a fellow worker who was noisily whistling near his desk. On another occasion he broke the nose of a telegraph operator with one punch in what was supposed to be a demonstration of boxing technique.

He was described as a "deadly serious kid who never learned to play."

When he was UP bureau manager in St. Louis, Pegler had found his $6 a week office boy incompatible and fired him. He did the office boy's chores himself and added the $6 a week to his $25 pay by creating fictitious office boys and cashing their checks under various phony names.

When World War I ended, UP counted its costs as $26 million in cash and the undying stigma of Roy Howard's premature armistice.

8

Becoming a World-Class Player

WHEN UNITED PRESS WAS LAUNCHED IT HAD ONLY ONE FOREIGN correspondent, Ed Keen in London. Americans, many of them immigrants, were eager to have news from the old country. Within two years Roy Howard had established bureaus in Paris, Rome and Berlin.

At its peak in the 1970s, the agency had eighty-one bureaus outside the United States, with more than 600 employees overseas, one third of the total staff.

World War I broke out and the demand for news from Europe grew even more. UP needed more reporters there. It would cost money.

Fortunately, Howard found a customer who would pay the freight for much of this expanded reporting. *La Nacion*, the leading newspaper in Buenos Aires, Argentina, where many European émigrés also lived, wanted unbiased news from Europe, which it was not getting from Havas, the French agency that had rights to all of South America under the existing world news cartel. Dispatches from Havas were notoriously biased for the French government.

La Nacion asked Associated Press, to provide service but the AP was also tied to the cartel and declined.

"We'll do it," Howard told *La Nacion*. In 1916 the newspaper was signed to a 10-year agreement. At first UP provided only a minimal service from Europe. But it quickly expanded, and Latin American clients were soon paying much of the cost of covering Europe.

The agreement with *La Nacion* "marked a watershed in the history of UP," according to Terhi Rantanen, an Indiana University scholar who published a study on wire service expansion.[1] UP became the dominant news service in all of Latin America and remained so until the 1980s.

United Press blossomed on the sunny side of the hedge. Everyone else had to live in the shade of the cartel, known as the "Ring." The three other major wire services, Havas of France, Wolff of Germany and Reuters of Great Britain had divided up the world into geographical spheres where each partner could gather and sell news exclusively.

The situation was becoming increasingly objectionable to newspaper publishers everywhere in the world. The "Ring" provided news to various smaller national services, but they could not gather or sell it outside of the cartel. In the United States, the Associated Press was a partner of the "Ring," having been given exclusive rights in North America in 1890.

UP, not a party to the cartel, had no way to produce a foreign news report except on its own although it did make exchange agreements with a few small foreign agencies independent of the cartel. They included the British Exchange Telegraph News Agency, Nippon Dempo Tsushin Sha (Japanese Telegraph News Agency), the Australian Press Association, Hirsch Bureau in Berlin, the Fornier Agency in Paris, later with Kyodo in Japan, TASS in Russia and, as late as 1971, Deutsch Press Agentur (DPA) in Germany.

Direct UP service to clients on the European continent began in 1921 when a line was opened from London to Frankfurt, Cologne, and Vienna. In Asia, direct service began a year later when clients in Peking and Tientsin came on the wire along with the *Orient Press* service in Korea.

In 1931–32 Reuters for the second time made overtures to bring UP into the "Ring" as North American member replacing the Associated Press. Reuters' director, Sir Roderick Jones, was selling AP news in Japan, mainly to blunt UP inroads. When he learned that AP was trying, behind his back, to take over the Japanese service itself, he backtracked and tried to build an alliance with UP. Karl Bickel responded that he would like to do it. Roy Howard also was in favor of it, even though it would have made UP part of the news cartel.[2] But the Reuters-UP combination failed to get started when Howard and Bickel learned that it would limit the company's sales and news-gathering opportunities throughout Asia and other parts of the world.

On this issue, AP's general manager, Kent Cooper, was in agreement with the UP chiefs. They wanted no exclusive news deals.

Again in the 1960s, Reuters and UP talked about merging news operations. A fourth serious play by Reuters to acquire UPI occurred in the 1980s. At that time, the cash-hungry UPI did sell its overseas picture service to Reuters.

Seeking its own network of correspondents, UP established bureaus in Madrid, Lisbon, St. Petersburg, Buenos Aires, Peking and other major news-producing world capitals.

Never loosening its grip on the purse, however, the UP held its foreign operations under tight financial fetters. Before World War I, Ed Keen in London was limited to an average of only 100 words a day by cable to New York. All foreign bureaus were expected to send by low-cost mail to New York, detailed advance material that would be used to pad out brief cabled bulletins later.

A selling point the UP had over its competition in the United States was that it had American reporters covering news in other countries. Written by U.S.-trained newspeople, for American readers, UP dispatches had an American flavor. Associated Press dispatches, mainly from Reuters, were written from a European angle and were heavy with British language usage.

The rapid, worldwide flow of news became a technical reality after World War I, which raised the intensity of wire service competition and gave the agencies a new challenge. Some national governments wanted to make the wires a tool of politics and diplomacy. The obvious way was by holding a grip on the means of distribution. United Press and Associated Press, both regarded freedom of communications as essential to their business.

In 1927, the League of Nations, then looked upon as a potential a world government, held a conference of press experts in Geneva. One hundred and twenty delegates representing the news business in thirty-six nations were on hand when the meeting was called to order August 24.

Kent Cooper of the Associated Press, Karl A. Bickel of UP, Moses Koenigsberg of International News Service as well as representatives of the *New York Times*, the Scripps-Howard papers, Hearst and others were there from the United States.

For four days the delegates discussed censorship, copyrights and the transmission of news.

Cooper and Bickel drafted a resolution that declared news agencies had a "property right" in their product, as defined by the U.S. Federal Court in 1917. A judge had ruled that news was like a fish that is free until it is caught and then the fisherman owns it.

Reuters and the other national agencies feared the resolution would weaken their monopolies. But surprisingly the sharpest criticism came from International News Service, the third major U.S. service.

INS had lost the 1917 U.S. Court case over news property rights when it was found guilty of pirating AP dispatches. At Geneva, Koenigsberg of INS spoke strongly against the Cooper-Bickel resolution. After acrimonious debate, on the final day, a compromise resolution was accepted. It said:

"The conference affirms the principle that newspapers and news agencies and other news organizations are entitled after publication as well as before publication to the reward of their labor and enterprise and financial expenditure upon the production of news reports. But the conference holds that this principle shall not be so interpreted as to result in the creation or encouragement of any monopoly in news."

The U.S. wire service chiefs also sought to guarantee freedom of their agencies to work in all countries, including those where government sponsored native news agencies claimed a monopoly.

Another resolution at the Geneva session declared that press copy should be given priority over ordinary private telegrams by communications companies.

What difference did these passionate debates at Geneva make in the collection and distribution of news? None. Even if the final resolutions had been clear and strict, there was no way to enforce them. It was a tempest in a teapot but it helped define issues that were to come up repeatedly in international news distribution.

The United States was not a signer of the League of Nations, which sponsored the Geneva meetings and never became one. These sessions were a preview of similar exhaustive and fruitless debate in the 1960s and 1970s by the United Nations Economic, Scientific and Cultural Organization (UNESCO), when so-called Third World countries wanted to control input and output of the major news services.

The newswire agencies were always in the forefront in the battles against restricting news collection or distribution or any attempt to license news reporters.

By the time World War II started in September 1939, United Press dispatches reached 251 newspapers in twenty-two countries in Europe. Growth in Europe was then crippled for the duration but resumed vigorously again beginning in 1945.

In a limited partnership prospectus in 1979 (which failed) the company said its largest foreign subscriber paid $876,805 for full service the previous year and the four biggest foreign clients contributed $2,655,201, or 3.6 percent of total revenue of the company.

A government could easily make it difficult for correspondents to function, and often did. In the Soviet Union after the Revolution, western reporters were not allowed to travel outside the city of Moscow. The United States imposed similar restrictions on Soviet reporters. Journalists, especially wire service correspondents, were often harassed, censored or given the heave by governments. Getting kicked out of Eastern European, South American and some Asian countries was almost routine for U.S. reporters.

The leaders of those countries wanted the wire service to distribute their propaganda. Governments regarded the press as a servant. But, in the case of United Press, they sometimes hesitated to clamp down because they knew it was objective and that it was popular.

A large newspaper client had more influence on the company than any government had. When *La Prensa* complained to UP about a story on the right wing Governor Carlos Lacerda in Guanabera in 1944, the staffer who wrote it was reprimanded.[3]

Governments themselves needed good information on events going on in the world. Wire services were the only instant source until CNN television news came along in the 1980s. UP stories were often ahead of official communications and became the basis for political decisions.

"The news choices they [wire services] make have a major bearing on the way the world views itself," a Twentieth Century Fund report said.[4]

Jonathan Fenby, a Reuters correspondent, authored that report. He identified the four major agencies, Reuters, AP, UPI and AFP, as the "town criers for the world."[5]

United Press always aggressively sought business around the world. When the war in Europe ended in 1945, the wire service's war correspondents, dressed in khaki and driving jeeps, went with the first allied troops into liberated countries and began putting together communications equipment and selling their news reports. They found the Europeans hungry for news of the world.

"In Belgium one UP man couldn't find any newspapers to sell the service to, so he signed up a butcher after convincing him that he would do better business if he was in touch with what was going on in the world" Fenby relates.

On August 25, 1944, the day the Germans pulled out of Paris and even before allied forces marched in, Jean De Gandt and Emilio Herrero, reopened the UP bureau at 2 Rue des Italiens. Herrero, a Spanish national, had been keeping a watch over the office during the occupation and had persuaded the Spanish Embassy to put it under diplomatic protection. A large sign on the door carried a Spanish Embassy seal. When the Germans were gone, Herrero and De Gandt went in and began preparing to resume operations. Joe Grigg arrived a couple of days later. He crawled up on the roof and rigged an antenna. Surprisingly, it easily intercepted the UP newscast being transmitted from London to South America. The report was promptly put on the wire to subscribers in liberated parts of Europe.

UP's spectacular growth after the war included new exchange pacts with various European agencies, including the Spanish EFE service, which provided 130 Spanish newspapers with United Press news.

The company always strove to live off the land, paying its way from revenue in the region where news was collected and taking out a profit if possible.

In foreign countries, as in domestic service, there was always pressure to make each bureau its own profit center. A bureau in a region was closed when there was not enough revenue in that region to support it, and a sales motive sometimes created a new bureau.

The Monterey, California publisher was promised a new UP bureau in his city. Richard A. Litfin, the sales representative told him the UP staffer assigned would be able to do local news as well as copy for the wires—and would cost less than a reporter's salary.[6]

Still, various division heads somehow were always able to claim that their department or division was profitable. Europe, Asia, every domestic division, the photo service, the sports department and financial service each asserted it was a profit center.

But somehow the company overall lost money yearly after the mid 1960s.

The needs of U.S. clients were usually paramount. "We like to think of ourselves as being international—we have the word in our name after all—but obviously when you get so much of your revenue from one country, that country is very important to you," UPI President Rod Beaton remarked in 1980.[7]

In Canada, the UP established a subsidiary, British United Press (BUP), in 1922. This stratagem gave the company certain tax advantages in Canada and lower "empire" cable rates. Bickel also launched a German United Press and he claimed credit for introducing UP into Italy, Spain, Denmark, Sweden and Russia.

UP/UPI set up national news services in several countries, including Chile and Argentina. When Argentine dictator Juan Peron ordered the local service shut down, UP executives were secretly relieved because the Argentine wire was not making money.[8]

BUP was maintained until after World War II when it became part of UP again. Then, in 1979, UPI operations in Canada were merged with the *Toronto Sun* Publishing Corporation and Sterling Newspapers Limited. UPI retained a 20 percent ownership. The service had headquarters in Toronto and bureaus in Ottawa, Montreal, Quebec City, Halifax, Winnipeg, Edmonton and Vancouver. It was called UPI of Canada and Patrick Harden was named general manager, with a staff of twenty reporters under Malcolm K. Hughes and ten photo staffers under Robert W. Carroll.

International News Service, the Hearst agency, began operating freely in Europe a few years after UP but was a weak competitor. The Associated Press, under Kent Cooper, continued to chafe under constraints of the "Ring," which it did not completely shed until 1967. At that point, the situation between the agencies had been reversed, AP was providing much more news to Reuters than Reuters was providing AP.[9]

The major European news agencies suffered from having to remain on good terms with their governments. In some cases, as in France, the home news agency, Havas, was directly subsidized by government appropriations and was notoriously subservient to the French government. In others, as in England, the government supported Reuters by contracting to buy its news and paying the agency to distribute royal propaganda. Reuters bowed to the British royal and parliamentary powers. Some smaller subsidized agencies gave their news free to newspapers. Some even paid editors to use their stories.

When, in the late 1930s, King Edward the Eighth was romancing Mrs. Wallis Simpson, a divorced American woman, to the displeasure of the country's established church and government, Reuters and the British press carried not a word about it until a few days before he abdicated the throne. United Press had no such inhibitions and gave its subscribers full reports as the royal romance progressed and officials and the royal family maneuvered to avoid a scandal.

Foreign governments frequently imposed outright censorship at one level or another.

At midnight on August 19, 1914, Pope Pius X died after a lingering illness. The Italian government immediately cut off all outgoing cables but not before Henry Wood, UP Rome correspondent, managed to send a coded cable, addressed it to Roy Howard's wife in New York and paid at the "ordinary" rate for commercial cables, which was more than twice the press rate but sometimes skirted censorship. Mrs. Howard understood the message, and United Press flashed the death of the pope. AP could not match it for six hours. This resulted in a public, inter-service tiff carried out, as many were in those days, on the wires and front pages of client newspapers. When the news of the pope's death was officially released, six hours after he died, the Associated Press put out a memo to editors saying that United Press had jumped the gun by five hours. UP, in turn, issued a statement pointing out that while its flash was four hours ahead of the official announcement it was within an hour of the pope's actual death according to the time given in the official announcement.

When the German blitzkreig subjugated and occupied European countries in 1939–1940—Austria, Czechoslovakia, Poland, Yugoslavia, Belgium, Holland, France—the Nazis quickly put limits on United Press. In 1941, the wire service was being used by 462 newspapers in thirty-eight countries or possessions outside continental United States. Its stories were transmitted in twenty-seven languages. Newspapers in the occupied countries continued receiving news, but were allowed to publish only minor, innocuous stories. Bureaus in Berlin, Rome and other occupied capitals were immediately shut down and American staffers repatriated in exchange for German and Italian journalists in the United States.

Following the hasty re-establishment of United Press in Europe after the war, when the UP was aggressively seeking clients, A. L. Bradford was transferred from South America to Europe as vice president replacing Virgil Pinkley. The latter had run European operations during the war. Bradford, with wide sales experience in Latin America, went to work signing what he called "Baby Prensa" contracts, which provided for UP to handle all of a newspaper's foreign needs and requests, as it did for *La Prensa* of Buenos Aires.

When Bradford signed a contract, Rob Roy Buckingham was appointed to the task of making it work. Buckingham recalled that he was dispatched to Paris to nail down a contract with the newspaper *L'Aurore*.[10]

During *L'Aurore's* period of trial service from UP, one of the top stories in France involved the French communist leader Thorez, who had just been released from a hospital in Russia after treatment for an unspecified disease. He was expected back in Paris but no one could find out when he would arrive. Bradford and Buckingham had a hunch that Thorez would come out of Russia through Berlin. Reporter Ed Korry and a photographer were assigned to the story. They were told to ride the trains between Helmstedt and Berlin every day and be on the lookout for Thorez. A week went by with no luck. New York began to complain about the expense. But Bradford kept the newsman and photographer on the train and after another two days it paid off. Korry spotted Thorez traveling incognito. UP got a good interview, gave it to *L'Aurore* exclusively, with a photo. The French paper signed a long-term contract.

The agency's European service got into the black with this and other Bradford "Baby Prensa" contracts. Newspapers like the *Helsingen Sanomat* and the *Daghens Nyeter* in Stockholm, EFE, the Spanish news service in Spain, ANI news service in Portugal, and *Al Ahram* in Cairo came aboard.

While European news agencies were directly and indirectly subsidized by governments, the U.S. agencies, UP, INS and AP, had at least one perk supplied by Uncle Sam. The State Department, seeking better relations with South American countries, negotiated a reduction in cable rates for news copy. It was reduced from 22 cents to 10 cents a word, and additional reception stations could pick up a "drop" for 2 cents a word. This was, in effect, a subsidy for U.S. services.

News agencies provide U.S. customers with vast quantities of copy every day on events happening in other parts of the world. Not much of it gets printed or used on television in the United States. Public figures, educators and even newspaper publishers frequently complained that the wire services were weak on foreign news. Massive volumes of world news were on the wires, but editors and readers preferred local news.

In small countries leaders complained that they only got wire coverage when there was a disaster or war. This issue was taken up by international organizations from time to time.

After World I, a number of international conferences on news distribution were held under sponsorship of the League of Nations. After World War II, they continued under the United Nations Educational and Scientific and Cultural Organization

(UNESCO). These meetings, like the 1927 Geneva meeting on news property rights, were attended by press and political leaders, including wire service executives and editors. The conferences gave so-called Third World nations a platform on which to raise concerns about the flow of news.

The three American agencies, United Press, Associated Press and International News Service were usually put on the defensive. Resolutions were introduced in the name of improving the exchange of news. The American wire services saw peril in any international rules or formalized guidelines on news collection and distribution. The wire services said the countries complaining the loudest of inadequate or unfair news distribution were often the most difficult places for correspondents to function freely and agencies to distribute news. Those countries seeking international press rules often expelled western correspondents or imposed censorship.

In Africa, the agencies made world news reports available to local media at very low and unprofitable rates. But even those small fees were difficult to collect because of political turmoil. A UPI representative once spent a whole week going from one minister or official to another in an African nation looking for someone to pay a bill. He finally found the right functionary and visited him. "He said he couldn't pay, pretending he didn't have our invoices. In fact, they were stacked up around him. I made him sign a check and caught my plane. The check bounced," the UPI representative reported later.[1]

Where there was a real lack of coverage, the wire services blamed it on financial constraints. They said they just did not have the revenue to be everywhere in force. In fact, according to the Fenby study, the major news agencies defied commercial logic by going into such places at all. Their long-range inability to make an acceptable profit from selling news of general interest internationally was obvious, said Fenby, but they nevertheless continued seeking customers throughout the world.[2] Competition among them remained stiff, keeping the losses higher. As late as the 1980s, some overseas subscribers could buy the full UPI news report for $100 or $200 a month.

UPI Vice President and Editor-in-Chief Roger Tatarian proposed that the U.S. agencies help Third World nations set up regional services. It never came to anything because critics in those countries were paranoid about the major news services and anything they might do, even help they might give. UPI did assist in development of a regional Mideast news agency.

Third World news people would not grasp the journalistic reality that man bites dog is news but dog bites man is not, airplanes that crash are news, airplanes that land safely are not news. Governments that make quiet progress are not as newsworthy as governments that have revolutions.

UPI and AP were usually glad to sell their news to national government-subsidized agencies. It often represented significant revenue. However, they were careful not to become dependent on this revenue as Havas and some other agencies did.

When the United States Information Agency wanted to purchase UPI and AP news and distribute an edited version to foreign newspapers the wire services objected.

They feared that their reports would be made into propaganda and that they themselves would find the free government version of the news competing with their own efforts to sell to overseas clients. The U.S. Congress sided with the news services and rejected the State Department's request for an increased budget to cover such a news service.

United Press International's unusual bookkeeping system made accountability confusing to managers. At one point in its history the South American operations were sending New York hundreds of thousands of dollars profit and the European division was losing money. The explanation was simple. European bureaus had big expenses providing news specifically for South America but the costs were charged to Europe and the profits credited to the Latin American division.

There were occasional labor problems in Europe as in the United States, and European countries had laws about employment, such as vacations and pensions, which sometimes surprised American executives of the company.

In August 1972, twenty members of the National Union of Journalists in England went on strike against UPI. Four U.S. citizens on the London staff joined the union and demanded to be covered by its contract. Managers kept the service going. The strike ended in less than two weeks when the journalists' union withdrew its support.

9

The Orient: Asia
Ernie and Friends

ROY HOWARD MADE UNITED PRESS AN INTERNATIONAL NEWS POWER
fifty years before UP became United Press International.

When United Press entered the Asia news market in 1909, linking up with Nippon
Dempo Tsushin-sha, the Japanese Telegraph News Agency, the only competition was
Reuters, which had an exclusive exchange agreement with Rengo Kokkusai Tsushin-sha,
the other large Japanese news purveyor.

Twenty years later, Associated Press, still fighting to break away from the international news cartel, signed an agreement with Rengo, replacing Reuters.

Through Nippon Dempo, UP served 230 Japanese newspapers and many Japanese
language newspapers in China, Korea and other parts of Asia. In Japanese United Press
was "Godo Tsushin" (news). It was usually called just "Godo."

After World War II the United Press came back into the Orient explosively under
vice president for Asia Miles W. Vaughn, who had been in Japan before the war, and
the flamboyant Earnest Hoberecht, who came in with the American occupation forces.

Vaughn was tragically drowned January 20, 1949, in Tokyo Bay while duck hunt-
ing with Sekizo Uyeda of Nippon Dempo, an American army dentist and a guide and
his son. Their boat overturned in a squall and they all drowned.

Vaughn had met Uyeda in 1925 when he first arrived aboard the President Pierce
to represent United Press in Tokyo. Their close comradeship had survived the war. In
1976, a monument memorializing the two journalists was erected at a Tokyo's Park
and an annual award in their names was established for a Japanese reporter specializing
in international affairs.

Vaughn was one of the few Unipressers who deliberately sought a career with
the agency and was committed to it for life. As a teen-aged boy in Winfield, Kansas, he was thrilled at the exploits of legendary UP reporter William G. Shepherd.
In 1916, Vaughn got a job in the Chicago bureau and subsequently worked in St.
Louis, Dallas, New York, Rio de Janeiro and New York as well as the Far East.

In his memoir, *Covering the Far East*, Vaughn recalled that the day he reported to
Edward Conkle in Chicago, the only question Conkle asked him was: "Can you spell?"

He said he could and was told to catch a train that night for St. Louis to take over the bureau there. When he arrived in St. Louis his predecessor handed him the key to the office and left town the same day. It was an exciting career-launch in the wire service and it thrilled Vaughn.

During his two long stints in Asia, Vaughn was often thought to be too friendly toward the Japanese. During the Japanese war in China he frequently wrote think pieces which were criticized as being slanted in favor of the Japanese. He was accused of being "too long in the land of the slant eyes." This was a rare accusation against a UP correspondent. Vaughn denied he was biased although conceding a close relationship with the Japanese. During the war in Manchuria, a Japanese general felt close enough to Vaughn to ask him to write the order which would instruct field commanders on handling the press.

"I asked for a typewriter and wrote the order on the spot," Vaughn said in his memoir. The order said correspondents were to be given every accommodation, including the best available quarters, transportation and communications. Since water in the war zone might be impure, "it would be wise to provide the foreign newspapermen with plenty of champagne and beer."

In December 1931, Vaughn was criticized for letting a Japanese government official write a statement for him to broadcast on a special NBC radio hookup to Japan. The statement defended Japanese military action in Manchuria.

Asia was a more costly area than Europe for news operations. Cable rates were much higher. When a major earthquake struck Japan in 1923 killing an estimated 100,000 people, United Press received the first dramatic 1,000 words on the devastation from its correspondent via urgent cable, at $3.60 a word.

"The press rate to and from the Orient is far too high to make it possible to send a large volume of news at anything but an almost prohibitive price," Bickel said. In 1926, the news agency was able to negotiate the press cable rate, then 30 cents a word, down to 18 cents a word for radio-teletype transmission via RCA between Tokyo and San Francisco.

Nevertheless, Asian service gradually expanded in volume and distribution until UP had many clients in China, Japan, the Philippines, India and Pacific Islands. It had bureaus in Hong Kong, Shanghai, Nanking, Singapore, Batavia, and Hawaii, then still a U.S. territory.

After World War II, United Press was able to use commercial channels to set up its own radioteletype connection, nicknamed "Cho-Cho-S," between Tokyo and the United States. Even so, communications from Asia to the New York cables desk were often chancy, as well as costly. Sun spots interfered with radio intermittently, sometimes disastrously for the report. A "washout" of a broadcast delayed all news. A partial washout could be nearly as bad. The first paragraph of a dispatch might be received and not the rest, or the last paragraph might come through leaving editors puzzling over what the lead was.

In 1966, the main editorial desk for outgoing relay of news to the Asian wire network was transferred from Tokyo to Manila because communications were better in the Philippines. Tokyo, under Hoberecht, continued to have administrative control over Far Eastern operations.

One of the service improvements made was the installation at Manila of a "split key," a switch that enabled editors to file separately to customers in the Philippines, Australia and other Asia points. News files could be tailored to the needs of the clients in the specific area. Stories of special interest to Manila no longer had to compete for the same wire space with news for Australia.

A huge amount of detail was involved in an innovation like this. Manila Bureau Manager Don Becker had to arrange with the commercial radio companies for new radio beamcast frequencies and schedules. Machines and desks in the bureau needed to be rearranged. Working schedules and routine of the staff had to be changed. Becker took a few shifts at each of the various desks himself to get a good feel and understanding of the new procedures. That's the way UPI handled things.

Commercial companies like Press Wireless, RCA and Mackay Radio were engaged to supplement the agency's own communications, particularly when "washouts" occurred in the company's own radio transmission.

Manila received incoming dispatches from throughout Asia, mostly by radio-teletype, telephone or commercial service. In some situations, duplicating reception methods were in place at the same time, with the second a backstop to minimize loss of copy in case the first route was down. Becker maintained Press Wireless transmissions to Manila from Kuala Lumpur as a second path because it was only 75 cents an hour, less than the cost of keeping a staff member on duty to receive direct transmission.

With the improved service to Australia, Charles Bernard, in Sydney, was able to negotiate a 10 percent increase in rates paid by the Murdoch newspapers and the Australian Broadcasting Commission. Leroy Keller, international vice president, congratulated Bernard on winning the increases. In the same letter he demanded that Bernard obtain matching increases at the *Sydney Telegraph* and other clients.

Karachi and New Delhi filed their reports via government Posts & Telegraphs to London because communications were better and cheaper at a penny-a-word.

Any major news event such as a meeting of a Colombo Plan conference in Karachi, Pakistan, required special communications arrangements. When Max Vanzi covered one of these meetings, he filed his stories by commercial cable to Singapore, where they were relayed to Manila and, from there, back to customers on the Asia wire as well as to New York and London. The Colombo Plan for Cooperative Economic and Social Development in Asia and the Pacific was formed in 1951 at Colombo, Ceylon (now Sri Lanka). It included governments of India, Pakistan, Ceylon, Australia, New Zealand, Great Britain, Japan and the United States. The wire service had clients in all of those countries. Full news coverage was essential.

In April 1966, UPI brought Pat Killen back from Kuala Lumpur to cover news in Washington of special interest to Asia. His travels for the news service were typical for the times. He had previously worked for UPI in San Francisco, Honolulu, Karachi, New Delhi, Singapore and Tokyo, where he helped cover the 1964 Olympics. Later, Killen would add UPI bureaus in Chicago and Manila to his resume.

United Press International had its problems with news written by native journalists whose use of the English language was weak. One staffer in Tokyo called it atrocious. However, the high caliber American staff in Tokyo and a few excellent native writers, working under Arnold Dibble and Al Kaff, could turn bad original copy into worthy journalism.

In 1966, the Tokyo staff included Joe Galloway, who covered the Vietnam war with distinction, several other Americans and Hank Sato, a very competent English-speaking Japanese man. Kim Willenson was in Bangkok and roved around Thailand, Cambodia, Laos and Burma. Ray Herndon was in Singapore and Malaysia. Charlie Smith, an expert on China affairs, was based in Hong Kong. Don Becker, Bob Ibrahim and Vic Maliwanag were in Manila and Charles Bernard in Sydney.

Incoming news for the Asia wire was received by radio-teletype and cable from London and New York. In Manila it was converted automatically into punched tape, which could be used to re-transmit the copy to Australia and other Asian points.

One of the annoyances of the complex system was that to try to pinpoint the source of a problem was frustrating. When garbled copy turned up in Sydney, Bernard complained to Manila. Manila said it was received there that way. Mistakes could have originated anywhere along the line. A dispatch about the Danish architect of the Sydney Opera House originated in Europe, passed through London, New York and Manila to Sydney. Bernard found finding the source of an error in the story like swimming against the current.

The Sydney *Telegraph, Herald* and the *Mirror*, when they wanted to show displeasure at UPI coverage of a news event or were upset with the service in general, did not say so directly. What they did was put an AFP (Agence France Presse) logo on UPI dispatches. Bernard noticed this and had to plead for a reconciliation with the newspaper to get UPI properly credited again.

Reuters dominated New Zealand in an agreement with the New Zealand Press Association. UPI made a small inroad in September 1966, selling a 2,000-word pony service for the *Sunday News* of Auckland for $140 a week.

At the end of World War II, Frank Bartholomew, vice president of the Pacific Division, visited the Philippines, Australia, and other Pacific areas that had been liberated, with an eye to business. Frank Tremaine was opening a bureau in Tokyo within days after the Japanese surrender in August 1945. Hugh Crumpler was ordered to leave one warship at sea and board another headed for Korea in early September to open a bureau in Seoul.

Earnest Hoberecht took over from Tremaine in Tokyo shortly after the bureau was opened and became a legendary character in the American community and the Tokyo Press Club and got the handle "Asia Ernie."

Hoberecht came from Watonga, Oklahoma, and worked for the Memphis *Press-Scimitar* before going to Hawaii and getting a job as a roustabout at Pearl Harbor. He got himself named editor of the navy newsletter there and began pestering UP for a job.

Tremaine, Hawaii manager at the time, hired Hoberecht to help with the sudden increase in news from the Pacific when the war started. In 1945, Hoberecht was lucky enough as a war correspondent to get assigned to the navy task force heading toward Japan for the final showdown and thus was one of the first Americans in with the occupation forces. He and Tremaine were on the battleship Missouri helping cover the Japanese surrender. Hoberecht became general manager for Asia in 1948.

Hoberecht regarded the Asia Division as his personal empire, and ran it as such. He also turned it into a cash cow that was a major reason UPI survived as long as it did. He was totally dedicated to himself and to UPI, in that order, but in equal measure.

He became a literary sensation in Japan early in the American occupation after World War II on the strength of several romance novels he wrote in a matter of weeks and had translated into Japanese.

The United States had imposed a ban on American books in Japan. Hoberecht filled the gap. He hastily wrote *Tokyo Romance*. The book was called the "worst novel of modern times" by *Life* magazine. But it was an instant best seller in Japan, which was starving to read about American culture. Ernie quickly produced several more romance novels. They sold in the tens of thousands and he became the best known American writer in Japan.

Hoberecht had hundreds of thousands of fans, many of them young women eager to learn how American males addressed matters of the heart.

James A. Michener, the distinguished American author, once wrote an article about Hoberecht's life in the Far East. Michener said when he went to lecture in Japan, he had never heard of the Oklahoman. Students and professors of literature stunned him by asking whether he regarded Ernest Hemingway or Earnest Hoberecht as the best American writer. Although Michener's article made fun of him, Earnie basked in notoriety and distributed copies to his friends.

Hoberecht was asked to help show the most popular Japanese movie actress, Hideko Mimura, how to do a kiss, something never before seen on the screen in Japan. He told her General Douglas MacArthur suggested kissing in movies would be "a step towards democratization." During Earnie's lesson, Mimura fainted, causing a national sensation that Earnie loved. He was then in demand as an instructor in kissing.

When a Karachi newspaper took offense at something Hoberecht did in India, it published a banner headline in red ink "Yip-Yapping Yankee Go Home" over Hoberecht's picture. Ernie again loved it and bought 100 copies of the issue to send to friends.

On Hoberecht's death in 1999, John F. Barton, a Unipresser who worked in Asia, said this about him:

"Anyone who worked for Earnie Hoberecht—be they friend or foe, and he had a lot of both, all of them richly deserved—may be forgiven if they have trouble believing he really is dead. Such was the man's energy and drive. I would have liked Asia Earnie a hell of a lot better if I had never worked for him. But the only way I knew him was as my boss, and he never let me forget it."

Hoberecht was ousted from his Tokyo realm when he seemed to be getting too strong. *Mainichi Shimbun*, in whose building the bureau was located, raised UPI's rent by 400 percent in 1964. It was probably legitimate. UPI had been paying at 1945 rates and Tokyo had become a high rent city. But Hoberecht reacted by sending the publisher a notice that the UPI service charge to Mainichi would also go up 400 percent. The newspaper at the time was paying the wire service the heaviest rate in Asia.

The *Mainichi* publisher called UPI President Mims Thomason, who told him to ignore the Hoberecht letter. Then Thomason moved to solve the Hoberecht problem.

Ernie had departed Tokyo right after sending the intemperate letter to *Mainichi*. Thomason reached him in India and told him to return to Japan via New York. Meanwhile he told Ron Wills, the business manager in Tokyo, to secure all the files in the bureau. Hoberecht had let it be believed he knew where all the skeletons were buried. Many UPI executives were nervous about that.

Hoberecht was fired in June 1966, and given $250,000 in severance pay.

Donald J. Brydon was named general manager for Asia. He brought back as Tokyo news chief, Arnold Dibble, who had parted with the company ten years earlier during a memorable public row with Hoberecht at the Foreign Correspondents' Club.

Currency exchange was always a problem for the wire service operating in many countries. It was difficult and sometimes impossible to convert earnings overseas into U.S. dollars. This situation occasionally made an overseas bureau flush with cash that could only be spent in the country. Six months after Hugh Crumpler arrived in Korea, the UP, along with AP and INS, were notified by U.S. Army occupation authorities that it could no longer convert Korean money into U.S. currency.[1]

Improvisation in providing service was especially important in Asia. When the UP sold its news report to the Nizam of Hyderbad, John Hlavacek and Robert C. Miller had to smuggle teletype machines into the country because the Indian government was running its own news service and did not want a competitor near.

The contract meant $100,000 annual revenue for UP, which was paid in advance. So the company was anxious to please the Nizam. It required that Hlavacek, the UP man in Hyderbad, live in the palace so he could be available to repair the teletype when it broke down. The Nizam also ordered that a Rolls Royce and driver be at Hlavacek's disposal at all times. When Hlavacek walked, the Rolls followed him along the road.[2]

In another fairly touchy negotiation, Hlavacek provided an author for Tenzing Norgay, the Sherpa mountain climber who accompanied Sir Edmund Hillary on his epic climb of Mount Everest in 1953. Hillary's team was English but Tenzing did not want an Englishman to ghost-write his story. So Hlavacek engaged Robert Musel, a very talented UPI writer, to do it. Both UPI and Tenzing profited.[3]

Censorship in some Asian countries was also a problem. In India during the regime of Indira Ghandi, she ordered censorship of outgoing copy. The UPI announced that it would identify all copy from its correspondents in India, Victor Vanzi and Kate Webb, with a line saying it had been censored. The government relented but required the correspondents to sign a statement that they would give "a full and balanced account" of events in the country, something which was taken for granted at UPI anyway.

In China in 1946, the government refused to allow UP correspondent Walter Rundle to travel out of Shanghai, even though China had a treaty with the United States permitting free travel. The Chinese based the restriction on the pretext that Rundle had a civil court case pending in Shanghai. It was a trumped up libel suit. The real reason behind the travel ban was to prevent him from visiting areas of China held by the communists.

10

Viva La Prensa

KENT COOPER, WHO HAD STARTED HIS CAREER WITH THE UP IN INDIANA, went to AP in 1910 and became an aggressive and formidable rival to Roy Howard. Cooper wanted AP to disentangle itself from the "ring" of international news cartels. He was restrained by the conservative AP general manager, Melville Stone. But in 1918, Cooper began a break from the cartels by stealing *La Nacion,* the largest newspaper in Argentina from United Press.

Two years later, in a dramatic head-to-head confrontation with Howard in Buenos Aires, Cooper also won a contract with *La Prensa,* the other major Buenos Aires daily.

Howard and Cooper had arrived in South America on the same ocean liner. At the offices of Ezequiel P. Paz, publisher of *La Prensa,* Howard was waiting in a room to see Paz while Cooper was in Paz' office negotiating with the publisher. Paz, a descendent of one of the most illustrious Argentine families, came out into the room where Howard was waiting and announced: "I am now a member of Associated Press."

Roy was stunned with disappointment. In a letter to his mother, he wrote, "On the 30th of May the UP had eight clients in Argentina, Chile and Brazil, yielding a profit of $85,000 a year. On the 31st of May the UP had one client in South America, on which it (we) stood to lose $104,000 a year if we continued to serve it."[1]

But UP and Howard did not leave South America, and in 1919, Buenos Aires Manager James I. Miller won *La Prensa* back from AP.

The United Press soon became the dominant service south of the border. As well as sending correspondents from the United States, the agency hired many native journalists. It provided internal South American news as well as news from Europe, America and Asia.

South America's proclivity toward revolutions and dictatorships gave the UP a curious advantage over local news operations. The local agencies were reluctant to initiate stories that might be found offensive by the regime, preferring the safer course of using United Press dispatches on the same stories.

Over the years, of course, UP came under restrictions by various regimes and sometimes their correspondents were expelled. In July 1924, the Brazilian government shut down UP and AP in Rio de Janeiro because the news services carried reports on a revolt in Sao Paulo that the government considered unfavorable. The services were allowed to re-open after a few weeks.

United Press was generally regarded as objective in all countries where it operated. Both South American and European government regimes themselves bought United Press reports even when these reports were kept out of local newspapers by censorship. One arrangement, established in 1931, provided news to Guatemalan dictator General Jorge Ubico.

The Guatemalan government paid $300 a month for an 8,000-word daily report, which was distributed free to local newspapers "as the government saw fit." AP signed a similar contract with Ubico. In 1946, a new government canceled the agreements, saying it did not want to exercise censorship, and the wire services were told they could sell directly to newspapers.[2]

The news report sent from Europe and North America, tailored especially for *La Prensa*, grew enormously. Cable transmission rates to Latin America were paid for by *La Prensa*, but UP could set up listening stations and receive "drop" copies of the "Chester"[3] radio-teletype circuit in Rio de Janeiro, La Paz, Caracas, Bogota, Guayquil, Montevideo and elsewhere at very little extra cost. UP opened bureaus and signed up clients throughout South America.

The relationship of "Prensa Unida" with the Buenos Aires newspaper was so close that many thought the wire service was owned by *La Prensa*. Nevertheless, the UP news report was unbiased and comprehensive and was respected by newspaper publishers and government officials as the premier source of news.

United Press transmitted up to 25,000 words daily in condensed news to South America. It was translated into Spanish and edited in the Buenos Aires bureau, the wire service's South American headquarters, where 100 journalists were employed. UP news went to every country in Latin America except Haiti and El Salvador. One hundred eighty-five Latin American newspapers and seventy radio stations received the service.

The prized South American service always received special attention at headquarters in New York. UP listened to its clients and complied, providing anything the editors asked for, even such mundane material as the price of Australian wool. UP correspondents wrote 1,000 words a day on routine meetings of the French government specifically to fill a South American request. Newspapers south of the border were more interested in solid news than spicy reports on the lives of celebrities.

The most influential client in South America was *La Prensa* of Buenos Aires, under Ezequiel P. Paz and later Alberto Gainza Paz. UP also served *La Razon*, an afternoon newspaper in Buenos Aires. Other customers included *La Prensa* of Lima, Peru; *Diario Illustrado* of Santiago, Chile; *Jornal do Brazil*, in Rio de Janeiro; *Diario Popular* of Sao Paulo; and numerous other dailies.

The agency provided not only news from the rest of the world, but also the news of Latin America itself. There were UP bureaus in Mexico City, Havana, La Paz, Caracas, Bogota, Lima, Guayaquil, Santiago, Montevideo, Rio de Janeiro, Sao Paulo and Panama, as well as Buenos Aires. The staff in South American bureaus at one time totaled 335 regular employees, supplemented by several hundred part-time correspondents in smaller cities.

News was going out as well as coming in. The South American bureaus sent large amounts of copy to New York for use on wires in the United States, Europe and Asia.

Soon the French Havas agency, which had the "ring" franchise in Latin America, was dwarfed in comparison with United Press.

Reuters showed up with an attempt to establish a regional news service in 1970, but it failed to gain enough subscribers to hold on against UPI. Associated Press also tried to encroach on UPI dominance with little success.

Ambitious local journalists wanted to work for UPI because the agency was highly respected and they knew they would have freedom to do their work objectively. By 1962, 70 percent of staffers in Buenos Aires were Argentinians and more than half the staff on the Latin American desk in New York was from South America. It was the only region where the UPI reporters outnumbered the opposition on every story.

In 1940 *La Prensa* received 11.5 million words of cable and radio news from outside the country and was paying $14,000 a week plus communications costs.

Rob Roy Buckingham recalls that when he arrived in Buenos Aires in February 1945, to head up the *La Prensa* desk, it was receiving dispatches directly from London as well as New York. "We organized and wrote tailored general war leads for *La Prensa* and edited all sidebars," he said.[4]

La Prensa had become the *New York Times* of Latin America under publisher Gainza Paz because of its complete coverage of politics, arts, science, music, theater and chess.

It was more than that. The newspaper was the post office for many of Argentina's European immigrants. Letters could be sent in care of *La Prensa* and always get forwarded to the subscriber. The newspaper also ran a medical clinic and a legal service for subscribers.

Chess was a national pastime in Argentina. *La Prensa* had a sign outside its offices on which it posted the move-by-move play of championship matches as flashed to the paper by UP, which carefully planned its coverage of every important chess match. When a world championship was played in Havana, the players were moved to a farm without a telephone to get away from excessive attention. UP installed a telephone line to a location near the farm and stationed a reporter there around the clock, at *La Prensa's* expense, of course.

The 100-member Buenos Aires staff ("Baires" as it was called at UP) included only a few North Americans: vice president Tom Curran and his assistants A. L. Bradford, W.W. Copeland, Hugh Jencks and Rob Roy Buckingham. Bill McCall was in Caracas, Jay Allan Coogan in Rio.

Bradford, the news manager, was one of UP's top journalists, having covered the Lindbergh flight and other stories as Paris bureau manager. Selling the service in South America, he played hardball. When *El Mercurio's* contract was coming up for renewal in Santiago, John Lloyd of AP tried desperately to move in and take the paper. United Press had very close relations with the Santiago police. Bradford got them to arrest the AP man and hold him in jail until the *El Mercurio* contract renewal was sewed up.[5]

When Juan Perón came to power after World War II and seized *La Prensa* in 1951, it was a heavy blow to United Press. The newspaper, up to then, had been more powerful than the Argentine government. It had fought tooth and nail against Perón. When he finally became dictator, he seized the newspaper and turned it over to the labor unions. *La Prensa* never recovered, although it was returned to Alberto Paz, nephew of Gainza Paz, in 1955 after Perón's fall.

During the Peron expropriation, UP stopped serving *La Prensa*. The newspaper subscribed to International News Service, the Hearst agency. Paz never forgot that. When United Press absorbed the INS and became UPI, La Prensa refused to add the "I" in its datelines.

In the mid-1960s, the Associated Press, in the person of Lou Uchitelle, gave UPI one of its rare setbacks south of the border. He signed about 100 small Puerto Rican radio stations for a Spanish-language report on island news. Although this was little more than a mosquito bite, UPI felt it had to react. A team of top Unipressers, including Wilbur G. Landrey, Don Becker, Francis McCarthy, Martin Houseman and Daniel Drosdoff swarmed through the island selling the UPI's Puerto Rico radio wire to small stations. These stations played UPI and AP against each other to squeeze rates. If it were not for the profitable *El Mundo* and the San Juan *Star* contracts, UPI would have been losing money on the island.

At headquarters in Buenos Aires, two desks were always functioning. One, called the "Messa Inglesa," was manned by Americans doing an English version of South American news to send to New York. At the other desk, dispatches from throughout the world were edited in Spanish for the South American wire. The communication system required the Spanish version to be sent to New York for transmission back on the "Chester" radio-teletype circuit. News was also received in Buenos Aires from Rio, Santiago, Lima and Caracas on radio-teletype in both Spanish and English.

The Buenos Aires bureau was a friendly, informal place to work. Local staffers called Vice President Bill McCall "Cowboy" because they learned he had a ranch in Montana. He didn't mind the informality although staffers under him said he could be a tough, mean boss at times.

UPI maintained national news services in Argentina and Chile through the 1960s and 1970s. Brazil, after a military coup in 1964, prohibited foreign-owned agencies from distributing local news, and the UPI wire was turned over to a Brazilian company formed by former UPI personnel. In Chile, UPI was unchallenged and had a large staff of local reporters.

The big story from Latin America in 1973 was the coup d'état that overthrew Salvador Allende in Chile. Art Golden, Santiago UPI manager, happened to be on vacation. Steve Yolen had come over from Sao Paulo to sit in temporarily for him. When the coup took place early on September 11, one of the first things the rebels did was cut communications.

On the scene, the six-person staff had an excellent view of the action. The bureau was on the ninth floor of a building across the plaza from the presidential palace. When the palace was bombed Unipressers flattened themselves on the floor as bullets started crashing through the windows. Oton Gutierrez, the Teletype operator, raised his head to take a look out the window. A bullet whizzed by, six inches from his face.

Rebel soldiers thought pro-Allende snipers were operating from the building and peppered the UPI office with machine gun bullets whenever anything moved near a window. Bullet holes were left in the bureau wall for years to commemorate the event. No one was injured. At one point a squad of nervous young rebels burst into the bureau ready to shoot everyone. When they realized they were dealing with news correspondents, they left.

Yolen managed to get a phone call through to Victor Doblado, a stringer in Mendoza, Argentina, on the other side of the Andes from Santiago.

"The next six hours were horrible," said Yolen. "The firing never ceased. Every now and again a round would come crashing through with a sound like a popping light bulb amplified a hundred times."

The staff kept the phone line to Doblado open for hours, giving UPI clients a dramatic account of the fighting until the line was eventually cut by the rebels. By 5 P.M. that day, the firing had subsided. The presidential palace was in flames. Allende was dead.

Horacio Villalobos, one of UP's intrepid photo stringers, came in with a picture he had taken of Allende's final public appearance on the balcony of the presidential palace shortly before it was seized. The picture made front pages throughout the world.

Yolen didn't leave the bureau for three days, sleeping on the floor along with several other staff members.[6]

UPI had to terminate its national news service in Argentina again when Perón returned to power in 1973 and was elected for a short-lived third term before his death. Perón wanted to force the media to use *Telam*, the government-run news agency. When UPI and Associated Press were shut down by Perón, a group of former UP and AP employees, with the help of newspaper clients, set up two competing privately owned agencies which soon shared most of the business in the country. One of them, Noticias Argentinas, later became an important client of UPI. The other local service, Diarios y Noticias (DYN), went with AP.

The 1960s and 1970s saw a great deal of violence in South America. Left-wing terrorist organizations operated in Uruguay, Argentina and Brazil. General Juan Carlos Ongania, president of Argentina from 1966 to 1970, was a target of serious anti-military riots in Cordoba and elsewhere. UPI covered it all.

In Buenos Aires, Augusto Vandor, a leading Peronist labor leader, was assassinated while U.S. Vice President Nelson Rockefeller was visiting Argentina in 1969. Anti-American rioters burned down thirteen supermarkets owned by the Rockefeller family.

UPI had a team of U.S. trained correspondents on the ground during the South American unrest. They included Marty Houseman in Santiago, John (Jack) Virtue in Sao Paulo, Albert J. Schazin in Rio de Janeiro, Carlos Villar-Borda in Colombia, H. Denny Davis in Mexico City and Stew Kellerman, Steve Harrison and Wilbur G. Landrey in Buenos Aires.

In 1970, the Brazilian government was under Emilio Garrastazu Medici, an army general. He did not impose censorship but in order to stay in business, media circulating within the country had to use severe self-control. If a newspaper crossed a certain line in criticizing the government, or if it reported the torture of prisoners, the newspaper would be shut down. Torture of political prisoners was, in fact, widespread. The government denied it and those who were tortured seldom survived to tell about it. The subject was out of bounds for Brazilian newspapers.

UPI had on its staff in Rio a former army officer who had good contacts in the military. Through those sources, correspondent Daniel A. Drosdoff was able to verify torture stories that filtered out from time to time. Brazilian newspaper publishers sometimes were able to print these stories if they were attributed to UPI.

In 1969, guerillas kidnapped American Ambassador C. Burke Elbrick. He was exchanged for fifteen prisoners held by the government. Later, West German Ambassador Ehrenfriend von Holleben was kidnapped and exchanged for forty prisoners. Swiss Ambassador Enrico Giovanni Bucher was kidnapped and exchanged for seventy prisoners.

Covering these delicate stories was always a challenge. When UPI got a tip that the guerrillas were about to release Bucher, Drosdoff took a cot to the office, slept there all night and received a phone call at 7:15 A.M. reporting that the ambassador had been released unharmed. Drosdoff was rewarded with the satisfaction of getting the news out 12 minutes ahead of the opposition.

In Montevideo on July 28, 1972, Hector Menoni, UPI manager for Uruguay, was kidnapped by members of an anarchist revolutionary group known as OPR-33. He was taken by force to what his captors called a "press conference" at which they denied they had tortured a previous kidnap victim. Menoni was released the next day. He said the anarchists accused UPI of spreading reports about torture.[7]

UPI's picture service accounted for at least half of the company's revenue in South America in the 1960s, according to Marty McReynolds, who was photo editor in Buenos Aires.

When German Ambassador von Holleben was released, Ted Majeski, picture chief in New York, sent a rocket ordering "all steps" be taken to ensure good picture coverage for DPA, a German agency which subscribed to UPI photo service. Scores of photos were transmitted for Germany, winning cables of gratitude from DPA. However when Alberto Schazin, bureau chief in Rio, asked the European Division to pay some of the $10,000 extra cost, haggling went on for weeks. It was finally decided that Europe would pay one-third, New York one-third and Brazil one-third. Such internal feuding over expense accounting plagued UPI everywhere its entire life.

When U.S. editors complained about a shortage of news from Latin America, one of UPI's best newsmen, Wilbur Landrey, was dispatched to Buenos Aires specifically to generate more Latin American stories for U.S. clients.

In 1970, the company began transmitting to New York by satellite to speed the process. None of these measures significantly increased the quantity of South American copy printed in North America, where most editors remained committed to priority for local stories.

The correspondents' position in South America always remained precarious. Pieter VanBennekom was expelled from Colombia in July of 1976 in a flap over a false bulletin, sent accidentally, which said the president had been assassinated. He was transferred to San Juan as Caribbean news editor and later became vice president for Mexico, Central America and the Caribbean, with headquarters in Mexico City.

Extremely good local sources were necessary for a wire service to operate effectively. In Santo Domingo on a business trip, Dan Drosdoff wrote a dispatch that detailed pervasive corruption in the government. Because of that, President Balaguer refused to let UPI reporters into the country to cover the 1978 election.

Drosdoff did not learn until later that what upset the dictator was not the report on corruption but a personal matter about which he was extremely touchy. The UPI correspondent had written that the president was suffering from glaucoma and was "half blind." Mentioning Balaguer's eye condition violated an unwritten law in the Dominican Republic.

Walter Logan, UPI foreign editor, wrote a letter complaining about this exclusion from covering the election. It had an unexpected response. Balaguer personally called UPI in New York and apologized, saying he had made a mistake and had been ill-advised. UPI was allowed back into the country before the voting, in which Balaguer lost.

Just before the 1968 Olympic Games in Mexico City, there was a bloody confrontation between soldiers and student demonstrators. Hundreds of students were killed. Mike Hughes, UPI manager for Canada, was there to help with Olympic coverage. He reported the riot and detailed casualties in the hundreds. The government admitted only that thirty-two students were killed.

UPI was in trouble. The publisher of a large Mexico City client newspaper, closely linked to the government, demanded a retraction about the large number of deaths. UPI President Mims Thomason was under heavy pressure to comply. The client was an important revenue source.

Hughes said Thomason personally met with him and asked, "Did you write that story?" Mike, worried, said yes.

"Is it true? Did you see it?" asked the UPI chief. Mike said it was true. He was there. He saw the bodies.

"Then I'm giving you a raise," Mims replied. The amount of the raise wasn't important. The company president's support for a staffer in a tight situation was the kind of glue that nurtured employees' fanatical dedication to their news service.

Sometimes native local reporters for UPI also got into trouble.

General Rojas Pinella of Colombia frequented the bull fights in Bogota. In September 1956, he entered the stadium and the compulsory cheer went up. Rojas Pinella noticed that not everybody was enthusiastic. His bodyguards began beating those who did not cheer.

The UP story reported that several people suffered fatal injuries. Rojas Pinella accused the UP reporter, Carlos Villar-Borda, of slander. He was found guilty by a government court, fined 7,500 pesos and had his news credentials lifted.

A big issue in Uruguay when the country returned to democracy in 1986 after 12 years of military rule was whether the government would grant army officers amnesty for human rights crimes. The newly elected president, Julio Maria Sanguinetti, publicly said there would be no amnesty, but privately he was negotiating with the army over the issue. He became very angry with UPI when the wire service carried a story quoting a top army officer as saying the government would not be allowed to put any officer on trial. The story demonstrated the president's problems with the military, and he was deeply embarrassed.

Sanguinetti sent a hot letter to Hector Menoni, Uruguay manager, accusing the UPI reporter, Zelmar Lissardi, of irresponsible journalism and fabricating information. Although Lissardi had his informant's quotes on tape, Sanguinetti was furious. Lissardi was made unwelcome in the presidential palace for the rest of Sanguinetti's term.

On New Year's Day in 1959, most Americans saw a banner headline in their newspapers over an Associated Press story from Havana which said Cuban dictator Fulgencia Batista had the rebels of Fidel Castro on the run and was about to exterminate them.

In fact, on that New Year's eve, Batista was packing his bags and warming up his plane's engines to flee to the Dominican Republic. He flew out of Havana that night, leaving Cuba to Castro.

The AP dispatch on Batista's "victory" was written from a handout that came from the presidential palace in Havana and had been personally dictated by Batista, who liked to think he was a journalist as well as a dictator.

The United Press International did not carry the erroneous story. AP and others who had picked up Batista's handout quickly sent corrections, but it was too late for most morning newspapers. How did UPI escape having the false report of Castro's rout? Was it better sources? Better analysis? Better thinking?

The truth was that Pedro Bonetti, night man at the Havana bureau, was not where he was supposed to be—absent without leave when the handout came in. He arrived in the bureau near the end of his shift and found the envelope with Batista's handout waiting unopened. UPI won one, thanks to a staffer goofing off.[8]

Castro expelled the American press, and it was not until 1981 that the island was opened again to correspondents after a visit to Cuba by eighteen publishers under the sponsorship of UPI. But the agency was forbidden to reestablish a bureau in Havana.

Unipressers in Latin America did have their lighter moments. Frank Breese, who went to Buenos Aires in 1938, recalls, "Despite recurring tensions and frenetic events which created an ambience of excitement, our personal lives were not directly affected. We lived quite comfortably. There was the Radio Bar for a lunch snack, The Helvetica for a cerveza or 'San Martin' after work. Everything was plentiful." On the waterfront there was a selection of small cafes, beer gardens, a zoo and boating facilities. Things became more austere when the U.S. entered the war in 1941.

Many journalists who became prominent in South America had their start with UPI, including the top editorial chiefs of both private Argentine news agencies and many newspapers. They were attracted to UPI for a variety of reasons, mainly the agency's reputation for integrity and competitiveness.

The sale of the UPI's international picture network to Reuters in 1983 was a blow to Latin American Unipressers who had grown up with the confidence they were working for the region's premier news service. The Latin American service suddenly lost half its revenue. Much of that revenue was profit because radiophoto transmissions were not costly. Fully staffed in 1983, the Latin America service deteriorated sharply within a few years.

Alberto Schazin, UPI's top Latin America executive; Luiz Menezes, vice president for Brazil; and Pieter VanBennekom, then vice president for Mexico and the Caribbean, gave serious thought to splitting the Latin American service away from UPI. They were planning to hold a meeting in Rio de Janeiro to discuss the idea. Mike Hughes, international vice president, called them individually and talked them out of it.

Even after the sale of the photo operation, South America sent some profit to headquarters but it was measured in thousands of dollars, not the millions cleared during the years of glory.

After Reuters bought the photo operation, the British agency rapidly replaced UPI as the premier news vendor in Latin America, hiring many former UPI correspondents, editors and photographers. Reuters also adopted UPI techniques such as filing dual reports in Spanish and English. However, remaining basically an economic news service, Reuters never captured the flair or influence of the old UPI in Latin America.

United Press International was losing ground in the 1980s in South America as it did everywhere else. From a full complement of dozens of competent English and Spanish writers and editors when the decade opened, by 1989 UPI had only one English writer for all of South America, Ann Harrison. She had only two years experience, one as an intern.

The South American countries themselves were changing. One by one old-line nationalist dictatorships gave way to elected governments in Argentina, Brazil, Uruguay and Chile. At the same time, the region was suffering a severe debt crisis, inflation and economic decline. Daniel Drosdoff, selling the service in those countries, said he had to carry around paper bags filled with nearly worthless pesos, australes and cruzeiros to pay hotel bills.

Schazin, who had risen to prominence in UPI in the 1970s and 1980s, abandoned the ship in 1992 to become deputy managing editor of *La Nacion*.

Luiz Menezes, who had started with UPI as a messenger and worked his way up to vice-president for Brazil, quit after the photo service was sold. He and Schazin had become wealthy working for the wire service, each owning several homes and cars, and both were well known around the best social venues. Menezes became an executive with Knight Ridder's *Commodity News Service*, which had once been a partner with UPI, and took many clients from UPI with him.

The company also lost its top North American staffers working south of the border: John Alius, John Virtue, Gary Neeleman, Claude Hippeau, Tracy Wilkinson.

Some of the Latin American native journalists working in New York on the "Chester" desk went on to good jobs in the United States, including Abel Dimant, who joined the *Miami News* in Washington and then moved to CNN (Cable News Network). Norberto Svarzman went to the U.N. press office, reporting for Televisa of Mexico and Telam, the state-run Argentine news service. Enrique Durand joined the Voice of America. Herman Beals went with Reuters in Miami.

In South America salaries were low by U.S. standards and given the volatile state of Latin American economies, a sudden devaluation could cut a paycheck by 90 percent overnight.

Some South American staffers benefited from the labor laws, which were more protective for employees than in the U.S. Luis Azuaje, a talented Venezuelan writer, was transferred from Caracas to Bogota in the early 1980s. United Press International had to pay him $10,000 indemnity under Venezuelan law.

A strike in Puerto Rico occurred when the 11-person staff abandoned the Newspaper Guild because of its leftist leaning and joined the Steel Workers Union. The Steel Workers took them out on strike and UPI had to bring in a half dozen North Americans to run the wire.

Those emergency transfers were made while UPI President Rod Beaton was away from New York headquarters. He was furious about the cost of the transfers and blamed John Alius, who, as manager there, had ordered the moves. Alius was demoted to sales representative. He then made so much money selling the service on commission that Beaton was even more annoyed.

UPI had been the most prestigious news agency in Latin America for three-quarters of a century.

11

A Visionary on the News Watch

THE BOOMING GROWTH OF UNITED PRESS IN ITS INFANCY WAS FUELED mainly by the restless energy of Roy Howard. Still, the fire continued, even when Howard resigned as president in 1920.

Howard had ensured the continuing growth of the young news agency nearly a decade earlier when he re-hired Karl August Bickel, a wealthy young man bitten hard by the news bug when a violent earthquake ripped open the ground under his dormitory at Stanford University.

At the time, Bickel was a free-lance contributor, or stringer, for the *San Francisco News*. So when the earth shook, he immediately headed for the office, hiking 30 miles through the devastation to take part in covering the 1906 San Francisco earthquake.

Bickel's reporting caught the attention of the *San Francisco Examiner* and earned him a full-time job. Even though he was a junior at Stanford, Bickel never returned to college.

Bickel was twenty-five when he first went to work for UP covering the Pacific Northwest from a bureau in Portland, Oregon in 1907. Just one year later, the dapper son of a wealthy Geneseo, Illinois, merchant left UP and bought an interest in the Grand Junction, Colorado, *News* and became its publisher.

Howard was impressed with Bickel's work in the northwest and persuaded him to rejoin the news agency in 1913 as UP's first full time salesman, based in Chicago. Bickel covered the territory from Pittsburgh, Pennsylvania to Denver, Colorado, and from the Canadian border to the Gulf of Mexico.

Bickel was bigger in stature, but he was a lot like Howard. He was a flashy dresser, never idle, hopping from one state to another to find new customers for UP. He moved up quickly. At the start of World War I, he was transferred to New York as the company's business manager. He was appointed general news manager in 1921 and, one year later, was named general manager.

In 1923, UP placed its fate in the hands of this young man who would prove to be a visionary. Bickel replaced W.W. Hawkins as president of the news agency. Hawkins had assumed the top spot when Howard resigned to become general business manager of the Scripps-McRae League of newspapers, forerunner of the Scripps-Howard publishing empire.

Bickel saw the world shrinking, with improvements in transportation and communications. He expanded UP's operations in Europe, opened the first wire service link to Russia, strengthened United Press' dominance in South America and took the agency to Japan and China.

Bickel's vision went beyond geography. In the early 1920s, he decided that an emerging medium, radio, had a future in news even though most newspaper publishers scorned broadcasting as a novelty.

In 1924, Bickel worked out a deal for the first mini-network of radio stations for news by setting up an election wire at WEAF, a New York radio station, with the election results broadcast through a dozen other outlets.

In 1927, Bickel wrote an article titled "The First Twenty Years," for *Editor & Publisher*. In that article the UP president boasted that the election news experiment had opened the way for radio news.

"At a time when competing press associations were fearfully regarding the development of radio broadcasting as possibly containing the germ of destructive competition, the United Press was first to welcome the radio, not as a competitor of the press association or newspaper, but as an invaluable ally," Bickel wrote. "When United Press took over the famous national 'hook-up' on the occasion of the general election in 1924 and through its cooperating client newspapers dominated the air that evening with election returns, the embargo on radio placed by other organizations crumbled and competition tumbled pell mell into line."

Bickel wrote a book, *New Empires*, published in 1930, in which he made the case that radio would become an important outlet for news. His vision of the future of broadcasting paved the way for United Press to become the pioneer of broadcast newswire services in the 1930s, while the Associated Press still disdained it.

Bickel worked toward providing radio stations with news, but his zeal caused mounting problems with his mentor. Roy Howard felt it was a mistake to serve radio because it might cause UP to lose newspaper dollars.

In 1934, Howard told Bickel, "I don't like the whole idea of selling to radio. But you and [Bill] Hawkins and Jack [Howard, Roy's son] think I'm wrong. So, go ahead and try it. If you fall on your face, it's your face."[1]

When in New York, Bickel lived at Gramercy Park and had a 75-foot yacht at the Larchmont Yacht Club. He also had homes in Sarasota, Florida and France. He profited substantially from the UP, but was privately well-off through his family and his wife, Helen, the daughter of a wealthy Portland, Oregon, hotel owner.

Bickel's determination to serve radio did not slow his efforts to increase and improve UP's coverage for newspapers. While he expanded both the scope and client base at UP, the tall, balding president never moved too far from the news desk.

He looked to improve the bottom line by boosting UP's prominence in both gathering and selling news.

Bickel undertook a vigorous solicitation of world figures to write special articles. These were sold separately by a subsidiary, the United News, which was begun in 1919 as a service for morning newspapers. Up to then, UP had been only a PM wire. After a few years, United News was absorbed into United Press, and United Features became its special articles service.

United News was staffed with some of the agency's top writers, including Westbrook Pegler, Raymond Clapper and Earl Johnson. It bought in-depth articles from William Allen White, the editor; J. M. Keynes, the economist; Robert T. (Bobby) Jones, the golfer; Major General Leonard Wood, commander of the "Rough Riders"; Edna Ferber, the author; Sir Arthur Conan Doyle, author of the Sherlock Holmes mysteries; Sinclair Lewis, the author; and many other celebrities and statesmen.

Benito Mussolini, the Italian Fascist dictator, was writing two articles a week for United News. Other statesmen lined up by Bickel included Raymond Poincaire, the French premier; Chang Tso Lin of China; and Vladimir Tchicherin, Soviet foreign minister.

United News was UP's entry into the morning field promising to provide "the word of the best authorities in international, political, industrial, economic, domestic or sporting fields as to what transpiring events mean to the man or woman who has only facts at hand, but desires to know more of circumstances and personalities involved."

When David Lloyd George retired after a dozen years in the British government, Bickel went to interview him. When he was leaving, Lloyd George's secretary, Florence Stevenson, stopped him and told him the diplomat needed money. Bickel told her if Lloyd George would write for his agency he would be paid $1,200 per article and 50 percent of the net if it exceeded $1,200.

The former British prime minister collected as much as $200,000 in one year for his special articles, which he continued for seven years with UP and United Features.

The crown prince of Germany, the Kaiser's son, was living in exile on an island off the Dutch coast in the winter of 1921–22. Bickel cabled London Bureau Manager Ed Keen to buy the prince's memoirs for syndication. Keen went to Holland but found the island isolated by ice. He cabled New York:

> PRESS BICKEL UNIPRESS NEW YORK
> CAN SEE ISLAND EXCOAST BUT IMPASSABLE FOR BOATS
> DUE THICK ICE STOP WHAT SHOULD EYE DO
>   KEEN

Bickel cabled back:

> PRESS KEEN UNIPRESS AMSTERDAM
> WALK
>   BICKEL

Keen did and signed the prince for twelve articles at $1,000 each.

Bickel and his wife were in Europe every year, traveled around the world twice, spent time in South and Central America.

His first trip to Russia was in 1922. The Russians agreed to buy a 1,200-word daily news report from UP and the government allowed the wire service to establish the first American news bureau in Moscow.

In the summer of 1923, he spent a month helping Rosta (later Tass) set up a modern news operation, from placement of desks in the office, to communications and equipment. He sent the Russian agency fifteen Kleinschmidt teleprinters, some of which were still in use thirty years later.

Bickel was in Moscow when the great Tokyo earthquake of 1923 occurred. He decided to go home by way of Japan, crossing Asia on the Trans-Siberian Railway. While in Japan, he sold the UP service to Baron Motoyama, head of *Osaka Mainichi* and to *Tokyo Nichi Nichi*.

A couple of years later, in 1925, the Russian communist government was negotiating for recognition by England and France. One of the conditions imposed by the European politicians was that Tass drop its agreement with UP and join the European news cartel. UP wires were replaced by AP news received through Reuters. A few years later when AP severed its cartel connection, Tass began taking both AP and UP.

Bickel went to Russia a dozen times in fifteen years. Aside from UP business, he spent much of his time there buying religious icons, some of them centuries old. The communist government was discouraging religion and dumping the icons and other religious art as firewood. Bickel sometimes got a bundle of icons for as little as 10 cents. He shipped them home as "household furnishings." When he visited Japan, he acquired numerous art prints there.

Among Bickel's personal interviews for UP was a talk with Hitler in 1933. "The whole German nation is behind me," the Nazi dictator told the UP president.

Bickel became a participant in one of the top news stories of the 1930s, the kidnapping of Colonel Charles Lindbergh's infant son. Lindbergh, hero of the *Spirit of St. Louis*, was a personal friend of Bickel. When the child was stolen, Lindbergh appealed to Bickel for advice on how to handle the press during his family's ordeal.

Bickel went incognito to Lindbergh's home and became Lindy's advisor. The flyer visited the UP bureau in disguise several times to confer with Bickel, but the UP president never disclosed to the news desk anything about his relationship with Lindbergh.

In 1921, John Graudenz was the first American correspondent permitted to visit the famine regions in Russia. He produced reports that brought the terrible effects of that disaster home to Americans. His stories greatly influenced the American Relief program for Russia.

United Press in 1922 had thirty-eight bureaus in the United States, 57,000 miles of leased wire. It had a nine-division structure: Pacific Coast, Mountain States, Southwestern, Central, Great Lakes, Michigan, Southern, Western Pennsylvania and New England.

James Henry Furay was foreign editor. His correspondents included E. W. Hullinger, the first permanent American journalist in Moscow; Webb Miller in Paris; Henry R. Wood in Rome; John Graudenz in Berlin, and a dozen other correspondents in Europe. The South American service was headed by James L. Miller in Buenos Aires.

Prohibition was big news in 1926. During a movement to repeal the Volstead Act, the United Press conducted a straw poll that indicated Americans favored repeal by seven to one. The Women's Christian Temperance Union blasted the UP survey as not representative, but it turned out to be on the mark. Prohibition was headed for repeal.[2]

United Press celebrated its twentieth birthday with a big splash—a dinner on April 25, 1927, at the Hotel Biltmore in New York at which President Calvin Coolidge was the main speaker. A 72-piece military band from West Point furnished the music. The 1,000 guests included publishers from throughout the world. The Coolidge speech was carried on national radio by NBC and was the lead story in the *New York Times* the next morning. The president warned Mexico against expropriation of American property.

When UP was twenty, the company claimed 1,100 clients, had thirty-six U.S. bureaus and twenty-eight in foreign countries. Key people under Bickel were: Robert J. Bender, general news manager; Ralph H. Turner, assistant news manager; Hugh Baillie, general business manager; Gilbert M. Clayton, assistant business manager; Clem J. Randau, sales manager; J. H. Furay, vice president in charge of foreign service; James I. Miller, vice president in charge of South America services, with headquarters in Buenos Aires; E. L. Keen, vice president and general European manager; and E. J. Bing, business manager for Germany.

In a speech in 1929 Bickel took upon himself to name the most important news figures of that year. They were, in Bickel's order of importance: President Hoover, King George and the Prince of Wales (tied), Colonel Charles A. Lindbergh, Benito Mussolini, Ramsay Macdonald, David Lloyd George, Henry Ford, Thomas A. Edison, George Bernard Shaw and Owen D. Young. The *New York Times*, in reporting the list, noted that it did not include any women or any sports stars.[3]

Bickel had been grooming Hugh Baillie as his successor for several years. He turned the presidency over to him in 1935, saying, "The press association is a young man's business." Bickel was fifty-three.

In his last official act, Bickel authorized the sale of UP news to broadcasters.

He retired to Sarasota, Florida, devoting himself to travel and art, relaxing by painting in oils. He became a good friend of John Ringling, the circus magnate, who had established a museum in Sarasota. After Ringling's death, Bickel made it his business to see that the Ringling Museum of Art would become a major institution. He donated many of his own valuable pieces to the museum and bequeathed the remainder of his art collection to the Ringling museum on his death in 1972.

During World War II, Bickel accepted a post as coordinator of inter-American affairs for Governor Nelson Rockefeller of New York. He also helped President Roosevelt reorganize the Latin America section of the State Department, and he helped Scripps-Howard set up a radio division.

Bickel wrote his own obituary in 1944, long before he died. In it he said he "took an active part in the promotion of the domestic service of the United Press, quadrupling its leased wire services in the United States and Canada and leaving the service with over 2,000 newspaper, radio and feature clients in forty-two countries."

12

The Sound of News on the Airwaves

THE PIONEERS OF HISTORY ALL BRAVED HAZARDS ... AND FOR ONE TRAIL-BLAZER of UP's radio news service, that meant living with country music.

Steve Snider was one of the first at United Press to write news "for the ear" when the wire service decided to start selling its world-wide reports to radio stations in 1935.

UP sent Snider and a half dozen other staffers to work at radio stations that had signed up for its news wire. These "live-in" staffers were called "processors" and their job was to take copy prepared for newspapers from the UP wires and rewrite that copy into news briefs using a conversational style better suited for broadcast.

Teams of UP "processors" moved into the newsrooms of WLS in Chicago, Illinois; KWK and KMOX in St. Louis, Missouri; WHO in Des Moines, Iowa; KARK in Little Rock, Arkansas; and KMA in Shenandoah, Iowa.

Snider, who later became a top sports columnist for UPI, was assigned to a desk in the WLS newsroom and told to help veteran broadcaster Julian Bentley prepare the opening 6 A.M. newscasts.

"It was tough getting up that early," Snider recalled, "but even worse, for me, was the loudspeaker piping country music into the newsroom. Country music was not my bag, but from 5 A.M. to around 11 or so, it was a continuing blast from people, whose names I believe, included the Arkansas Woodchopper, Lulubelle and Skyland Scotty."

Snider said he learned a lot from Bentley. "Mostly, I just watched Bentley work up the copy in his own fine style and I wrote during the crunches."

Snider and most of the radio "processors" worked with UP newspaper Teletype copy. However, those in more remote markets had to rely on so-called "pony" reports, phoned in on conference calls from UP bureaus. The UP "pony" readers for this emerging broadcast service included Walter Cronkite and Westbrook Pegler. Pegler went on to become a syndicated newspaper columnist.

Louis Milliner was a UP "processor" who worked in a cramped office just off the main studio at KARK in Little Rock. He wrote broadcast news reports from three daily "pony" feeds from the Memphis (MP) bureau.

Those "pony" reports were made up from items on the newspaper wire, news that bureau manager Pat Walsh gathered from around the state and a sprinkling of features from UP's mail service called the "Red Letter."

The Little Rock "pony" was usually read by Walter Logan, who later became a decorated war correspondent and foreign editor for UPI. The phone calls were transcribed by KARK secretary Gladys Welch, who later married the "processor" Milliner.

Milliner said he was transferred from Little Rock to KFDM in Beaumont, Texas, for similar duty. At Beaumont, he relied on a receive-only Teletype printer that relayed copy from the Dallas (DA) bureau. He also, for some reason, inherited a Hallicrafter SuperSkywriter radio, which came in very handy in March of 1937.

Milliner said he was returning to the bureau when a paper boy told him there would soon be an "extra" edition about an explosion at a school in New London, Texas, that had killed hundreds.

"When I arrived at the bureau, I was ready to put out bulletin copy for the radio station," Milliner recalled. "However, Dallas forgot to file it to us on the wire and I couldn't reach anyone at the bureau."

Milliner used his short-wave radio to tune into an East Coast station that used UP news, copied the story of the explosion and handed it to a waiting announcer.

The following morning, the Dallas relay wire began with the explosion story and it ran for one solid hour.

"I told the announcer that was all I had," Milliner said.

"That's all we want," the announcer responded.

The decision to serve radio stations was a daring move by United Press because it flew in the face of fierce opposition from newspaper publishers determined to restrict the use of news on radio.

UP's visionary president, Karl Bickel, had opened the door for the bold move in 1924, when he set-up a mini-network of radio stations to carry reports of the general election that vaulted Calvin Coolidge into the White House.

Bickel's right-hand man, Hugh Baillie, boasted that he "processed" the election material for radio at station WEAF (later WNBC & WFAN) in New York. He said two Morse wires were set up to serve a chain of stations going as far west as Minneapolis and Des Moines and deep into Dixie.

Baillie recalled that Graham MacNamee broadcast the reports after using a musician's triangle to interrupt the programming and alert listeners to the fact that there would be new election returns from United Press.

Radio broadcasting was in its pioneer stage and, according to Baillie, somewhat informal. He said Will Rogers drifted into the studio at 195 Broadway from the nearby Follies and ad-libbed for about 10 minutes about the returns, for free.[1]

That one-night stand created a crack in the publishers' wall of opposition to radio news that eventually brought down the barrier.

In 1928, UP, AP and INS all agreed to provide radio stations election returns in the bitter presidential race between Al Smith and Herbert Hoover.

In 1933, the American Newspapers Publishers Association (ANPA) made a move to harness the momentum of radio news. The ANPA worked with the two major radio networks, CBS and NBC, to form a cooperative called the Press Radio Bureau. In order to join the Press Radio Bureau, the networks agreed to withdraw from covering news and limit their news broadcasts to two five-minute periods daily, one in the morning and one in the evening. News would be provided without charge by AP, UP and INS.

The Press Radio Bureau was ideal for the Associated Press, anxious to protect its member newspapers from the intrusion of radio news. AP ran a double-page ad in *Editor & Publisher* promising that it would not sell its news services to radio stations and that it was "the only exclusively newspaper press association" in America.

"In this changing world—one thing as yet unchanged," AP boasted.

The Press Radio Bureau agreement did little to halt broadcasters' movement toward providing news. The compact actually opened the door for entrepreneurs and it did not restrict UP or INS from selling directly to radio stations.

In March of 1934, Herbert Moore, who had worked at CBS with former UP staffer Paul White to form a short-lived Columbia News Service and had been a United Press employee, formed an independent news gathering organization to serve radio stations exclusively. Transradio Press Service claimed it was serving 100 radio stations by the end of the year.

Facing the threat of new competitors, UP President Hugh Baillie picked up the campaign of his mentor, Bickel, and endorsed an ambitious plan to establish the agency as the premier news wholesaler for radio. Baillie worked with central division manager Thomas Curran in Chicago selling contracts to radio stations and assigning "processors." Curran recalled that he instructed staffers to avoid sibilants, long sentences and unpronounceable words. As UP "processors" moved into more and more radio stations, Baillie okayed a plan to produce a national broadcast wire.

The initial radio newswire was set up in 1935 at the UP bureau in the *Chicago Daily News* Building and was run by Ed Brandt. The new wire, written in broadcast style, reached most of the points that had been served by the "processors," many of whom moved to Chicago to work in the bureau on the radio wire. The main drawback for the new wire was that it did not reach the East Coast or the West Coast because of wire costs.

At the turn of the decade, UP started another broadcast wire from the New York bureau. The New York wire, carefully cultivated under the direction of Phil Newsom, soon became UP's main broadcast wire. However, the Chicago bureau continued to file its own version for clients in the Midwest and Southwest. The Chicago wire initially ran only as far west as Denver. UP soon set up a relay operation in Denver (DX) with staffers there filing a broadcast wire to the West Coast. It was made up from the Chicago wire and western news that Denver staffers processed from newspaper wires.

A handsome and charming man-about-town, Newsom assembled an impressive New York staff of writers and editors who pioneered many of the standards for broadcast news writing in the early 1940s. Newsom and his staff produced a 42-page "United Press Radio News Style Book" in 1942. It was a forerunner for most of the manuals on writing for the ear.

Newsom explained in the book, "At an early stage in this news service, United Press editors learned that news for broadcasting required a writing technique differing clearly from that of newspaper writing, that radio news style must be fashioned for the ear, not for the eye.

"Words, phrases, sentences—every element—must be chosen for effectiveness and clarity when spoken."

The book sold for 75 cents and quickly became a standard reference in hundreds of radio newsrooms. The manual advised broadcast news writers to "use words used in everyday conversations," and to read back copy "out loud" to make sure that it was "listenable."

The tiny "United Press Radio News Style Book" grew through five major rewrites into a 436-page manual that covered both print and broadcast style. That 1990 edition was titled "UPI Stylebook."

The radio wire became United Press' fastest selling product, mainly because the agency made it an all-in-one service for radio stations. The product included world and national news packages designed for 1-minute, 5-minute and 15-minute broadcasts as well as sports and financial news and features.

The same 60-word a-minute AT&T Teletype circuit that carried the radio wire to nearly 3,000 radio stations by 1955 also carried state and local news packages for clients in the larger states. For 15 minutes every hour, the wire was divided into individual state segments when state bureaus were able to transmit their own radio copy. Many regions designed state news packages similar to the national radio report to move during these 15-minute periods, which were called "splits" because the local wire was split away from the national circuit.

The rates charged for the radio wire varied according to the station's market. Full-powered (5,000 Watt) radio stations in the large cities like Chicago paid far more than the low-powered stations in smaller markets. Most of the small market stations got the complete, around-the-clock service for less than they paid a single employee, including the janitor.

The popularity of the radio wire helped United Press quickly expand in several areas. Because the radio wire was an "all-in-one" service, UP had to add state news reports in every state in which it had a strong radio client base. This meant more staffers covering news at the grass-roots level, which, of course, improved service and sales to newspapers.

By the end of the 1950s, the radio wire was serving stations in every state and was AT&T's longest dedicated circuit. UP years later maximized the advantage of leasing such a wide-ranging communications circuit with a frequency modulation system that allowed the news service to pack nearly thirty teletype circuits onto a single line. The system was called sked-4.

There was one major communications problem with the radio wire. The circuit ran from New York, snaking through every state to every customer, all the way to the West Coast, the Gulf Coast and finally back to New York. It was called a round-robin circuit. Trouble on any segment of the long line knocked out service to every radio client on the other end of the circuit.

In 1957, UP radically advanced its communication system by replacing the cumbersome "round-robin" circuit with a series of six web-like segments, centered in Chicago, Atlanta, Boston, Pittsburgh, Dallas and San Francisco. The state segments were split from the six centers, or hubs, and any wire trouble could be isolated.

At the same time, United Press moved its national radio department from New York to Chicago, ostensibly to locate the main radio production bureau into the central hub of the new communication system. However, that rationale was weak because AT&T could "split," or divide, the wire into individual circuits by remote-control.

The decision to move the radio news headquarters more likely involved economics and internal politics. UP's New York radio department had grown quickly under the direction of Newsom, Harrison Salisbury, John J. Madigan, John N. "Jack" Fallon, and Arnold Dibble. There were more than fifty full-time staffers producing the national radio segment

In Chicago, Central Division Manager Bert Masterson had an idea of how to solve the problem of overstaffing in the New York radio department and, at the same time, increase his own fiefdom in Chicago. Many believed the ambitious sales manager hoped eventually to move all of UP's national editorial operations to Chicago.

Masterson worked with the broadcast sports editor, Dean C. Miller, in New York and persuaded the company's top executives that the cost of transferring the department to Chicago would soon pay for itself by reducing the staff to about thirty-five writers and editors.

When the radio department moved to Chicago in the fall of 1957, Miller was named national radio news manager. Fewer than twenty from the New York staff made the move. Some were absorbed into other departments and a few left the company. One staffer from each of the company's six divisions was transferred to Chicago to give the new department an "All-American" look and eliminate the spectre of editorial decisions being made by the "big city" people.

Charles E. Ahrens, central division radio editor, who had handled the old Chicago radio wire relay, joined the new radio department. Ahrens was a master of tight, accurate broadcast copy. Agency insiders said that the no-nonsense Ahrens changed UP's slogan from "Around the World, Around the Clock," to "Around the World, Around the Clock, Around Five Lines."

The leaner national radio department was able to keep up with the fast-breaking events of the 1960s, but for most of that decade, it was strictly a re-write operation, with staffers converting newspaper copy into broadcast packages around the clock.

The national radio report was made up of seventeen news packages, each designed for five minutes on the air. These World In Briefs (WIBs) were supplemented by five World

News Roundups, designed for 15-minute newscasts, and a set of World News Head-lines, scripted for one-minute, on the hour breaks. There were also regular sets of sports headlines, briefs and roundups and the latest scores, and packages of business and market news. An in-depth feature package moved during the overnight hours.

The popular World in Brief news packages brought UP its first direct radio news sponsor. The ESSO oil company contracted with the agency to produce several sets of WIBS to certain specifications. The ESSO WIBs had to be ten to twelve items on world news with each item running thirty to forty words. ESSO then offered incentives for its dealers across the country to sponsor these special world news shows with local broadcasters. This meant that the local broadcaster had an automatic sponsor when it bought the UP broadcast wire.

In the 1960s, with a growing number of television clients, the Radio Wire became the Broadcast Wire. It also incorporated a new UPI service for radio stations, voice reports from the news scene.

The UPI Audio service opened in 1958 and served radio stations voice reports from reporters, sometimes with the voice of the newsmakers. These were called "actu-alities." The audio cuts were sold on an individual basis and were transmitted to clients on standard telephone lines.

William R. Higginbotham, a World War II correspondent and European news manager, had been working for UPI Newsfilm (later UPI Television News). He provided the editorial direction along with Bob Hewitt, while C. Edmund Allen, a longtime New York executive, handled the internal politics and sales. Allen was broad-cast sales manager, in charge of all radio network business.

Phil Bangsberg, an audio editor in the early 1960s, recalled working in the cramped audio section of the UPITN newsroom.

"A client would phone in, give his ID for billing, and be dropped into the audio tape running on one of two Wollensak tape recorders. The client simply waited until the tape recycled, then rang off.

"The charge wasn't much and the service drew a consistently strong response."

Bangsberg said as UPI Audio got more ambitious, the service began offering live voice reports from news scenes. The audio service put a summary of available cuts on the Teletype wire, calling them "billboards."

"High tech, it wasn't," Bangsberg said. "We had just ten phone lines. The cuts from reporters and news sites were recorded on small reels with long leaders at each end. Each leader had a narrow metallic strip pasted on. When the strip hit a sensor on the Wollensak, it automatically rewound and played again."

The network's version of high tech came when UPI bought the Audio service's major competitor, Radio Press International, in 1966. In addition to picking up a number of new clients, UPI hired some of RPI's engineering staffF Chief Engineer Pendleton Stevens, Bill Wilson and Frank Sciortino. The trio quickly brought the audio service to state-of-the-art standards. Sciortino would later run the audio operation from New York.

Peter S. Willett, general manager of broadcast services, said UPI bought RPI without spending a penny. Peter Strauss, owner of RPI, had placed a call for LeRoy Keller, a UPI vice president who was out of the country at the time, Willett recalled. The message wound up on the desk of assistant national sales manager Richard Fales, who knew that RPI had been looking for a buyer and had approached the Associated Press.

Fales called Strauss, who was indeed interested in selling his audio network to UPI. Fales relayed the news to Willett, who realized the acquisition of RPI would enhance UPI's audio service.

Next followed a series of calls between Fales, Willett, UPI President Mims Thomason and General Manager Frank Tremaine. Fales then met with Strauss and proposed a plan that required no up-front money from UPI, but, if the merger was successful, could produce more revenue for Strauss than that offered by AP.

The owner of RPI quickly signed off on a contract that would allow UPI to take all of RPI's equipment and the contracts of any willing RPI clients. In exchange, UPI promised to pay Strauss 50 percent of all revenues UPI collected from former RPI clients for three years. It was a win-win deal and in January of 1966, RPI was merged into UPI.

Willett was a young renaissance man who had been a reporter and sales executive in the Southern Division and business manager and Central Division Newspictures manager in Chicago. He had been brought to New York to help Communication Manager James Darr develop computer operations, beginning with computerized stock prices.

The two men had worked out the initial planning for UPI's Information, Storage and Retrieval System (IS&R) on cocktail napkins at the Boul Mich bar near the Chicago bureau.

In 1967, UPI Editor Roger Tatarian appointed Willett to the newly-created title of general manager of broadcast services and put him in charge of both the National Broadcast Department in Chicago and the audio service.

At the time, UPI seemed to be losing its big lead over AP in broadcast business after dominating that market for 30 years.

UPI top management felt that the National Radio Department in Chicago should be working more closely with audio. National Radio news manager Dean C. Miller was thought to be too concerned with maintaining his independence.

Willett transferred Miller back to the New York bureau where he was named business editor. In 1968, Willett named Billy Ferguson editor of national radio. Thomas L. McGann was appointed broadcast bureau manager and John I. Pelletreau became broadcast news editor. Charley Ahrens was named broadcast sports editor and Weber F. Trout, who had once handled the old Denver broadcast relay, was appointed feature editor.

Willett believed an effective audio service could greatly enhance sales of the broadcast wire.

In the 1950s, when he was selling the services in North Carolina, he had helped set up an experimental service, collecting taped voice reports and "actualities" from individual radio wire clients and playing them back for other radio clients. The service gave a surprising boost to broadcast wire sales in the state.

As Central Division business manager, Willett traveled to Indiana to make a sales swing with Eugene "Jep" Cadou, a former INS man who was a legend in Hoosierland.

On the first day, the two made eight station calls and signed eight audio contracts. Willett recalled that after the final call that day, Cadou, in his late sixties, went to sleep on the elevator as they left the radio station. His head nodded down and his cigar started to burn a hole in his tie.

"Jepper," Willett said, giving him a nudge in the ribs, "I don't think your heart is really in this."

"Oh no, kiddo," Cadou responded after putting out his smoldering tie, "I love to sell this stuff, if I just didn't have to listen to it."

Cadou called the audio network the "shouting-down-a-rain-barrel-service" because its sound quality did not compare well with ABC, NBC, CBS and Mutual radio networks. Those networks used program-grade (5 KHz) while UPI Audio relied on voice-grade (3 KHz) telephone lines.

Several of the audio network's most familiar voices had worked for Radio Press International, including Don Fulsom, Pye Chamberlayne and John Chambers. Chamberlayne spent most of the next thirty-seven years with UPI Audio, most of it covering congress and later doing a special, stylized newscast. Fulsom left after nine years, but was back with the network in 1999 covering the White House. He filed the last news cut that UPI would ever transmit in 1999:

"65: :35 V WH HSE (UPI'S DON FULSOM) PRESIDENT CLINTON IS CELEBRATING HIS BIRTHDAY AND PREPARING TO FLY TO MASSACHUSETTS TO START A NEARLY TWO-WEEK FAMILY VACATION."

Like the rest of UPI, the audio network was a training ground on which many top news broadcasters started or sharpened their skills. The UPI Audio alumni included Merrilee Cox, Bill Greenwood, Duff Thomas, Roger Gittines, Roger Norum, Tom Foty, Scott Peters, Stan Sabik, Ed Kerins, Craig Smith, Mike Aulabaugh, Dennis Gulino, Morrie Trumble, Bill Reilly, Bob Fuss and many more.

As well as the core staff of full-time audio staffers, hundreds of regular UPI staffers throughout the world filed voice reports and actualities on news events they covered.

These staffers sometimes lacked the "voices" and articulation of the full-time broadcasters, but Willett said they made up for it with believability and an intimate knowledge of the stories they were covering. He cited the voice reports from Henry Shapiro in Moscow along with Don MacKay and K.C. Thaler in London, which he said kept UPI Audio well ahead of the competition throughout the Cold War in Europe.

Willett said UPI's large world-wide staff of seasoned reporters gave UPI Audio an advantage over the big three radio networks. He said UPI Audio thrived on overseas reports from Joseph Grigg, Karol Thaler, John Barton, Robert Musel, Mike Keats, Richard Growald, Ted Shields, Bill Sunderland, Richard Longworth, Peggy Polk, Bill Bell and Aline Mosby

As it grew, UPI Audio added bureaus in Saigon, Los Angeles, Chicago, Dallas and Miami. Some of the network's most memorable broadcasts came from Vietnam. Roger Norum was rolling his tape recorder in the field when his colleague, photographer Charles Eggleston, was fatally shot by a sniper. Seven years later, UPI's Alan Dawson filed the final broadcast report from Saigon as helicopters were taking off from atop the U. S. embassy.

Broadcast wire sales, bolstered by Audio, did well through the 1960s, and by the end of 1971 UPI had 3,361 radio and television stations using it. Despite a gain of ninety-one radio stations and ten TV stations during 1971, there were signs of problems on the horizon.[2]

Associated Press was cutting into UPI's broadcast empire. The AP, mainly through a rate war, claimed in 1971 that it had 3,000 broadcast clients. In 1974, AP followed UPI into audio service.

Another challenge was the expanding and diversified needs of the broadcasting media. Radio, television, cable television and large, medium and small market radio stations all wanted specialized news reports. This was even before the Internet swept into the news business in the 1990s.

The National Broadcast Department developed an alphanumerical newswire for CATV (cable television) in 1971 and UPI launched another cable service called "Newstime." It fed CATV stations a news script to be read by an anchor off camera, coordinated with UPI news pictures and audio cuts. It was carried on a satellite feed. However, both of UPI's cable services were doomed when Ted Turner opened the Cable News Network in 1980.

To meet the diversity of broadcasters, the agency's broadcast services began an effort to customize the Information Storage and Retrieval (IS&R) computer system introduced in 1972 for newspaper circuits. Editor Billy Ferguson and News Editor Paul Harrall of the national broadcast department worked with UPI Managing Editor Paul Eberhart and communications chief James Darr to give the IS&R system more flexibility and enable the computer to handle all regional, as well as national, news for newspapers and broadcaster.

By the time UPI launched Regional Information, Storage and Retrieval (RIS&R), the second generation of computerization, the company was plunging into bankruptcy.

13

Rock-'em!
Sock-'em! Baillie

WHEN KARL A. BICKEL WAS PRESIDENT OF UP, HE GROOMED HUGH BAILLIE to be his successor and it was a good choice. Baillie was a tough police reporter, crew cut on the top and square-jawed.

Called "flat top" by the UP staff, Baillie was pleased when a profile writer said he had "the aspect of an old-line Prussian military officer." He had done some boxing and had been a fullback at University of Southern California.

Baillie tried to get into newspapering as a cartoonist in Los Angeles. Fortunately for his eventual career, no cartooning job was available at the Los Angeles *Record.* They offered him a slot on the sports desk. He covered baseball games and boxing matches, but his ferocious ambition soon had him out of sports and onto murders and bank robberies. Before he was twenty-five, he was writing three columns for the paper. One was whimsical verses about local events, under the pseudonym "Jim Frothingham." Another was a Broadway-style gossip column with the by-line "Reformed Officeboy." The third was a running series exposing local vice. He used the byline "John Danger." Young Baillie carried a pistol for protection and once used it to frighten off two men who assaulted him.

The *Record* was a Scripps-Howard newspaper, and it loaned Baillie to the United Press to cover the trial of Clarence Darrow, the famous lawyer accused of bribing a jury. Afterwards he accepted full-time UP work and kept up a hectic pace for forty years with the wire service, twenty of them as president of the company.

Pursuing news passionately for United Press was Baillie's life. When he became a vice president, he had to deal with the business end. But what he liked was punching vivid verbs and active adjectives into a typewriter and slapping a news story onto the wire. After the Darrow trial, in 1915, the UP posted him to San Francisco, where he filed the West Coast news wire, editing and padding-out the tight Western Union telegrams sent from Denver, where the UP main wire ended, and adding regional and local items.

In a few months, he was back in Los Angeles as bureau manager. In 1916, he was transferred again to San Francisco. His UP career then took him to Portland, Oregon,

Chicago, New York and Washington. When he became president, he made the whole world his bureau, reading the wire every day and showing up wherever he saw a good story to report himself or jolt his staff to action.

When Karl Bickel became president of UP, he told Baillie, then general news manager in New York, that if he was going to get to the top he should have some business-side experience. Baillie said the business end of the company was "as attractive to me as a case of smallpox." But he went on the road for a couple of years selling the service, then was brought into headquarters to become sales manager and soon business manager of the company. In 1931 he was made executive vice president and Bickel's chief lieutenant, running both news and business departments while Bickel disengaged from day-to-day decisions and took to globetrotting.

Although the business side of UP was less fun for Baillie than news, he didn't neglect it. He reorganized the company structure into regional divisions, with headquarters at Chicago, San Francisco, Kansas City, Atlanta, London, Tokyo, Buenos Aires, Berlin and Sydney, giving the managers some autonomy from New York.

He never could be mistaken for a bean counter. His view was that UP was a news organization, not necessarily a profit center for the E.W. Scripps Company. He frequently told bureau chiefs to "pull out all the stops" on a good story and hang the cost.

Baillie liked to do some travelling himself. On July 27, 1932, he was in Germany interviewing Chancellor Franz von Papen. It was his first news-making interview with a world leader and he was impressed at getting to talk to Von Papen. The story was a good one because the German leader publicly announced for the first time that the Versailles Treaty, which imposed harsh limitations on Germany at the end of World War I, was dead. Germany would re-arm and take back its lost colonies by force if necessary.

Baillie, although still only a vice president, realized he got the interview because he was the representative of an important world news agency. His rank in UP gave him an entree that lower-echelon newsmen did not have. Fred Kuh, the UP bureau man in Berlin, was well-informed and acquainted with German issues and officials in Berlin, but he could not get an interview for himself. For "the chief," he was able to set it up. It was always the job of the local bureau manager to grease the way for "flat top." He or she had to get hotel reservations, negotiate the interview and brief Baillie on the person he would be interviewing, the background of the country or region, and suggest questions.

Baillie could write. He sometimes asked his local editor to look over his copy— never to soften what he wrote, however. New York editors had the final editing responsibility. On one occasion three words in one of his dispatches were changed. He blew up.

He became president of the company in 1935 and continued seeking interviews with world leaders and the famous. He had them with Premier DeGasperi of Italy; Premier Jan Christian Smuts of the Union of South Africa; Premier Laval of France; Mussolini, the Italian dictator; Maxim Litvinoff, Soviet Commissar of Foreign Affairs; Hitler; Emperor Hirohito of Japan; Baron Carl von Mannerheim, of Finland; Chiang

Kai-Shek, of Nationalist China; Stalin (by cabled questions and answers); Syngman Rhee, President of South Korea; British General Bernard Montgomery; President Franklin Roosevelt; General Douglas MacArthur; Secretary of State Cordell Hull; President Harry Truman; President Warren Harding; President Woodrow Wilson; General George S. Patton; President Calvin Coolidge; James Jeffries, the world champion boxer; William Jennings Bryan; Lord Northcliffe; President Eisenhower; British Prime Minister Clement Attlee; Neville Chamberlain,[1] another prime minister; and Japanese Ambassador to the U.S. Admiral Kichisaburo Nomura.

These interviews always made news and showcased the United Press as an important player in world affairs. For example, in the exchange with Stalin in October 1946, the Soviet leader made one of his first declarations of the cold war, charging that the "incendiaries of a new war [are] foremost Churchill and those who think like him in Great Britain and the United States."

Baillie was not in every case able to get to the person he wanted to interview. In 1944, a few weeks after Paris was liberated, he told Joseph Grigg, the newly appointed Paris bureau manager, that he wanted to interview General Charles de Gaulle, who was forming a new French government. "He wanted to get the French leader to say he supported the United Press effort to re-establish news distribution in liberated France," Grigg recalled. De Gaulle had rebuffed all attempts by reporters to interview him.

"We got to the government headquarters and Hugh marched into the general's office and threw a question at him in English, 'Can we expect full freedom of the press in postwar France?' De Gaulle, who spoke English very badly, did not answer the question but shot back, 'This IS your interview, Mr. Baillie' and shut the door on the UP president," Grigg said.

"That was the prize brush-off," Baillie snorted as he and Grigg left the building.

Arriving back at the press headquarters in the Scribe Hotel, said Grigg, "We sat down and concocted a story reporting that UP President Hugh Baillie called on General de Gaulle, head of the new French government and 'discussed with him the possibility of opening a news service in liberated France, which the general said he warmly favored.'"

"Who's going to deny that? and we certainly did discuss it with him," Baillie insisted.[2]

In his memoir, *High Tension*, Baillie recalled the meeting with de Gaulle. He said the tall French leader, in full uniform, "looked down his long nose disapprovingly" and gave him the most hostile reception he had ever had.[3]

Employees of United Press considered Baillie a good boss. He knew what was news and he was passionate about getting it on the wires. One of the first lessons given to every Unipresser was to be prepared for a phone call from Baillie. He wanted to know everything going on and often called the nearest bureau. He expected enthusiasm.

"I sometimes phone and ask what's doing and am told 'nothing doing,' or 'everything under control.' It's thought to be the proper answer. The lid is on. All is peace. If I had ever given [Roy] Howard or [William] Hawkins such an answer in the old days, they would probably have thought I was taking sedatives. Anytime we have a nice quiet situation of nothing doing, we are in a coma," Baillie said in a letter to A. L. Bradford of the Paris bureau.[4]

His "Rock 'em! Sock 'em! Whambo! Zambo!" cable messages to "ALL" became part of UP lore. In the summer of 1952 during the Korean War, he sent this rocket to the staff in Seoul and Tokyo:

> "LET'S REVIVE KOREAN WAR. BRING IT BACK TO LIFE. NOW IT'S MERELY ANOTHER BOER WAR. AMERICAN TROOPS WHO ARE OUT THERE AND THEIR PEOPLE HERE DESERVE BETTER TREATMENT THAN THIS. LET'S HAVE FIRST PERSON STORIES FROM TROOPS UNDER FIRE FIRST TIME. SUGGEST SCENES DRESSING STATION, MILITARY FUNER-ALS, EVACUATION WOUNDED BY HELICOPTER, BRINGING UP SUPPLIES, JUST AS IF IT WERE ALL BRAND NEW. SUGGEST INTERVIEW NEW TROOPS ARRIVING, OLD ONES DEPARTING WITH BATTLE-WON MILITARY DECORA-TIONS. ALL THIS BATTLEFIELD STUFF SHOULD BE VIVID AND RAW BECAUSE OTHERWISE IT WON'T GET PRINTED. KOREAN WAR WHICH NOW SOMEWHAT FORGOTTEN IS REALLY ONE BIGGEST COSTLIEST DILEMMAS THIS COUNTRY'S HISTORY SO SUGGGEST WE REMOBILIZE INTEREST ACCORDINGLY WHILE OPPOSITION IS SLEEPING. LET'S GIVE IT THE WORKS ON NEWSPICTURES ALSO."
>
> —HB

One of E.W. Scripps' business principles was to motivate his top employees by allowing them to buy shares in the company that could be paid for in dividends. Thus, they could get rich if the managers spent frugally and earned good dividends, which they did—as much as 36 percent a year profit in the early days. This motivation helped earn the company a reputation for penury that stuck with it. Baillie, as president, did very well financially under this system although he never became as wealthy as his predecessors, Roy Howard and Karl Bickel.

United Press grew and gained prestige under Baillie, but weakness in the "financials" started in the 1950s and eventually cost Baillie his job. Roy Howard told him the UP should be making more money. Baillie passed the blame on to business manager Jack Bisco in 1952. "There has to be a better showing or else," he warned. Bisco began using what might be called "creative bookkeeping" or "cooking the books" to enhance the bottom line. The situation came to light and Baillie was fired as president on September 26, 1955, by a letter from Charles Scripps, head of the parent firm, who cited the "unorthodox bookkeeping."

Baillie's dismissal did not come with a public humiliation. He was kicked upstairs to chairman of the board. He had no interest in the mundane chores of a board of directors and afterwards always insisted he wanted to be remembered simply as 20-year "president" of United Press, the period when he was leading and prodding a staff of 1,500 young, hotshot newshands, goading them to wade through the blood and guts of a war and tell people what was happening.

His pugnacity once nearly cost him his life. He and Bert Brandt, an Acme photographer, were returning to the press camp from Aachen on the Western Front in World War II. It was dusk and their jeep crashed into a debris of a truck that had been blown up on the road. Baillie was thrown through the windshield of the jeep. He was wearing his helmet and this saved his life.

For Baillie, as for one of his heroes, General George S. Patton, war was an occasion for glory and manhood. In 1943 he went into Sicily with Allied forces. He visited the front lines throughout Europe. Later, in another war, he was with General MacArthur at the invasion of Pusan, Korea.

When not on the scene himself, he was spurring his correspondents on with fireworks cables. "Tell those guys out there to get the smell of warm blood into their copy. Tell them to quit writing like retired generals and military analysts, and to write about people killing each other," he said in a message to the European news manager. If there was no war going on, Baillie could get excited about whatever was news—disasters, heroic exploits, tragedies, even a political campaign. He liked to shake things up. He sent Lyle Wilson, UP's leading Washington byline, over to London to cover a British election, hoping it would stir some interest in the story in the United States.

UP staffers loved their volatile boss and snapped to attention when he came through the newsroom kicking a wastebasket and shouting orders to get more color and smell into a story.

If anything came ahead of United Press in Baillie's life it was his Scottish (you'd be in trouble if you said "Scotch") heritage. Once when he heard singer Maxine Sullivan belting out a swing version "Loch Lomond," which he considered sacrilegious, he was so annoyed that he called the radio station manager and threatened to pull out its UP service. The disk jockey did not take this instruction very amiably and so he played the record again. Baillie followed through with his threat, ordering the service to be cut. It took some sweet-talking by UP sales manager LeRoy Keller to appease the customer and get it back on line.

On another occasion, Baillie chopped a radio station because an announcer reporting an item on the Stone of Scone, rhymed scone with stone instead of the correct "skoon." Drambuie is an expensive Scotch liqueur and its spelling is tricky. Someone in the New York bureau once spelled it incorrectly and "Flat Top" saw it. His reaction was totally uncharacteristic. A firing could have been expected. Instead Baillie handed a bottle of Drambuie to the offending staffer. "Maybe you will spell it correctly next time," he said. Perhaps Hugh had been mellowed by a touch of the Drambuie he kept in his desk.

In New York, Baillie lived in a swank apartment at 450 East 52nd Street. Clare Booth Luce, U.S. diplomat and wife of Henry Luce of *Time Magazine,* lived in the same building. One day Hugh found himself in the elevator with Mrs. Luce. In a friendly way he said to her: "Mrs. Luce, that was a fine speech you gave last night at the U.N."

Mrs. Luce bestowed on him a devastating glance and said: "Mr. Baillie, please learn how to spell my name." The UP story had misspelled "Clare."

When Baillie moved from Manhattan to Connecticut, he wanted a vanity license plate for his car saying "HBNX" Baillie's UP code for messages. Someone else already had that combination. It turned out to be Harry Brewer, a Teletype mechanic in the New York UP bureau. Brewer gave up the license so that his boss could have it.

Although Roy Howard hired Baillie, the two men never became close. "They never got along, and forty years later, RWH played a major hand in jerking the rug from under him," said Baillie's son, Hugh Scott Baillie, Jr.

"Rip-Roaring Baillie" was the title of a *Saturday Evening Post* profile published in July 1946. The author, Jack Alexander, called the UP president "one of the last news executives in the Hollywood tradition." He described him as "an erect, scowling man with the bearing of a Prussian general." Baillie was proud of that description. "He was irrepressibly flamboyant. He wore a fresh white carnation to work every morning, sat at a gigantic mahogany desk with a three-foot wide globe beside him and a naked steel bayonet as a paper weight," Alexander wrote.

Not surprisingly, Baillie had stomach ulcers. Several times his insides began bleeding dangerously and he would have to spend time in a hospital. In an attempt to relax his life style, he took up golf. The game frustrated him. When his ball hit a tree, Baillie proceeded to thrash its branches with a club, a companion reported.

To everybody in the company his presence was often a message on the wire like the following addressed to "ALL."

"Gentlemen, United Press is the greatest news service in the history of journalism. It is our responsibility to keep it so. But what's going on here? I write this as we are in the midst of absorbing a licking on British planes shot down by the Israeli…The news report is in a down draft. A bad one. I see no excuse for getting beaten on official announcements. I am sick of hearing that 'The censor did it to us' or 'The wire failed' or 'The copy was lost in the relay,' etc. ad nauseam. Furthermore, we have fallen into a bad habit of showering posies on ourselves for thoroughly routine performances on big stories. Why shouldn't we cover these things better than anyone else? That's expected of us. We have got to rock 'em and sock 'em like athletes trying to stay on the squad. Let's have a big improvement, effective today. If anybody can't be bothered to go along with this, let him quit. Let's reduce interoffice correspondence about 50 percent, which will save a lot of everybody's time for the news report….Yes, you Unipressers, this is the alarm clock you hear ringing!"

On the receiving end of such a rocket, a staffer told Jack Alexander, "You know that you're being conned, but you don't mind being conned by such an expert con man, and you go forth armed to perform miracles. It has a peculiar effect on you. You grumble about the dough, yet you have a lovely, unreasoning loyalty to Baillie and the UP. I suspect there is something spiritual about it. Your AP counterpart is getting two hundred and seventy-five a month for living expenses, and your allowance is eighty-eight. So what? You're probably younger than he is, and he's mixed up with a more hierarchical outfit than you are. You know that you can start as green as grass in the UP and advance on your own merits. But after you've advanced, where are you? It's all very contradictory."

Baillie believed deeply that competition among news services was one of the country's chief blessings. It made the American people the best-informed in the world, he said. "We are covering, play by play, the greatest show on earth—for today's readers, not for posterity."

To be sure that people knew about United Press, Baillie commissioned composer Paul Lavalle to create a "United Press March." He hoped it would become as popular a band piece as the "Washington Post March," which was written by John Philip Sousa, director of the Marines band, for a children's festival June 15, 1889, sponsored by the *Washington Post*. The UP March was played for the first time December 9, 1952, at the Belasco Theater in New York. Baillie had the company's best New York reporter, Doc Quigg, cover the story and UP photographer Ford Bond documented it with his speed graphic.

The UP president was thrilled, and couldn't see why everyone else wasn't. He wrote in his diary two days later that he had talked to Charles Scripps. "He said he had heard the march, and that the band seemed to miss a couple of beats. Such enthusiasm! Such appreciation for getting his company a march that will be heard for years!"[5]

Baillie thought radio stations would use the United Press March as a tag for their news broadcasts. Few did. But the tune found its way into an unlikely spot in history. Baillie wondered if he could get it played during the coronation of Queen Elizabeth in London. Robert Musel, of the London bureau, was a musician of some note and had connections. He relates what happened:

"Like other top UP executives of the era, Baillie had the endearing belief that his staff could do anything. So it wasn't worthwhile telling him the music in this ancient ceremony was heavily traditional. But, as it happened, I had always moonlighted as a songwriter and was known as such to the musical establishment, one of whom just happened to be the leader of the band of the Irish Guards.

"And so the impossible came about. UP reporter Jack Fox was on the balcony of the Berkeley Hotel in Piccadilly with the UP President when the Guards marched by. He reported that Baillie actually had tears in his eyes as he gasped 'They're playing our song!'"[6]

The United Press office was on the 12th floor of the *Daily News* building at 220 East 42nd Street. Like anyone else, Baillie sometimes had to wait for an elevator to take him to the street. He didn't like to wait. So a button was installed on his desk connected to a bell in the lobby. When he jabbed the button, the dispatcher in the lobby was supposed to send the next elevator directly to the 12th floor for the UP chief. One day an elevator filled with people heading up to floors above stopped at the 12th floor to discharge a passenger. Baillie entered, ordering "Down!" The operator was so intimidated that he took the elevator, with its load of passengers, down to the lobby immediately and before going up again with the other passengers.[7]

Hugh Baillie and Earl Johnson, the vice president for news, lived close to each other in Manhattan, but Johnson did not like Baillie much and called him "that bull in a China shop." The two often met when they went out from their apartments about 10 P.M. in the evening to buy the early editions of the *Mirror* and the *Daily News*. Johnson complained to another New York staffer that Baillie was always "lurking around wanting to tell his troubles, that he had been double-crossed by someone at UP. Earl didn't want to hear it."[8]

In his passion for a news report that would get attention, Baillie once admonished the troops: "LET US NOT EVER GET TOO SOLEMN TO LET A LACY FART."

14

Today's News Today

"TODAY'S NEWS TODAY" WAS THE SLOGAN OF UNITED PRESS IN ITS
appeal to afternoon newspapers. The urgency of getting news on the wire was captured
in the title of *Deadline Every Minute*, an account of the company's first fifty years, by
Joe Alex Morris, published in 1957.

UP also wanted the news wires to be interesting. Interviews and human interest
stories were encouraged, in contrast to AP where Melville Stone wanted only a straight
recitation of "the facts."

A 1929 United Press guidebook called for staffers to avoid "bromidic" expressions
in writing news.

> "Nothing so ruins newspaper copy as bromidic expressions. Here are some
> which should be avoided, and every bureau manager knows plenty more
> belonging in this category: *Setting the stage, behind closed doors, took steps, pris-*
> *oner was grilled, conducting an investigation for 'investigating, an investigation*
> *was under way today*—when used as the lead of an overnight story; *probe or*
> *quiz for investigation, flayed, combing the country, nationwide dragnet*—or in
> fact—*any dragnets when applied to pursuits.*"

Such clichés were found all over the UP wires in 1929, and were still found plen-
tifully in 1930, 1940, 1950, 1960, 1970, 1980 and 1990. While supervising editors
called for less trite writing, newsmen with a deadline every minute seldom had the
time to use Roget's Thesaurus.

But at least the UP writing had something over its opposition. Karl Bickel once
remarked that in AP's halls, "news was not presumed to be authentic unless it was
supremely dull."[1]

In a later guide for UP staffers, Boyd Lewis, a New York editor, advised: "Let the
event tell itself. The news is the big thing, not the writer's clever phraseology. Keep the
writer behind the story."

Typical of the operations of a small UP bureau manager in the 1920s was that
experienced by Frank Bartholomew in Portland, Oregon. Bartholomew was later to
become president and chairman of the board of UP.

When he started in the small Portland bureau on February 12, 1921, he recalled in his memoirs, "My duties were to read the local news of the *Journal* and select material. Also, to do any incidental checking by telephone or legwork to confirm facts and to get the news into a pony telegraph report for transmission by Western Union to clients in the area. Some papers received a basic 500 word report for the entire day, 250 in mid-morning, another 150 at noon, and a wrapup final 100 words later. A small list of more affluent newspapers received 750 words a day."

In the larger bureaus there was a "routiner" or "kitty" for each job. This was a minute-by-minute rundown of what should be moving on the wires throughout the day. The kitty often ripened into a grimy sheet of yellow teletype paper filled with scrawled margin notes. It was an essential tool for getting the job done, especially when the regular staffer was absent and someone else had to take care of a wire.

The key staffer in the bureau was the wire filer. He or she was manager of the wire, editing copy for the teletype operators to send, making decisions on which dispatches should be transmitted and which could be trimmed, held back or discarded.

Boyd Lewis' guidebook said the wire filer "often must cut and discard when the pressure mounts. He must always do so qualitatively, not quantitatively."

It was a complex job. Besides selecting dispatches from the mass of copy available, the filer had to handle weather forecasts, grain and poultry markets, local sports scores. These routine items were extremely important to client newspapers and broadcasters.

During the ski season, a delay of a few minutes in the daily ski report, which described conditions at the leading resorts, was sure to bring several telephone calls.

The day President Kennedy was shot and important news was pouring from everywhere in the world, Richard Harnett, the wire filer in San Francisco, was ordered to interrupt the flow of assassination copy to move a local chicken market report.

An urgent news development was a "five beller." The operator tapped a key that rang a bell five times in the customers' wire rooms, alerting editors. A bulletin called for ten bells and was a single paragraph followed by urgent adds as the story developed. Often a "first lead" would be used when new developments merited rewriting the story from the beginning. Second, third or fourth leads might be required on a breaking story over one news cycle.

The teleprinter, on which all this material arrived in news offices, was invented in 1914 and had replaced Morse transmission by the 1920s.[2]

Although the writer Upton Sinclair called Associated Press "the most powerful and most sinister monopoly in America," there was more genuine and heated competition during the 1920s than any other time in American history, with AP, UP and INS in the fray as well as several smaller agencies.[3]

By the close of 1928, UP had 952 newspapers in the U.S. and Canada, and 1,150 worldwide. Most of them were afternoon newspapers. The service was supplying news in nineteen languages in forty countries. It had twenty-eight foreign bureaus and fifty-one in the U.S. and leased more than 105,000 miles of telegraph wires.

The UP in the 1920s and 1930s became a viable alternative to the AP for many newspapers. The AP was respected as the more authoritative basic report, but many editors preferred stories from the United Press because of their variety and liveliness compared to the AP report.

AP wanted to be the only news service in America. Its by-laws forbade any member from dealing with any other news agency. It had a deal with Western Union under which the telegraph company would move only AP news.

The cooperative loosened up only gradually under pressure from the courts, from publishers and from United Press competition.

After winning "property right" to its news reports in the case against INS that was finally decided by the Supreme Court in 1919, AP sought to go one step farther. It issued a directive to members ordering them to post notices telling their employees they were forbidden to send out any version of the news to other news agencies, no matter how differently it may be worded from the story given to the Associated Press. AP claimed that all of the 80,000 employees who worked for newspapers in the United States were also AP employees. The cooperative had the power to enforce its rules by heavy fines upon newspapers.

The AP news report was "as dry as dust," Dewey M. Owens, a well-known journalism commentator, observed, while UP and INS had sprightly writing.[4]

Managers were rarely called into headquarters to be indoctrinated. All of this made UP very different from the tightly organized and supervised Associated Press.

Despite its opposition to AP's practice of serving only one newspaper in a city, the UP, in the 1920s, introduced something similar. It was the "cumulative equity" contract. This was designed to give the client an equity value in its arrangement with UP, which could be turned into cash if the UP service was sold to a competing client. The device was used frequently to deny service to customers the UP did not want, such as strike newspapers and would-be publishers attempting to start shoestring news operations in competition with established customers.

United Press was reorganized financially in 1928. Voting power was lodged in 2,500 common shares and 70,000 shares of preferred stock were issued. They were promised a $6 annual dividend requiring UP to earn at least $420,000 a year.

In its growing role as a major news vendor, the United Press, in 1929, gained the attention of publishers and politicians. It was responsible for opening public scrutiny of U.S. Senate votes taken in executive session.

During the first half of the century, the Senate frequently went into executive session to discuss matters the members preferred the public not to know about, such as the confirmation of appointments. Paul R. Mallon, chief of the United Press Senate staff, managed, occasionally, to get the breakdown of senators voting pro or con on such matters.

In May 1929, a secret vote was held on the nomination of former Senator Irvine L. Lenroot for a federal judgeship on the Court of Customs Appeals. Mallon got the roll-call from his sources and put it on the wire. Hell broke loose the next day when some senators saw, in print for everybody to read, how they had voted. These senators demanded an investigation of the "Lenroot leak."

Mallon was called before the Senate Rules Committee. He declined to disclose his source. The Senate wasted a good deal of time debating what to do about Mallon's reporting. Should reporters be banned from the gallery? Should every senator be required to testify under oath that no leak occurred in his office? After a month's debate, the senators came to the realization that secrecy was indefensible and decided that votes taken in executive session would be made public.

In 1931, the UP moved its headquarters from the Pulitzer Building on Park Row to the *Daily News* at 220 East 42nd Street, taking the entire twelfth floor and half of the eleventh floor as well as some space on the third floor, a total of 14,000 square feet. It was the second move in the company's history. In 1908, one year after it was founded, UP had moved from the Park Row Building to the Pulitzer Building, which housed the *World*.

The company matured during the 1930s. With this came unionization of employees. The American Newspaper Guild, which belonged to the Congress of Industrial Organizations (CIO), petitioned the National Labor Relations Board on May 12, 1937, for an election among editorial employees in the continental United States.

The man behind the Guild movement in the wire services was Morris Watson, a left-leaning newsman who had been fired by AP for union activity. The U.S. Supreme Court ordered AP to reinstate him but he resigned a short time later to become a full-time union organizer. The UP was high on his list of targets.

As well as reporters and editors, the Guild claimed office boys, clerks, tabulators and some employees not directly engaged in writing or editing. Hugh Baillie wanted to exclude all non-writing employees from the bargaining unit but in the end. most were included. The company and Guild signed their first contract on June 23, 1937, covering 450 employees in sixty-six bureaus in the United States. It provided for a 5-day, 40-hour work week in 11 large bureaus and a 6-day, 48-hour week in 55 smaller offices.

Throughout the entire life of the company, UPI fought a simmering battle with the Guild over bureau managers in smaller bureaus. Management said that as supervisors they were exempt under federal labor laws from the union's jurisdiction. The National Labor Relations Board ruled otherwise, in favor of the Guild. But management condoned and even encouraged violations of the contract. Provisions on hours and overtime were seldom observed by managers except when the union took action.

It was not unusual for the manager of a small bureau to earn less money and work more hours than the people under his authority.

Lewis Lord, manager of the Columbia, South Carolina, bureau in the 1960s, described his day: "I usually opened the bureau at 5 A.M. and worked until 5 or 6 P.M. On Saturdays, I worked from 6 A.M. until 2 P.M., except on days when there was a football game or a Nascar race that I would cover. I remember one Saturday in 1964 when I rode in the morning in an army helicopter to a crash scene near Augusta, covered a South Carolina-Clemson football game in the afternoon and staffed a Goldwater for president rally at night."

Lord said his only staff employee, Bill Cotterell, failed to put paper in the machines before leaving one night and he felt he had to call the error to Cotterell's attention.

"If you keep this up," he told Bill, "you will never make bureau manager."

Bill raised his head. His frown broke into a broad grin, and he responded: "You promise?"

The bureau manager in Reno, Nevada, when writing to New York to ask for a pay raise, said he was embarrassed because his staff members sometimes opened the company mail and saw his paycheck, which was lower than theirs. The response from New York was: "From now on, your check will be sent in a separate envelope." A raise would have to wait.

Many managers were actually glad to see the Guild win increased wages because their own pay was geared to the Guild scale. They got pay raises a few months after the union people won theirs.

Teletype employees, who had been organized earlier into the Commercial Telegraphers Union, an American Federation of Labor craft union, had a "union shop." All employees in that department had to become members of the CTU.

15

Covering Kings and Kidnappers

THE RUNNING NEWS STORIES OF THE 1930S INCLUDED THE DEPRESSION in the United States and political tension elsewhere in the world. Bureaus in Europe were busy with wars in Ethiopia and Spain, the coronation of an English king and abdication of another for his love of an American divorcee. United Press went at them with Baillie's whambo! zambo! enthusiasm.

When King George VI was crowned in England, reporters for "empire" newspapers cabled colorful word pictures of the spectacle—the beauty of the women, the gaiety of the crowds, the worshipful homage of the king's subjects.

United Press accounts told of the brilliancy and dignity of the occasion but, besides that, they reported the extravagant expenditures for the coronation display. The UP dispatch pictured prosperous Englishmen seated in the expensive street stands tossing their lunch baskets to the street. It also described how the half-starved men and women in London's army of unemployed rushed in like squirrels to seize the discarded crumbs.

This kind of graphic reporting brought praise from journalism critics in the United States, including *Harper's Weekly* and *American Magazine*.

Unable to match the AP in depth of staffing, UP editors tried to get attention for their news by a more exciting, more sensational kind of reporting.

In the fall of 1936, the hottest running news story was the love between Edward VIII, king of England, and Mrs. Wallace Warfield Simpson, a married American woman.

Edward, who had been ruler of the empire for less than a year, was in love with the American beauty and wanted to marry her. Would the king give up the throne for love? Would he sacrifice his amour to preserve the tradition of the monarchy? It was the obligatory topic of conversation among tea-sipping ladies and beer-drinking men. American newspapers wanted everything on this story. It had page one ingredients—royalty, money and sex.

The other royalty knew the story. Leaders of the government knew it. Parliament knew it. The Archbishop of Canterbury knew it. Chimney sweeps and charwomen knew it. Newspaper publishers knew it. But not a word was printed in British newspapers.

On October 16, the king invited Lord Beaverbrook, owner of the *London Daily Express*, to Buckingham Palace for a talk. Edward was a bit ill at ease. When he finally got to the point, he asked the publisher to play down the expected divorce of Mrs. Simpson. He wanted Beaverbrook to get the rest of the British press to suppress the divorce story. Mrs. Simpson, the king told the publisher, ought to be "treated like any other American citizen" getting a divorce in England, with perhaps a small notice on an inside page. And so, on October 27, 1936, when Mrs. Simpson was granted a divorce at Ipswich, England, from Earnest A. Simpson, the newspapers in England printed only a paragraph or so.

The British government and the Church of England wanted leading newspapers of the country to undertake an editorial campaign against the speculated Edward-Simpson marriage. Beaverbrook warned, correctly, that this would only bring the affair more attention.

On Wednesday, December 9, 1936, United Press reporter Dan Rogers was at work in the London bureau when Tosti Russell, a stringer, popped in as he did occasionally. A handsome man, with a black mustache, Russell was privately on good terms with Queen Ena of Spain, then in exile in Britain.

Russell told Rogers that Queen Ena, who was on social terms with Britain's royal family, had confided to him that Edward would have to abdicate the throne if he wanted to marry the American, and that he would do so.

Rogers rolled a book of flimsies into his typewriter and wrote: "Sources usually unimpeachable have informed United Press that the king will abdicate."

The story was on the mark but the reverence of the British about their royalty caused every London newspaper to pass on it. In the United States, speculation and excitement increased. A. J. Liebling, in his "Wayward Press" column for *New Yorker* magazine, said Rogers had the story right.[1]

UP President Hugh Baillie, by coincidence, was travelling to Europe on the same ship on which Lord Beaverbrook was returning from America to England that December. When the two men were chatting on the deck, Beaverbrook told Baillie the British press was not censored but "had merely come down on the side of tradition."[2]

At a meeting in Warwick House, the residence of Lord Rothermere, publisher of the *Daily Mail*, a group of newspaper executives discussed how to handle the problem of media attention to the king's romance and expected marriage. Beaverbrook and other leading British newspaper publishers agreed to keep the lid on the romance story. It should be assumed, they decided, that "the king's friendship with Mrs. Simpson was strictly a part of his private life" and not a subject for the public to read about in their newspapers.[3]

The London *Daily Mail* denounced in print the United Press and others who covered the story as "foreign scandal mongers."

On December 10, Edward formally abdicated the throne to marry "the woman I love." The next day, Parliament endorsed the abdication. Then, finally, it hit the English press in a big way.

In the 1930s, the United News, the UP's service for morning newspapers, concentrated its efforts on quality journalistic analysis stories by its own correspondents, and by noted persons recruited to do byline stories. One who wrote for United News was Benito Mussolini. The Italian Fascist leader had been a reporter himself for *Popolo d'Italia.*

Webb Miller had worked with Mussolini covering a political conference in Cannes France in January 1922. "Mussolini trotted around with the rest of us, carrying his notebook and pencil; nobody paid any attention to him at all," said Miller. Nine months later Mussolini had taken over Italy and was a dominant personality in Europe.

In 1932, Miller had an audience with the Italian dictator in Rome. "Ten years ago this week we were reporters together at Cannes on the same story. Well, I am still a reporter," said Miller as they shook hands. Mussolini laughed, put his hand on Miller's shoulder and said, "Maybe I shall be a reporter again, too."[4] Mussolini later wrote two articles a month for United News.

United News also carried serialized features including the letters of Napoleon, which were in the public domain. Its stable of big-name writers included the novelist Sinclair Lewis. On January 18, 1936, Hugh Baillie and his father were visiting Lewis to discuss articles when the writer jumped from his chair and exploded at some criticism from Baillie. He ushered the UP president out while shouting invectives at him. That ended the Sinclair Lewis series.

Other writers engaged by United News included William Allen White, the distinguished editor; J. M. Keynes, the economist; Bobby Jones, the golfer; General Leonard Wood; Sir Arthur Conan Doyle of Sherlock Homes fame; and Edna Ferber, the poet.

UP was gaining prestige throughout the world. Tom Morgan, Rome bureau chief, wrote to Bickel in June 1932, that at a meeting of the "allied agencies" in Europe the main topic "turned out to be exclusively a question of how to handle the formidable United Press competition which is now prevalent in practically all the territory of the allied agencies."[5]

The Paris bureau of UP always kept a female on the staff. The fashion shows were a female beat. In 1929, Mary Knight, an attractive, young American, went to Paris for excitement and cultural ambience and was looking for a job. Ralph Heinzen, the UP manager, hired her.

He almost fired her when she turned in her first story on a fashion show. "No! No! We can't use stuff like that," Heinzen shouted. "It's the dresses you are sent to describe, not the furniture and the flunkies and how people in the audience look!"[6]

In her five years with UP, Knight made herself a "newsman"—a title women of the press prized in those days. She interviewed princes, politicians, diplomats, a world heavyweight fighter and handled the day-to-day routines of the bureau.

On January 3, 1932, World War I French Commander in Chief Marshal Charles Jacques Joffre was under a death watch. INS had already reported erroneously he was dead. To check out the report, Knight went to the hospital where he was thought to be a patient. Aware that she might be stopped by security she carried a bouquet of flowers. She ducked her head into every room as if looking for a sick relative. When in one room she saw Joffre's family standing around the bed, she knew the general was still alive but probably in grave condition. "*Excusez moi*," she said, and dashed out. She had the information she needed.

Paul Doumer, the thirteenth president of France's Third Republic, was shot to death on May 6, 1932 by Paul Gorgouloff, a mad Russian. When seized, the Russian claimed to be the Lindbergh kidnapper and gave authorities other strange stories. He was suspected of faking insanity, tried and sentenced to the guillotine.

Knight wanted to cover the execution but Heinzen assigned another staffer, Reynolds Packard, a senior Paris reporter. Even if Heinzen were willing to send her, women were not allowed to be official witnesses at an execution.

Guillotine executions were carried out before dawn in a public square. Parisians, finishing off a night on the town, often gathered for these events.

Knight was determined to see it. She borrowed some male clothes, pulled a cap down on her head and made her way in the middle of the night to the square where the guillotine had been readied. She was standing with the reporters, not far from Packard, when the blade fell and Gorgouloff's head rolled into the basket, blood spurting from his neck. The two-piece corpse was taken away and the cobblestones quickly hosed down.

Reporting to work at her usual hour that morning, one of the other staffers to whom she had told her intention to see the execution, asked, "Mary, did you go?"

"Yes," she said, "I borrowed men's clothes and saw it."

Heinzen, feet up on his desk reading a newspaper in typical bureau manager's pose, overheard the exchange. Throwing down the paper he yelled, "Mary! Christ alive! Snap to it and let's get going." He knew a good story.

Knight turned out a sidebar about the experience that was widely used.[7] New York cabled Paris for a picture to go with her story. The very feminine Knight made "the most improbable looking man you ever saw," said Wallace Carroll, also on the Paris bureau staff at the time.[8]

When Mary Knight came home to the United States on vacation, she was a minor celebrity and was interviewed as the gutsy American girl who sneaked into a Paris guillotining. UP sent her out on promotional appearances.

On May 20, 1927, at 7:52 A.M., Charles Lindbergh took off from Roosevelt Field, Long Island, New York, in the *Spirit of St. Louis*. He had five sandwiches and a thermos of coffee. "Will that be enough?" he was asked.

"If I make it, that will be enough. If I don't make it, that will still be enough." Lindy was more concerned about how much gasoline could be force-fed into his plane. The tanks were topped off at 4,458 gallons.

A prize of $25,000 awaited the first man to fly the Atlantic alone. For newspapers, this was another stupendous story that could sell thousands of "extras."

That night, hundreds of people were at Le Bourget Flying Field outside of Paris, hoping to see Lindbergh fly in. Almost every reporter on the continent was there. John O'Brien, Jane Dixon and Ralph Heinzen were the UP staffers. The news service had also hired a half dozen stringers. Heinzen sent them out to occupy every public telephone booth at the field, keep the lines open and "Don't let anyone else use the phones."

When the *Spirit of St. Louis* touched down, there was a frantic rush for telephones. At one phone, when the UP stringer would not give it up, frustrated rival correspondents dumped over the booth with the UP stringer inside.[9]

Reporters Dixon and O'Brien were tossed around in the surging crowd. When they found each other, Jane Dixon's clothes were torn and she had lost a shoe and her hat.

The UP flash was received by newspapers seven minutes ahead of AP, according to a report in *Fortune* magazine. On a story of this much interest, that was a tremendous beat.

The kidnap and slaying of the flyer's infant son, Charles Lindbergh, Jr., five years later, on March 1, 1932, was another news sensation around the world.

The baby was stolen from his nursery in the Lindbergh's home. A ransom note was left.

Desperate to get his son back, Lindbergh negotiated with several parties claiming to be intermediaries. He paid $50,000 ransom to one of them, but the child was not returned.

Two and a half months later, on May 12, William Allen, a working man, stopped his truck to answer a call of nature. He was squatting in the bushes alongside the road when he saw a child's body partially buried. It was baby Lindbergh.

The ransom money serial numbers had been recorded. These bills began showing up in neighborhoods around the Bronx. Walter Lyle, a gas station attendant, accepted a $10 gold note from a customer. It looked suspicious and he took down the plate number of the customer's car.

Bruno Richard Hauptmann, a Bronx carpenter, was arrested two and one-half years after the kidnap. He was found guilty and executed in 1936. That was also a major news event of the decade.

As circumstantial evidence piled up against the German immigrant the newspapers were ravenous for every detail. Evalyn Walsh McLean, estranged wife of the publisher of the *Washington Post*, paid $100,000 to a man named Gaston B. Means. He was a con artist who said he could get the baby back for the Lindberghs. He went to jail, but Mrs. McLean never got her $100,000 back.

Hauptmann's trial in the town of Flemington, New Jersey, attracted 150 reporters from throughout the world. The UP team covering the trial included Sidney Whipple, Harry Ferguson, James C. Austin and Jane Dixon, with others coming up from the New York bureau as needed. UP hired Norma Saunders, daughter of the Hunterdon County sheriff, as a messenger, hoping she might have some inside source possibilities.

UP, like the other agencies and newspapers, set up a mini-bureau in Flemington. Special telegraph circuits were installed in an improvised pressroom on the second floor of the courthouse. Wires dangled and snarled around desks.

The one small hotel in the town was not nearly adequate for the crowd of reporters and curious. Residents put their extra rooms up for rent and made a killing.

The trial began January 2, 1935. Evidence against Hauptmann was circumstantial—the money, a home-made ladder found near the crime, the weakness of his alibi, handwriting samples matching ransom notes and eyewitness testimony of the gas station attendant who had recognized the ransom money.

It was high drama. An endless procession of automobiles from New York and other cities brought the morbidly curious to the scene. State police, resplendent in their horizon-blue uniforms and flaring yellow-striped breeches, guarded the entrance of the courthouse. An admission pass was required. Reporters, prospective witnesses, court attaches, telegraph operators had red, blue, yellow, and white tickets.

At least 1,000 people clamored for admission every day. They included clairvoyants, amateur "experts" in crime detection, spokesmen for various participants, U.S. senators, Broadway actresses, Hollywood stars, society women, social reformers, ministers, professors, prostitutes, preachers, publicans, concert singers, crooners.

"Unfortunately for the working press, it appeared most of these celebrities managed, in one way or another, to obtain their tickets," Whipple said.

The newspapers were ravenous. The *New York Journal* asserted informal custody of Mrs. Hauptmann, guarding her day and night as closely as her husband was guarded by the state of New Jersey.[10] This did not stop a Mr. Whitney from claiming to be her agent and offering to sell her version of the trial to various newspapers.[11]

UP's lead reporter, Whipple, had to match rumor for rumor. He and the other Unipressers rushed around Hunterdon County chasing down fantastic tales about surprise mystery witnesses or "startling new evidence." Dignity was in flight and the circus was in town. Whipple had to stop people from chopping up his telegraph wire for souvenirs.

Newspapers and intermediaries made offers as high as $150,000 to Hauptman to give them his story, "How I killed the Lindbergh baby." No story was too weird or impossible to find its way over the wires and into the newspapers. Ten minutes after the latest sensation hit the streets, all the competing correspondents were being queried by their editors and a new wild-goose chase would begin.

Once Whipple wrote three paragraphs of a lead, yanked it out of his typewriter and tossed it toward a wastebasket. A woman picked up the ball of paper and thrust it under Whipple's nose. "If you autograph it I'll pay you five dollars for it," she said.[12]

Police tapped press telephones to keep abreast of what reporters were finding out on the case.

Whipple, telephoning from his hotel room, looked out a window into a window of the telephone company exchange across the street. When he picked up his phone to call the UP bureau, he noticed a state trooper in the telephone exchange pick up a set of headphones and plug himself into a line.[13] That was a remarkable coincidence, he thought. So he hung up and called again. The trooper again picked up his headphones.

"I'll have to go to another phone," Whipple told the UP desk. "I can see a state trooper listening to us." He then saw the startled officer drop the earphones in surprise.

Sandor S. Klein was sent from New York to help cover the verdict, which came down February 13, 1937. All the reporters and editors were tensed for the day. Every preparation they could think of had been made. The UP strategy to get on the wire first was to post Klein at the rear door of the courtroom. Across the hall in a small room where a teleprinter was installed Harry Ferguson manned a desk beside the teletype operator. Whipple and James C. Austin were in the courtroom.

For UP's main wire service competition, Associated Press, the Hauptman verdict was a disaster. At 10:31 P.M. AP put out a flash: "GUILTY. LIFE." The flash sped around the world.

Earl Johnson, UP's news chief standing by the wire in New York, started receiving calls. He sent a rocket to Flemington, "OPPOSITION FLASHING HAUPTMAN GUILTY WITH LIFE SENTENCE." The message was slipped to Whipple in the courtroom. He passed a note back: "JURY IS STILL OUTSIDE COURTROOM. IF AP IS RIGHT IT IS NICE TO HAVE WORKED WITH YOU."

For 15 minutes the AP bulletin was the only news from the trial. Editors put out "extras" with the verdict. The *New York Times* had truckloads of newspapers speeding around the city.

When the verdict was actually announced. Whipple scribbled it on a slip of paper, handed it to Austin, who passed it over the transom of the door to Klein. Harry Breuer grabbed it and passed it to Ferguson. Teletype operator Edward Bungue tapped out the flash.

United Press was far behind with its flash. But it was correct, "GUILTY AND CONDEMNED TO DEATH."

The Hauptman trial, and the AP's blunder on the verdict, helped United Press establish itself as a reliable news service. Like Roy Howard's false armistice flash, the erroneous AP Hauptman flash was never forgotten in the news business.

In a curious follow-up the Associated Press used its error in a promotion piece. It quoted George B. Armstead, managing editor of the *Hartford Courant*, in a letter to AP chief Kent Cooper. "It must be grand to preside over an organization so far famed for accuracy and speed that when it makes a slip it becomes a national sensation."

Presidents and other government officials often find fault with news reporting. Sometimes they make comments, usually off the record or in passing, critical of "the press" or "the media."

Seldom are they specific but on one occasion in 1939 when Americans were gripped in an intense debate over isolationism and the European war, President Franklin D. Roosevelt took United Press to task very heatedly.

A UP dispatch on July 13 said Roosevelt and Secretary of State Cordell Hull "were reported in administration quarters today to have disagreed on the language of a neutrality message."

Ronald C. Van Tine, head of the agency's Senate staff, wrote that Hull wanted to soften the wording of a message Roosevelt proposed to send to Congress. The Senate Foreign Relations Committee was stalling on a Roosevelt-proposed law that would permit the president to give increased help to Great Britain and its allies.

UP sources, unidentified in the story, said Hull was afraid Roosevelt's strong words might anger the German and Italian governments and further antagonize members of Congress who favored U.S. neutrality in the European crisis.

Roosevelt saw Van Tine's story in the Washington *Times-Herald*. The president was livid. He summoned UP's Washington chief Lyle Wilson to the White House and administered a sharp scolding. He also issued a signed statement accusing the UP of "falsification of the actual facts." The story, Roosevelt said, "represents the limit of any decent person's patience." He specifically named the UP and said he didn't want to criticize the Associated Press, which did not have the story. He said he and Hull had not decided whether any speech or message on neutrality would be issued and if so, what the content might be. "That is the truth, and it is a great pity that this simple truth, of which the press has been informed, has been disregarded by a press association."

However, it turned out that a message was, in fact, sent to Congress the next day and it incorporated what UP had reported was Hull's viewpoint.

This was not the last unhappiness Roosevelt had with the Scripps-Howard owned agency. When the U.S. entered the war, the president, in a public appearance, said only one person turned down a request from him for help. It was Roy Howard. Roosevelt wanted Howard to go to Latin America as a U.S. representative to talk to leaders there about the American war effort. Howard refused, giving the excuse that he was unable to speak Spanish or Portuguese.

The president said Howard, along with the *Chicago Tribune* and Hearst, were members of "the Clivenden Set," referring to a British association that favored appeasement.

Thereafter Roosevelt rebuffed several appeals by Howard to grant him an interview. The enmity between Roosevelt and Howard dated from the 1932 presidential nomination race in which the Scripps-Howard newspapers supported Roosevelt's opponent, Al Smith, for the Democratic nomination.

Another dramatic running news story of the 1930s was the disappearance of Amelia Earhart near Howland Island in the Pacific. United Press had a special correspondent aboard the *Itasca,* the Coast Guard's vessel coordinating the search for her plane. As an example of how news was received from remote places in those technically impoverished days, here is one of the messages that Howard Hanzlik sent to UP San Francisco from the *Itasca* on July 3, 1937. It was transmitted by radio from the ship. The re-write person in San Francisco had to put the story in shape for the wire.

RDO USCG ITASCA CK222 PRESS COLLECT 1545 HST 3 (JULY); **UNIPRESS SANFRANCISCO**; FROM ELEVEN THIRTYSEVEN AM JULY SECOND (ALL TIMES GIVEN HST) TO NINE AM JULY THIRD ITASCA COVERED APPROSIMATELY [SIC] SIX THOUSAND SQUARE MILES AREA NORTH AND NORTHEAST HOWLAND EXTENDING HUNDRED TWENTYFIVE MILES NORTH AND SIXTY MILES

EAST CRUISING AT SEVENTEEN KNOTS EAST WIND
FIFTEEN MILES SCATTERED CLOUDS MEN AT STATIONS
TENSELY ALERT LONG WAIT CAPPED BY ANXIETY SEARCH
FELT DEEPLY MEN WORKING WITH GRIM EFFICIENCY
GREAT CONCERN OVER WHY SHORT OF FUEL IN AIR
ONLY APPROXIMATELY TWENTY AND HALF HOURS
SHOULD HAVE HAD SEVERAL HOURS MORE FUEL WHY
AMELIA NEVER GAVE POSITION HER RADIO EVIDENTLY
NOT WORKING PROPERLY ITASCA REQUESTED EACH
BROADCAST GIVE POSITION NEVER GIVEN STOP AT
EIGHT FORTYTWO AMELIA RADIOED QUOTE HALF HOUR
FUEL LEFT NO LANDFALL POSITION DOUBTFUL UNQUOTE
LAST MESSAGE NINE FORTYTHREE QUOTE LINE OF POSI-
TION ONE FIVE SEVEN DASH THREE THREE SEVEN AM
CIRCLING PLEASE GIVE RADIO BEARING UNQUOTE HER
VOICE SOUNDED VERY TIRED ANXOUS ALMOST BREAK-
ING LACK INFORMATION FROM AMELIA MAKING
SEARCH DIFFICULT LAST NIGHT AT SIX FIFTY PM SAILING
EAST INVESTIGATED SEEMING LIGHT FLASH HORIZON
PORT BEAM NO RESULT ELEVEN THIRTY PM STARTED BACK
TOWARD HOWLAND SEVERAL TIMES EXCITEMENT
AROUSED STARS LOW ON HORIZON SEEMING FLARES
DAY BREAK SMORNING SEEMING SMOKE HORIZON
INVESTIGATED FUTILE

SEARCHING FULL SPEED TODAY AREA HUNDRED FIFTY
MILES NORTHWEST HOWLAND HUNDRED MILES NORTH
WEATHER SAME YESTERDAY

The top ten stories of 1940, as chosen by UP editors, included one that had never been written: what was going on in Russia?

"This is the first time that something which has not been reported has ever received enough votes to qualify among the first ten on the annual list," said Earl J. Johnson, vice president and general news manager. "Our editors felt that if the facts about Russian influence on world affairs were not shrouded by official secrecy and censorship, the Russian story might be among the most important of the year. The big thing we do not know about Russia is the extent of her influence on Tokyo's operations in the Far East and on Germany's plans in the Balkans."

The Russian non-story was listed tenth by the editors polled. The third-term election of President Roosevelt was first, the Battle of Britain was second and the fall of France was third.

Each year the wire services went through the routine of polling newspaper editors to pick the big stories of the year. Sometimes they broke it down into two lists, "news impact" and "significance."

In the May 1933 issue of *Fortune* magazine, Stephen Vincent Benét, the author, wrote a lengthy, penetrating study of the United Press that characterized the wire service throughout its life:

> The strongest bonds that hold UP together, and what it boils down to, when the sentiment and the wisecracks are both skimmed off, is an actual and genuine love of the game. Unipressers are bound in an unusual esprit de corps, hard to define but nonetheless real. No doubt it has something to do with UP's fearless independence and with its leaning toward liberalism. Perhaps it is based on the fact that UP was the underdog and is now worrying the somewhat august AP. Other factors may well be that UP is an organization of young men, average age about twenty-eight—from small towns and midwest colleges of journalism, plain fellows of Nordic stock with scarcely a Harvard B.A. among them, and every UP executive has come from the ranks.

Benet observed that wire service people had power but he added, "Power is theirs only so long as they do not use it."

16

Following the Armies

THE FIRST MAJOR INTERNATIONAL CONFLICT AFTER WORLD WAR I WAS
the assault by Italy against Ethiopia in 1935. It was the last rattle of European imperialism. Mussolini, the Fascist dictator of Italy, attempted to take over a large chunk of
Africa by force.

The trouble for Mussolini was Ethiopia and the trouble in Ethiopia was a great
embarrassment for the League of Nations, which had been set up after World War I.
Haile Selassie, emperor of Ethiopia, complained to the League about Italy's aggression.
Article II of the League's covenant required it to take "every measure effectively to
safeguard peace."

Other nations like England, France and Belgium, which had their own colonies in
Africa, wanted to stay out of the Ethiopian tangle and hoped it would blow over. The
world organization was helpless and its failure lead to the collapse of the whole postwar
international political system.

Selassie's army was a collection of primitive tribesmen, sometimes with only spears
for weapons. The Italian army's base was across the border in Eritrea, an adjacent
Italian colony. In the summer of 1935 Mussolini sent large numbers of troops down
through the Suez Canal to Eritrea and prepared the Italian people for war.

Dan Sanford, UP stringer in Addis Ababa, was a close friend of Haile Selassie.
During that spring he filed frequent reports indicating increasing concern about
Italian hostility. A war, or at least an international incident, was brewing.

United Press chief Hugh Baillie thought so. In June he sent Edward J. Beattie, one of
his star reporters, down from Berlin. Beattie had just returned from Asia after covering the
Japanese-Chinese conflict. In Ethiopia he was the first American reporter to get an interview with Selassie. In the interview, the emperor expressed great distress over the situation.

T. J. "Frank" Rohrbaugh was hired to help Beattie and Herbert R. "Bud" Ekins
was sent to Harrar, another dusty town in the Italian territory.

Webb Miller, the celebrated UP war correspondent who was then European manager
based in London, decided sadly that another war was at hand. He had covered every
war since the U.S.-Mexican border fighting in 1914 and was less than enthusiastic

about seeing this one. It would be bloody, terribly one-sided and, in Miller's view, the last gasp of imperialism. In his memoir, *I Found No Peace,* he expressed the thoughts he had while waiting for the fighting to start.

"My emotions were tangled and conflicting when the question of going to witness another war arose. I was disgusted by the hypocrisy, two-faced maneuvering, and double-dealing of the British, French and Italian statesmen and by the prospect of watching the aggression of a nation with all the modern resources for slaughter upon an ignorant, backward, comparatively defenseless people."[1]

Miller went to Rome to get credentials for Africa. It took him a month, but in September he finally was issued press card Number 1, and set out for Eritrea. An Italian ocean liner was to depart with a group of correspondents a week later. Miller did not wait. He went immediately to the Naples waterfront and found a transport, the *Esperia,* readying to leave for Alexandria, Egypt. Miller had no ticket and since the ship was sold out, the boarding officer would not let him get on. He tells in his memoir how he then pretended to be a dumb foreigner who could not understand the message. He kept heading up the gangplank, repeatedly being turned back. He ultimately told a couple of lies and bribed a ship worker to put his equipment on the vessel. With his things already on and the *Esperia* about to sail, the boarding officer became so frustrated he let him board.

Landing at Alexandria, Miller was just in time to catch the twice-a-week plane to Khartoum. Again, he had a problem because the flight was sold out. Miller knew better than to try to bribe the sanctimonious British crew of an Imperial Airlines plane. Using heavy charm and a few more fibs, he talked the English captain into ordering the passengers already booked to reduce their luggage so that he could get on the plane. He even managed to get all of his equipment aboard—tent, bug spray, field canteen and other supplies for an expected rugged tour of duty. From Khartoum, the only city in the world deliberately built with streets laid out forming a Union Jack, he hopped an Italian plane to Asmara.

Another reporter had beaten him there: Floyd Gibbons of International News Service.

Mussolini, who had written stories for UP in the past, was at that time writing articles for the Hearst newspapers. The Hearst connection gave INS a lead in getting credentials and transportation.

INS and UP were the vanguard of a journalistic swarm that eventually reached several hundred correspondents. They arrived in the hot, dusty, fly-infested city of Asmara, home of 10,000 primitive and gentle tribesmen. Asmara jumped from "a sleepy, obscure provincialism into headlines throughout the world," Miller said.

There were another 120 correspondents in Addis Ababa in May 1935.

Miller wrote that Asmara's dusty streets "bustled with the most exotic assortment of humanity I had seen outside India. Eritrean big shots in white nightgown-like shammas, wide Stetson-like hats and black cloaks strode about in barefooted dignity or rode dwarf mules followed by a half dozen trotting barefooted retainers."

His first dispatch included a description of the house of prostitution the Italians had set up across the street from a Catholic church. He described the bill of fare at the brothel: enlisted men in the morning at 10 lira; noncoms in the afternoon, 20 lira; and officers during the evening and night, 30 lira.

The biggest complaint correspondents covering the Ethiopian war had was the flies. Every one of the reporters at some point wrote a dispatch about the thick, disgusting, clinging flies, which clung to one's face and body, crawling into the nostrils and ears.

Count Galleazzo Ciano, son-in-law of Mussolini, was in charge of an Italian Air Force squadron. He flew Miller and Gibbons on a leisurely patrol over the hills where 200,000 well-armed Italian soldiers were poised. A few thousand native tribesmen were gathered on the Etheopian side of the border, armed with spears, shields and a few rifles, preparing to defend their country. Miller wrote a 2,000-word dispatch from Asmara on October 1, 1935, setting the scenario in detail and hinting that military action was imminent.

Never reluctant to pull out the stops on an important story, Baillie told Reynolds Packard and his wife, Eleanor "Pebe," both then UP staffers in Paris, to catch a ship leaving Marseilles in two days for Alexandria.

"Isn't there anything sooner?" asked Eleanor. UP also hired another reporter, Ben Ames, and sent him to Addis Ababa, the Ethiopian capital.

On October 2, correspondents in Asmara were told that the Italian army would move at 5 A.M. the next day. Miller wrote another detailed, descriptive story and left it with the censor in Asmara, telling him to file it by cable as soon as action began. He then drove with an Italian officer to an outpost on Mt. Coatit in the hills overlooking the valley where the drama was expected to unfold. He and Gibbons were there watching through binoculars as the panorama began to stir. Italian troops waded across the river into Ethiopian territory. There was very little opposition, none against most of the probes.

Miller persuaded an Italian telegrapher at the mountain outpost to send a flash back to Asmara, to be forwarded from there by several different routes to Rome, Paris, London and New York.

Rome newspapers subscribing to UP had extras on the street before the government's official announcement of the invasion. Miller's dispatch made headlines everywhere in the world. In the United States it was a seven-hour beat. Associated Press chief Kent Cooper, more conservative than Baillie, held off getting correspondents to the front, thinking war would be avoided.

When Miller and Gibbons, moving with the Italian army, reached an outpost inside Ethiopia, they were concerned there would be no way to get their stories out. At a pause in the march, the Italians told them a courier was leaving for Asmara in 15 minutes.

"Here were Gibbons and I with the biggest newspaper story since the world war—sitting on top of a mountain with a grandstand seat witnessing the beginning of a war—and we had only fifteen minutes in which to write. It was a reporter's nightmare." He managed to get 620 words out of his portable typewriter in time to catch the courier.

Wire service newsmen fought each other fiercely to hit the wire first. But they also had the good sense to recognize a situation in which they needed to work together. Miller and Gibbons were the only reporters on the scene. They could both go on with the Italian force and gather information competitively but probably have no way to get it to their wires.

So they agreed on a deal. Gibbons would go back to Asmara and handle any developments there. Miller would go with the troops marching into Ethiopia. Any news either obtained would be shared with the other. In later wars such "pool" reporting was organized by the military commands, but in 1936 in Africa, it was a voluntary agreement between the two men who were the only ones who could inform the world about the Italian drive into Ethiopia.

Miller went with the Italian army through the extremely rugged mountains, mostly on foot, to Adowa, a town in Ethiopia. From there he was allowed to send only twenty-five words by military communications back to Gibbons. Then he set out to trek the 260-plus miles back to Asmara on foot, on donkey, on truck and the last few miles by car. He passed through Danakil, a town credited with having the highest temperature ever known, 161 degrees Farenheit in the shade. When he reached Asmara he was so physically beat that a doctor told him he must get away from the thin air on the 6,600-foot plateau and give himself a long rest.

But the UP reporter went with Italian forces on another assault, on the town of Makale.

Late in the fall, Miller went back to London where he spent Christmas, then crossed the Atlantic to the United States. He was sent on a lecture tour covering forty cities, telling Americans about the war in far off Africa. Everyone in the country sympathized with the black tribesmen of Emperor Selassie and saw Mussolini as the bad guy. Miller visited the White House and found President Franklin Roosevelt eager to know everything he could about the Ethiopian war.

Back in Africa, Reynolds and Eleanor Packard were working out of French Djiboutrie where they had arrived October 6. They interviewed French colonial and British officials in the area. Eleanor went to Aden where British troops were expecting an attack by the Italians, while Reynolds went to Zeila, a British port on the Red Sea, to see if the embargo on arms shipments to Africa was working. A few weeks later, in November 1935, the Packards were separated again by their jobs, Eleanor going to Cairo and Reynolds to Asmara to help Miller and his crew.

Eleanor Packard noted in her diary that the presence of a white American woman caused some sensation in a locale inhabited by an army of 200,000 men. At Massawa, just before they were going separate ways, the Packards tried to take a walk but had to abandon it because "thousands of soldiers and dock hands gathered around us to catch a glimpse of "la donna bianca" (the white lady).

While the Packards were having dinner at an outpost one evening, the Italian soldiers gathered around her and asked if they could serenade "la donna."

On another occasion she went with Reynolds to take a bath in the river. She put on her bathing suit and a robe and they hiked through the woods to the river, looking for a quiet spot. They suddenly came on a riverbank where about 200 naked Italian soldiers were soaping themselves in the water. The captain in command of the detachment came to the rescue. "Attention! About Face! March to shore! Don drawers! Return to your bathing!"

Eleanor Packard was not the only woman correspondent who covered the Ethiopian war. Others were Eleanor Meade of *Transradio Press* and two French women reporters representing *Journal of Paris*.

Later, when she had rejoined Reynolds in Asmara, she said the two of them "had a wonderful tent, at the UP's expense, equipped with oilskin floor and windows with mosquito netting" while about 200 other correspondents were going crazy with the flies and dirt.

A new Italian commander in Asmara, General Pietro Badoglio, told correspondents there would be no news for them and they would be confined to the city until the action was over. Most of the reporters went home. Reynolds and Eleanor stayed.[2]

When Addis Ababa was taken, censorship was relaxed and the Packards were allowed to follow the army to the captured capital. They stayed at the Imperial Hotel. In the next room was Count Ciano in command of an Italian Air Force bomber squadron.

They met in the hotel corridor and Mrs. Packard invited Ciano to their room for a drink. She had managed to bring a bottle of White Horse Scotch with her to Addis Ababa. This little gesture of hospitality to the Italian official was to figure importantly for UP several years later in Rome.[3]

Coverage of the Ethiopian war was very expensive. But headquarters approved anything the correspondents needed. The Packards' luxury tent was on the expense account.

Webb Miller's expense chits included: canvas bag for camping; provisions in field; three pack and riding mules and feed; boy's wages; Mauser rifle and ammunition; etc.[4] Baillie afterwards reported that covering the war cost the service $4,000 a day.

War correspondents had achieved an elevated rank in journalism. It was a glamorous and dangerous assignment. People attracted to reporting wanted to go to the fighting.

The writer Evelyn Waugh, who was in Africa in 1937 for the *Daily Mail* of London, wrote a novel, *Scoop*, which became a classic as a parody of the foreign correspondent's role. His leading character, Boot, through a confusion of names, gets a job covering an African country. When being interviewed for that job by the editor of a London newspaper he asks:

"And all the papers have reports from three or four agencies?"
Editor: "Yes."
Boot: "But if we all send the same thing it seems a waste and if we all send different news isn't it very confusing?"
Editor: "It gives them a choice. They all have different policies so of course they have to give different news."[5]

Hugh Baillie always wanted to be close to a big story. He was in Rome with manager Virgil Pinkley when the Ethiopian war broke out. Pinkley spoke Italian and had contacts in the fascist government. On October 2, 1935, Baillie was at Pinkley's penthouse apartment having lunch with a group of newspeople when Pinkley got a phone call from one of his sources saying the war would be declared at 3:30 P.M. that day.

Most of the reporters present thought it was a hoax, but Baillie took no chances. He went immediately to the UP bureau and ordered two telephone lines to London to be held open for the rest of the day—two because something might interrupt one of them. The UP chief himself was in the huge throng of people in the Piazza Venezia who were shouting "Duce! Duce!" and raising their hands in the fascist salute when Mussolini appeared on his balcony that afternoon and announced the war.

Baillie wrote in his diary: "Crowds were surging, soldiers marching, and, presently, bands playing, regimented civilians parading, children singing patriotic songs over the radio, Caproni bombers roaring and swooping over the housetops."[6]

The next morning Webb Miller's bulletin arrived and was on the streets before the government had confirmed the advance. "The Italian invasion into Ethiopia began shortly after dawn today when fascist legions poured across the Mareb River."

The Rome bureau had opened lines to Berlin and Zurich as well as London. The line to Berlin proved worth the extra cost. Since Italy and Germany were allies, there was better phone service. That relay saved UP 27 minutes in getting copy to London.

When the war had started, Baillie noted in his diary that taxi drivers in Rome stopped giving change for a fare, with the non-sequitur comment, "There's a war on." It led to some arm-waving discussions between passengers and the taxi drivers, the UP president wrote in his diary.

On the following day, October 4, Baillie had an interview with Mussolini. The dictator asked the UP president if he were on Italy's side. Baillie's response: "We are favorable to you to the extent that we are not unfavorable to you. It balances."

During the meeting, the Italian dictator did not confine himself to answering questions. He wanted to make it a sort of diplomatic exchange over U.S.–Italian relations. At one point, he pulled a sheaf of papers from his desk and waved them at Baillie. "These are copies of Miller's dispatches from the front. I am keeping close watch on everything that is written. We do not want anything but the truth to come out."

Webb Miller's personal comment on the Ethiopian war: "I told myself that my duty as an objective reporter compelled me to stifle my personal opinions and sit in the grandstand, watching and describing the parade, not to join the procession carrying the banner. And I knew that a writer who detested war made the best correspondent because the scenes impinged more vividly upon his senses."[7]

Late in 1935 there was a lull in the fighting and most of the correspondents went home. Reynolds and Eleanor Packard of UP, Christopher Holme of Reuters and Eddie Neil of AP had to stay. They made up a bridge foursome and played from 10 A.M. to 10 P.M. "to stop us from going mad," said Packard.[8]

The Spanish Civil War, 1936–39, was of great interest in the United States because it involved taking sides, either pro-Franco, the Fascist rebel, or pro-Communist, the government which had taken power in Madrid. Many American volunteers went to Spain to fight against Franco. Newspapers wanted good, accurate information every day. It was the kind of challenge that invigorates wire service reporters and editors.

Hugh Baillie told the New York State Chamber of Commerce on January 7, 1937, that no one was better informed on news in Europe than Americans who read their newspapers.

"Americans are made aware, acquainted with events of world significance which occur in many countries, even before the inhabitants of those countries are made aware of them," the UP president said. "American newspapermen covering the war have a tremendous responsibility in these precarious days when a steady flow of accurate information is so essential to the formation of intelligent public opinion."

Baillie, not able immediately to go himself, sent Webb Miller, his top correspondent in Europe, to take a look at the war front. It was Miller's tenth war. He returned to Spain several times during the conflict.

Reporting the facts with the correct focus became difficult in the Spanish war because modern techniques of propaganda were used intensely on both sides. A reporter for the *New York Times* was thrown out of the war zone at the rebel headquarters at Burgos in the hill country by Franco's forces because that newspaper refused to call the government in Madrid "reds" and repeatedly called Franco's troops "insurgents." They wanted to be called "loyalists."

In September 1936, United Press correspondent Jean Degandt was reported missing, along with INS correspondent H. R. Knickerbocker. They were said to have been jailed at Caceres, according to army officers in Badajoz. The UP had last heard from Degandt Saturday night, September 12. He was then in Seville and about to start northward into the war zone. UP people worried but Degandt checked in two days later, safe in Seville along with Knickerbocker.

When the "loyalists" were nearing Madrid, Henry Gorrell drove out to see if he could find some action to report. He found it—more than he wanted. A small band of rebels appeared on the road ahead of him brandishing machine guns. Gorrell dived from the car and scrambled for a ditch. A column of tanks showed up, moving fast toward him. He was taken prisoner and accused of being a spy for the government. He was summarily sentenced to be shot the next morning.

The officer who interrogated Gorrell told him, "We have killed 300 reds on the road today and you are the first man to come out alive."

Just before sunrise he was released without explanation. He hurried back to Madrid.

In August that year, 1939, Gorrell was transferred from Madrid to London for a new assignment, covering another war, the one breaking out on the European mainland.

Spain and Africa were not the only places reporters had problems. On September 11, 1936, Gorrell, then correspondent in Rome, filed a story on communist agitation in Italian cities. The Italian Press Ministry had announced the arrest of twenty persons in Terni for passing out leaflets and posting flyers supporting the Communist side in the Spanish war.

Gorrell's dispatch reported the Terni trouble and similar demonstrations in Grosseto, Leghorn and Rome. The Ministry of Information called him in and demanded he explain this story. Gorrell said his information came from reliable stringers. The press ministry itself had announced the arrests.

Nevertheless, the UP man was ordered out of the country. The U.S. Embassy intervened but was unable to get more than a 24-hour extension for Gorrell. Officials of the Fascist regime told the embassy the UP story gave "the false impression that a widespread communist plot had been discovered" in Italy.

Gorrell was the third newsman expelled from Italy after the Fascist regime of Mussolini took over.

UP then sent him to Spain to help cover the war there. His dispatches made him a well-known by-line in the United States.

By August 1939, Mussolini had booted out twenty-three correspondents. Herbert. R. Ekins of UP was the twenty-fourth. The fascist government was so annoyed by a UP story that it ordered the agency to shut down all operations in Italy. It was the most drastic step taken against any foreign service.

The offending dispatch had suggested that Mussolini was ill. Ekins, who was previously a correspondent in Asia, was in Rome only five weeks when he picked up a report that Il Duce had suffered a stroke while reviewing troops, fallen to the ground, and been taken to a military hospital nearly unconscious.[9]

Knowing such a story would not get through fascist censorship, Ekins telephoned it to London, veiling the dictator's reported illness in baseball slang. "This is Bud here," Ekins told the London desk. "The pitcher of Italy's national baseball team collapsed on the ground and was carried off the field."

The London editor who took the story on the telephone was sharp enough to decode the item. UP filed a dispatch under a London dateline, attributing the information about Il Duce's illness to "sources" in England.

When arrested in Rome, Ekins protested that he did not originate the dispatch and had nothing to do with it. Mussolini's press representatives told Ekins Il Duce had nothing against the correspondent personally but wanted to discipline United Press. Ekins was treated courteously by the police. Escorted by two policemen, he went to the train station where a half dozen other American reporters saw him off, all wondering who would be next to go.

U.S. diplomats who immediately attempted to intervene on behalf of UP were told that Minister of Press and Propaganda Dino Alfieri and Foreign Minister Count Ciano were both out of town and that police had carried out the expulsion without consulting higher authorities.[10]

It was the first time the Italians had closed down all operations of an international wire service. Policemen were posted at the door of the UP Rome bureau and telephone service was cut off. It was a very serious matter for the agency because there were clients in Italy who were paying for the news service.

Ed Keen, European general manager, and Virgil Pinkley, European business manager, hastened to Rome to see what could be done. Hugh Baillie happened to be in Paris at the time. Reynolds Packard, the veteran foreign correspondent, had just returned to the French capital on vacation after covering the Spanish war. Baillie ordered him off to Rome immediately.

Packard was accompanied by his wife, Eleanor. Baillie thought it might be helpful because she knew the Italian Foreign Minister, Count Ciano, having met him while covering the Ethiopian war.

Baillie, along with J. I. Miller, UP vice-president for Latin America, and Paris Bureau Manager Ralph Heinzen went to the Paris train terminal that night, August 14, 1939, to see the Packards aboard the Rome Express.

Packard fumbled for his tickets but could not find them. The train was about to pull out. Baillie, exasperated, asked his colleagues to pool their cash to buy new tickets. They were digging in their pockets when an excited Frenchman came running along the platform shouting "*Les billets, les billets!*" Packard had stopped at a store to buy some cigarettes for the trip and accidentally left the tickets on the counter.

On the train the Packards had a few drinks to settle down. The next morning they were met in Rome by brothers Ralph and Aldo Forte of the now idled UP staff. At their hotel room Aldo told them the report that Ekins picked up about Mussolini's stroke was false. The dictator had appeared on the balcony of the Palazo Venezia the next day to prove it.

Because the bureau had been closed down, Forte said, he could not send a corrective story.

The following day, Packard visited U.S. Ambassador William Phillips, who had gone to Foreign Minister Count Ciano and assured him Ekins did not originate the erroneous story but it had been picked up in London from anti-fascist sources. Phillips related what happened then:

"Count Ciano very politely interrupted me, saying, 'Excuse me a moment and listen to this.' He then turned on a recording of the telephone conversation between Ekins and the UP news editor in London. I could hear Ekins, whose voice I know, saying, 'This is Bud here.' He then went on to say that the pitcher of Italy's national baseball team had collapsed on the ground and was carried off the field. And it was quite clear to me, and I am not a baseball fan, that the pitcher was obviously Mussolini.

"I was convinced then that Ekins had not told me the truth and that here I was out on a diplomatic limb, defending a correspondent who had misrepresented the facts to me and thus compromised me and the embassy. So I am not disposed to do much more about the incident, nor do I have the impression that the State Department would want to push this matter."

That evening the Packards repaired to the Albergo Ambasciatori bar for a drink. They had just ordered when suddenly, "everybody snapped to attention and even those seated at the tables jumped to their feet," Packard recalled.

Count Ciano had entered the bar. The Italian official noticed Eleanor Packard. He went over to the Packard's table and, smiling, greeted her. He recalled that she had served him a glass of White Horse in her room at the Imperial Hotel in Addis Ababa.

After a few pleasantries, the subject of UP's Rome bureau was raised. "When do you think we might be able to open up again here?" said Packard.

Ciano paused for a few moments and then said: "Now, let me see. We have to respect protocol and foreign policy. We have to be severe with British and Americans because they aren't too friendly and use baseball slang to report that Il Duce had a stroke he never had. So. Today is Wednesday. You must cool your heels a few days more. Let's say next Monday, the beginning of the week. You open on Monday. That's a decree from the Foreign Ministry. I'll fix it up."

"Do we need anything in writing?" asked Packard.

"Not a thing. My decree is enough. Il Duce will initial it. So all the best." He rose, smiled, gave a fascist salute, then rejoined his own party.

After four days closure, the bureau was allowed to resume serving Italian newspapers, and a week later was permitted to file news to London again.

Packard was a wire service Ernest Hemingway, a hard drinking, swashbuckling, bearded journalist. His lifestyle was known then as "Bohemian." He once said he chose journalism as a profession because it allowed him to be "a boozer, whoremonger and nonconformist."

The UP Rome bureau was on the fourth floor of a ramshackle office building at 54 Via Della Mercede. The building also housed the Associazione della Stampa Estera. This was the club for foreign journalists that Mussolini had established and subsidized in hopes of keeping the foreign press friendly. It helped concentrate the correspondents in a place where they could easily be watched and their telephones could be tapped.

The Packard's remained in Rome for three and a half years. On December 10, 1941, they and other American and British correspondents were interned. They were exchanged in June 1942, for Italian journalists in the U.S. and Britain.

17

Biggest Story of the Century

UNITED PRESS SENT 150 OF ITS BEST AND BRIGHTEST AND CERTAINLY ITS most ambitious into the action of World War II. Five reporters were killed, more than one dozen were wounded and scores more were imprisoned by the Germans, Italians and Japanese.

It was a coveted though dangerous assignment, a good story, for both veteran correspondents tested in earlier wars and young reporters hoping to make their mark in journalism.

Edward W. Beattie had covered wars in China, Ethiopia and Spain. So had Henry Gorrell and several others. Beattie was on the scene in Warsaw when Germany invaded Poland.

Walter Cronkite's credentials included stints in the Kansas City and Austin, Texas, bureaus and a brief tour on UP's cable desk in New York before going overseas in 1941 to cover the war in Africa and Europe.

These newsmen reported the gritty, muddy action of the war with a dedication that was a stereotype for the wire service war correspondent.

Beattie was so anxious to be a reporter for the UP that when he graduated from Yale University in 1929, he began showing up in the New Haven, Connecticut, bureau, answering the phone and doing rewrites at no salary. Boyd Lewis, the bureau manager, got a phone call from L. B. Mickel, superintendent of bureaus. "You got young Ed Beattie working there for nothing?" Lewis said, "Well, he wants to do it."

"Jeez!" said Mickel, "Bickel [UP president] and Edward's father are old friends and Bickel said to him at a party last night, 'What's young Edward doing these days?' Beattie replied, 'Working for you for nothing.'"

Ed got on the payroll the next day at $25 per week. He soon transferred to Washington and then Europe.

Beattie had seen the Axis military machine building. First, when he covered Ethiopia's surprising defeat of the Italian army, then as a correspondent in Berlin.

In August 1939, he was on a fishing vacation in the little village of Valsjobyn in Jamtland near the Arctic Circle in Sweden. A telegram at midnight August 22 began: "Hate interrupt vacation but view today's developments advisable you get Warsaw immediately." It was from Webb Miller, European news manager. Germany and Russia had announced their military pact agreeing to make a joint meal of Poland. Beattie rushed to Warsaw. He rang up $1,000 in cable tolls his first day there, filing news reports to Amsterdam and New York.

In his memoir, Beattie told of a strange encounter as the Nazis were closing in on Warsaw. He and Larry Lehrbas of the Associated Press were leaving the Polish capital. They stopped overnight in the town of Nalechow. In the morning, as they were having breakfast, a well-dressed woman came to their table. "She asked in good English whether we were going to Romania. It brought us up with a start. We had been living for three or four days in an atmosphere of growing defeat, without admitting it to ourselves. 'Hungary would do just as well,' she said, 'I'm staying here. I can't go.' Her husband was in the Polish army in the north.

"'Would one of you take a button for me to the French consul in Bucharest?' she asked. She was wearing a blue and white print silk dress with big three-quarter-inch buttons. I said I would," Beattie related. "Then she said, 'I should tell you, it is a diamond. It is worth $20,000. I want the consul to send it to my sister in Paris. It will be safe there. I am quite willing to trust you. There is a chance this way that it will get to Paris. Otherwise, the Germans will take it.'"

Beattie took the button and tucked it into the inside pocket of his wallet. Nobody ever asked to examine his wallet. When he reached Bucharest, he looked at the gem. It was blue, intricately cut and flawless.

"The end was unromantic," said Beattie. "I carried it up two flights of crooked, back stairs at the French embassy and gave it to M. Choppin de Janvry, with the address of the sister in Paris."

The French official pulled out an envelope, sealed the stone in it and tossed it into the safe on the wall. "It will leave with the pouch next week," he said. Beattie was surprised that he was not asked how he came into possession of the gem.[1]

During his stop in Bucharest, Beattie stayed at Hotel Metropole, which had a UP ticker in its lobby for the benefit of guests following the exciting news events of those days. The UP bureau in Bucharest was mainly a relay point, originating little or no copy of its own but funneling dispatches from various correspondents and other European bureaus to London and New York.

Arriving back in the German capital, Beattie learned that "being a foreign correspondent in Berlin was not very pleasant," when Hitler began the blitzkrieg. There was no official censorship, but he always heard "the faint click-clack of the machines the Gestapo used to record your conversations." An added concern was that the Nazi regime could "expel any offending correspondent on a few hours notice." It didn't matter much anyway, he said, because German news sources had dried up for Western correspondents.

Propaganda minister Joseph Goebbels did one favor for foreign correspondents. He classified them as "heavy labor," which entitled them to double food rations.[2]

In 1940 when U.S. entry into the war seemed imminent, UP strengthened communications and drew up elaborate plans for various eventualities. The Copenhagen bureau, which had existed only for incoming services to Danish clients, took on the excitement of the war story that was building. Harold Peters, who had covered the Spanish War, arrived there from Buenos Aires. He bought desks and chairs and installed telephone and teleprinter communications.[3]

By the time the United States entered the war, United Press was on the story in full force and in full competition with Associated Press, International News Service and Reuters. UP correspondents were with the armed forces at all major military operations and on top of news stories back home.

In the early days of the war, UP tried to hire all the trained journalists it could find. The job was attractive to young men and women aspiring to be writers. It gave them a chance to participate in the great struggle, with a fair amount of glamour assured. In the case of men whose physical condition made them 4-F and exempt from the draft, a correspondent's job was a chance to go to war. The draft's drain on UP's staff also opened some key jobs for women. In New York, Elizabeth Poston was assigned to the night cables desk that handled the bulk of the war stories for morning newspapers. Poston later recalled that after the war she became the first woman ever to write the main United Nation's story for Am'ers. Another woman, Joan Younger, was assigned to the New York day desk and handled key copy for afternoon papers. In Washington, Helen Thomas was moved from a local desk operation to the national staff where she covered many of the federal agencies.

At the front, correspondents for competing agencies often worked closely together, sharing living quarters and information for their stories. Sometimes this happened because only a limited number of reporters were allowed at go with the troops. Pool arrangement required a reporter to share stories with his or her competition. Often correspondents shared information anyway because no reporter could cover a whole front by himself.

Beattie worked and traveled very closely with Larry Lehrbas of the AP. They often exchanged notes so that each could write a complete dispatch. They shared living quarters and transportation.

Beattie spent the next five years covering the war in Europe. On September 12, 1944, he was jeeping with two other reporters near the Loir River to report on the surrender of 20,000 Germans in that sector. They ran into a German ambush and were captured.

The Germans were in headlong retreat at the time and not very interested in prisoners. Next day they released John Mecklin, who had been with UP in North Africa and Italy but was then working for the *Chicago Sun*. Beattie and Wright Bryan of the *Atlanta Journal*, who had been wounded in the incident, were taken to a German prison camp and held until the war ended.

When Germany invaded Poland in 1939, Fred Oechsner, Berlin bureau chief, was escorted by a Nazi press relations officer to a town on the German-Polish border and shown 25 mutilated bodies. He was told that they were German civilians murdered by Poles. Oechsner asked the German officer how he could be sure they were not Polish civilians murdered by Germans. The officer replied: "You are exaggerating your objectivity." United Press did not use the atrocity story.[4]

When Russia attacked Finland, Webb Miller and Norman Deuel were sent to Helsinki, Herbert Uexkuell went to the northern front where the Finns were fighting the Russians. These reporters telephoned their stories to Copenhagen, which also received copy from reporters in Stockholm, Oslo, Bergen, Trondheim and Kirkenaes.[5]

The moment a call came through to the Copenhagen bureau, a staffer rolled a sheet of paper into the typewriter and started taking dictation. As this was happening, another staff member opened the teleprinter line to Amsterdam. As the communiqué came in, it was ripped from the typewriter of the dicationist in two or three-line pieces and handed to the operator sending to Amsterdam. There it hit the direct cable to New York, where it could be teleprintered almost instantaneously to clients in the Americas, Asia and back to Europe. Under perfect conditions a communiqué moved from Helsinki to San Francisco in under ten minutes.[6]

Miller, Deuel and Uexkuell alternated trips to the Finnish front lines.

From London, communications chief Harry Flory had his wife hand-carry to New York a message outlining in detail what would be done if the London office were bombed out or had to be abandoned in the expected invasion of Britain.

"If things get tough and there has to be an evacuation of our present headquarters, we have an emergency office with BUP [British United Press] in Birmingham, equipped with telephones, teleprinters, private lines, etc. We would hope to maintain a skeleton staff in our present location as well."

The memo detailed emergency communications, which had been arranged. Flory added: "There is almost unanimous belief in England by those who aren't still complacent, that an invasion definitely will be attempted. We are doing everything possible to be prepared. In the ensuing confusion, you would probably be receiving direct the individual products of numerous staffers."

Similar arrangements were made by Ralph Heinzen in Paris. He planned to move the bureau to Tours and Bordeaux if Paris was taken. But he cabled that staffers would "remain in paris longs possible then decamp by bicycle onestep ahead stop morale all swell but transmission difficulties accumulating."

In early October 1940, German airplanes were pounding London every night with massive bombing raids in the Battle of Britain.

"It started on September 7," recalled Wallace Carroll in an interview. "Our office was in the *News of the World* building, just off Fleet Street. It was a three-story building but had a tower going up another two stories. A year earlier I had installed a telephone on the roof, with a line into the bureau. On that afternoon the sirens sounded. I told the man on the desk, 'This may be it,' and went up to the tower. The German bombers came out of the west, right past the House of Parliament, maybe at 4,000 feet. They came in perfect formation, eight of them. They went down along the Thames and St. Paul's to the docks where they went into their dive, unloading bombs. I dictated an eyewitness story to the desk man in short takes. He handed it to the Morse operator, who sent it to the cable office and censor, and it went right through to New York."

When the all clear sounded, Carroll went back down to the bureau and wrote a night lead. Walking home to Stafford Court that evening, he heard the sirens for the night bombing raid. As he was passing Buckingham Palace, two bombs exploded in the royal courtyard.

William Dickinson, who was the night wire filer in London, received phone calls from UP President Hugh Baillie and News Manager Earl Johnson every night. The bosses wanted a rundown on what was going on. To cover these calls, Dickinson kept notes on his desk ready to rattle off the day's developments. "Of such little things, apparently, is this business made," Dickinson wrote in a letter to his parents.[7]

Despite the bombings and heightening war activity, Americans in London were interested in the World Series being played between Cincinnati and Detroit that autumn. The bureau sent a query to New York: "Beleaguered exiles would greatly appreciate daily World Series scores and batteries." Cincinnati won the Series four games to three.

When Germany declared war on the United States in December 1941, American correspondents in Germany and Italy were rounded up and interned. They were held in the Bad Nauheim prison camp until the next spring. Interned Unipressers included Joe Grigg, Jack Fleischer, Glenn M. Stadler, Clinton Beach (Pat) Conger, Fred Oechsner, all of the Berlin staff, and Robert Best, of Vienna. Reynolds Packard and his wife, Eleanor, Allen Tuska and Livingston Pomeroy of the Rome Bureau were interned at Siena, Italy. Ralph Heinzen of Paris was also interned.

Richard C. Hottelet had been arrested in March 1941, on charges of "espionage for an enemy power." His seizure was in retaliation by the Germans for President Roosevelt's suppression in the United States of *Transocean News*, a German agency. Hottelet was released in July 1941, in an exchange for German nationals arrested in the U.S.

When the correspondents at Bad Nauheim were repatriated in May 1942, Robert Best, 46, was conspicuous by his absence. All the other American correspondents left Vienna for Berlin once the Nazis occupied the city, but Best stayed. Berlin chief Fred Oechsner went to Vienna, to tell Best that UP no longer needed a full-time correspondent there and he could take a transfer or become a stringer. He chose the latter and also became a stringer for CBS and other news agencies. He was soon picked up by the Germans and imprisoned with the other American news reporters at Bad Nauheim.

Two months before the repatriation of the correspondents, Best disappeared from the camp and soon was heard broadcasting on Goebbels' English language propaganda station. William Shirer, author of *Berlin Diary* reports that, ironically, Best's South Carolina twang was recognized in the German broadcasts by a Jew, whom Best himself had helped leave Austria.

Best was railing against the United States, using the name "Guess Who?" He called his country the "Jew-nited states."[8]

Before he disappeared from the internment camp, Best had written a self-profile for the inmates' newsletter in which he said that after graduating from Columbia University Journalism School, he had traveled throughout Europe and had been "a cook, cotton mill hand, detective agency patrolman, dishwasher, ditch digger foreman, farm laborer, handbill distributor, lecturer, movie actor, Pullman conductor, salesman, school teacher, soldier, night watchman, wood chopper and surveyor's lineman."

Best had been UP's correspondent in Vienna for nineteen years and had a colorful reputation there. Shirer, in his *Berlin Diary* entry for March 1938, when the Nazis seized Vienna, writes:

> "Over at the Cafe Louvre, Bob Best of UP is sitting at the same table he has occupied every night for the last 10 years. Around him is a crowd of foreign correspondents, male and female, American, English, Hungarian, Serb, all but Best in a great state of excitement, running to the phone every five minutes to get some news or give it."

When Best was called to the telephone and returned he was able to tell Shirer and the others that the Nazis had arrived in Vienna. He had good sources.

According to Richard McMillan, another UP correspondent in Austria, Best also had won fame in Vienna as a rake. "A lady friend, reportedly a Hungarian countess, used to dress in riding breeches, seize a stock, and roam the city streets shouting: '*Haben Zie Herr Best Gehesen?*' (Anyone seen Mr. Best?) When she found him in the company of another heart throb, there were fireworks! Oh, la la! *Mon dieu! Quel disastre!*"[9]

When the war ended, Best was arrested, tried as a traitor and given a life sentence in a federal penitentiary. He died in 1952, still in prison, after suffering a stroke.[10]

In November 1942, Leo S. "Bill" Disher was aboard the U.S. Coast Guard cutter *Walney* with the Allied fleet invading North Africa. He was one of eight UP correspondents covering the action. The others were Walter Cronkite, Walter Logan, Phil Ault Clinton Beach "Pat" Conger, E. A. "Ned" Russell, Chris Cunningham and John Parris.

The French fleet put up a strong, if useless, fight before surrendering. The Walney, assigned to ram through a ring of booms outside the port of Oran, was hit by several French Navy shells and blasted out of the water. Disher was standing on the bridge of the cutter. He had a broken ankle suffered earlier in a fall and was on crutches. He had a chest life preserver and a second one wrapped around the ankle.

Shrapnel punctured the chest preserver. Disher found himself with his head under the ocean surface and the life preserver on his leg holding him upside down in the water. He afterwards said he had to climb up his leg to keep from drowning.

Disher managed to swim to shore. When medics looked at him they found twenty-six wounds. He received the Purple Heart and, after a long recovery, helped cover the Normandy invasion.

A Stanley-Livingston incident occurred when Walter Logan was rescued from the sea after a ship had been sunk under him in the Mediterranean.

"I was picked up by an American LCI. I saluted the captain and introduced myself: 'Walter Logan, United Press, New York.' He returned the salute, replying: 'Kenneth P. Leake, United Press San Francisco.'"[11]

Dan Thrapp, who was in the Buenos Aires bureau when World War II broke out, got itchy to get back to the United States and join the armed forces. Thrapp was a mule lover. He, Charlie Pollak of the Buenos Aires bureau, and Malcolm Bissell of AP set out from Argentina riding mules heading north. At LaPaz, Bolivia, they abandoned the mules for faster transportation to America.

When he joined the army, Thrapp was able to use his mule expertise in the China-Burma Theater. He rejoined UP in 1946 and helped cover the Greek civil war.

When Germany seized most of Europe, nearly 200 UP client newspapers were lost in occupied countries, but at the same time, dozens of U.S. newspapers added UP service, so the company continued growing steadily.

All correspondents with the armies were in some danger. United Press managers repeatedly told correspondents not to take chances. But they did. In September 1943, Henry Gorrell was with British General Bernard Montgomery's forces marching into Tripoli. Gorrell talked officials into letting him fly on a bombing mission that took him closer to the war than he needed to be to cover it. The plane he was aboard came under heavy enemy fire. Several crewmen were injured, including a gunner in the nose of the plane.

Gorrell crawled to the injured man in the nose of the bomber and gave first aid. The man later died of his wounds. Gorrell was awarded the Air Medal by President Roosevelt for "extreme gallantry in conduct under fire," the first given to a correspondent in the Middle East Theater.

Gorrell had already become a legendary foreign correspondent. He had been expelled from Italy, went to Spain to help cover that war and narrowly escaped death by firing squad when seized by government troops because he spoke Spanish with an Italian accent. He was reporting in Athens early in 1941 when the German armies invaded Greece, driving a British expeditionary force out in a harrowing retreat.

When the allies fought their way back into France on the Normandy beaches, Gorrell was chief UP correspondent with the American invasion armies. His report on the Normandy landing was the first eyewitness dispatch from the bloody beach. He also filed the first news story from Cherbourg where he accompanied American troops.

Gorrell had begun his career in 1929, with a year on the Kansas City, Missouri, *Journal-Post* before becoming a writer for UP. After the battles and blood of the war, he left the wire service and was editor of a Veterans' publication in Washington, D.C. He died in 1958 from a stroke at forty-eight.

Edward Beattie and Walter Cronkite were together in London's Bloomsbury, section, just leaving the Ministry of Information, when air raid sirens sounded and they heard what sounded like an airplane engine sputtering, just clearing the rooftops with a tail of flames and finally crashing with a huge explosion several blocks away. It wasn't an airplane. It was the first of Germany's V-2 rockets that tortured London during much of 1944.[12]

United Press President Hugh Baillie was also in London when the V-2 attacks began. Although the British refused immediately to confirm that the explosions heard were German bombs, Baillie went to investigate the sites of two explosions. He found his agency's London staffers at each of the craters. European News Manager William R. Higginbotham was examining the site of a bomb blast in Chiswick, and reporter

Sam Hales, who had been with UP in Kansas City, was poking around a crater in another section of London.[13]

Cronkite landed a big assignment when he was chosen as one of eight correspondents to fly with the American bomber fleet, which was raiding German targets every day. The eight reporters were given a week's training, including how to fire, load and field strip a .50 caliber machine gun. The Geneva conference on warfare prohibited correspondents from using weapons but the rule was ignored by many correspondents.

When he was squeezed into a B-17 for a raid on Wilhelmshaven, a German submarine base, Cronkite got everything he wanted and an experience he didn't expect—firing the machine gun at a German fighter.

He wrote in his memoirs that he missed the target. But he came back with a story which made many newspapers around the world: "I have just returned from an assignment to hell, a hell at 17,000 feet, a hell of bursting flak and screaming fighter planes, of burning Forts and hurtling bombs."

Cronkite said he was a little embarrassed about the "purple prose," but it was the kind of dramatic dispatch that won headlines.[14]

Aldo Forte, was stationed in the Berne, Switzerland, bureau after escaping from Rome. He disguised himself as a mountain climber, cut his way through the barbed-wire barrier on the border and went back down into German-dominated Northern Italy to get an exclusive story on the feeling of the people there about the Nazi regime which had taken over. Less than a year later, Forte again crossed the frontier to get a first-hand report on the operations of the Maquis, the French underground.[15] Forte was back in Italy with his brother Ralph in 1944 to re-open the Rome bureau.

At the start of the allied offensive across the Rhine in February 1945, UP had a power team with the armies sweeping through Germany. Among them were Robert Vermillion, Richard McMillan, who had been wounded in the Africa fighting, Clinton B. Conger, Chris R. Cunningham, Leon Kay, Boyd Lewis and Ann Stringer.

Stringer was hired by UP after her husband, Bill Stringer, was killed in a German bombing. Bill had worked for UP in South America but was a correspondent for Reuters when he was killed. Ann was a blue-eyed beauty with long dark hair and nerves of steel. Romanian Prime Minister Groza asked several American correspondents, "When is Ann Stinger of the United Press coming back? She had the most beautiful legs in Romania."[16]

When Ann showed up on the streets of Juelich on the German front line, fellow Unipresser Jim McGlincy recalled, "Everywhere we went, unshaven and dirty infantrymen, who couldn't remember when they'd last seen an American girl, grinned, started waving and gave Ann their stories. When bullets whined or shells screamed, the rest of us ducked but Ann just wrinkled up her brow and scribbled more notes."

On April 25, 1945, the Russians were pressing on Berlin. Stringer flew with an American spotter plane that landed in a clover field across at Torgau on the Elbe. Russian soldiers across the river sighted her and shouted, "Bravo, *Americanski!*" They waded across the river to greet her. The plane had gone back to its base, so the Russians helped her get back across the river and catch a ride to Paris to file her story of the first dramatic link-up of American and Soviet troops.[17]

At the same time, the Germans were retreating hastily northward in Italy. Mussolini was attempting to escape disguised as a German officer and his whereabouts was not known by the allies. However, he was recognized by anti-Nazi partisans, who killed him and his mistress.

UP reporter James E. Roper picked up a tip from the Italian partisans that Mussolini was in Milan. He and a couple of other reporters headed for the city, passing retreating German troops no longer interested in challenging anyone. Roper wrote the first report on the Italian dictator's fate:

> BY JAMES E. ROPER
> **MILAN, APRIL 29** — (UP) THE PEOPLE BENITO MUSSOLINI HAD RULED FOR TWO DECADES PAID HIM THEIR LAST TRIBUTE BY HANGING HIS REMAINS HEAD DOWN FROM THE RAFTERS OF A GASOLINE STATION IN MILAN'S LORETO SQUARE.

There they spat upon their fallen leader, shot his body in the back and kicked his face into a toothless, pulpy mass....His mistress, Clara Petacci, and sixteen other Fascists who were with him were also killed by the mob.[18]

UP editors in London, New York and other bureaus who handled copy and dictation from correspondents in the field had more to do with getting their stories into the client newspapers than the reporters themselves. Some of the best journalists were on the "war desk," editors like Harrison Salisbury, who went on to a distinguished career in Moscow for UP and later with the *New York Times*. The bureau war desk could make or break a dispatch.

Sometimes the war desk was imperfect. In 1943, the Russians began a counter-attack against German forces near Stalingrad. One morning the *New York Times* published a front page story from United Press about Soviet troops making a 100-mile advance in one night. The *Times* added a map, illustrating with arrows the towns captured.

Next day the *Times'* editors learned that the UP dispatch had a significant error. The story, filed by Henry Shapiro in Moscow, quoted a Russian communiqué that said Soviet troops advanced to Iganogrov. Salisbury, on the desk in New York, looked at the bureau's war map and found a town by that name about 100 miles from where the Russians were the day before. If the Russians reached Iganogrov overnight it meant that German tanks were being routed.

"The fact was that in Russia, Iganogrov is like Washington or Jefferson. Every state has a town with that name," said William Mandel, an expert on Russian geography. UP had the wrong Iganogrov.[19] The *New York Times* was so embarrassed by the mistake that it boycotted UP war copy for a month. UP recovered by covering a number of large tables with European maps and hiring Mandel to stand by the cable desk in New York every night and advise the lead writers about the terrain on the Eastern Front.

18

Getting Back to the Philippines

THE JAPANESE WAR OF AGGRESSION IN THE FAR EAST BEGAN IN the 1930s. By 1938, the conquering forces of the Rising Sun had subdued Manchuria, taken Peiping and were coming down on Hangkow, then the capital of China.

Roy Howard had been on the Japan/China battlefront in 1933. He afterward always saw that the United Press was well represented in the Orient.

On December 13, 1937, the *Panay*, an American gunboat loaded with foreigners being evacuated from Nanking as the Japanese army approached, was bombed and sunk in repeated attacks by Japanese planes.

UP correspondent Weldon James was aboard the *Panay*, along with several hundred people being evacuated from the Chinese city. He was the only wire service reporter on the ship and delivered a dramatic first-person account of the attack.

The Japanese at first denied the incident. A few days later at a news conference in Shanghai, they conceded their planes had made the attack but there was no apology. The Japanese indignantly asserted that the American gunboat had violated international rules by firing back at the attacking planes.

The U. S. government did not want to upset the Japanese emperor and took steps to minimize the event, including the confiscation of film showing Japanese planes making the attack.[1]

James was at the Shanghai press conference when a Japanese officer spoke of the American shooting at Japanese planes. The UP man, who had been at the scene, could not help but burst out in response: "You're God-damned right! And of course you won't be able to believe it, but we were trying to hit them."

John R. Morris was in charge of the UP bureau at Shanghai. Doris Rubens, who had studied at Columbia University for a doctorate in clinical psychology, took some courses in journalism and was looking for adventure. She wanted to go to China. The editor of the *New York Post* told her if she did some freelance reporting the newspaper would buy her stories.

In Hong Kong, Doris met Morris, who offered her a position in the Hangkow bureau. She arrived in October 1938, and found herself among many of the top foreign correspondents in the world, who had come to report on the Japanese-Chinese war.

Not long after her arrival, Generalissimo Chiang Kai-shek and Madame Chiang fled the city, setting up headquarters at Chungking. Most of the correspondents followed, including Mac Fisher, UP's bureau manager in Hangkow. Morris asked Rubens if she would stay in Hangkow to run the bureau. Three days later, the Japanese marched in. That winter, Doris was the only American reporter in Hangkow. Writing daily stories about the Japanese occupation, she forgot completely about becoming a doctor of psychology.

The American gunboat *Oahu* was anchored in the port to safeguard American diplomats still there. Rubens was able to get the Navy to transmit her stories in order to avoid Chinese censorship.

In the spring of 1939, Rubens left Hangkow along with all the remaining American nationals. U.S. Navy Admiral Yarnell took them aboard his private yacht, Isobel, and sailed up the Yangtze escorted by two gunboats.

Rubens then went home to New York by way of Shanghai, Harbin, the trans-Siberian railroad and Paris.

A year later, she was swept up in an even more perilous experience in the Philippines. She had married Thurston B. Macauley, and they went to Manila ten months before Pearl Harbor. When the Japanese conquered the Philippines, the Macauleys fled into the hills and were sheltered by Filipino resistance guerillas in the jungle. But the Japanese learned of their presence and threatened to kill all the Filipinos in the area if they harbored Americans. So they surrendered and were imprisoned until the liberation.

In addition to bureaus in Hangkow, Shanghai, Peiping and Hong Kong, UP had an office in Tientsin. The Japanese occupied that city. On September 28, 1939, armed Japanese plainclothes police raided the UP bureau on the top floor of the American Radio Service building. Six Japanese officers ransacked the files and read bureau correspondence. They also entered and searched the ARS office, which handled press copy and business communications. The purpose of the intrusion was never explained. The Japanese at the time controlled most of China and were notorious for gratuitous violence against Chinese and non-Chinese alike. During the raid on the UP bureau, a Chinese employee was slugged by a Japanese officer for no apparent reason.[2]

The Japanese bombing of Pearl Harbor on December 7, 1941, touched off a storm of activity for the wire service in the Pacific and Far East. The raid itself was reported by Frank Tremaine, Honolulu bureau manager, his wife, Kaye, and William Tyree, a staffer. Awakened before dawn by the bombing, they telephoned bulletins to San Francisco until communications were cut a few hours into the attack. No news reports were allowed from Hawaii for several days. In the weeks, which followed, correspondents throughout Asia came in with news of the Japanese advances.

Some of the most dramatic activity took place in Shanghai where the UP staff included Karl Eskelund, a Danish-born reporter, whose wife, Paula, was expecting a child at the time. When the Japanese began arresting foreigners in Shanghai, the Eskelunds fled and hid in a farmhouse outside the city. Japanese soldiers entered the house and made a search. They came into the room where Karl and Paula were hiding but did not look under the bed where the couple lay holding their breath.

Shanghai bureau manager Robert "Pepper" Martin and staffer William McDougall made a dramatic escape. They got past a Japanese checkpoint by posing as drunks stumbling home. The Chinese underground took them from safe house to safe house until they reached territory held by the allies. From China, McDougall flew to Java to help cover the war there.

When the Japanese were moving on that Dutch base, most Americans fled hastily. McDougall told the New York desk he would file "one last story" and then get out. He missed the last plane to Australia, then boarded a small freighter, the *Poleau Bras*, along with 240 refugees who had crowded aboard. The ship was strafed and bombed out of the water the next day, dumping survivors into the ocean.

McDougall swam to several lifeboats but those who got there first pushed him away, saying there was no room. A devout Catholic, while treading the black water, he made a promise that if he survived he would become a priest.

He saw another lifeboat and persuaded its passengers to let him aboard. They got to the shore. Many of the survivors were machine-gunned on the beach by Japanese troops. McDougall and a few others managed to hide in the jungle but were soon captured. He was imprisoned for three years at a notorious Japanese prison camp. The food ration was a few spoons of rice each day.

The reporter cared for other inmates. Many were suffering without medical care. McDougall did the best he could, but every day a half dozen or so died.

He collected scraps of paper and pencils and kept a diary, which he put in a bottle and buried in the prison grounds.

United Press and his family thought he was dead.

Fast-forward to 1945 at the Singapore UP office: in walks a 70-pound ghost, Bill McDougall.

He went home, took a Nieman fellowship at Harvard, then carried out the pledge he made in the treacherous water off Java. He became a priest and was a beloved pastor in Salt Lake City, Utah, for many years. He went back to the Pacific and, miraculously it seemed, found his buried diaries, from which he wrote his story, *Six Bells Off Java*.

Robert T. Bellaire, Tokyo bureau manager, Richard C. Wilson of Manila and George E. Baxter, Hong Kong manager, returned to the United States along with 1,500 other Americans and anti-Axis nationals aboard the Swedish liner *Gripsholm*, which arrived in August 1942. The Japanese had accused Bellaire of being a spy and beat him when he refused to write a propaganda statement for them during his imprisonment. While being held, he wrote forty pages of notes and memorized them before discarding the paper.

Joseph F. McDonald, Jr. was an engineer on Wake Island when the Japanese seized the Pacific outpost at the beginning of hostilities. He was also a stringer for UP. He was reported killed in December 1941, while working with a volunteer anti-aircraft crew.

However, on February 20, 1942, the Navy turned over to UP a dispatch from him written on December 20, 1942, leading to the belief he might be alive. He turned up in a Japanese prison camp in 1945.

The Pacific war competed for news space with the late stages of the European conflict when Russian troops were advancing on Berlin. On February 1, 1945, the Pacific story was the clear winner. It reported the rescue of 513 American prisoners on Luzon in the Philippines.

Franz Weissblatt of UP was in a Bilibad Prison in Manila. He had been captured when the Philippines fell to the Japanese in 1942. Doc Quigg was one of the UP reporters with Gen. MacArthur's troops when they liberated the Americans. He gave this account:

> "The night was pitch black, but I felt my way around the wall and along the corridor toward a hum of excited voices.
>
> "Suddenly I sensed, rather than felt or saw, someone beside me. I stuck out my hand, even as did Stanley in darkest Africa those many years ago.
>
> "'I'm Quigg, United Press,' I said.
>
> "The Dr. Livington of Bilibad Prison grasped my hand fervently.
>
> "'Weissblatt, United Press.' he replied."

Later, Weissblatt told about his capture.

> "I ran into a Japanese ambush while riding with a scout car detachment of the 26th Cavalry on January 7, 1942, on Luzon. The whole detachment of 15 men and an officer were knocked off. I was the only one who came out alive.
>
> "We had gotten in back of the Japanese lines and during an intense burst of small arms fire, I was shot in the leg. Then a mortar shell burst right over the car and I was knocked unconscious. When I came to, the other fellows in the car were dead.
>
> "I started to haul myself out but saw the Japs and dropped back on my belly. They gave a whoop and yanked me out onto the ground, inspecting my wound.
>
> "The Japs immediately stripped all my clothes off. Then, as I lay there on the ground beside the scout car, they filed by, one after another. There wasn't one who didn't kick me or spit on me or hit me with his rifle.
>
> "Every time one of them hit me I called him a dirty son-of-a-bitch. That relieved my feelings."[3]

He said he was moved around for thirty-five days without hospital attention, lost sixty pounds in the first thirty-five days of captivity and was without clothes all that time. When Weissblatt was liberated in Manila, he had a list of 6,000 prisoners who had died on Luzon. He said he spent hundreds of hours collecting the names. Many were victims of the infamous Bataan Death March.

Weissblatt's wife, Vivian, was interned at Santo Tomas only four blocks away, but Weissblatt didn't see her during their entire imprisonment. They were reunited when the Americans seized Santo Tomas. Vivian was among 50 prisoners wounded by a Japanese shell in the final fighting. 20 people were killed. When Weissblatt got out of Letterman Hospital in San Francisco, he said he wanted to go back and be on hand for the invasion of Japan.[4]

Frank Hewlett, another UP correspondent in Manila when the Japanese invaded the Philippines in 1942, left with General Douglas MacArthur for Bataan and Corregidor. His wife, Virginia, stayed as a volunteer nurse at Santa Catalina Hospital in Manila. She was interned by the Japanese while Frank went on covering the war in Australia, India, Burma and other Pacific battlefronts. When U.S. forces liberated Manila, he was reunited with Virginia at Santo Tomas.

Hewlett, Carl Mydans of *Life* magazine and Hal Steward, a military correspondent, were with an 800-man lightning motorized unit racing into Manila while General MacArthur's main force was attacking from another direction.

When they reached Santo Thomas prison, Frank dashed in and up a staircase. He met his wife making her way down. She was emaciated, down to less than eighty pounds, and it took a moment for him to recognize her. Then he swept her into his arms singing, "I found Virginia. I found Virginia. She's just fine!"[5]

Unipresser Francis McCarthy also met relatives at Los Banos prison camp when he came in with the U.S. liberating troops. His brother Floyd and sister Marion had been living in Manila when it fell to the Japanese. "Floyd embarrassed me by running up and down the corridor of the barracks and shouting. 'I told you my kid brother would come to rescue me. Whoopee!'" wrote McCarthy later.[6]

The turning point in the Pacific naval war was the Battle of Midway in the spring of 1942. It was reported by William Tyree, who watched the action from the bridge of a cruiser.

In an interview later, Tyree gave this account:

> "Correspondents and the crew had a snack of sandwiches and oranges in the cruiser's ward room before dawn. In the midst of the meal the bugler sounded an alarm that meant we had contacted the enemy.
>
> "I stuffed a chocolate bar into my pocket as we scrambled to battle stations. That was all the food I had for the remainder of the day. But it was no hardship. There was so much action, so much drama and excitement that there was no time to think of anything else....
>
> "Until dusk our forces repelled repeated attacks which reached a climax in a fanatical Jap thrust with torpedo planes.
>
> "I raced from one vantage point to another on the bridge in an effort to keep track of the action. It was spectacular to see our fighter planes shooting down the Japanese aircraft, including their vaunted Zeros, which burst in flame as they were hit.

"Everyone cheered as we blasted two torpedo planes from the sky. One of them exploded so near we could see the body of the pilot in the flaming wreckage. His rear gunner turned a final, desperate, strafing burst of gunfire on our bridge. Bullets spattered the armor sheeting across my chest. I wasn't conscious of being in danger. I only remember joining my shipmates in a round of curses which left my throat raw for days afterward."

Like other correspondents, Tyree was assigned a sailor to assist him and he had easy access to the ship's officers. "Actually," he said in an interview a few weeks later, "there was too much information available for today's space-cramped newspapers."

War correspondents weren't in action constantly. Many hours were spent playing poker. Robert C. Miller was a two-theater reporter, Europe and the Pacific. He said in his diary he lost $10.60 in a game one July night aboard a warship in the Pacific.

Walter Logan, while killing time aboard the U.S.S. *Calvert* off the East Coast, said the poker stakes were astronomical among the men who did not know if they would be alive for another day. "My original stake of a few hundred dollars grew by leaps and bounds and before the voyage was over I had won more than thirty thousand dollars."[7]

Practical knowledge Miller picked up included how to keep his diary in a condom so that if the ship got shot from under him, his notes would not be ruined. "It's sacrilegious to use them for that, but it's practical," he wrote on August 5, 1942 as the fleet approached its destiny in Guadalcanal.

The reporters who covered the war had their worries. Miller wrote in his diary: "There are exceptionally good possibilities that I may not come out of this alive, but I'm satisfied as I haven't wasted much time. It would be a dirty trick to check out before the thing ends." After a few weeks he pulled strings to get out of Guadalcanal. After several weeks in Hawaii, giving speeches, getting drunk and writing about the action, he was anxious to get back to the front.

Two years later, Miller was in Europe. In September 1944, his left arm was shattered when he was hit by shrapnel. Still undaunted, with the withered arm he went on to cover a half dozen other wars including Korea and Vietnam.

Lisle Shoemaker filed a first-hand account of the Iwo Jima invasion. His copy arrived at the UP in Hawaii in a blood-soaked envelope. The messenger had been shot getting off the island.[8] Shoemaker wrote: "When we landed on the green beach under Suribachi's ugly nose, we sprinted 10 feet up the sloped beach and dropped into the coarse black volcanic gravel. Machine gun bullets kicked up spurts in front, back and sides. Mortars crumped along the entire beach.

"From there it was run and fall, from shell hole to shell hole. In my fourth one, a Jap sniper spotted me. Every time I stirred to get out, a bullet whizzed by. Then I stuck up my empty helmet. He shot at it four or five times then stopped. It took three hours of this lunging and sprinting to reach a little sand hill at the top of the beach, only a few hundred yards inshore."[9]

Bill Tyree saw Iwo fighting from the sky. He described the island as looking "like a fat pork chop sizzling in a skillet. Iwo was smoking from end to end." In a small plane at 1,000 feet he could see the Marines dashing inland from the beach.

American soldiers, generals, admirals, privates, maintained their sense of humor with correspondents. In October 1944, Admiral Chester W. Nimitz held his usual briefing. With serious demeanor, he read to the reporters a communiqué.

Powerful Allied naval forces have attacked a portion of the Japanese fleet lying at anchor near the entrance to Fusan harbor on the southeast coast of Korea. Twenty-six of approximately eighty ships in the harbor were set afire and the remainder dispersed. In a later engagement, more than 70 Japanese vessels, including warships and transports, were encountered by the Allied fleet and sunk. The devastating blow has isolated enemy armies in Korea and cut them off from their home bases."

At the end, Nimitz smiled and added: "This communiqué, incidentally, is dated late June 1592." The correspondents sighed with relief, then laughed.

The ancient communiqué misled a few news broadcasters in the United States when the AP transmitted it line by line as the admiral spoke, with the punch line at the end as Nimitz had given it. The AP text moved through the relay at Hawaii and got onto the AP wires, misleading rip-and-read announcers. A quick advisory by AP New York was needed to explain the situation.

The United States had broken the Japanese secret diplomatic "Purple" code before December 1941, and at least seven reporters knew about it but never disclosed the fact.

Lyle Wilson, Washington manager for UP, was called at 8:30 A.M. on November 15, 1941, and invited to a secret press conference to be given by General George C. Marshall. Also invited were the bureau chiefs of INS and AP and reporters from *Time, Newsweek*, the *New York Times* and the *New York Herald Tribune*.

Marshall told the newsmen that the United States was "on the brink of war with Japan." Then he made a disclosure, which, if anyone had leaked it, might have changed the course of the war.

"We have access to all the information the Japanese are receiving concerning our military preparations, especially in the Philippines. In other words, we know what they know about us, and they don't know that we know it."[10]

Throughout the fighting, the ability of the United States to read Japanese coded messages was never disclosed and gave the American forces distinct advantages. At that time General Marshall correctly believed that he could trust American newsmen not to leak an important national military secret.

Hugh Baillie, president of the company, hustled around the battlefronts of both Europe and Asia, encouraging his correspondents, promoting the service and filing his own colorful dispatches.

After a 10-week trip visiting American troops around the world, Baillie published "Two Battlefronts," a collection of dispatches he had written.

The war ended in 1945, first in Europe and then in the Pacific, after Hiroshima and Nagasaki were destroyed by atomic bombs.

United Press had prematurely reported the end of World War I and was never allowed to forget it. At the end of World War II, it was Associated Press that reported Germany's surrender prematurely, twice.

On April 28, 1945, the agency had put out the following bulletin, which made banner headlines throughout the country, including a "victory extra" by the *Chicago Sunday Times* with a two-word, huge type, front page: "GERMANY QUITS!"

SAN FRANCISCO, APRIL 29 (AP)—GERMANY HAS SURRENDERED TO THE ALLIED GOVERNMENTS UNCONDITIONALLY AND ANNOUNCEMENT IS EXPECTED MOMENTARILY, IT WAS STATED BY A HIGH AMERICAN OFFICIAL TODAY.

In Washington, UP and other reporters instantly dashed to the White House press office. President Truman, annoyed when he was interrupted during an important meeting, told them, "There is no foundation for the rumor. That is all I have to say."

AP hung to its false story throughout the evening, telling editors it was "an accurate and factual account of a statement to AP staff men by Senator Tom Connally in San Francisco." Connally told other reporters he "didn't say anything like that."

A few weeks earlier, International News Service had flashed a German surrender. Most papers' telegraph editors, in that case, waited for a confirmation from the AP and UP, which never came. After the INS error, John S. Knight of the *Chicago Daily News*, in a dig at UP and INS, passed along one of his telegraph editor's comment: "They [AP] make mistakes, too, but not on the ending of a war."[11]

But that's exactly what AP did a month later.

Edward Kennedy was AP correspondent in a group of sixteen reporters brought to General Eisenhower's headquarters in Reims, France, to witness the surrender. Each of the correspondents had pledged not to put out the story until it was officially released by Eisenhower, who wanted to coordinate the announcement with British leader Winston Churchill and, especially, with Stalin in Moscow. The Russians' exact battlefield situation on the Eastern Front was not known.

Kennedy phoned his story to London twenty-four hours before the official release. The AP dispatch, as with Roy Howard's 1918 story, touched off victory celebrations around the world. Eisenhower was angry. He said the AP premature release imperiled the cease fire and damaged Ike's credibility with the Russians because he had promised there would be no announcement until they were ready.

Other correspondents covering allied headquarters were furious. They jointly signed a letter to Eisenhower asking him to discipline the AP. Eisenhower banned AP from filing any news from Europe "due to self-admitted deliberate violation of SHAEF (Supreme Headquarters American Expeditionary Force) regulations and breach of confidence." He said the wire service management was responsible, as well as its correspondent Kennedy, because it had defied a request to pull back the story.

Ike's order suppressing AP was rescinded within a day, but Kennedy remained blacklisted. The veteran AP writer, who headed the agency's team in Europe, said he broke the secrecy pledge because the military had no right to require such a promise from reporters.

The outcry by journalistic groups over the Kennedy flash resulted in his being quietly severed by AP the next year. However, the agency helped him get a position on the Santa Barbara, California, *News-Press*. Three years later, he became editor of the Monterey, California, *Peninsula-Herald*.

At the end of the war, British censors reported that they had handled more than 900 million words of press copy through London between 1939 and 1945. The wire services produced 270 million of those words. Six hundred to 800 U.S. correspondents served in the European Theater, suffering 149 battle casualties.

The UP had a staff of 150 full-time war correspondents and several hundred part-timers covering the war. They moved 25,000 to 35,000 words a day by cable and telephone.

Five women held credentials as UP war correspondents during World War II. They were Hazel Hartzog, who worked in the Pacific Theater, Dudley Ann Harmon, Corinne Hardesty, Eleanor Packard and Ann Stringer, who covered action in Europe. Two other women had reported for UP from China in the early stages of the war, in Chungking—Betty Graham, who later went to INS, and Dorothy Rubens, who covered the fall of Hankow to the Japanese.

During the fighting, well-staffed bureaus were maintained in neutral places like Zurich, Berne, Madrid, Lisbon and Ankara, Turkey. Bureaus also stayed open in Stockholm and Vichy, France. Even in Berlin, several German staffers tried to maintain the UP bureau after the war broke out. However, the Nazis ordered that the UP leave and turn the bureau over to a Japanese agency.

During the early days of the Nazi attack on France, Glen M. Stadler attempted to maintain the Paris office. On June 13, 1940, he stayed awake all day expecting the Wehrmacht to arrive. That evening, he lay down under the desk for a rest and was awakened by noise of activity. He ran down stairs. It was time to go. He got on his bicycle and headed for the U.S. embassy. At the Place de l'Opera he ran into German traffic officers and saw the Eiffel Tower crowned with swastikas.

When Paris was liberated, Stadler was waiting to reopen the UP service. At Antwerp, local employees were also found waiting to help crank up the wires.

American correspondents in World War II had no qualms about being biased on the side of their country. The Japanese were "Japs," and the Germans were the "Hun."

United Press front-line correspondents wrote special stories supporting an American war bond drive. Reporters contributing to the project were John R. Morris, Far Eastern manager; Richard W. Johnston on Tarawa; Robert C. Miller, Guadalcanal; George E. "First Wave" Jones and Frank Hewlett from Pacific battlefronts; and Edward W. Beattie and Walter Cronkite in Europe. The series was edited by Boyd Lewis and put on client wires in July 1944.

In 1939, there were 800 American or American-trained correspondents in Europe, compared with about twenty in World War I, according to Alistaire Cooke, the British journalist, historian.[12]

The D-Day invasion was covered by 450 reporters who filed 2.5 million words, 106,000 feet of film and 25,000 photos in the first five days of the second front.

Webb Miller of UP is counted as the first American journalist killed in World War II, but it was not on any battleground. He died late one night in 1940 in a blackout when he fell off a train just outside Clapham Junction while going to his country place for a rest from the hectic pace of news in London. His body was found the next morning.

His death was ruled an accident, although there was some speculation that he was depressed about starting off on coverage of this, his eleventh war, at age forty-eight, and may have committed suicide.

German propaganda agents put out a story that he was the victim of British secret police because his dispatches were not sufficiently pro-allies. That report was ridiculed and not repeated, even by the Nazis. The United States honored Miller by naming a Liberty ship for him. He was survived by his widow, Marie, and a son, Kenneth, then eighteen, who later worked for United Press.

Besides Miller's accidental death, four other UP correspondents died in World War II. They were: Harry Leslie Percy, who died of malaria in Egypt on April 20, 1942; Brydon Taves, killed at age 29 in the crash of a plane in the Pacific on the day after Christmas 1943; John Julian Andrews, lost on a B29 mission from India on November 5, 1944; and Jack Frankish, killed on December 23, 1944, by a stray German bomb. Harry Leslie Percy also had a Liberty ship named for him.

On vacation in Belgium, Frankish saw a bomb blow up outside his hotel and went out to look. A second bomb exploded, killing him and injuring several other correspondents.

Taves was one of the first correspondents to receive the Purple Heart medal, in 1945, when the U.S. began awarding battle medals to war reporters. *Editor & Publisher*, the journalism magazine headed by Robert U. Brown, an ex-Unipresser, had lobbied for the decoration for correspondents injured alongside soldiers.

The Purple Heart was also awarded to Joe Custer who lost an eye during the Coral Sea battle on August 8, 1942, when he was aboard the cruiser *Astoria*. Other Unipressers honored with the medal were Leo S. Disher, blasted out of a ship in the allied landing in Africa in 1942; Eleanor Packard for injuries in a jeep accident in Italy; Walter F. Logan, hurt in a mine explosion near Medjez-el-Bab, Tunisia, in 1942; Robert C. Miller, whose right arm was smashed by bomb fragments at Verdun in August 1944; Edward V. Robert, struck in the left shoulder and hip by shell fragments at Brest September 1, 1944; James E. Roper, hurt in a dive-bombing raid near Rome July 3, 1944; Virgil Pinkley, struck in the neck by machine-gun bullet in Libya in December 1941; Frank Hewlett, who suffered a leg-wound in his capture by the Japanese in December 1941; and Richard D. McMillan, a British citizen, hit by a shell fragment near Cherbourg, France, June 25, 1944. Walter Briggs was wounded on the British front lines in Burma.

Hewlett also received a commendation from the First Cavalry Division for his role in the liberation of Manila early in 1945. He was at the lead of a "flying wedge" into the city, where his wife was a prisoner. Medals for valor under fire went to Unipressers George E. Jones, Robert Vermillion and Richard W. Johnston.

19

Serving Milk in Omaha

AT THE END OF 1949, THE UP ASKED ITS EDITORS TO IDENTIFY THE TEN people who had made the greatest impact on the first half of the century. Franklin D. Roosevelt placed first, followed by Hitler, Thomas Edison, Winston Churchill, Henry Ford, Nicolai Lenin, The Wright Brothers, Albert Einstein, Joseph Stalin and Louis Pasteur (even though Pasteur died in 1895).

The beginning of the second half of the century was a challenging time for the country and for United Press, with the cold war heating up, the Korean War threatening to go nuclear, and worldwide economic problems. Looking back from two generations later, the 1950s were understandable, the struggles were clearer than those of the following decades. The "McCarthy era" was fading, and nothing so politically volatile appeared on the horizon. The next big war would not break out for another ten years. The United Press had the vigor of youth but was in fact passing its middle age.

In 1950, veteran foreign correspondent Reynolds Packard published a novel, *The Kansas City Milkman.* It was a thinly disguised and exaggerated version of wire service life, set in the UP Paris bureau of "IP" (Interworld Press Association). Though with negligible literary merit, the novel was reprinted in two paperback versions, *Dateline Paris*, and *Low Down.*

The original title, *Kansas City Milkman*, came from an instruction often issued by United Press editors to their novice reporters: "Write it for the milkman in Omaha." Packard changed the milkman's hometown.

His IP executives and staffers were so modeled on UP people that some individuals could easily be recognized. IP President Homer Rockwell, sending "whambo! zambo!" rockets to Paris, was easily recognized as a caricature of UP President Hugh Baillie, who, of course, noticed this.

One day, getting into the elevator at the *Daily News* Building with company attorney Ezra Bryan and others, Baillie said, "Ezra, let's sue Packard."

The attorney replied, "Well, Hugh, everybody in this elevator knows who he was writing about. If we sue him, the whole world will know." There was no suit.

"There is no time for literary fancywork or groping for words," says the novel's narrator, IP's Clay Brewster, instructing a new correspondent. "You just bang out the copy as fast as your fingers can tap the keys and it flows into cliché molds."

Kansas City Milkman became a cult book among wire service people. Now out of print, a copy is a prized possession of any Unipresser who has it. Even Associated Press people were fascinated. Stan Meisler of AP, wrote that he "could see all our work mirrored in his pages, all the frenzy, all the speed, all the ambition, all the mediocrity, all the cynicism….Every foreign correspondent or wire service reporter that I know seems to fit somewhere in Packard's pages."[1]

The book overflows with situations wire service people recognize. A Paris correspondent flashes to the world that the premier survived a vote of confidence in the French Assembly. He had actually lost by two votes. Paul Kester, IP's Paris manager, halts his underling from sending a correction.

Instead Kester concocts a new flash, "RECOUNT DEMANDED IN ASSEMBLY."

Then, after a pause, another flash, "RECOUNT OVERTURNS PREMIER VOTE." This brings a congratulatory cable from New York. "WE EXCLUSIVE ON VOTE RECOUNT."

By 1950, all UP wires had been converted from Morse telegraphy, which required a receiving operator to take down the dots and dashes, to teletype, which transmitted words in printed form. These machines clicked out yards of cheap yellow paper in the wire rooms of newspapers and in UP bureaus.

Teleprinters had been first used in 1914. They were gradually speeded up from 34 to 60 words a minute.

In 1951 a significant improvement came, the teletypesetter, called "TTS." The new machine printed with upper and lower case type and "justified" the lines to make them the correct width for newspaper columns.

TTS transmission created a one-inch paper tape with a pattern of punched holes. The tape could be fed directly into a Linotype machine at the newspaper plant, thus eliminating the jobs of Linotype operators. The new technology raised some nasty labor issues related to automation in the newspaper industry.

The International Typographical Union, which represented the Linotype operators and printers at newspaper plants, called numerous strikes. The biggest walkout shut down New York City newspapers for weeks.

The fight was carried into smaller shops also. In Reno, Nevada, when the *Evening Gazette* and *Nevada Journal* were struck by the printers on June 29, 1959, both UPI and AP came to the rescue of the publishers by rushing in TTS equipment overnight, through the picket lines. This enabled management to produce the newspapers.

The TTS issue was a watershed for the ITU's efforts to halt technical printing advances in newspaper production.

The pay rate for United Press newsmen under the American Newspaper Guild contract in 1950 was $47.50 a week for beginners and $110 for those with six years of experience.

Newspaper employees organized by the Guild, a unit of the Congress of Industrial Organizations (CIO), had a local in each city where it had a contract with the newspaper. Wire service employees, being distributed in many cities, were represented in negotiations by the parent American Newspaper Guild rather than the local chapter.

Some union members thought they could do better by having their own nation-wide "local" of all wire service people. They succeeded in chartering the Wire Service Guild in 1957 for employees of AP, UP and INS, numbering in all about 2,400 in the United States.

As it turned out, the Wire Service Guild was not strong enough to keep up with major newspaper guilds. Only about 60 percent of covered employees belonged to the union. They found themselves falling behind the best newspaper pay rates.

Besides the natural conflict between employer and employee on wages, UP management had the additional problem of staying on good terms with newspaper publishers in smaller cities. Those papers did not want to see the agencies paying reporters more than they paid theirs.

In 1957, the Guild negotiated the first pension plan for UP news employees, providing an initial $2 weekly company contribution. The first beneficiary of the pension plan was Justus De Vries, who retired in New York and received his first pension check in April 1960.

The Commercial Telegraphers' Union, an AFL (American Federation of Labor) craft union representing the "punchers," went on strike against UP in 1950 in a walk-out that lasted six weeks. Management and sales personnel learned how to operate Teletype transmitters and were able to keep the news flowing.

Bureaus located in newspaper buildings had especially serious problems because printers and other union employees of the newspapers refused to cross the telegraphers' picket lines. In San Francisco, the bureau in the *News* building was moved to a storefront across the street and most of the transmission was moved to Moraga, 40 miles east of San Francisco, where UP had its West Coast international broadcast receiving station.

The strike ended unfavorably for the union and its bargaining power was permanently crippled.

By 1960 the CTU had a pay scale of $137 a week for operators with three years experience. In the contract, awarded by an arbitrator, the union also won contributions of $6 a week into a pension plan.

The Guild never had a union shop at the wire service. Editorial employees were not obliged to join the union as the telegraphers were. Many did not, sometimes because they opposed unions on principle and sometimes because they thought they could get ahead with their bosses by staying out.

Some wanted it both ways, paying the Guild the equivalent of the dues but refusing to sign a membership card. Scott Baillie, son of the UP president, regularly sent a $35 check to the Guild but never joined.

In 1976, Guild membership at UPI was 76 percent of eligible employees.

During negotiations in the mid-1970s, when the union was comparing UPI salaries with higher Associated Press rates, a management spokesman remarked, "They may also use bigger paper clips than we do."

The Guild seized on this remark and issued badges with the image of a paper clip on them. Management took the protest too seriously and shipped all bureaus quantities of large size paper clips. Small paper clips were out at the wire service.

After personnel costs, the company's biggest expense was wire haul, the cost of buying space on commercial telegraph circuits or satellites. UPI and AP, aided by some publishers, fought to keep telegraph rates down and to preserve the special rates, which had been established on press lines. The FCC (Federal Communications Commission) controlled these rates.

At a hearing on October 13, 1959, the UPI presented a 57-page argument against a requested increase, saying it was "unjust, arbitrary, capricious and unlawful." These kinds of protests often resulted in a compromise. There would be an increase but it would be lower than the transmission companies asked for.

In the 1959 case, UPI argued that an increase only a year earlier had boosted wire costs by 15 percent. The proposed 18 percent boost would increase the cost by an additional $738,000 a year bringing the cost for its 49 leased wires to $5 million.

In July 1960, the FCC approved a $2.25 million rate increase for wire service leased lines. The commissioners reasoned that press customers were in effect being subsidized by other leased line users. "If subsidies are required, they should be supplied by the general public," the FCC said.

The wires contended that the commission's rate policy, which guaranteed the telegraph companies a 7 1/2 percent profit, was in effect a "subsidy" as well, but the argument lost.

Some, concerned about the economics of the wire services, observed that the AP and UPI, by including line costs in their charges for news, were, in effect, selling telegraph services for the communications companies as well as selling news.

Fights over telegraph rates occupied management time and sweat throughout the UPI's history. The wire charges were a much more important matter for the cost-conscious agency than they were for the Associated Press, which automatically passed on all increases to its members.

In January, 1978, AT&T was given a 39 percent increase in rates for leased wires and on May 12, 1981, it got a 16.4 percent increase which raised UPI's annual cost by $1.6 million to $11.6 million. The wire service said this "significantly impaired UPI's ability to continue to effectively disseminate the news."

Louis Blanchard Mickel, known to everybody in United Press by his initials "LBM" on approved or disapproved expense accounts, retired in January 1957, after 45 years with the company. He was from Soldier, Kansas, a town of about 300 souls.

He worked in Chicago, St. Louis and Kansas City before coming to New York where he became Superintendent of Bureaus and gained the appellation "Save-a-Nickel

Mickel." As the company's cash curator, his job was cracking the fiscal whip on bureaus and staffers throughout the world.

The word "downhold" became UPI's trademark. It was derived from messages sent to all bureaus periodically to hold down expenses. "DOWNHOLD" was accepted by the cable companies as a single word, saving cable money right there.

Mickel was asserted to be "father of the downhold." But he denied paternity. He told a group of ex-Unipressers in Detroit in 1957: "When I joined the UP in 1911 'downhold' was already the watchword."[2]

Thousands of ex-Unipressers enjoyed being members of the Downhold Club, which never became a formal organization but carried on informally for many years. Its members enjoyed nothing more than occasional get-togethers at which they exchanged war stories about their days with UPI, which many declared were the best of their lives.

At one meeting, Mickel was chosen "Chief Worthy Downholder" and his signature appeared on membership cards which affirmed that the bearer "being dedicated to the proposition that nothing is so cheap it can't be done cheaper" was "entitled to no special privileges, consideration or credit whatsoever."

Downholders did not want elections, by-laws or dues. What they wanted were occasions to meet for a few drinks and lots of deep nostalgia for UPI.

They gathered at Toot Shor's in New York and at Frank Bartholomew's vineyard in Sonoma, California, entertaining themselves for hours with such pursuits as creating verses about company expense accounts. One of these had the chorus attributing everything to "Mickel, Bickel and God."

On Mickel's retirement, Karl Bickel, who had retired earlier, sent him a telegram. "You are among the last of the tight little band of middle western kids who shook up the whole world's jaded and worn journalistic system."

Bickel may not have meant it that way, but "tight" was the operative word.

Hugh Baillie wrote Mickel telling him people couldn't retire from UPI.

> "You are tied to the organization like a Siamese twin joined at the brains. That was, and is, the secret of success of the United Press....If we triumph in Budapest [a Unipresser] feels the glee in Rio....If we get a kick in the pants in Outer Mongolia, he senses the pain in Montana if that's where he's working at the moment. This is the mystique which makes the UP click, the amalgam which holds it together."

The first half century of United Press was recorded in *Deadline Every Minute*, a semi-official history written by Joe Alex Morris and published by Doubleday & Co. Morris had been a Unipresser for 15 years but was freelancing at the time he was engaged by Hugh Baillie to do the history. Baillie urged staffers around the world to submit material for it.

Academics called the book a house history. but "*Deadline*" was the only comprehensive wire service history available for many years.

Louis Lyons, in a *New York Times* review, said: "If its emphasis seems almost wholly on speed and scoops, that is clearly what has conditioned the life of reporter Morris, his colleagues and their agency."[3]

On December 27, 1951, Acme Newspictures became United Press picture service. They had been separate entities. Acme was a subsidiary of Newspaper Enterprises Association, which, like UP, was part of the E. W. Scripps Co. Mims Thomason, later to become UP president, was transferred from Central Division manager in Chicago to New York to run the photo service. Scripps officials hoped to get news photos and news dispatches better coordinated.

The Soviet Union put the first man-made satellite, *Sputnik*, into orbit September 30, 1957. United Press dominated the story the next day in major American morning newspapers, including the *New York Daily News*, the *Washington Post, Chicago Sun-Times* and *San Francisco Chronicle*.

Thanks to the contacts of Moscow bureau manager Henry Shapiro, The Soviet feat had been predicted in United Press dispatches from Moscow during the previous week.

Most UPI hirings were haphazard. You walked in the day they need somebody and you got the job if you would settle for the low starting pay. The company had an application form and a screening process on paper, but it seldom was used in practice. Bright people eager to work for the wire service were a dime a dozen. The bureau manager usually made the decision, although sometimes a new staffer was hired on orders from New York or the division headquarters.

When Gambal Nasser nationalized the Suez Canal in 1956 the Egyptian president shunned interviews by western correspondents. A young woman, Pat Herman, was in the Middle East, trying to get into a news job. She had worked briefly on a newspaper in Texas.

"I was so naive, so green, it didn't occur to me not to, so I asked for an interview," Herman said. She talked to the Egyptian president for a half hour and sold the interview to UP. She was promptly hired to cover the Sinai war.

Edith Kermit Roosevelt, Teddy's granddaughter, turned up in the San Francisco bureau and was hired as vacation replacement for Horace Benjamin, the office boy. This was the bureau's lowest ranking job. It consisted of sorting the mail, running errands and "making books." The books were used by news staffers writing stories. One copy would go to the newspaper wire, another to the broadcast desk.

The books were made by folding newsprint sheets in half and slipping a sheet of carbon paper, black on both sides between them.

"Edie" was in the back room, her face smudged with carbon and black blotches on her dress when UP President Hugh Baillie visited the bureau. As was his custom, he went around pumping the hand of every staffer.

Accompanied by Division News Editor Ron Wagoner, he went back to the storeroom and was introduced to Miss Roosevelt. He was only there a moment, but as he and Wagoner walked back into the main bureau, Baillie told the division news editor: "That's a by-line we've got to have."

Miss Roosevelt found herself suddenly a by-line columnist in Hollywood although her writing about the stars required the help of several veteran Los Angeles staffers.

In June 1957, United Press celebrated its 50th anniversary. Congratulatory messages came from President Eisenhower, the Pope, the Premier of Japan, Chancellor of Germany and other world figures.

Time magazine called UP the "world's most enterprising wire-news merchant." The *New York Times* said, "A strong esprit de corps among its staff members, a fierce competitiveness that placed a premium on enterprise and a forceful style of news presentation helped the agency to develop into a major press service."

At that time the company was in its heyday. It had 4,833 newspaper and broadcast clients and had about 4,000 employees worldwide. It had 400,000 miles of leased wires in the United States and radio printer service to thirty-two cities in Europe, Africa, the Middle East, the Far East, Australia and island points.

Events marking the anniversary included a luncheon at the Metropolitan Club in New York where certificates were given to thirty newspapers that had subscribed to UP service since its beginning.[4] President Frank Bartholomew told publishers the company was having an "exceptional" year, which gave it "a strong starting point for the half-century ahead."

20

Getting into China

IN 1956, A CRITICAL DEBATE AROSE BETWEEN PRESS ORGANIZATIONS and the U.S. government over whether American news agencies could send reporters to China to report on conditions under the communists. The United States still recognized the government on Taiwan as the legitimate representative of China. The State Department repeatedly refused to grant passports to newsmen to visit the mainland.

Diplomatic writers believed the communist Chinese were seeking a rapprochement with the United States because they regarded the Soviet Union as a closer threat. The overtures were spurned by U.S. Secretary of State John Foster Dulles, who had organized SEATO (Southeast Asia Treaty Organization) to oppose what he thought to be Chinese expansionism.

At that juncture, the Red Chinese sent special invitations to a few American correspondents, specifically named, to visit Peiping. These included Robert C. Miller of UP.

Dulles announced that any correspondent who went to China would lose his U.S. passport and might be arrested. News organizations protested strongly against the ban. Hearings were held by the Senate Foreign Relations Committee. Julius Frandsen of the Washington UP bureau presented a statement saying free access to the news at its source outweighs other considerations.

Four correspondents, including Miller, planned to accept the invitation to China, even without passports. Miller, who had joined UP in 1938 as a University of Nevada student, was a foxhole reporter, not a diplomatic correspondent. He wondered why he was invited. He said later he thought it was because he once shared a cigarette—a Chinese "Peace" brand cigarette—with a few Chinese representatives at a meeting in Australia held to discuss the Melbourne Olympic Games.

A cable to Miller from Madame Kung Pang of the Chinese Department of Foreign Affairs said, "YOU HAVE BEEN GRANTED A 30-DAY VISA TO ENTER THE PEOPLES REPUBLIC OF CHINA."

Earl J. Johnson, UP's news chief in New York, immediately cabled Miller, "PROCEED HONGKONG AND AWAIT INSTRUCTIONS." Enroute, Miller stopped at Singapore where UP correspondent Wee Kim Wee informed him that the State Department had again threatened to prosecute any reporters going to China.

Nevertheless, Miller planned to go on, but before the next flight to Hong Kong another cable from Johnson ordered him to "RETURN SYDNEY SOONEST."

Frank Bartholomew, UP President, told Miller later that a Justice Department representative had visited Lyle Wilson, Washington manager, and said the pending plan to merge UP and International News Service would be opposed by the government if a UP reporter went to China. State Department pressure was also exerted on a dozen other news organizations, which had no merger plans.

In Miller's opinion, the correspondent said many years later, this surrender on the principle of press freedom "allowed the blinded and ear-muffed American public to be skidded into an East-West war in Vietnam that might have been limited to what it should have been: a dirty little civil war between North and South Vietnam, not the international conflagration that killed and crippled tens of thousands of Americans."[1]

Dulles, in a letter to the *New York Times* Publisher Arthur Hays Sulzberger, argued that constitutional guarantee of press freedom applied to the distribution of news and not to its collection. He suggested American news agencies ought to hire foreigners to cover news in Peiping for them. The UP replied that the American people needed reports from American journalists.

Fifteen years later, the State Department relented. In 1971 "ping pong diplomacy" saw the admission of several U.S. correspondents into China. UPI was not among them through its own fault.

The U.S. table tennis team, led by Graham B. Steenhoven, had made a poor showing in a tournament at Nagoya, Japan. China saw an opportunity to exploit its team, which had dominated the tournament. The weak American "ping pongers," along with others from Canada, Colombia, Britain and Nigeria, received unexpected invitations to play in the Peoples Republic of China. The Chinese intended to get recognition—if not diplomatically, at least in the sport of table tennis.

UPI hired Geraldine Resek, who was with the U.S. team but was not a journalist, to report on the games in Peiping.

Albert E. Kaff, UPI vice president in Tokyo, was alarmed when he learned that AP, the opposition, was sending a full-time experienced staff member, John Roderick, to cover the event. NBC was also sending an American reporter, John Rich.

How could these services get into forbidden China? In a frantic call to Peiping, Kaff learned that the reason UPI did not get admitted was because the agency had not applied to go and the others had.

When the tournament started, however, UPI in Tokyo began receiving excellent reports from a freelancer, Julian Schuman, who offered his service for $150 a day. Kaff speculated later that the Red Chinese had assigned Schuman, a sympathizer with the Communist regime, to cover for UPI because they wanted as much publicity as possible for their "ping pong diplomacy."

Difficulty in covering China continued for years. Americans received only sketchy news from China picked up by travelers or heard on Chinese radio broadcasts.

A breakthrough came the next year, in 1972, when President Nixon visited China, accompanied by eighty-seven U.S. reporters. This trip initiated a friendlier relationship between the two countries.

Nixon dumbfounded the world by flying to Peking to end the standoff that had dominated U.S.-China relations since 1949 when the communists drove Chiang Kai-shek from the mainland to Taiwan.

Stewart Hensley, UP's diplomatic reporter, was with an advance group of correspondents who accompanied Secretary of State Henry Kissinger there to smooth the way for the president's visit. They were met in Shanghai by the "Revolutionary Committee for Press and Radio," which provided each of eighty-seven American reporters with an interpreter and a guide.

Su Yuan-chien was assigned to Hensley. He was a very pleasant guide, showing the UPI reporter the Great Wall and other sights. However, when asked at lunch what happened to Lin Piao, Mao Tse-Tung's designated successor who had disappeared, the Chinese guide answered: "Have some more soup."

The Nixon-Mao meeting was more like a Hollywood production than a news event. "Everything seemed carefully organized for us," observed Bill Lyons, UPI photo representative who also was with the press group.

A press center was set up in the west wing of the Cultural Palace of the Nationalities. "It had bowling alleys and a basketball court, but no typewriters, no paper," said Hensley. He said twenty-two tables were arranged with white tablecloths and exactly 154 chairs, the precise number of foreign correspondents on hand. Pig-tailed waitresses in white jackets "never allowed a correspondent to remain without a cup of green tea."

Usually emotionless reporters, perhaps because they had little else to do, were affected emotionally by the drama, feeling that they were in on important history being made. Walter Cronkite, then with CBS, said when the Chinese band played the Star Spangled Banner for Nixon's arrival "We all felt a chill run up our spines."

White House UP reporter Helen Thomas, who arrived in Peking on *Air Force One* with Nixon, said it was "the most exciting story I have ever covered.

"Everything was news," including such urgent information as the disclosure that you could buy an acupuncture doll in Peking for less than $1.

"It was a joy to have my editors ask via transpacific satellite 'What's Pat [Nixon's wife] wearing?' What's the menu? and 'What does your hotel room look like?

"This was the first time they ever cared," said Thomas. There were no news conferences during the Peking summit, but a communiqué released when the U.S. delegation moved to Shanghai revealed that the two nations would work to resume diplomatic relations.

Ronald F. Cohen, overnight editor in Washington, was on the phone with Thomas as she dictated a stream of information about China. UPI had decided to keep the phone line to Shanghai open for hours despite the heavy cost, so that a flash would not be delayed.

While Thomas was dictating from a telephone on the second floor of the Shanghai hotel, Hensley picked up the press release downstairs, flipped through the pages to find the news, then headed for the phone upstairs.

The veteran State Department correspondent was a heavy smoker and suffered from emphysema. Still, he raced up a long flight of steps ahead of everyone else. Helen handed him the phone. Cohen, in Washington, was poised for a flash.

"I could hear Hensley huffing and fighting for breath," Cohen recalled. "It was scary. I was afraid Stu might pass out. It seemed like forever before he was able to talk and give me the flash."

Before one of the rare public events at which reporters were allowed, Ron Ziegler, White House press aide, coached a reporter to ask the question: "Mr. Nixon, What do you think of the Great Wall?" It was asked.

The president, smiling for photographers, replied: "I think the Great Wall is a great wall."[2]

An international event of this magnitude required UPI and other news agencies to pull out the stops. UPI was represented by a full team, including Thomas, Hensley and photo chief Bill Lyons, plus reporter Norman Kempster, Audio correspondent Donald Fulsom and photographers Frank Cancellare and Dirck Halstead.

UPI did benefit from the trip. The cordial meetings between Nixon and Mao resulted later that year in agreement between UPI and Hsinhua, the offical Chinese news agency, for an exchange of news and pictures.

The narrow slit in the Bamboo Curtain also made it possible for a limited number of American journalists to get U.S. visas to visit the Chinese mainland.

With the situation softening, the UPI in May 1972, organized a two-week visit by twenty-five American newspaper executives to China, led by Rod Beaton, president of UPI. This was followed in September by the UPI hosting eleven representatives of Hsinhua, for ten days in the U.S. Beaton later made a second trip with a small UPI team to work out details of the news exchange.

There were many nettlesome details both political and technical. The Chinese demanded that UPI use the term "China mainland" instead of "mainland China." This quibble had something to do with the United States diplomatic ties with Taipei, at odds for years with the mainland.

In 1975, President Ford visited China. UPI's versatile writer Richard Growald went with him. In one of Growald's stories he reported that Chinese press officials had a "terrible and wonderful way to answer any request." It always was: "That's no problem at all—it's impossible."

Growald's dispatch carried direct quotes from a Chinese official who met privately with Henry Kissinger. Other correspondents were outraged because the meeting had been held in private at the Great Hall of the People and when it ended none of the participants made any comment to reporters waiting outside. The UPI correspondent was accused of fabricating the quotes, shocking prevailing journalistic ethics.

Kissinger reportedly confronted Growald and asked him where he got the quotes. Growald responded, "I have my sources."

In 1978 when diplomatic relations were formally agreed on, twenty-seven American correspondents went to China for the ceremonies.

Chinese officials put on a show of liberality for the newspeople, allowing them to visit the Great Wall and other sights. But every correspondent and photographer had a Chinese chaperone throughout. UPI photographer Rickio Imajo shot a picture in a Peiping beauty shop while his host watched, puzzled at the photographer's interest in that shop.

Robert Crabbe of UPI reported that when he got aboard a crowded subway train, a Chinese soldier offered him his seat. Crabbe said he tried to decline but the soldier stood up, grabbed him by the collar and threw him into the seat.

On January 30, 1979, after seven years of negotiations, an agreement was announced between the Peoples Republic of China and the United States permitting an exchange of news. The UPI, AP and the *New York Times* could open bureaus in Peiping, and the New China News Agency could open a bureau in Washington.

Crabbe and Aline Mosby, who had worked in Moscow and Paris, were assigned to Peiping by UPI. When the Associated Press learned that UPI was going to assign Mosby to the post in China, it decided to change its staff in Peiping to include a woman, Victoria Graham.

United Press International and other western agencies had continuing problems in communist countries of Asia and Europe. Anthony J. Cavendish, a top UPI diplomatic correspondent, sent a dispatch from Ludz, Poland, reporting that five persons were injured when police suppressed a strike of streetcar workers. He was accused of "tendentious" reporting and ordered to leave Poland within a week.

Cavendish told the Polish police that he had seen hospital records of the five injured. An official replied that the use of the phrase "at least" implied there were more than that number. The transit workers strike was one of the first displays of Polish protest against Soviet rule. *Trybuna Ludu*, a newspaper published by the government and controlled by staunch communists, editorially criticized First Secretary Gomulka for failing to quell the strike instantly.

"No strike, particularly in public utility enterprises, is a proper way of settling even the correct demands of the strikers," the Soviet controlled paper said. That was the beginning of the end for Soviet hegemony.

After World War II, a large Eastern and Central Europe service had been started by UP. Prague, Czechoslovakia, became its hub, largely owing to the fact that money earned in the Eastern bloc countries could not be converted into western currency. So bills and salaries in the region were paid with the Czech kronas.

Because of the abundant Eastern bloc currency, employees in Prague found it easier to get pay raises than staffers in other parts of Europe. But they had other things to worry about. The Czech government continually harassed western news services because they were bringing in unfiltered news from the West.

Helen Fisher, an American on the Prague UP staff, became a target of Czech secret police, who planned to arrest her and try her as a spy. Dick Clark, Prague manager, was tipped about the plan. He got on the telephone to Fisher and ordered her to leave immediately for Switzerland, ostensibly to cover a ski event.

Because Fisher was then out of reach, the communist regime turned, instead, to William Oatis of the AP. He was imprisoned as an alleged spy and tried in a widely publicized show trial.

Other staffers in Prague who were in jeopardy got help from UP in escaping from the country. Among them were Ivan Zverina and his wife, Czechs, who were smuggled out and worked for a time in Germany, then moved to the United States.

In January 1957, Norman Gorrell of UP and nine other western correspondents visited the kingdom of Yemen where clashes with Great Britain were occurring along Yemen's border with the Western Aden protectorate.[3]

On the other side of the world, President Sukarno of Indonesia launched an attack against United Press for reporting on a brief military insurrection in northern Sumatra in December 1956. The dictator said the foreign press was interfering in his country's internal affairs by putting out stories that led to criticism of his government.

Sukarno's problems with rebellious factions in his military forces continued and attacks against the western press continued. In May 1957, Jack Russell, UP bureau chief in Jakarta, was called in and lectured because his stories "had not received official clearance."[4]

Sukarno served notice to the UP that he was "entitled to restrict the dissemination of news" concerning the rebellion.[5]

In Haiti, another new revolutionary government, headed by President Francois Duvalier, seized power. U.S. officials feared civil war would break out in the Caribbean nation. They warned 1,500 American citizens living there to leave. Duvalier's military junta, which had deposed Paul E. Magloire as president, accused UP reporter James F. Cunningham of meddling in the country's internal politics.

Cunningham had reported the death of Shibley Talamas, an American citizen, while in the custody of Haitian military authorities. Talamas had been assured he would not be hurt, Cunningham reported.[6]

When Cunningham returned to the United States on vacation in February 1958, he was denied permission to return to Port-au-Prince. He was told his "tourist" admission had expired.[7]

In 1950, when Joseph Stalin was in poor health, a garbled rogue transmission caused a problem for UP. The "undertime" wire, which clients were not supposed to be on, clicked out the following:

"X';ADF STALIN ...OKRRSSX###
EAD 444"

It was unaddressed, unsigned, had no dateline, did not carry any bells, and appeared as garble on a wire that was supposed to be dead. No half-witted editor would have taken it as a legitimate news flash. But a few radio stations, which had been accidentally left on the wire, seized it and broadcast that Stalin was dead.

The next day, New York editors saw fit to send out a memo to all the agency's customers explaining that the transmission with Stalin's name in it was a mystery and probably originated in the phone company.

In 1950 Russ Jones of UP won the agency's first Pulitzer Prize for his dramatic eyewitness reporting of the Soviet Union's military suppression of a budding revolt in Hungary.

When the crisis loomed, Jones made his way from Germany to Budapest. He filed a dramatic running story as Russian tanks rolled up the street in front of the bureau. His bulletins stopped only when Soviet soldiers presented themselves at the door of the bureau.

Under Hugh Baillie, the UP had boycotted the Pulitzers because Baillie believed the selection committee was biased against UP. Kent Cooper, general manager of the Associated Press, was on the Pulitzer Prize Board from 1931 to 1956. During that period the AP received 14 Pulitzers and UP not a single one, although it was generally acknowledged in the news industry that UP dispatches were often more professionally and vibrantly written than the AP's.

In 1954 when noted author Ernest Hemingway was lost in Africa and thought to have been killed in a plane crash, AP reported perfunctorily that he was found alive.

The UP lead said: "Ernest Hemingway walked out of the jungle today, carrying a bunch of bananas and a bottle of gin. 'My luck, she is running good,' he said." Eugene Patterson, on the desk in New York, was writing from sketchy information called in by a stringer in Entebbe, Africa.[8]

When Marshal Petain, the French traitor of World War II, was dying imprisoned on Ile d'Yeu off the coast of France in 1951, UP in Paris set up plans to be informed when the general died. Robert Ahier was sent to the island from Paris. As a back-up measure in case telephone communications were cut, a fishing boat near the island was engaged to radio the news to another fishing boat at Brest, which would relay it to the Paris bureau by telephone.

One night, John Law, the Paris overnight staffer, received a call from Ahier: "Petain is dead. Petain est mort." He repeated three times in each language then the line went dead.

Law sent the flash and bulletin.

New York sent back:

"CONGRATS PETAIN. OSN UNHAS."

An hour later another cable from New York:

"CHEERS PETAIN. YOU STILL EXCLUSIVE."

Then, after another hour:

> "YOU STILL EXCLUSIVE WITH PETAIN DEATH. DISREGARD
> CONGRATS. OSN HAS OFFICIALS DENYING PETAIN
> DEAD."

Bill Landrey, who was on the Paris staff at the time, recalled that Bureau Manager Joe Grigg called him at 2 A.M. and ordered him into the office.

"I dressed, got on my bicycle and pedaled as fast as I could across the Seine to the office," said Landrey. "Joe was writing a lead:

> "MARSHAL HENRI PHILLIPPE PETAINE RALLIED MIRACU-
> LOUSLY TONIGHT AFTER DOCTORS HAD ALREADY
> PRONOUNCED THAT HIS HEART HAD STOPPED."

Grigg's "rowback" lead reviving Petain became a UP legend. Petain died a short while afterward, on July 23, 1951.[9]

When called to account for his error, Ahier explained that he had overheard the Petain death report from another reporter on the island.

Throughout United Press International's life, it had arrangements with other news services to exchange news. At one time it served 39 foreign agencies. They ranged from the Kyodo in Japan, DPA in Germany, and TASS in the U.S.S.R. to Antara in Indonesia, KNA in Kenya and PARS in Iran.

When UPI grew stronger in a country, the exchange arrangement was often discontinued. The reasons for these agreements and for ending them were varied. It might be the number of clients in the country, the foreign exchange rates, availability of communications facilities, the political scene in the country, or the availability of personnel with appropriate language skills.

An agreement with the South African Press Association was terminated in 1957 when UP saw an opportunity to sell radio news directly to broadcasters in the region. George Peeples set up a bureau in Johannesburg with a staff of 11 resident reporters.

As one tactic in the East-West cold war, the U.S. government mounted a propaganda blitz throughout the world. Activity by the U.S. Information Agency (USIA) aimed at influencing public opinion abroad against the Soviet Union swelled until 1957. The USIA was spending $113 million a year, and its chief, Arthur Larson, was asking Congress for $144 million for fiscal 1958.

Legislators, with Democratic Senator Lyndon B. Johnson in the forefront, wanted to slash that budget. Johnson said the USIA wasted more money than any other agency in government. Larson appealed to the Senate Appropriations Subcommittee, saying his agency had "awesome responsibilities" to offset communist propaganda.

The debate involved United Press because the USIA was, in effect, giving away a modified and propagandized version of the news that it was getting from the wire services and which UP and AP were trying to sell in foreign countries.

In a letter to the subcommittee, Frank Bartholomew, president of UP, said the USIA should be limited to reporting official acts of the U.S. government and possibly the reaction to them.

Frank Starzel, Associated Press general manager, on the other hand, said free distribution of the news by a government agency was not "harmful or disadvantageous" to the AP—which depended less on foreign clients than UP. Nor did a letter from International News Service object to the activities of the USIA. UP stood alone on that issue. The appropriation for 1958 was eventually cut by $50 million.[10]

21

A Forgotten Raincoat

THANKS TO A CONSCIENTIOUS BUREAU MANAGER AND A FORGOTTEN raincoat, United Press was able to alert the world to the start of the Korean War.

Jack James, UP's bureau manager in Seoul, scored a significant beat when he made the first report of the invasion of South Korea by the North on June 25, 1950. Not even the U.S. government or the United Nations had any report of the action until United Press dispatches began moving. It was a two hour 40 minute beat.

In New York, Eugene Patterson and Charlie McCann, two veteran editors, were on duty. "Bulletin! Break 'em up!" Patterson shouted. The flash was on the wire in seconds. This was late Saturday and near closing time for Sunday morning newspapers.

Patterson recalled: "AP, as usual, tried to pee on it (the UP report) with one of their patented doorholders: 'We are checking reports that…' But Julius Frandsen in Washington was already informing General Omar Bradley of the Joint Chiefs that they had a war on their hands."

The *New York Times,* in a historic case of journalistic arrogance, refused to print the story because AP had not "confirmed" it. The *Times* editor later wrote United Press an unusual letter of apology "for letting AP talk him out of printing our scoop and thus missing an edition on the start of a war," said Patterson.[1]

James' beat was partly luck. But it was not pure luck.

As a responsible bureau manager, he went into the office every Sunday morning to check the wires, while most correspondents took the day off.

James had planned a picnic later in the day, but was going to the bureau first. It started to drizzle and he remembered he had left his raincoat at the U.S. Embassy press room. He would stop and get it.

A U.S. military attaché saw James hastening to the press room. Assuming the UP correspondent knew about the North Korean invasion, he asked, "What do you hear from the border?"

Up to that point James had heard nothing about the invasion, but the officer's question gave him the scent of a story. "Not much. What do you hear?"

"I hear it's started everywhere but Eighth Division Area," the officer told James. That was enough. The picnic was forgotten.

There had been warnings of a communist buildup north of the 38th parallel, which divided the country after World War II, but on that weekend there was no indication of anything imminent. Half the Korean army was on weekend leave. Experts thought if an invasion occurred, it would likely be after the rainy season, in August.

James began phoning around. He hesitated to file anything to New York until it was sourced. There had been many false alarms. Dependable information was hard to come by. Telephones to the border area were down. Military radio facilities were swamped.

Going over to the Korean Defense Ministry, James found generals asking him what he knew about the invasion. After two hours of digging, he was certain something was going on at the border, and he knew it was deadline time for Sunday morning newspapers in New York. He filed a bulletin saying the North Koreans had "launched general attacks along the 38th parallel." He advised the desk not to call it a war at that point because it might be no more than a probing action.

A half hour after filing the bulletin, James saw North Korean airplanes dropping bombs on Seoul. This removed his doubts.

UP's break ahead of all opposition at a crucial time for U.S. newspapers strengthened the agency's credibility. An aggressive effort was launched to stay ahead on the war that President Truman called a "police action," but cost 50,000 American casualties.

Reinforcements were quickly sent: Rutherford Poats and Peter Kalischer from Tokyo and Charles Moore and Glenn Stackhouse from San Francisco. The battlefront staff also included Robert Bennyhoff, Bob Vermillion, Doc Quigg, Joe Quinn, Robert C. Miller, Pete Webb, LeRoy Hansen, Fred Painton and Murray Moler. Earnest Hoberecht, Tokyo chief, was backed up by Frank Tremaine and Ralph Teatsworth.

Charles Corddry, UP's aviation expert in Washington, was sent over to do stories on the air war.

The American Unipressers were aided by the Japanese staff in Tokyo and by Korean George Suh in Seoul, who was able to provide reports from the South Korean capital after the city was taken until the communist invaders arrested him. He was not released until Seoul was liberated.

Harry Ferguson, with experience in World War II, was named foreign news editor in New York to supervise war coverage.

Within two days of the outbreak of fighting, Hoberecht arranged to lease the only 24-hour radio-teletype circuit from Korea to Tokyo for UP's exclusive use. This gave the service an advantage throughout the war. Other correspondents had to wait in line to use military communications when available, or wait their turn on the single telephone line to Tokyo. Several hundred correspondents showed up and communications became chaotic.

United Press spent $1,000 a day just getting copy from the war front by telephone, radio and cable. Reporters called from anywhere they could get access to a telephone.

Hoberecht also bought around-the-clock radio-teletype service from Tokyo to New York. News was relayed through a receiving station at Moraga, California. The circuit was called the "Jagcast."

At Moraga, east of San Francisco, dispatches were transcribed and relayed instantly on a special cross-country wire.

Commercial radio-teletype facilities of Press Wireless, Mackay and RCA, were also used. Urgent copy went two or three separate routes to ensure prompt delivery.

Reporter Robert Vermillion was one of the first correspondent casualties in Korea. He jumped with the 187th Airborne Regiment at Suchon in the first parachute assault of the war, broke a few bones landing and had to be hospitalized.

Peter Kalischer landed in Korea early enough to accompany American troops on their first foray against the North Korean invaders. He saw U.S. troops being overrun by the enemy and barely escaped capture himself. His dispatches were the first with detail on the dramatic hand-to-hand battle scene.

On the Fourth of July 1950, Kalischer was in a foxhole overlooking a road near Osan. He was with a small band of U.S. troops when a line of twenty Russian-built tanks appeared only yards away and opened a torrent of fire at them. The American troops had only their rifles to fire back and soon broke into headlong panicked retreat. Kalischer and a few other survivors found shelter in a farmhouse.

The next day an enemy broadcast announced Kalischer was a prisoner, but he wasn't. He made it to Taejon and filed his account of the North Korean onslaught. He quoted an American soldier who told him, "I never saw such a useless damned war in all my life."

Colonel Marion P. Echols, public information officer for the U.S. army in Korea, did not like what he considered negative reporting and he cracked down on Kalischer. When he went to Tokyo on a break from front-line duty, Echols pulled his credentials, saying he had given aid and comfort to the enemy.

General MacArthur summoned Kalischer and Tom Lambert of AP, who had also been kicked out of Korea. He told them they could go back to the front but warned them to be careful.

Robert Bennyhoff, who had come in the first wave of correspondents, was the only reporter with South Korean forces when they drove an invading force back across the 38th parallel. He had attached himself to a ROK (Republic of Korea) army unit trying to drive back the invaders. The only other Americans with this army were a small group of military advisors.

Bennyhoff improvised the best communications system on the battlefront.

"Somebody had sent us, by mistake, an RTT (Radio Teletype Truck), complete with microwave transmitter" he recalled in an interview for this history. "There was a technician who set it up but no one knew how to punch a Teletype."

Bennyhoff made a deal with the officers to send their military traffic if they would let him use the facility for his own stories. Besides being able to file his copy to UP, he read much of the military traffic.

"I saw a battle order saying the unit was going to cross the 38th parallel next morning at 4 A.M. The United Nations had been saying the border would not be crossed," he said. Bennyhoff wrote a story in advance and sent it to the press headquarters at Taegu, telling them to hold it until he called.

"Sure enough, we went across the parallel about eight hours after they told us we weren't going to do it," said Bennyhoff.

After moving eight miles into North Korea, he hitched a plane ride back to the ROK army's headquarters, went to his Teletype truck and filed another detailed dispatch on the intrusion into North Korea. Since he was the only correspondent with the ROK unit, United Press had its exclusive.

A dozen other correspondents rushed to the scene but Bennyhoff had the radio truck parked in a wooded area away from the headquarters. For several days, he alone was able to file stories on the action, getting them out hours before the opposition.

Bennyhoff knew there was still some telephone service functioning in Korea. On a hill watching a battle between North Korean and South Korean tanks, he picked up a field telephone and asked for "Danger." That was the 24th Division headquarters. When he got it he asked the operator to put him through to "Scotch," the Taegu base. He asked the operator there if he could be put through to Tokyo. Reaching the Tokyo operator he asked if the line could be patched to New York. A few moments later he was talking to a desk man in the New York bureau.

The UPI man in the New York was surprised.

"Bennyhoff? I thought you were in Korea."

"I am," said Bob, "I'm sitting here watching a tank battle." UP had an eyewitness account direct from the battlefront. It was a brilliant communications scoop. "We could hear each other perfectly," he said. "Remember, this was long before we had satellites."

Peter Webb of UP was confined to quarters at 8th Army headquarters in Korea, accused of premature disclosure of the death of Lieutenant General Walton H. Walker.

Webb and a correspondent for the *London Daily Mirror* were on a road near Seoul when they came upon an overturned Jeep with stars stenciled on its frame and a pool of blood underneath. A pair of dark glasses, Walker's trademark, lay in the mud.

Webb hurried to the nearest field hospital, where he heard a surgeon telling a group of officers Walker was dead. Webb had already phoned the story to Tokyo when he was ordered to hold it for an official release. Webb called the Tokyo desk but the news was already on the wires. Webb was released then but a week later MacArthur imposed full military censorship.

When Rutherford Poats was rotated back to Korea from Tokyo after a short break from the front, he borrowed four homing pigeons from the *Mainichi* Shimbum. Japanese reporters in Tokyo routinely used pigeons to send copy and film to their office to avoid the city's heavy street traffic.

The UP bureau was on the eighth floor of the *Mainichi* building. The pigeon cage was nearby, just outside the men's room door.

After getting back to the war front, Poats clipped dispatches on their ankles and launched them on two successive days from a Korea airstrip.

William Prochnau, in a book about the war,[2] says the pigeons arrived in Tokyo eleven days later, their feathers bedraggled. However, Poats himself, in a war reminiscence in 1996, said, "These undoubtedly communist-bribed birds never reached our Tokyo editors."

The pigeon flop was the least of Poats' experiences at the battlefront. One day he and Ken Kantor, previously with UP but then with NBC, were driving along with a detachment of Marines fighting to retake Seoul following General MacArthur's bold troop landings at Inchon.

North Korean planes appeared overhead and began strafing the column. "We all dove into a gully beside the road," recalled Kantor. "I landed on top of Poats, pushing him into the mud.

"As Rud grimly turned his buried mucked up face toward me, I realized we had landed in what the military not so euphemistically called a 'piss trench.'"[3]

By midwinter 1950–51, United Press was moving 30,000 words a day from Korea and was able to get the first paragraphs of a dispatch on the wire in the U.S. while the story was still being dictated by a reporter on the front.

The Inchon landing, covered by Robert C. Miller, took place September 19, 1950. Miller wrote that "never before in the history of amphibious warfare had a more successful assault been made." To get his story out ahead of the opposition, Miller used an old wire service trick. He filed a hold-for-release dispatch, leaving it with the censors at Pusan before the invasion force sailed. He told them to transmit it when the landings occurred. Miller then went on the beach in the sixth combat landing of his UP career. The others had been in World War II.

Robert C. Miller caused some soul searching when he came home from the war in the spring of 1952 and told a meeting of editors that dispatches coming from Korea were sometimes "pure fabrication" and that he and other reporters had filed them because the stories were issued by "responsible military headquarters."

Earl Johnson, general news manager of UP, said the Korean War was "the first war we have covered without military censorship."[4] But, in fact, there was censorship. The U.S. army issued a directive to all its commanders telling them what could be reported. These commanders advised correspondents what the restrictions were and what would happen if they were circumvented. What had been changed in contrast to other wars was that news dispatches did not have to be submitted to a censor before they were transmitted. Instead, reporters were told what was off limits and that they would be disciplined if they violated "security."

Ironically, this censor-free policy was criticized by correspondents and news agencies. They didn't know exactly what they could publish without getting into trouble. Military commanders imposed local and unwritten rules.

When the U.N. command decided it had to institute understandable rules for everybody, it made them tighter than any previous censorship in U.S. history. Reporters could not use the word "retreat," and were subject to court martial for undefined infractions of security.

On the home front, the Defense Department asked United Press and other agencies to refrain from carrying news about call-up of National Guard and Reserve units and troop movements.

Dispatches from Korea were prepared for client wires by the "war desk" in New York for the first year of the conflict. The "war desk" was transferred to the San Francisco bureau in 1951.

The Korean War was not a declared war with the entire country physically and emotionally involved. Much of life in America went on as if Korea was no more than a distant geographical region.

On a quiet Sunday in the spring of 1951, it was disclosed in Korea that the communists had agreed to negotiate for a truce.

Frank Bartholomew, Pacific Division Manager, was relaxing at his vineyard ranch in Sonoma, California. He called the San Francisco bureau as he often did to get a news fill-in. Dick Harnett, who was manning the Sunday shift, told Bartholomew about the truce talk announcement. Bartholomew asked for details, said thanks and hung up. He called the bureau an hour later to say that he had made a flight reservation to Tokyo and was leaving that night for Korea.

When he arrived at the United Nations press headquarters below the 38th parallel, he and other correspondents were told they could not go to Kaesong, where the truce talks were to take place. They were to remain at a press camp twenty miles south.

Bartholomew was a UP vice president and the senior correspondent at the scene. He fired off a telegram to General Matthew B. Ridgeway, commander of UN forces. "I am sure you do not want all the news coming from the conference to originate with the communists," he told Ridgeway. "The American people need their own reporters at the talks."

Speaking for sixty-one correspondents who had arrived at the press camp, Bartholomew braced Colonel Andrew J. Kinney, who was in charge of the preliminary arrangements. Bartholomew said American news reporters must be allowed to cover the truce meetings, whether the communists liked it or not. Kinney agreed to allow twenty correspondents to accompany the truce delegation to the talks, with the pool to change each day.

Bartholomew was in the first group. A communist military checkpoint stopped the convoy and said the correspondents could not go on to Kaesong. This resulted in Kinney calling the entire delegation back to base.

The truce negotiations got under way a few days later, with the UN reporters present at the talks. At the end of each day, the correspondents were transported by truck back to UN lines. UP had a jeep and driver waiting to grab copy from the reporter who attended the meeting and rush it back to the press camp to be phoned to Seoul.

When "Bart" was not in the pool, he was the jeep courier. Earnest Hoberecht, UP's Tokyo chief, was waiting at the camp to take the dispatch and dictate it by telephone to the Seoul bureau.

Hoberecht wrote in his memoir[5] that Bart drove the jeep so recklessly fast that he picked up the name "Hot-Rod Bart." One day the competition services, INS and AP, joined forces to beat Bart to the telephone. One driver would take the copy for both services and the other would cut off Bart's jeep.

When Bartholomew saw the "enemy" vehicle cut in front of him, he turned off the road and sped across an airstrip, arriving at the press camp three minutes ahead of the AP jeep. After a day of that, the army halted the race by imposing a speed limit.

No speed limits were needed for the long and rancorous truce negotiations, beginning at Kaesong in North Korean held territory and moving to Panmunjom in a demilitarized zone near the 38th parallel. The truce was not effectuated until July 27, 1953.

22

Embracing the "I"

ON SATURDAY, MAY 24, 1958, A STORY MOVED ON THE UP AND INS wires from New York, numbered NX1.

NEW YORK MAY 24 (UPI)—THE UNITED PRESS ASSOCIA-TIONS AND INTERNATIONAL NEWS SERVICE JOINED FORCES TODAY AROUND THE WORLD IN THE CREATION OF A SINGLE NEWS AGENCY NAMED "UNITED PRESS INTERNATIONAL."

THIS IS THE FIRST DISPATCH OF THE NEW SERVICE WHICH WILL EMBRACE THE LARGEST NUMBER OF NEWSPAPER AND RADIO CLIENTS EVER SERVED SIMULTANEOUSLY BY AN INDEPENDENTLY OPERATED NEWS AND PICTURE AGENCY.

Ironically, Associated Press, the enemy of both UP and INS, scored a beat over them on their own story. A day earlier, on Friday afternoon, the Dow Jones wire carried a brief bulletin saying the merger was in the works. AP picked up the Dow Jones report and distributed it. An official of Hearst, the owner of INS, had released the news to D.J. before disclosing it to employees of INS.[1]

UPI's merger story went on to say that an agreement for the consolidation of the two services was signed on May 16. The delay of its announcement was to arrange the physical wire changes. It was a complex operation, switching clients, moving wires and equipment, and coordinating changes so that the flow of news continued without interruption to clients of both services.

There was also a rumor that the Justice Department was breathing heavily in the shadows, with the threat of an antitrust injunction against the plan.

Everyone agreed that economic considerations were the most important factor in the merger. Neither UP nor INS had been able to make a profit while competing with each other and against the Associated Press, which, as a cooperative, did not have to prove itself financially. In the mind of Frank H. Bartholomew, UPI's president, another very important consideration was the opportunity to add all the Hearst newspapers to UPI wires.

The idea of merger between the two smaller news services had been simmering for years. On October 8, 1926, the AP declared that Hearst was responsible for an "ever-recurring evasion and nullification of the obligations" of AP members. It threatened to pull the plug on fifteen Hearst newspapers.

In order to deal with the problem, Moses Koenigsberg, who was running INS, proposed that the wire service be separated from the Hearst newspapers and made an independent company.

A committee appointed by Hearst, consisting of Koenigsberg, Victor H. Polachek, Bradford Merrill and Morrill Goddard, urged William Randolph Hearst, Jr., to seek a consolidation of INS with United Press. Hearst responded immediately in a coded letter signed with his code name, "Doctor." He said UP executives had submitted a proposal and he would be undertaking negotiations.

Koenigsberg later said the possibility of a merger with UP was nearly destroyed at a meeting between Hearst and Roy W. Howard. Howard visited Hearst's San Simeon castle on the bluffs overlooking the Pacific Ocean. "Mr. Hearst, you know how to run newspapers, but we know how to run a wire service. Why not join INS and UP?"

Hearst's reply: "Well, you know, a mother is always fondest of her sickest child. So I guess I will just keep INS."

Koenigsberg said Hearst was offended by Howard's remark, even though it was innocently intended.[2]

During the following three decades, UP officials occasionally turned come-hither eyes at INS but the desire was not reciprocated.

In 1955 under Hugh Baillie, UP made a serious effort to combine the picture services of the two agencies. Mims Thomason, UP vice president, and Frank Tremaine, who headed UP photo operations, met with Seymour Berkson of the Hearst Corporation in New York. Berkson was against any merger, Tremaine recalled.

When Frank Bartholomew succeeded Baillie as president, he was obsessed with the idea of taking over INS. He raised the possibility of a merger whenever he was negotiating a service agreement with the Hearst newspapers.

One of Bartholomew's neighbors at his vineyard in Sonoma, California, was E. D. Coblentz, a prominent San Francisco attorney who happened to be on Hearst's legal team. "Bart" cornered his neighbor occasionally and pressed the merger idea.

In November 1956, Bartholomew and a Scripps attorney met with Jacob D. Gortatowsky and Kingsbury Smith, of INS, at the Brook Club in New York. Smith opposed any merger. He insisted that INS had status as a major news service and had employees as dedicated to their organization as UP people were to theirs.

The two sides agreed to keep the talks secret and meet again in two weeks. They did so at a hotel in Santa Barbara, California, where Gortatowsky often vacationed. The motivation for secrecy was to keep the proposal out of the sight of the Justice

Department, which was then touchy about news media mergers because newspaper consolidation was eliminating competition in many cities.

Robert O'Dell, who owned the Santa Barbara hotel and was a friend of both Bartholomew and Gortatowsky, almost scuttled the secrecy inadvertently. He thought it would be nice to have a record of the meeting of the two top wire service executives together and called in a photographer to take their picture in the lobby. At the sight of the waiting camera, Bart and Gorty heeled back into the elevator and headed "up."

The talks were interrupted early in 1957 so that Bartholomew could discuss the matter with the UP board of directors.

The board met February 11 in New York. It "turned out disastrously," Bartholomew wrote in his memoir. "Roy Howard would not permit me to finish my presentation, condemning vigorously and dramatically most of the basic steps taken."

Howard said he could negotiate a better deal in two days with Hearst. Bart challenged him to do it. Howard said he'd have it done in 48 hours.[3]

The UP president said afterward he made a mistake by taking it to the board at that stage. He said he had more trouble selling the idea to the UP board than he did to Hearst people.

Nothing more happened until July when Bartholomew, attending the annual Bohemian Grove campout in Northern California, talked with Charles E. Scripps, who was at the campout that year. Charles was then the top executive of the E.W. Scripps Company, which owned UP. Bartholomew persuaded him to support a merger at the next UP board meeting in September.

Charles quietly talked to others in the Scripps structure and, at the September meeting, the consensus was to go ahead with the merger. Roy Howard then supported it. Bart resumed talking to Jacob D. Gortatowsky, the Hearst point man.

When Bart left on a European vacation in 1957, he asked LeRoy Keller, UP's sales manager, to become "caretaker of the conversations" on merger during his absence.[4]

Keller recalled later, "I spent the summer courting Charlie McCabe, who had worked for United Press before joining Hearst and was publisher of the *New York Mirror*. 'Bart is determined to get this done,' I told him. 'You know both sides of it. You worked for UP and now with Hearst. I want you to tell me what you think it will take for Hearst to let loose, give up INS.'

"He said, 'I have done a lot of thinking about it. To get it done you will have to give Hearst stock in United Press, maybe not 50 percent, but some equity.'

"I said, 'All right, if that's what it will take, I will see what I can do.' I went back to Bart with this and he said, 'Ho, ho, ho! You know Roy Howard is not going to permit that.'"

They then had lunch with Howard and presented the idea. Keller won a two-dollar bet from Bart when Howard agreed that Hearst could be given a minority ownership position in a merged service.

Keller went back to Charles McCabe, who then back-tracked and said it would have to be a "50-50" deal, with Hearst owning half. The UP executives knew that would never be accepted by Scripps-Howard. However, by getting McCabe to start talking merger, "we were on our way," Keller recalled.

Although not signed until the middle of May, 1958, the consolidation had been agreed to in principle eight months earlier, in September, 1957. That was when top Hearst and Scripps-Howard officials gave their consent to the consolidation. The specifics and arrangements were put in the hands of Bartholomew and LeRoy Keller of UP and Gortatowsky and Smith of INS.

In the final deal, Hearst got five percent of UPI. Keller said this amount was decided on the basis of what INS was worth. "We laid the equities on the table and you could see they didn't deserve more than five percent," said Keller[5]

Keller, the UP vice president, was a quiet, shrewd operator who had learned how to handle business matters delicately.

At a crucial point in the merger talks, Keller was invited to a dinner party at the Waldorf-Astoria Hotel, sponsored by Spyros Skouras, the Greek financier who was backing Twentieth Century Fox, with which UP was working in television news.

During the reception, Keller recalled later, "I spied Dick Berlin, who was then the big Pooh-bah of Hearst. I walked across the room to where he was standing. 'Mr. Berlin,' I said, 'it's a shame that we can't come to a conclusion on this merger with INS.'"

To the astonishment of Keller, Berlin said, "I'm in favor of it. Why don't you get going with it?"

Keller wanted to be sure. "We understood you were blocking it," he said.

"No. Go ahead, get the deal done," Berlin told Keller.

Bartholomew was out in his vineyards in California. "I called him and he said he'd be right back in New York," recalled Keller.

Keller went back to Charles McCabe the next day and told him what Berlin, a higher ranking Hearst official, had said.

Bartholomew then invited Gortatowsky and other leading executives of the two organizations to a lunch ostensibly to honor Karl A. Bickel, retired UP president who lived in Florida but was in New York on other business. The lunch was held at the Pinnacle Club, and when Bickel was asked to say a few words he spoke enthusiastically about the desirability of a merger of UP and INS for the good of both.

Then followed several meetings between Gortatowsky, Kingsbury Smith, Keller and Bartholomew at the Plaza Hotel. Things seemed to be going forward.

Another meeting was held at the Union League Club, with Charles Scripps attending. Scripps almost sank the ship again when he suggested that Bartholomew and Gortatowsky might have to step aside and let the principals, Roy Howard and Richard Berlin, finalize the deal. Gortatowsky was offended. The next meeting, scheduled to be held at the Southern Newspaper Publishers Convention in Boca Raton, was called off.

Retired UP President Hugh Baillie was a strong supporter of the consolidation, which he gave the code name "Company X" back in 1954. On November 30, 1957, he offered Bartholomew a suggestion in a letter:

"One other suggestion about Company X, and that is, never let the opposition become aware that we are as anxious for it as we actually are, or they will stall further and exert every effort to gain the advantage."

Responding to Baillie, Bartholomew wrote:

"Charles [Scripps] just telephoned from Cincinnati asking details concerning the shrinkage of the market in which we operate domestically, and other statistical material seemingly intended to support his belief—and my conviction—that Company X must be brought into being. It is not desirable, it is imperative."

Early in December 1957, negotiations did get down to serious terms in Miami. Gortatowsky and Kingsbury Smith stayed at the Fountainbleu Hotel, Keller and Bartholomew at the Kennilworth. They did not want to be seen together. The meetings were held alternately in private rooms at the two hotels.[6]

The Associated Press happened to be holding a meeting in Miami at the same time, and a *Miami Herald* reporter noticed that executives from all three news agencies were in town. The *Herald* reporter did not know what was going on, but he made a guess that the Associated Press might be getting ready to absorb the two smaller agencies. AP repudiated the suggestion and issued a public denial on behalf of itself, UP and INS.

Mims Thomason, UP vice president; Ezra Bryan, Scripps attorney; Ray McCauley, INS lawyer; Tom Edwards, an attorney retained by Scripps-Howard; and Glen Offenbacher, lawyer for UP, were called in to work on the language of a merger agreement.

To maintain momentum in the negotiations, the next meeting was held on Park Avenue, New York, with Jack Howard present, along with Bartholomew and Mark Ferris and Barney Townsend for Hearst.

At that point, Bartholomew wrote a letter outlining the situation and possible outcomes. Jack Howard approved it. The next meeting of the lawyers and key executives was held in Suite 1901 of the Beverly Hotel. The lawyers had come up with seventeen pounds of paper.

On Friday, May 16, in Suite 404 of the Drake Hotel, the papers were signed. Bart broke out a few bottles of wine from his Buena Vista Vineyards.

With so many people in on it already, secrecy became difficult. Small leaks developed. On Friday, May 23, Bartholomew received a telegram from the Justice Department saying that no steps should be taken until the department had a chance to check into a report from the American Newspaper Guild that the wire services were planning to reduce competition in the news business.

Twenty United Press division executives were called to New York and informed about the negotiations in a secret meeting at the Commodore Hotel. They were told that, to help get the new company in financial shape, there had to be a round of layoffs. Twenty UP news people and four Teletype operators were being given notice.

Announcement of the merger had been scheduled for Monday, May 26, but when the Justice Department expressed interest, a decision was made to ignore the caution and make the deal a fait accompli that weekend, with an announcement at noon Saturday. Bartholomew said a Justice Department lawyer called him the next week and said, "I suppose you think we cannot unscramble those eggs."

They couldn't be unscrambled. UP had moved in on INS offices around the world on Saturday and consolidation of wires and facilities was completed in less than twenty-four hours.

Among the delicate issues in the agreement was the addition of the "I" into the logo. Kingsbury Smith and other Hearst people wanted it to be "International United Press." The UP side wanted it to remain simply "United Press." They compromised by adding "International" at the end.

The Justice Department announced May 29 it had decided to take no action because INS was a "failing corporation." The Hearst agency had lost money for the previous fourteen years, totaling millions of dollars. UP had shown "some profit" from foreign operations in recent years, the government said, but overall losses and the total financial situation of both agencies was "not particularly favorable."

Two days earlier, Senator Estes Kefauver, Tennessee Democrat, had urged the Justice Department to block the merger. He said it presented small newspapers and radio stations with "an absolute monopoly" on national news because they could not afford the higher priced AP service.

The merger was also criticized by Congressman Emanuel Cellar, Brooklyn Democrat, who urged laws, eventually passed, requiring advance notice of corporate merger plans. Representative Wright Patman, Texas Democrat, suggested that UPI would play down news of government actions on company mergers because of its own consolidation. None of these objections became significant in UPI's future.

Almost all INS employees were given dismissal notices immediately. The American Newspaper Guild said 385 of the 415 employees in its jurisdiction were fired. Fewer than fifty INS people were kept on in the new service although more were rehired by UPI in the following weeks. Most of the INS management was retained at the outset. Besides the news people, INS had 150 clerical employees and sixty-five teletype operators who received notice. All those fired were given severance at two weeks pay for each year of service.

Some of the ex-INS employees found positions at newspapers. Wire service experience was the best journalistic training a job candidate could have. Still, five months after the merger, some of the 485 INS staffers who had been laid off were still looking for jobs. A group of them tried to launch a new wire service, News Associates, Inc., but it lasted only a few months.

Kingsbury Smith, who had started as a copyboy with INS in 1924, was general manager of the service. He opposed the merger with UP but under orders from Hearst, was a key figure in the negotiations and was named vice president and associate general manager of UPI. But it was only a nominal title, he did not want to participate in the merged organization.[7]

William Randolph Hearst Jr., Jacob D. Gortatowsky and C. O. Markuson of Hearst Corp. were added to the UPI board of directors.

The merger put approximately 5,000 UP customers and 3,000 INS clients on the integrated wire. Some of these already had both services.

United Press-Twentieth Century Fox Movietone and Hearst's International News Television, were not included in the merger. Nor were King Features, the Hearst syndicate, and United Features, a subsidiary of UP.

At the last minute, Scripps-Howard demanded that United Features be pulled out of the merger deal for fear of complications with King Features, the Hearst feature agency. UP executives were not fully conscious at the time of what that would mean. The loss of the United Features proved disastrous. UFS had been generating substantial income for UP and, in 1950, United Features signed Charles Schulz to draw the "Peanuts" comic strip for the syndicate. Newspaper publishers were very interested in their funny papers. The ability of a UP salesman to help a newspaper get Snoopy could have made a difference in getting a UPI contract signed.

The merger of UP and INS reduced the number of major international news agencies from six to five, UPI, AP, Reuters, AFP and TASS. Together they provided the news for 98 percent of the world's countries.

The comment on the UP-INS merger from AP General Manager Frank Starzel was: "We have seen this merger coming. It is both a product of the times and added testimony to the strength of the AP cooperative structure. I'm completely confident the AP staff throughout the world will meet any and all challenges the UPI offers."

Frank Bartholomew viewed this remark as a declaration of war by AP against his new agency. "We're not at war with the AP," he said. "Our plans are for improving the standards of news service."

UP and INS executives had to apologize to their staffs for denying or stonewalling them on the merger rumors before it actually took place. Earl J. Johnson, UP's editor-in-chief, told *Editor & Publisher* he had been evasive at the direction of the lawyers. Kingsbury Smith of INS apologized to the INS staff for not giving them more warning. Two weeks earlier he had dodged a direct question about merger plans.

Five senior INS people in New York were asked to join UP: James Kilgallen, senior writer; Tom Breslin, personnel manager; Phil Reed, assistant general manager; Ken Smith, promotion manager; and Paul Allerup, managing editor. Kilgallen, Smith and Allerup took the offer and were given similar jobs with the merged service.

INS ace correspondents Bob Considine, Louella Parsons, Phyllis Batell, Barry Faris and Pierre J. Huss stayed with the Hearst organization. INS foreign correspondents were asked to switch, and a few did, including Charles Arnot who later left to join ABC News.

Jep Cadou, Indianapolis INS bureau manager, became a regional business representative for UPI. The Washington bureau was strengthened editorially by the addition of eight staffers from among the thirty-two at INS in the capital. They included:

Bill Theis, who became chief of the UPI Senate Staff; Al Spivak, who had been INS White House reporter; Joseph Hinshaw; William Unstead; Sam Fogg; William Zimmerman and Thomas Ross; all of whom who meshed easily into the UPI news operation.

Among INSers around the country who began functioning under UPI by-lines were David Oestreicher in Denver, Shelby Scates in Dallas, Russell Boner in Hartford, Joseph St. Amant and Ronald "Rick" du Brow in Los Angeles, Harry Stathos and Leslie Whitten in Atlanta, Hortense Myers in Springfield, Illinois, Barney Seibert in Milwaukee, George Brown in Detroit, John Nagel in New York and Howard Babcock in Cleveland. Ed Stein of INP became associate picture editor for UPI.[8]

In an article about the merger, *Time* magazine characterized the three American news agencies this way: "On a coronation story, editors could rely on the AP for the dimensions of the cathedral, the UP for the mood of the ceremony, and the INS (sometimes) for an interview with the barmaid across the way." *Time* aroused the ire of Hearst columnist Bob Considine by also characterizing INS as "splash and dash journalism."

The biggest immediate benefit from the deal with INS was the acquisition by UPI of all the Hearst newspapers as subscribers. However, that was not an unmixed blessing. More than half of INS's customers already had United Press service. Some even demanded a rate cut for losing INS.

Another plus, which only the employees of a miserly wire service could appreciate, was that many poorly furnished UP bureaus around the country inherited the best desks and typewriters from the poorly furnished INS offices. In San Francisco, a dozen dilapidated wooden desks at UP were replaced by heavy steel furniture from INS. This furniture, although old in 1958, served UPI for another forty years.

Not as a direct consequence of the merger, but made easier by the destruction of a competitor, UPI raised its rates by 9.28 percent for all subscribers in 1959. The boost was laid to increased cost for labor and communications lines.

The Saturday of the merger remained vividly in the memories of staffers on both sides. Al Webb, manager of the one-man UP bureau in Greensboro, North Carolina, said he had a telephone call from Miles Wolff, editor of the *Greensboro Daily News* on the previous Thursday asking about a rumor he had heard of the merger.

"He hated UP and was afraid of getting stuck with us if INS failed," said Webb. "I called Southern Division Manager Rhea Eskew, who told me there was nothing to it. I passed this on to Wolff. Then I was driving to a weekend outing when I heard on the radio about the deal. On Monday I had an irate phone call from Wolff."

UP Agriculture Editor Bernie Brenner was working in his yard in when his wife called him to the phone. Joe Myler told him somberly, "I have to inform you no longer work for United Press." There was a pause and he added, "You are now working for United Press International."

Rod Beaton, who was later president of UPI, said the decision by Scripps-Howard to hold back United Features "really whomped us in the head." Although UFS was not a substantial revenue producer when the merger occurred, it later became one when William Payette was put in charge and developed cartoonist Charles Schulz and "Peanuts."

The cash flow of United Features was tremendous in the late 1960s and 1970s. A widespread misconception among Unipressers was that "Peanuts" was paying the bills, but UPI received no direct cash flow from UFS.

United Features contributed substantially to the Scripps company and thus indirectly helped UPI. The link through Scripps ownership also sometimes gave UP salesmen an advantage in selling the wire service if United Features could be persuaded to serve a newspaper prospect. "We used Snoopy in Europe to get contracts for our other business," said Beaton.[9]

Bartholomew said in his memoir that the merger with INS was "the outstanding accomplishment of my seven-year presidency at United Press."

By coincidence, a separate and completely unrelated "UPI" news services that had existed for twenty-five years folded at about the same time that UP became UPI. United Press of India, a privately owned news agency established in Calcutta in 1933, had 25 bureaus and 130 subscribers before it went out of business in 1958.

Displeasure at adding the "I" waned quickly in the newspaper business, but for some it was never accepted. Eziquel Gainza Paz, publisher of the Buenos Aires *La Prensa*, refused to add the "I" to the logo on wire stories. His reason was that INS had replaced UP and served *La Prensa* during the period that dictator Juan Perón had expropriated it.

Some other newspapers, including the *San Francisco Chronicle*, also used "UP" without the I. Bill German, Chronicle editor, said that Scott Newhall, editor at the time, was "devoted to old things and old ways. He drove an old Packard automobile. He insisted the newspaper call it United Press because that's the way it had always been."

Besides, German said, the Chronicle liked UP but didn't like Hearst because it was in a bitter face-to-face competition with the *San Francisco Examiner*, a Hearst paper. He said the "I" would bring "a Hearst label into the Chron." He said also that "International" might not fit in a credit line.

23

Film News as "Art"

TOM SCHAEFER WAS THE STEREOTYPICAL PRESS PHOTOGRAPHER OF THE 1940s. Obnoxious, overweight, out of shape, the pockets of his rumpled suit filled with flashbulbs, a cigar butt clamped tightly in his teeth, grunting commands from behind a bulky Speed Graphic.

Schaefer figured the world owed him a front seat to the scenes of history and nothing could stand in his way.

The pushy Acme "shooter" had perfected most of the rude habits that made many press photographers outcasts, particularly with the newsmakers they seemed to push around.

But to former president Harry S. Truman, Tom Schaefer was a good man and a friend.

Peter S. Willett had real doubts that Schaefer was really a friend to the ex-president and was tired of hearing the veteran news photographer boast of the day in 1948 when Truman told Schaefer, if he ever needed a favor, to let him know.

Schaefer said Truman figured he owed him a favor because Tom set up the former president's favorite news picture.

On the evening of election day in 1948, the *Chicago Tribune* was so confident that Republican presidential candidate Thomas Dewey was going to beat Truman that just after the polls closed, it ran an early, extra edition with a bold headline proclaiming "DEWEY WINS."

Schaefer had been assigned to shoot pictures of Truman's news conference the next day and he brought along one of those extra edition *Tribunes*. Tom said he gave the paper to Truman and told him to hold it up as he posed for pictures from the rear of his campaign train.

A smiling Truman held high the *Tribune* headline "DEWEY WINS" as Tom and many other news photographers snapped the famous picture, but Schaefer apparently got more.

Willett, who was manager of UPI's Central Division photo operations in Chicago, recalled a day when Schaefer was responsible for finding a prominent speaker for the annual Chicago Press Photographers meeting.

"Tom was moaning that there was no one available and griping that the job of finding a big name had fallen to him," Willett remembered.

Willett said he realized it was a great time to call Schaefer's bluff about his tight friendship with the former president.

"Why don't you call your old buddy Truman," Willett chided, "you said he owed you a favor."

Schaefer puzzled briefly, then nodded approvingly, grabbed a phone and, in a matter of minutes, was on the line with Truman at his home in Independence, Missouri. Much to Willett's surprise, Truman not only remembered Schaefer, but he checked his schedule and told Tom he would be glad to travel to Chicago and address the news photographers.

Willett said Truman made the trip, addressed Chicago's press photographers and allowed Tom to drag him around like a trophy for introductions.

Press photographers, particularly those in the wire services, had been pushy as well as quick, inventive and fearless. Unlike their pen and pad brethren, "shooters" couldn't hang back and rely on sources.

Covering violence, like wars and riots, meant getting as close as possible to the action. Still, UPI "shooters" competed for assignments to dangerous war zones like Vietnam, where a total of 135 photographers were killed.

Bill Snead, manager of UPI photo operations in Saigon in 1968, recalled his brief friendships with some of the eager young photographers who died in combat.

Snead said that many of the UPI photographers tried to follow the footsteps of Japanese photographer Kyoichi Sawada, who once worked on the picture desk in Tokyo. Sawada won an assignment to Vietnam by going there on his vacation and taking combat pictures that won wide play for UPI. Sawada's Vietnam photos also won a Pulitzer Prize in 1965 when he was just 29.

In February 1968, another Japanese photographer, 28-year-old Hiromichi Mine arrived in Saigon for a second tour, begging to get into the field the very next day. He was killed barely a month later when a U.S. Marine armored personnel carrier he was riding in hit a booby-trapped bomb. Sawada accompanied Mine's body back to Tokyo.

Sawada was killed two years later in Cambodia when he was driving near the outskirts of Phnom Phen and was ambushed by Khmer Rouge troops.

The death of Mine created an opening in Saigon and it was filled by Kent Potter of the Philadelphia bureau. Potter struck it off quickly with bespectacled Charles Eggleston, a fearless veteran of many helicopter forays into Vietnam action.

Eggleston was eager to travel to the nearby Tan Sun Nuht airport where the Viet Cong were waging heavy action against U.S. forces. Eggleston drove to the airport with "Radio" Roger Norum of UPI's audio network. When they arrived, Vietnamese rangers were flushing out the Viet Cong near the airport. Norum started his tape recorder and was interviewing Eggleston when the fearless young reporter was shot in the head by a sniper and killed instantly, the brutal sound of his death recorded on Norum's tape.

Shortly after Eggleston's death, Snead left Vietnam and UPI. But young Kent Potter remained on the front and, shortly after visiting Snead in Philadelphia during a home leave, he returned to Vietnam and was killed in 1971.[1]

The UPI's Picture Department's roots reached back to even before United Press was formed in 1907. It began as part of Scripps Newspaper Enterprise Association (NEA) in 1903 and one of its first pictures NEA provided for its clients was the Wright brother's airplane in flight. At the time, the picture had to be engraved on metal, transferred to lightweight, cardboard mats and distributed by mail and courier.

NEA pioneered time-saving photo techniques. In 1910, it used the first darkroom on wheels to develop pictures of Teddy Roosevelt returning to New York from an African safari. It was considered a feat of speed when NEA got pictures of the Dempsey-Firpo fight in New York across the country to the West Coast by plane and train in forty-five hours.

Improvising ways to get pictures from the camera to the subscribers was the heart of the wire service photo business. When Bob Dorman covered an around-the-world flight in 1924, he snapped the plane landing in Labrador, a remote area where it was necessary to physically transport the film to New York.

Arrangements had been made for the photographers to sail from Labrador to Boston on a Navy destroyer. Before reaching port, Dorman hired a speedboat to pick him up from the ship and get him on land before the ship docked. He raced from the waterfront to an airfield where he hired a plane that flew him to New York. He packed his film in an inner tube, which he dropped from the plane into the East River, where another boat had been posted to pick it up and rush it to the bureau.

Another time, NEA's Harold Blumenfeld chartered a seaplane to fly out to the steamship Leviathan, land near it and snatch up film that was tossed from the liner's deck into the ocean attached to a float. Harold said he dangled precariously at the end of the wingtip to grab the package. His seaplane then skimmed to a takeoff and flew back to New York. The pictures were the first shots of an airship crash that had occurred in France a few days earlier.

By 1924, NEA was experimenting with wire and even radio transmission of pictures. In July 1928, when Gene Tunney defended his world heavyweight championship against Tom Heaney, Acme hired a private ambulance, parked near Madison Square Garden and built a mini-darkroom in it. As soon as the first shots were made, a runner dashed with the film to the ambulance. The driver turned on the engine, took off, siren screaming, while staffers in back developed the film. The destination was the American Telephone and Telegraph Company transmitter, which was engaged to transmit the pictures across the country.

AT&T was the only commercial service that had equipment to transmit photos. Whoever got to the transmitter first had the first transmission. Acme was usually first, but the Associated Press then bought the AT&T system and the Scripps agency had to create its own equipment and facilities.

The company's first telephoto transmitters were used during the 1936 political conventions. Since they were a new system, NEA backed them up with a squad of carrier pigeons to fly from Phiadelphia to New York with a packet of film clipped to their legs. Unfortunately, a storm blew up and forced the birds down in Trenton, New

Jersey. They didn't show up in New York until the next day. Luckily the telephoto wire system had worked.

NEA didn't give up on the pigeons. They were used afterwards to fly film from news events, ocean liners, race tracks, sports stadiums. But soon the birds were replaced by a colorful band of human jockeys on motorcycles.

When the armistice was signed at the end of World War I, pictures were flown to New York by dirigible.

The NEA spun off its news photo business into Acme in 1925. Scripps-Howard merged Acme into United Press in 1952. At that time, only fifty large city newspapers subscribed to the photo service because of its cost.

Scripps hoped the consolidation would result in better photo/story coordination. Newspaper client editors had been constantly complaining that pictures came without a matching story or that a story came without a matching picture.

However, the marriage between UP and Acme was strained for a long time. Picture editors complained that the news desk did not inform them quickly enough about breaking events. Sometimes calls from newspapers asked for "art" to go with a story they had received. Top UPI managers found it necessary to continually harp on photo and news staffs to work together more closely. But the two sides never were fully blended.

A picture opportunity could vanish instantly. If you didn't get there before the fire was out, all you could shoot was the smoking embers. A word reporter, on the other hand, could always search for witnesses to provide quotes for a story.

There was also residual resentment by veteran Acme photographers over being absorbed into the UP. Some photo veterans consciously or unconsciously disdained the "pencil pushers" on the news side.

Separate locations for the picture bureaus were not unusual, even when the photo service moved into the *Daily News* Building in New York, the picture department located itself on a different floor. When the San Francisco news and picture bureaus moved into a single space in a new building, the photo manager insisted on having a glass wall between his bureau and the newswire editors.

Rewrite staffers working the telephones were supposed to alert the photo desk on a breaking story. But with a telephone cradled on your shoulder, taking a hot story from an outside reporter or stringer, it was easy to forget or be unable to make a phone call to the photo desk on the other side of the glass.

When cameramen were dispatched by the photo desk, they did not always remember to alert the news side so that a reporter could go along to the news site.

Some photographers thought the separation from writers was an advantage to their work. "We were dispatched instantly, while AP photographers were delayed in order to coordinate with the reporters," said one UPI photographer.

Press photographers have to maintain a despotic bearing in their work. They give arbitrary commands to presidents, princes, dictators, movie stars and athletes. When Queen Elizabeth visited the United States and was being photographed in San Francisco a UPI cameraman was heard to shout: "Hey! Queenie! Turn this way!"

Wire service photographers began using 35-millimeter cameras when improvements in film made enlargement to 8x10 inch prints good enough for newspaper use. This meant the quick demise of the classic news camera, the bulky Speed Graphic, whose popping flashbulbs had become the trademark of press on the scene.

United Press International owned the world's largest archive of news photographs. It had every newspicture made by NEA, Acme and UP/UPI photographers as well as shots picked up from local newspaper cameramen and hundreds of stringers.

Frequently, the photo itself had a story. At the funeral of President Kennedy in 1963, UPI published the heart-touching shot of little "John-John," standing beside his mother, saluting as the cortege carrying his father's body passed.

Stanley Stearns, whose film that shot came from, was one of many UPI cameramen covering the funeral march. His film was sped by messenger back to the UPI photo lab in Washington, where it was developed, printed and given a caption.

Ted Majeski, UPI's top photo editor, was in the bureau making the selections of prints to be put on the telephoto network. Examining film through a magnifying glass he noticed the frame with Jacqueline Kennedy and a little boy next to her. It looked like the child had his hand up in a salute. "Can we crop this for just the boy saluting," he instructed an aide.

Allan Papkin, who was working in the darkroom in Washington that day, recalled, "we had to put the printing easel on the floor of the darkroom and get on our hands and knees to focus on the part of the picture they wanted," he said.

The result was the single most remembered picture among the thousands shot during those four days in which the lives of Americans paused, stunned by the assassination of their president.

Having to invent its own transmitting equipment back in the 1920s gave UPI technical momentum which kept it ahead in new equipment throughout its life. The wire service invented and sometimes manufactured its own machines, usually in collaboration with laboratories and manufacturers.

In the 1960s UPI introduced a facsimile system it called Unifax, which transmitted pictures that arrived in the newspaper editor's office as finished prints. They did not have to be developed again in the client's darkroom. At first the faxed photos were not as sharp as those sent on telephoto. But for small newspapers, they were a godsend and television broadcasters used them on evening newscasts without having to operate a darkroom.

Pictures could be transmitted only on "voice quality" lines, for which the telephone company charged higher rates than for data transmission. It took seven minutes to transmit one picture, so photo editors became very selective in the shots to use. One of the frequent frustrations encountered was having someone pick up a telephone and ruin the transmission.

A photographer, out of town on an assignment, sometimes was able to develop and transmit pictures back to the UPI bureau from a client newspaper's dark room. Few clients had transmitting equipment on hand and so such an assignment required the photographer to cart along a portable transmitter—only barely portable, bigger than a typewriter.

Continued research brought improved facsimile machines. Unifax II, a hugely improved machine, was introduced in 1974. This instrument became the industry's universal machine for photos, producing semi-glossy prints almost equal to telephoto. Unifax II, developed with E.G.G. Inc. of Salem, Massachusetts, was used by many newspapers and even by the Associated Press. *Industrial Research* Magazine cited it as one of the top 100 products developed in 1974. A desk-top receiver, it produced sharp 8x10 prints completely dry, cut and stacked.

A modified version of the machine was capable of receiving radiophotos and became widely used through the world, particularly in Latin America. Some were still in use thirty years later. Finally, they had to be retired for lack of parts.

The facsimile machines were very profitable for UPI. The company was still collecting rents on some of them in the early 1990s when the wire service had long since stopped using it for its own photo transmission.

In 1972, picture transmission went satellite, which proved to be more reliable and better quality than land lines.

In the early 1970s, before the women's rights movement took hold, so-called "cheese-cake" photos of scantily clad females were a darkroom staple and caused some differences of opinion. The Associated Press Managing Editors organization took up the subject.[2]

Many "cheesecake" photos originated in Australia, being transmitted to London for the *Star,* a tabloid with a clientele that appreciated the pulchritude. The shots usually originated from a promoter seeking publicity for female entertainers.

UPI received about a half dozen of these pictures a week. The most "appealing" was put on the telephoto circuit, usually in the middle of the night or on a weekend when traffic was light.

Rupert Murdoch's News Ltd. was a good UPI client. Cheesecake specials for his *News of the World* were selected carefully and sent from Sydney to London through a circuit to Hong Kong and New York. The transmissions were carefully monitored and copied at every intervening bureau to become souvenirs for posting on the wall of the darkroom.

The sexy pictures did not interfere with other news photos on the wire, and editors, of course, were free to discard them. But some publishers and editors thought they should not be put on the wire. They complained to UPI.

In October 1971, photo chief Ted Majeski was put on the spot. He received letters asking why such pictures were carried on the wire. Heeding the complaint, he issued an order to quit transmitting them. But when they stopped appearing on the wire, Majeski received an equal number of letters asking why they were dropped. So they came back, but were limited.[3]

UPI photographers won their share of honors. David Kennerly won a Pulitzer Prize in 1972 for his feature pictures in the Vietnam war. A native of Oregon, Kennerly worked in Los Angeles, New York and Washington for UPI before going to Vietnam.

In 1986, when UPI was falling apart, the owners sold the entire picture library to the Bettmann Archive, a picture agency founded by Otto Bettmann in 1935. He owned five million photos he had already collected, to which it added the 11.5 million UPI pictures. The Bettman archive was sold in 1992 to Orbus, Inc., a company owned by Bill Gates, the Microsoft billionaire. Corbis Corp. sold digitalized versions of the newsphotos to anyone who wanted them.

Being a press photographer was sometimes a dangerous occupation. You had to be near the shooting to get good battle pictures. Domestically, photographers covering demonstrations, police actions and sports events sometimes became the target of a policeman's baton, a demonstrator's wrath or a fullback's leap over the front line.

During the Berkeley demonstrations in May 1972, Terry Schmidt was clubbed on two or three occasions. Sam Mikulin was knocked off a bridge at San Francisco airport while taking pictures of a rally for presidential candidate Barry Goldwater. He spent six months recovering from his injuries. Scores of other UPI photographers were hurt on the job.

In 1981, UPI introduced its digital darkroom at its new $2.5 million New York headquarters. This completely revolutionized the newspicture operation. Pictures could be edited, stored and transmitted electronically. When digital cameras came on the scene, the use of film wasn't necessary, although by that time, the UPI was in no position to buy the $15,000 digital cameras needed for press-quality work.

The digital system could hold 200 8x10 pix and receive or transmit seven pictures simultaneously. When pictures moved from European headquarters in Brussels

News photographers shooting table at 1960 Democratic National Convention in Los Angeles. Gary Haynes, shown behind the UPI logo with camera and telescopic lens. Others not identified.

to New York, the system automatically changed the format to conform with national standards.[4.]

Photo satellite transmission was tested in 1981 to complete the system upgrade.

Darkroom hands included the "squeegee boy" at the bottom, who used his rubber scraper to press water out of prints. Some of them moved on to a "shooter" or photo editor. Arthur Fellig, who was a squeegee boy at Acme, later became a noted art photographer. He kept the name "Weegee" he had picked up at the wire services. Some of his photos were sold at an auction in February 2000, for $256,300.

UPI won eight Pulitzer Prizes between 1960 and 1980.

- In 1949, for a picture of baseball great Babe Ruth slumping towards home plate in his final appearance at Yankee Stadium.
- In 1960, for a shot of a Cuban being executed.
- In 1961, for a stabbing scene of a Japanese politician.
- In 1966, for a picture of a Vietnamese mother and children wading to escape bombs.
- In 1968, for a rescue feature picture.
- In 1968, for another Vietnam war picture.
- In 1972, for Indianapolis hostage scene.
- In 1980, for coverage of execution of Kurds and former police officers of deposed Shah of Iran.

UP had a commercial photography department. This unit made photos for public relations, advertising and other customers. In most cases the service was separated from the news photo department and had its own personnel and laboratories.

The UPI's "picture people" performed fantastic feats in finding dark rooms for processing film, which required total darkness. Frequently, a hotel bathroom was handy. In 1964, Gary Haynes commandeered a men's room near the meeting room where President Lyndon Johnson was giving a speech. He had a sign printed on hotel stationery "OUT OF ORDER" and taped it on the door of the restroom. Haynes filed the initials "MRP" on the caption for "Men's Room Photos."

On another occasion, covering the racial news in Oxford, Mississippi, a team of UPI photo staffers spent a week in a cramped hotel room amidst chemicals, transmitters, dryers, an enlarger and processing trays.

Before digital electronic cameras, news photographers often had to work in difficult environments for the wet chemical processing. At a football game in Green Bay, Wisconsin, the liquids froze. In temperatures above 100 degrees at Bogalusa there was no ice to keep the developer cool enough.

In Charlotte, North Carolina, in the early 1960s, UPI had its photo operation "in the broom closet on the 12th floor of the Liberty Life Building," recalled Al Webb. He said the enlarger and transmitter were in the bureau area shielded by a black curtain to diminish light.

Since there was no water in the broom closet, Webb and his photo assistant Tom Balch "souped" their film and prints across the hallway in trays on the floor with water from the urinals. Sometimes the UPI staffer accidentally stepped into the chemical trays arranged on the floor and in the darkness.

The St. Louis bureau of United Press International in 1970. The bureau was located on the newsroom floor of the *St. Louis Post-Dispatch*. Pictured are bureau manager Jim Wieck (foreground), teletype operator John Michalski (left) and reporter Laszlo Domjan (right). (UPI photo from the Jim Wieck files via Wieck Photo DataBase.)

24

Camelot to the Moon

THE 1960S DEFINED THE NEW UNITED PRESS INTERNATIONAL.

From Camelot to the Grassy Knoll, Vietnam to the Congo, the Berlin Wall to a motel balcony in Memphis and, finally, to the very surface of the moon, UPI was forced to prove its worth.

UPI reporters, photographers and editors battled the bigger and better equipped Associated Press around the world to document, day by day, the big and not-so-big events that marked this decade of change.

Early in the decade, UPI, for a change, came up with truly superior resources to take full control of the biggest story of the fledgling Kennedy administration, the ill-fated Bay of Pigs Invasion.

Always strong in Latin America, UPI had some of its top reporters tracking Cuba as it moved from a Caribbean playground for the wealthy to become America's closest communist threat.

Francis L McCarthy, a career Unipresser who was at Pearl Harbor December 7, 1941, and covered the Pacific War until it ended, was in charge of the Havana bureau in the late 1950s. McCarthy covered the rebellion headed by Fidel Castro and managed to get on the wrong side of the soon-to-be Cuban premier.

McCarthy had good contacts with the regime of Cuban dictator Fulgencio Batista and got a tip from a high-level source that Castro had been slain. He checked out the report by having one of his Cuban reporters call the army outpost where Batista's army was fighting Castro's rebels. An army officer confirmed the report and McCarthy filed the story. The report was false and infuriated Castro against McCarthy and the wire service he worked for. McCarthy added fuel to the fire when he refused an invitation to come to Castro's mountain hideaway to see that Castro was alive, mainly because he feared it was a trick.

When he achieved power in 1959, Castro began putting pressure on the UPI and other American agencies in Havana.[1]

McCarthy was named Latin American editor in 1961 and was transferred to New York. Reporter Matt Kenny was named manager of the Havana bureau, which included veteran correspondents Martin P. Houseman, Adolfo G. Merino and Pedro Bonetti.

Rumors of an imminent invasion by exiled anti-Castro forces, backed by America's CIA, were widespread in Havana when acting bureau manager Henry Raymont and Merino attended a party at the Argentine Embassy on Sunday, April 16. Kenny was on leave in the states at the time. Raymont and Merino were discussing the rumors with the Argentine ambassador when a captain of Castro's army arrived with his wife and children to seek asylum for his dependents. He said that an invasion force was landing in Las Villas Province and he had been ordered to the front.

Raymont borrowed the ambassador's phone and gave the UPI cables desk in New York its first confirmation from Havana that an invasion was underway.

Raymont and Merino were arrested a short time later, and Raymont called Houseman at his home to tell him of the invasion and the arrests.

At the UPI Havana bureau, Houseman used a radio-teleprinter circuit to read reports of the invasion from the cables desk and a secret "listening post" that UPI had set up in Miami just weeks earlier.

The "listening post" had been setup and managed by Francis L. McCarthy, and it gave UPI huge beats over the AP on the early news of the ill-fated incursion.

Frank Eidge, the Miami (MH) bureau manager in 1961, recalled getting a call from McCarthy in the second week of April with an urgent, secret assignment. He was told to open a new UPI office in Miami immediately. It was to be separate from the established bureau and in a location that could include living quarters. Also, it had to include space where communications equipment and radio receivers could operate effectively. He was told the equipment was on its way and that more staffers were being sent to Miami.

Eidge rented a suite and rooms at the Dallas Park Hotel in Miami. Among those arriving, in addition to McCarthy, were a dozen news reporters and Mike Alanso, a Cuban exile. Alanso was a technician who had worked in the Havana bureau during the civil war, monitoring Castro's clandestine radio.

McCarthy and his staffers, using McCarthy's contacts in the Miami-based exile invasion force and the sophisticated monitoring devises, swept the play for the first several days, but there was NO word from UPI's staffers in Havana.

Houseman and the other Havana staffers had gathered a lot of information, but they could not get it out of Cuba. Castro's army was blocking all telephone and telegraph traffic. A militia unit was assigned to watch the UPI bureau.

Finally, on the evening of April 18, reporter Norman Cornish of the UPI Washington bureau got a telephone call through to Houseman. Cornish had flown to the U.S. military base at Guantanamo Bay on a military flight for the press. He persuaded an operator to place a collect call to the UPI bureau.

Houseman reported that Raymont and Merino had been arrested and that thousands of suspected counter revolutionaries had been taken into custody. He also was able to shoot down some of the radio reports from the Miami exiles, including one that Castro's Air Force had been destroyed and that Ernesto "Che" Guevara had been killed.

Houseman and Cornish agreed to try for a similar phone hook-up on the following day, but Houseman was behind bars by that time. After one month, Houseman was repatriated with other U.S. citizens aboard a Pan Am charter flight to Miami. The "Bay of Pigs Invasion" had been crushed in 72 hours.

One of the most important battles between UPI and AP started late in 1963 when Lee Harvey Oswald assassinated President John F. Kennedy in downtown Dallas. The entire news world was witness to UPI's leading coverage on this fast-breaking story.

The two news wholesalers fought on mostly even terms in the following years as they strove to cover the growing civil rights conflict, the war in Vietnam and the East-West cold war that touched off an all-out race to be first in space.

Both UPI and AP were pressed near their limits in 1968 as one earth-shaking event after another rattled the world. Starting with the Tet offensive in Vietnam, the news spotlight moved to the assassinations of civil rights leader Dr. Martin Luther King, Jr., and presidential candidate Senator Robert F. Kennedy; the Russian invasion of Czechoslovakia; campus turmoil; urban riots across America; President Lyndon B. Johnson's decision not to seek re-election; and the mayhem in the streets of Chicago during the Democratic National Convention. The 1968 barrage of pressure news stretched all the way to Christmas week when America launched three Apollo 8 astronauts into orbit around the moon.

At the end of the decade, in the summer of 1969, a man landed on the moon and came back to earth, which will likely go down as the most memorable event of the twentieth century. The moon landing of Apollo 11's *Eagle* and astronaut Neil Armstrong's historic first step upon the lunar surface was an astounding story to report.

Still, UPI faced battles beyond reporting the news. The decade also challenged those who transmitted, distributed and sold the product and the corporate leaders charged with pulling it all together while, simultaneously, keeping the bank account solvent.

The technology and engineering, which allowed America to put men on the moon, also changed the way things were done on earth, with dramatic advances in computers and communications. Americans, who watched live television of two astronauts walking through the lunar dust a quarter of a million miles away, were changing their expectations about news coverage.

To stay competitive, UPI was forced to move ahead on all fronts despite spiraling costs and a shrinking bottom line.

The real winners of the war between AP and UPI were the retailers of news, the newspapers, radio and television stations. The two news agencies strained to offer these clients more news, delivered faster and at the cheapest possible rate. More importantly to the public, the feuding wire services provided the Fourth Estate a system of checks and balances.

This was evident in the fall of 1961 when United Nations Secretary-General Dag Hammarskjold was killed in a plane crash in a Northern Rhodesia jungle.

Hammarskjold was en route from Leopoldville in the Congo to Ndola in Northern Rhodesia to confer with President Moise Tshombe, who was leading a move by the province of Katanga to break away from the Congo Republic.

Ray Maloney, UPI's correspondent in Elizabethville, had driven to Ndola to cover Hammarskjold's visit. Colin Frost and Andy Borowick were there for AP. Reuters and other news agencies were also there to cover the talks. The reporters were kept away from the airstrip at Ndola by security police.

The airport did not have much traffic and when a small plane landed just before midnight and its passengers were whisked off in limousines, the correspondents assumed they had seen Hammarskjold arrive. Maloney phoned Mike Keats, UPI's man in Johannesburg, to dictate a brief lead on the Congo story placing the U.N. secretary general in Ndola.

Keats recounted the events of later that night. "The motley crowd of reporters dispersed to night clubs, bars and other assorted diversions. But Maloney was still at the airport when a security guy arrived to report who had arrived and who hadn't—the latter being Hammarskjold."

The security officer told Maloney that Hammarskjold's pilot was waiting for daylight to land.

Maloney phoned Keats, waking him up, and explained the confusion and need for a corrective lead making it clear the U.N. chief was not there yet. "I got dressed and drove to the office, punched up Ray's corrected story and went home," said Keats.

When he arrived in the Johannesburg bureau the next morning, Keats found an urgent message from London:

"ROX HAS HAMMARSKJOLD MEETING TSHOMBE AT NDOLA. YOU HAVE HIM UNARRIVED AFTER KILLING MALONEY'S ORIGINAL STORY. HOW PLEASE?"

The AP story had made headlines around the world. Maloney's original report did not make it to client wires in the United States and the only lead from UPI that American editors and news directors saw had Hammarskjold waiting for daylight to land.

Billy Ferguson, who then was the overnight editor of the national broadcast wire in Chicago, recalled that clients were demanding that UPI match AP's story placing the U.N. diplomat at the meeting. Ferguson said some clients wanted UPI to hedge its story by quoting one of the TV networks, which were also reporting Hammarskjold safely on the ground.

However, UPI's editors decided to wait for the facts. It was now daylight in Ndola and there still was no sign of the secretary-general's plane. Keats was besieged with urgent messages.

The mystery of Hammarskjold's missing plane was solved later in the morning when one of Keats' contacts in Northern Rhodesia reported that the wreckage of a United Nations plane was found by the Northern Rhodesian Air Force in the jungle many miles from Ndola. Hammarskjold and seven others were killed in the crash.

More often than not, it was just solid planning and fast, sure action that gave UPI or AP the beat on a story rating a 10-bell flash. That was certainly the case in the summer of 1963 when both wire services geared up for the anticipated death of ailing Pope John XXIII.

Bill Sunderland, UPI Rome bureau manager at the time, figured that the first word would come from either of two sources, the Vatican Press Office or Vatican Radio. He assigned his seven staffers to man the press office around the clock and maintain a telephone connection to the bureau.

He knew there might be problems if the announcement came on Vatican Radio, which he felt was the more likely source. The station broadcast in twenty-four languages, including Latin, and since the death could come at any time, it would be announced in whatever language was being used at the time. Sunderland polled his reporters, photographers, teletype operators, accountants and other support workers and came up with protection on one-half of the languages, much of it thanks to newsman Ernest Sackler, who was fluent in many. Still, there were a dozen languages used by Vatican Radio, including Swahili, that would find UPI lacking.

The staff continuously monitored the radio. Sunderland recalled: "At one point, they suddenly cut off a broadcast and began playing funeral music, which we took as a sure sign that the announcement was to follow. Then the station went dead for the longest 45 minutes of my life. Finally, they resumed broadcasting and, sure enough, it was in Swahili. Luckily, it wasn't the Pope's death."

When Pope John XXIII did die on June 3, it was announced by the Vatican Press Office. Staffer Rufus Goodwin phoned Sunderland with the flash and it was on the wire within seconds, several minutes ahead of AP.

AP's in-house log said UPI was first because AP's Rome bureau manager toppled over backward in his chair when he got word of the Pope's death and thus delayed the transmission of the flash.

The election of a new pope was always world news. In 1958, when Pope John was elected, there had been widespread confusion among reporters.

In a time-honored custom, the cardinals, meeting secretly in the Sistine Chapel, burned the ballots in a small stove after each vote. They added dry straw to produce white smoke proclaiming that new successor to Saint Peter had been chosen. Wet straw added to the burning ballots was supposed to produce black smoke indicating failure to reach a majority.

At 11:52 A.M. on October 26, 1958, what appeared to be white smoke emerged. Vatican Radio announced that the white smoke indicated the 262nd successor to Peter had been elected. UPI and other news agency reporters watching from perches on rooftops also saw white smoke and flashed the news.

But the smoke kept getting darker. Four minutes later Vatican Radio began to have doubts. Seven minutes later it was definitely black smoke.

At 6 P. M. the same day another cloud of smoke belched forth and Vatican Radio again announced that a pope was elected. But five minutes later the smoke turned black again. A new pope was not elected until two days later. By the time Pope John XXIII died June 3, 1963, the Vatican had set up a chemical process to assure the right kind of smoke to elect the next pope.

In the 1960s, UPI proved to many in the news media that it was a good idea to have at least two sets of eyes and two minds guarding the public's right to know.

A massive buildup of nuclear weapons by cold war enemies, the USSR and the United States, and the fact that any of the many political brushfires going on could expand into a nuclear holocaust was a threatening menace.

UPI diplomatic reporter Stewart Hensley wrote a story on January 9, 1960, saying the U.S. would propose a nuclear test ban. It was immediately denied by the U.S. administration, but a month later President Eisenhower announced a "sweeping new proposal for a nuclear test ban."

Hensley was a 30-year veteran of the UP and was its chief State Department reporter. He had covered the China-India-Burma theater in World War II and had been in fifty countries for UPI, traveling with Presidents Eisenhower, Kennedy, Johnson and Nixon. On those assignments he often worked with Merriman Smith and other UPI reporters.

When he was in India, Prime Minister Nehru once said to him, "Hensley, you know more about India than anyone I know. You ought to write a book about it." Hensley replied, "Mr. Prime Minister, I have been here for seven months. After six months I knew everything there was to know about India. But after seven months I have questions."

Smith and Hensley, when they were with President Eisenhower in Chile, experimented with the use of walkie-talkie radios, then fairly new technology. At their hotel in Barloche, a resort near Santiago, the two UPI men carefully plotted their strategy for covering the president's motorcade through Santiago.

1975 New York City, UPI Editor H.L. Stevenson, and UPI General Manager Frank Tremaine.

Using a photograph of the city skyline and a map of its streets they picked out the tallest building and arranged for a telephone to be installed on its roof. Hensley would station himself there with a small desk, chair and typewriter. Smith would accompany the motorcade from the airport.

The plan worked perfectly. Smith's dictation on the walkie-talkie came in loud and clear to Hensley, who was able to move a dispatch to New York while the parade was still inching its way through the crowded streets and competitors were stuck in the throng.

The walkie-talkies were used again when Eisenhower visited Montevideo. A small riot occurred during the parade there, police subduing protestors with tear gas. UPI got it on the wire first because of the radio.

Hensley earned another page in wire service lore when he and a *New York Times* reporter covering the war in Burma could not find any transportation. They bought an elephant, rode it to their destination and then sold it. Hensley had trouble getting New York accounting to OK refunding the difference between the elephant's purchase and the sale.

Hensley and Smith were both heavy drinkers and smokers. James Anderson, Hensley's successor at the State Department, recalled being with Hensley in Scotland, en route home from Vietnam with Secretary of State William P. Rogers.

"Toward the end of the trip Stu collapsed. The next morning he called Dottie Wood on the London desk and asked whether they wanted a lead on the Rogers trip. She stunned him by telling him he had dictated 600 words the night before and it made perfect sense." Hensley died soon after that at the age of sixty-two.

At the LBJ Museum, there is a letter Merriman Smith gave to President Johnson in 1966 shortly after Merriman Smith, Jr., a helicopter pilot, was killed in Vietnam. "This young army captain, husband and father was a professional, but he was no killer. As I wrote you when he shipped out last year, he was anything but gung ho, but a well-trained young American going to work," Smith wrote.

"Please try not to take these things personally, Mr. President. Yours is the awesome responsibility of command and we want you to exercise it as surely and confidently as possible. My boy did not die for an empty cause, nor was he a war maker. His hope was yours, Mr. President—peace and, at least, a chance at a better life for others."

President Johnson maintained a fondness for most reporters and a keen interest in the media despite the growing editorial criticism of his presidency over the war. He had UPI and AP Teletypes running in the Oval Office and often called the UPI Washington bureau to complain or point out problems with news stories.

Al Spivak, UPI's second in command at the White House under Smith, recalled that Johnson called him immediately after one of his stories had cleared on the wire. "You've got the wrong lead on your story," the president barked.

After a brief discussion, Spivak agreed the president was right. "I did have the wrong lead," the veteran reporter said.

Helen Thomas joined Merriman Smith in the White House press room in 1960 after John F. Kennedy was elected president. Her assignment was to cover the president's glamorous wife, Jacqueline.

Thomas was named UPI's Senior White House Correspondent in 1970 when Smith, possibly despondent over the death of his son in Vietnam, committed suicide.

The 25-year-old Thomas had joined United Press in Washington in 1945, one of the women hired to take the place of UP staffers who went to war.

It was Thomas' relentless energy and ambition that helped her keep her job when the GI's came home. She moved from the radio desk to cover some of the federal agencies in 1956. Eventually, Helen's drive carried her to the top of her field as chief White House Correspondent for UPI and dean of the White House press corps. But, even at the top, Thomas did not relax. She was usually the first reporter to check into the White House newsroom at 6:30 A.M. and rarely left until the president was tucked in for the night. Helen was virtually married to her work, often canceling plans for vacations when they interfered with her White House responsibilities.

When she finally found time for a private life and married in 1971, she chose a fellow White House correspondent, Douglas Cornell, of the Associated Press. He died in 1975 after a battle with Alzheimer's.

Thomas remained at the White House for thirty years, firing sharp questions at eight U.S. presidents. She became a celebrity in her own right and UPI's most recognized reporter. She left the company in 2000 at the age of 79.

Thomas was a prolific reporter. When she accompanied President Richard Nixon on his historic trip to China in 1962, she kept a valuable phone line from Shanghai to Washington open for hours by dictating a steady stream of information and observations on the newly-revealed mysteries of communist China. The energetic Thomas wore down several staffers in Washington who wilted trying to keep up with her dictation.

Almost all Washington reporters found it hard to keep up with the stocky daughter of Lebanese immigrants. One White House correspondent told a group of friends that what he most admired about Helen were her legs. When his friends recoiled at such a seemingly sexist remark, the correspondent explained he had often seen Helen beat reporters half her age sprinting from an airport tarmac to a pay phone.

Citizen Band radio communication was introduced for news coverage in New York in 1960 when Soviet leader Nikita Khrushchev attended a United Nations General Assembly meeting. New CB radios were borrowed from a supplier. These units needed batteries that were very bulky. Aline Mosby, covering Khrushchev at the Soviet embassy, carried her radio equipment in a baby carriage.

Mosby was able to dictate running copy to the bureau in the Daily News Building when the Soviet leader made an unscheduled appearance on the balcony of the embassy and engaged in a raucous shouting exchange with reporters, as well as during his unpredictable tirades and comments when he entered and left the building.

"We were getting copy on the wire before many of the reporters were able to get to a telephone," said Bill Sexton, in charge of the New York bureau news desk.

UPI had an all-star staff covering that U.N. meeting, with Khrushchev and Fidel Castro of Cuba in the city. The team included Moscow manager Henry Shapiro, Mosby from the Moscow staff, Bruce Munn, chief U.N. correspondent, former Havana bureau manager Francis McCarthy, Hensley, and three dozen other reporters.

At the peak of East-West tension over the Berlin Wall in January 1962, a United Press International dispatch drew vigorous protest from West German authorities.

One night twenty-eight people, including a 78-year-old paralyzed woman and a child of 8, crawled through a tunnel from the East Zone controlled by the Soviet Union to the West Zone in the hands of the western Allies.

Berlin was isolated in the Soviet-controlled part of Germany. A British, American and French foothold in part of the city had been maintained only by the dramatic and massive American airlift of supplies a few years earlier.

The East Germans built the wall separating the two sectors of Berlin in 1961. It was intended chiefly to keep East Germans from fleeing to the more prosperous western sector. Armed guards were posted at the wall and a number of people were shot attempting to cross the "no-mans-land" buffer on the east side of the wall.

A group of East Germans surreptitiously entered a house in the buffer zone on that January and, over a period of several weeks, they dug a 90-foot tunnel under the wall.

Correspondents in West Berlin learned of the escape of the twenty-eight people on January 24. West German authorities said they had cut their way through a section where the wall consisted of barbed wire fencing. The people had escaped, but the official West German report about how they escaped was a deliberate lie. UPI had interviewed the escapees and reported they did not cut through barbed wire but crawled through a tunnel. When East German police learned this they went to the house in the buffer zone and found the tunnel.

Officials in West Berlin called the UPI story a "tragic indiscretion." Indignation against the wire service grew. The news agency reported that its informants called the tunnel escape a "one shot" deal. German officials said, however, that as many as one hundred more people were hoping to leave East Germany through the tunnel and were prevented when the house was seized.

25

Getting into the Tube

THE NEWS INDUSTRY BEGAN COMPUTERIZATION IN THE 1960S AND UPI was on the leading edge, launching computerized stock market quotations in 1962.

Text wires were a challenge because, although words could be processed at very high speeds, printers that could handle copy at those speeds were not yet available. By 1969, UPI and AP both were experimenting with ways of handling news efficiently using the new high-speed transmission technology which was advancing faster than machines could be invented to handle it in newspaper offices.

A significant advance in TTS (teletypesetter) tape service was inaugurated by both AP and UP in 1951. By the '60s, UPI had more than 600 TTS client newspapers. Larger newspapers began using tape because of improvements in Linotype equipment. Machines were available that could handle 750 lines an hour. The newspapers were also weakening union resistance to automation.

At UPI, a national TTS wire for afternoon papers functioned during the overnight from 2 A.M. to 7 A.M. when it was split into regional wires that were edited at division points. There were thirty-four regional wires in all.

UPI developed a communications breakthrough in 1967 with a system called "Sked 4." The new system split voice-grade telephone circuits into as many as forty-four one-way channels or twenty-two two-way circuits that could carry all of the news wires at much lower cost than separate wires. UPI technicians had discovered in 1964 that under FCC regulations a "Schedule-4" voice-grade wire could be multiplexed into several electronic segments for sending data. Western Union Company, which leased some telegraph lines to the news services, fought against use of the system before the FCC, causing a two-year delay in its implementation. UPI had equipment made to order by Lenkurt Electric Company. The first application was a transcontinental "back-bone" wire linking bureaus on which they could send stories and message traffic to New York to be edited before it was put on wires seen by clients. It was quickly expanded to carry UPI wires to newspapers and broadcasters.

Computers were changing the rules of newspaper production and news distribution by the '70s and UPI was determined to stay on the leading edge. Wire service writers had always turned out copy by typewriter on paper. The paper went to an editor who penciled it up and turned it over to the Morse or teletype operator.

UPI hired Data Dimensions Company for $1 million to develop a computerized editing system. In 1972, the New York UPI bureau received the first dozen computer terminals. They were large, box-like desk machines about the size of a microwave oven. Manufactured by the Harris Company, they were the best available and cost about $30,000 each.

Writers and editors typed on a keyboard and their sentences appeared on a greenish screen, about twenty lines showing at any time. The rest could be seen by pressing keys to scroll up or scroll down.

The new machines were called VDTs (video display terminals) but the staff immediately called them "tubes." That name came from the main part in the VDT, a cathode ray tube.

The best thing about the tubes was that you could correct or edit the news story by back-spacing. No more xxxxxxing over errors or rolling in a new sheet of paper to start over.

When the reporter's copy on the screen was ready, a tap on the "send" key fired it into the big computer in New York, where it was saved on large reels of magnetic tape. The editor could call it up on his screen, edit it and dispatch it onto the customer wire with another few keystrokes.

The first VDTs had a failing that caused otherwise clean-minded men and women to explode in army language. There was no fail-safe backup. If you punched the wrong key, or if there was a power loss, your copy vanished and you had to start over reconstructing the dispatch. Later VDTs had batteries that saved everything unless it was deliberately killed.

Over the first ten years of computerized desking, UPI went through three generations of "tubes." New versions were smaller—some not much larger than a typewriter. They came with advanced skills and at a much lower cost.

The VDTs in the newsroom were components of a revolutionary computerized wire setup created by the company's brilliant communications chief, James (Jimmy) Darr. The system was called IS&R (Information Storage and Retrieval).

Computerization took hold in the news business rapidly. At UPI, typewriters were moved back to the storage room, taken home by staffers as souvenirs or just thrown away.

After New York went onto IS&R, other geographical sections of the company network were put on the system over a two-year span.

By 1974, UPI had more than 400 video terminals throughout the country linked to its two central Sperry-Univac computers in New York, each of which could store thirty-three million words. The IS&R was implemented in Canada in 1977 and Europe in 1978.

A few reporters didn't want to abandon their typewriters. Some swore they would not touch a VDT. There were, in fact, a few resignations over the issue. However, the tubes could handle news copy so much more efficiently than the old way that even the stubborn quickly accepted them.

The news still arrived at most clients on teletype printers whose "chug chug chug" was the theme music of the news business. But soon smaller, faster, quiet printers were developed and the familiar old Model 19 and Model 15 teletypes faded away. In Hawaii a couple of old teletypes were moved directly from the UPI bureau to a museum.

During the transition to computers, UPI's editorial, sales, communications and computer executives split into two camps on how the computer should be used to serve clients. One group, headed by Jimmy Darr, wanted to allow clients to dial-in to the UPI database and shop for what news and information they wanted. Under Darr's "demand" service, clients would contract for UPI services on a multi-year basis and be given different levels of clearance based on their needs and rates.

Travis Hughs, a smooth-talking sales executive who had moved from Texas to New York, had a different approach. He wanted to continue delivering news to UPI clients by wire, but using sophisticated high-speed equipment. Hughs' plan, called "DataNews," used 1,200-word-a-minute printers and electronic selectors that would allow UPI to tailor its news reports to newspapers by basic categories.

Most of the editorial managers who helped plan and implement IS&R backed Hughs plan because of its potential to serve all of the news service's clients. Many editors also worried that sharing its database with newspapers might create the same "carbon-copy" mentality that hobbled AP's independent pursuit of news. The Associated Press requires its clients to provide carbon copies of all of their stories to the local AP bureau. These carbon copies often substituted for AP coverage of a news event.

Hughs' plan prevailed and UPI introduced "DataNews" in 1975. "DataNews" and a similar high-speed service for broadcasters called "CustomNews" became UPI's main news delivery systems.

"DataNews" used coding developed by the American Newspaper Publishers Association in 1974 to support computer sorting of news by categories. For example, the code line at the top a dispatch would have an "s" for sports, an "i" for international news, an "f" for financial and so forth. With this coding, newspaper computers could distribute copy to the appropriate editors. There were also priority codes: "u" for urgent, "b" for bulletin, etc.

UPI later developed a greatly expanded coding system that allowed "CustomNews" clients to choose from a large menu of topics and even sort copy by geography, as well as very specific news categories. A client could choose to receive all copy from its own state, but only very selective copy from neighboring states, Washington and selected foreign points. Each client could totally tailor its own news and information package.

The UPI computers, programmed by Data Dimensions Company to transfer copy directly to client computers, caused an "abstract" to print out on small, quieter, high speed Extel printers at subscribers' offices. The abstract was the first paragraph or a few lines of a dispatch, along with information as to its category, length and originating bureau.

Electronics at each receiving point could be remotely programmed by long distance to pick up only the material the customer was entitled to.

Moving to computers created a serious personnel situation. What to do with about 100 teletype operators who were no longer needed? The Commercial Telegraphers Union and the company settled it peacefully. Older operators were offered early pensions. Younger operators were invited to try out as editors. Having already done editing on behalf of less than perfect wire filers, many operators spent the rest of their careers as editors and wire filers.

In 1975, UPI offered various "supplemental" news and feature syndicates free transmission of their material via its "DataNews" high-speed wire. The *New York Times* news service became one of the first users of the UPI system, distributing its copy on "DataNews" wire in April 1976.

The University of Georgia School of Journalism was set up with a link to UPI's computers to teach students electronic news editing.

Newspapers covering the Montreal Olympics and the 1976 national political conventions in New York and Kansas City were offered use of UPI terminals to send copy to their home offices. At the political conventions, UPI itself moved 100,000 words a day from the press rooms.

United Press International moved another step ahead in technology when it teamed with RCA American Communications Inc. at the ANPA convention in Anaheim, California, in 1977 to demonstrate the use of satellites for transmission. A six-foot dish antenna was shown to be reliable in picking up transmissions, even voice for the audio service.

UPI's computerization had many advantages, including faster delivery of the huge stock lists. The sports department was able to have the computer format small-font "agate" material such as baseball box scores and standings. Long lists of golf scores could be listed almost instantly, sorted by scores or alphabetically.

In the case of the stock market, much of the computerization was done before the data reached the wire service computers. UPI was surprised in 1975 when it received a bill from the New York Stock Exchange seeking $1,500 per month for using its computerized list. The exchange said the charge was to cover technical costs of its high speed operation.

UPI and AP protested to the Securities and Exchange Commission, which regulates the exchange. They said stock prices were public information and should be available without charge. The charges would double their cost of running the stocks on their wires, they complained. It was a violation of the First Amendment of the Constitution for the exchange to withhold the data, the wire services argued.

Since there really was a cost in producing the computerized list, the wires' case was not good. However, the Stock Exchange reduced its fee from $1,500 per month to $750. Associated Press agreed to this. UPI continued its futile protest to the SEC but lost the argument.

In 1981, UPI began an arrangement with Lexis-Nexis, a computer search company serving many newspapers and libraries.

At the time there were a half-million home computers in the United States and the market was expanding by 10,000 per week. The internet had not yet been widely developed and home computers were in their infancy.

By the end of the 1970s, UPI's Univac computers in New York were growing obsolete although less than a decade old. Management, under Rod Beaton, persuaded the Scripps owners to invest $10 million in a new communications center in Dallas. It had its own building, costing about $2 million, and two new 90/80 Univac computers worth $6.5 million, plus ancillary equipment.

The Dallas center opened on the Fourth of July 1980, and was the first such installation in the world designed and built specifically for news distribution.

The technology may have been primitive by today's standards, but it was a revolutionary advance from the 1960s and earlier communications schemes like the "pony" telephone reports. Going back farther, an arrangement worked out for the Stillwater, Minnesota *Evening Gazette* in 1916. The *Gazette* received its news by streetcar.

Joe Morgan, who was with UP in Minneapolis, recalled the set-up. "An office boy would walk three blocks to the bus route with a roll of printer copy. He was supposed to hand it to the driver of a bus heading to St. Paul. The bus driver might or might not stop to collect the packet.

"At St. Paul's main intersection, the bus driver would toss the roll of paper out onto the street. There, a Western Union messenger was to pick it up and put it on the streetcar to South Saint Paul, where, at the end of the line, the motorman would pitch the packet into a snowbank. Someone from the newspaper could pick it up from the snowbank if all the previous exchanges were carried out."[1]

In the 1970s, technical costs of running a wire service were becoming so expensive that Beaton made another pitch for joint physical facilities with the Associated Press. At a meeting of editors in Oklahoma City, August 13, 1970, he said the two services did not need to maintain separate delivery systems at the cost to each of millions of dollars.

"I personally believe that the time has come when our industry must try to rationalize some of the things we're doing through more intelligent use and sharing of communications and other facilities," Beaton said. He said it could be done "without any diminishing of meaningful competition."

Beaton's plan made sense for the newspaper clients, who were paying for both systems. As satellite transmission came in, there was no reason why one receiving dish on the roof of a newspaper could not pick up both the AP and UPI reports, as well as other broadcast data. UPI and AP news would be separated by electronic filters attached to the equipment, with no danger of mixing them. Beaton said this alone could save the industry up to $11.5 million a year.

An agreement was urgent, the UPI chief said, because land line rates of the transmission companies were rising by $4.3 million a year for UPI. There had been a 10 percent rate increase at the end of 1971 and a 35 percent hike for the wire services lines in January 1974, amounting to $4.5 million dollars. James Darr, communications chief, said the company was already paying $216,488 a month for leased wires and it would jump by $94,220 with the increase. Satellite transmission could eliminate most of the land lines.

Technical chiefs from both services, David L. Bowen of AP and Darr of UPI, said a joint system could avoid anticipated transmission cost increases.

"I can guarantee that AP and UPI will continue their vigorous competition. We would share this communications system but this is really no different than the current situation in which we share the ATT system," Bowen said.

Under Beaton's plan, a jointly owned non-profit corporation would be formed to handle the technical services. He repeatedly pleaded with the industry to insist on such an arrangement.

Nevertheless, the Associated Press refused to seriously consider technical cooperation. Because the joint equipment sounded reasonable to publishers, AP executives said they would go for the idea, but they insisted on control and imposing a disproportionate amount of the cost on UPI. AP said it would not allow UPI to attach more than one client to one satellite dish, which was an important part of the arrangement UPI wanted.

The 1977 demonstration at Anaheim had used a six-foot dish. Later, UPI developed a satellite system using 18-inch receiving dishes. Clarence Zaitz, a West Coast UPI sales representative, demonstrated one by hanging it outside a hotel room window.

Both computers and electronic satellite transmission relied on electricity.

Tuesday, November 9, 1965, was a memorable day on the Eastern Seaboard of the United States. A power failure blacked out a huge area, trapping people in subways and elevators at precisely 5:28 P.M.

When the lights went out in the New York UPI bureau on the 12th floor of the Daily News Building, there was no great surge of excitement. Unipressers were trained to take things in stride.

Roger Tatarian, editor-in-chief, made his way to a storage cabinet and found an oil lamp. His next move was to go for a cup of coffee. Of course the coffee machine was not working, so Tatarian sat down at his desk and began planning how to cope with the situation.

Telephones were still functioning. Tatarian called the Chicago bureau and told them to find out what was going on in the blackout and to handle the "blackout" story. Washington was called and told to take over filing the national trunk wires. Other bureaus were alerted by telephone to handle various chores that usually were done in New York.

London was told to file its material by telephone to Washington. Tokyo was instructed to telephone San Francisco with its news. The report for South America, usually translated into Spanish in New York, was to be filed in English from Washington.

The photo staff spread its chores out in similar fashion. When the lights went back on, everything returned to routine.

Twelve years later, at 9:34 P.M., July 13, 1977, power went out again at UPI headquarters in New York. Terminal screens went black. Printers stopped buzzing. Activity came to a halt.

Editors stayed in their chairs, assuming it was a momentary interruption of electricity. However, lights did not come back on until 5:30 P.M. the next day.

Twenty hours without power was an eternity for a wire service.

When the lights went out and the computers went dead in New York, all the wires emanating from editorial headquarters clunked to an eerie quiet in bureaus around the world.

A "deadline every minute" wire service could not sit back and wait for a resumption of power. Technicians immediately began converting the system to manual functioning on emergency power so that some news could move.

Telephones were functioning, so, as in the power failure of 1965, the New York bureau linked itself to the Washington bureau by several telephone lines. Washington took on the job of filing to regional centers around the world. Some copy was sent between bureaus by facsimile, which uses telephone lines.

UPI had obtained a diesel generator after the 1965 blackout but it was inadequate to handle the needs of 1977.

Lou Carr, on the desk in New York, phoned around the country and obtained story skeds for the A.M. news budget. Don Mullen and Joe O'Brien set up conference calls to division points and dictated dispatches that could be moved in regions not affected by the blackout. Some important customers were telephoned individually and stories dictated as they were in the old "pony" days.

Mel Laytner was going off duty, waiting to catch an elevator, when the power went off. In the day's fading light he went back into the bureau. He knew where candles and flashights were stored, in a locker along with the riot helmets for use in covering another kind of emergency—on the streets. He was feeling his way there when he ran into Bobby Ray Miller, overnight editor.

"Laytner, give me 450 words on the blackout," Miller barked.

Tom Foty was at home in Riverdale. He telephoned the audio office to tell them he would go to police headquarters in New York to help report on the blackout. In his pitch dark garage he found a flashlight, got into his car and drove carefully in the eerie darkness on Harlem River Drive. He was flabbergasted because there was no skyline, the lights were missing.

In Albany, also without power, staffers got out typewriters, typed copy and sent it to customers by telephone photofax, alternating pages of news with photos.

UPI did not have a serviceable communications backup. Associated Press did and was able to get news out more quickly using emergency generators. Needless to say, UPI began planning an emergency power system when the lights went on the next day and put in an order for a new generator and other equipment which, according to Beaton "would sustain an acceptable level of service in an emergency."

A backup system using huge batteries was established in the new Dallas communication center. The communications department also moved to the Dallas center.

The new computers in Dallas were linked to UPI national and division bureaus in Boston, New York, Washington, Atlanta, Pittsburgh, Chicago, Dallas and San Francisco. These so-called "data-links" gave those bureaus complete access to all data in the computers as well as the ability to file to and manage all customer circuits.

Smaller bureaus, using slow-speed circuits on the "Sked-4" system, could only file their copy to these division points. This caused a problem since many of these bureaus had filed state newspaper and broadcast wires. Establishing full data links from all of the fifty states to the computer would have been cost prohibitive.

To solve the problem, UPI established "news centers" in Boston, Pittsburgh, Atlanta, Dallas, Chicago and San Francisco to file newspaper and broadcast state wires to all states within their divisions. Many staffers were transferred from state headquarter bureaus to the division points to help produce those state wires. Reporters in the outlying bureaus filed their stories to the division points where they were edited for newspaper wires and re-written for broadcast circuits.

Computers were changing the geographical boundaries for UPI. Editors and writers in the San Francisco office were able to produce news and broadcast copy for Montana as quickly and easily as they did for California.

New York bureau celebration 1974 on the second anniversary of UPI's Information, Storage and Retrieval (IS&R) computerization. From left: Lou Carr, Jimmy Darr, Walter Logan, Edie Cahill, Al Bruce, Don Mullen, Mike Hughes, Travis Hughs (mostly hidden behind Hughes) and Jeff Grigsby.

26

You're Supposed
to Be Dead

"MISS WEBB," SAID THE CAMBODIAN LIEUTENANT, "YOU'RE SUPPOSED
to be dead."

It was Saturday, May 1, 1971, Catherine M. Webb was huddled in the dawn on
Highway 4 with five other journalists when the officer approached them.

The six had been captured by North Vietnamese troops on April 8 after wandering
frantically in the jungle no-mans-land for 24 hours during a firefight between Vietnamese communist troops and Cambodian paratroopers who wanted to get the North
Vietnamese out of their country.

Miss Webb was supposed to be dead. Three weeks earlier two Cambodian officers had
found a woman's body near where she disappeared, identified it as Webb and cremated it.

"This is Kate. Jimmy and I are alive and well," she told Khauuv Bun Keang, who
had been holding fort at the Phnom Phen bureau since she failed to return from a
news-hunting expedition. "Jimmy and I are alive and well," Kate had to tell Khauv
several times before it sank in.

After a two-day trek through the jungle from the hidden communist camp, the
North Vietnamese had brought the captives to the road and fled back into the jungle.
The Cambodian unit, which found them, took her to a telephone.

Kim Willenson, a UPI staffer in Saigon, rushed to the Cambodian military outpost as soon as he heard the good news.

"Alive," correct. But "well" was an optimistic half-truth. Webb was nearly destroyed
with malaria, swollen, ulcerous feet and other debilities suffered in her twenty-three
days as a captive of the North Vietnamese in the jungle.

Webb's companions in captivity, who were with her when she was seized, were
Chin (Jimmy) Sarath, UPI staff driver, Toshiichi Suzuki, a newsreel correspondent for
a Japanese agency, and four Cambodian photographers.

Like other reporters in the sullen, dirty war, she had been frustrated by dubious handout material from military headquarters. Reporters always want to get
news where it is happening. This small group of journalists was fifty-seven miles
outside Phnom Pehn on Wednesday, April 7, 1971.

Webb looked up and saw the clear blue sky dotted with white parachutes. Cambodian paratroopers were landing to a greeting of heavy fire from communist positions on the other side of a road. She and her companions abandoned their jeep on the road and tried to flee through the jungle. They found themselves tripping over dense growth and telephone cables strung through the trees by the North Vietnamese who had elaborate camps set up in the Cambodian "sanctuary" near the border with South Vietnam.

The correspondents were slowed by hunger and, especially, thirst in the tropical heat. A band of communist soldiers approached and quietly took them prisoners.

During her twenty-three days with the enemy, Webb said she was treated well. She smoked cigarettes with her captors, listened to them singing, listened to stories about their side of the war, was given the same food and water as her captors had, and was interrogated gently and considerately. They wanted to know whether she was an American, whether she was with the CIA, and why she was risking her life out on that road.

She responded honestly. She was not an American. She was a New Zealander. She was not with the CIA. She worked for UPI. She was out on the battlefront because she wanted to report what was going on. She was just a reporter, not a "foreign correspondent."

The communists let her listen to *Radio Hanoi*. She was surprised to learn it was pirating United Press International news reports.

Xuan Loc, Vietnam, April 16, 1975—from left, UPI audio correspondent Bill Reilly, UPI correspondent Leon Daniel, two weeks before the fall of Saigon.

"They treated us very well," Webb told other reporters when she got back to Phnom Pehn. "They gave me pills and penicillin when my feet swelled up. They gave us toothbrushes and toothpaste, hammocks and other things. They even built a wash stand for us."

Much of her time in captivity was spent moving through the thick jungle from place to place. This was the communists' way of avoiding Cambodian air attacks.

Going to Vietnam originally for an Australian newspaper, Webb had joined UPI as a stringer and then was hired as a staff reporter. She left the wire service in 1969 but returned to the Pittsburgh, Pennsylvania, bureau, then got back to Southeast Asia as Phnom Pehn bureau chief.

She had been reported dead. Her friends and relatives had mourned. Unipressers in bureaus from Saigon to London had held memorial drinking parties, exchanging Kate Webb stories. When she turned up safe she became the UPI's most celebrated war reporter in Southeast Asia. Her account of the experience moved in a series on the wire and was afterward published in a UPI promotional booklet titled "On the Other Side of the War."

Other UPI women who covered the Southeast Asia war included Maggie Kilgore and Tracy Wood. They worked the same jobs as the male staffers and often had to endure added inconvenience and embarrassment. Men could go behind a tree but women had to squat.

She told historian Philip Knightly, who reported it in *First Casualty*: "The first time I went out, there was a bit of a fire fight and I was so scared that I wet my pants. I hoped the GIs would think that it was sweat and that no one would notice. Then I saw that some of the GIs had wet pants, too, and it didn't matter any more."[1]

Southeast Asia had been a French colonial territory until after World War II. In 1954, the French were driven out by natives insurgents. A communist faction headed by Ho Chi Minh set itself up in Hanoi in the north. South Vietnamese, mainly anti-communist Catholics, established their base in Saigon, with a government under Ngo Dinh Diem.

Diem's regime was shaken by an abortive coup at the end of 1960. The rebels were called Viet Cong and had ties with the Communists of the North. Four hundred people were killed in the fighting.

When President John F. Kennedy sent 200 U.S. military advisers to Saigon to support the Diem regime, only a half dozen foreign correspondents were based in Saigon, including Ray Herndon of United Press International. During the following decade, more than 600 journalists came to the country to report on a war that ultimately engaged a half million American troops.

In April 1962, Cornelius Mahoney Sheehan, a Harvard graduate, who had been in the Army in Asia, was hired by UPI in Tokyo and sent to Saigon.

"Neil" Sheehan was "as green as Irish grass," according to William Prochnau, author of *Once Upon a Distant War*.

Sitting at the American officers' club bar, an army officer told Sheehan that 200 Viet Cong had been killed in a battle forty miles south of Saigon. The correspondent verified with other officers that there had been a skirmish at My Tho. He went with the story and the 200 killed. Next day he learned that there had been a battle, but only fifteen Viet Cong were killed. UPI had to roll back from 200 to fifteen dead, the kind of embarrassment that singes a wire service's reputation.

But Sheehan matured quickly under fire, Prochnau said, "He also became one of the best correspondents ever to set foot in Viet Nam, becoming a legendary figure."

The Vietnam War was different from every other war America fought, for four reasons: uncertainty about objectives; secrecy about what was going on; political intrigue, locally in Vietnam and internationally among the major powers; and a divided America.

These things were all reflected in reporting the war and presented continuing problems for correspondents covering the fighting and the rebel movement to overthrow the corrupt Diem regime.

One example cited by historians was the exaggeration of Buddhist opposition to Diem. This opposition was not as important in the country where it occurred as it was pictured in the world press. It was presented as a major, deep, widespread religious feeling by the dominant religion. But, in fact, it represented only the pro-communist element of the Buddhists.

The correspondents for AP, UPI and the *New York Times* courted the rebels to the point that they received special invitations to witness and photograph self-immolations on Saigon streets.

In July 1963, a faction of Buddhists, siding with the Viet Cong, took up protests in Saigon and kept the news media advised. On July 7, nine American correspondents were attacked by about twenty South Vietnamese secret police while covering a Buddhist protest. Several reporters, including Neil Sheehan of UPI, were slightly injured. Robert J. Manning, U.S. assistant secretary of state and a former UPI staffer, told reporters he would investigate the situation but nothing came of it.

As Saigon bureau manager, Sheehan carried heavy responsibilities and often quarreled with Tokyo on what to cover and what to ignore. Tokyo bristled when Saigon failed to interview General Paul Harkins, the U.S. military commander, who had made himself available for interviews. When other services showed with Harkins' comments, Tokyo queried Sheehan and received back a cable bearing a touch of the reporter's annoyance.

NONE RESIDENT CORRESPONDENTS BOTHERING INTERVIEW HARKINS ANYMORE BECAUSE TEDIOUS MONOTONY HIS REMARKS STOP WE LEAVE HIM TO VISITING FIREMEN STOP THIS STORY UNLENDS ITSELF TO INTERVIEW TECHNIQUE STOP WHY YOU QUERYING ME HARKINS INTERVIEW STOP SHEEHAN.

At the end of October 1963, Hoberecht ordered Sheehan to take a break, come to Tokyo for vacation. Neil didn't want to. He wanted to be in on the Diem "kill."

As fate would have it, Diem did fall on November 1 while Neil was in Tokyo. In an unusual friendly gesture for a competing news agency, David Halberstram of the *New York Times* and AP's Malcolm Browne had cabled Sheehan to get back to Saigon so he wouldn't be scooped by them. Sheehan claimed afterward that the message was kept from him. Other Tokyo staffers say Sheehan did not look at the "live" spike.

UPI coverage of Diem's fall was handled by Ray Herndon, who had been in Vietnam longer than Sheehan and had not committed himself to the cause of the insurgents. Herndon crawled with the rebels' tanks as they drove into Diem's palace.

The succeeding government of Nguyen Van Thieu proved to be nearly as corrupt as Diem.

Sheehan remained bitter about this episode, particularly when the Pulitzer Prize board gave Browne and Halberstram a prize for their reporting. Sheehan thought he should have shared. The prize seemed to have been awarded more to celebrate bringing Diem down than for good, objective reporting.

There was reason for Saigon correspondents to be frustrated. Getting accurate news out of Vietnam was a chaotic job. U.S. spokesmen insisted they could not give information because it was South Vietnam's war. The South Vietnamese made themselves unavailable for questions or lied about what was happening.

President Kennedy said the American soldiers were there only as advisers. When the bodies of American soldiers were brought in, U.S. spokesmen said they could not comment. In February 1962, a directive known as Cable 1006 told U.S. military officers in Vietnam it was "not in our interest to have stories indicating that Americans are leading and directing combat missions" even though they were. Officers denied that Americans were flying the helicopters and that napalm was being dropped, despite the fact that every reporter knew it was happening.

Direct military censorship was rejected by American officials and no guidelines were issued. Reporters were left to ferret out news and then risk the consequences of publishing it.

UPI's Bob Ibrahim said military commanders required reporters to "abide by the accepted ground rules" without knowing exactly what those ground rules were. The only known rule was that if a correspondent broke voluntary censorship, not only the offender but every reporter for the agency could be discredited. "They allow a reporter to make an error and then they lower the boom. The military is prosecutor, judge, jury and executioner. There ain't no appeal," said Ibrahim.[2]

Joe Galloway covered an action in which the U.S. First Cavalry division demolished a North Vietnamese regiment at Plei Me. Military spokesmen called it an important victory. The following day, however, an American battalion stumbled into an ambush in the same area and was nearly annihilated. The division suffered 151 killed, 121 wounded and four missing. The Army said the casualties were "moderate."

In comparison to the entire Army force in the country they were, but for the unit involved, the loss was certainly "heavy." Officers had concealed the casualties even from General William C. Westmoreland.[3] He learned about the heavy loss from Galloway.

When correspondents complained that information was being withheld, they were stonewalled or lied to and they didn't like it. Barry Zothian, State Department spokesman in Saigon, commented, "Hell hath no fury like a wire service scooped."[4]

In one of the early battles in 1963 at Ap Bac, South Vietnamese troops behaved cowardly, refusing to fight. The American officers directly involved complained about it to reporters, but U.S. officials stonewalled all inquiries about the action, even though the blatant Vietnamese cowardice had cost American lives.

As the war accelerated, the press corps in South Vietnam grew from forty correspondents at the beginning of 1964 to 282 in January 1966. One hundred ten of them were Americans. Later more than 600 reporters and photographers were accredited but less than a third of them actually covered any combat.

UPI's Arthur Dommen was the first to report that B52 bombers were conducting strikes against communist infiltration routes in Laos. His dispatch filed on December 18, 1964, said U.S. planes had been attacking communists in Laos for months. The raids became an issue when other news media picked up the story.[5]

On the last day of January 1970, as the South Vietnamese people celebrated Tet, their most festive holiday, Viet Cong forces attacked all the important cities and towns in South Vietnam. In Saigon, they assaulted the presidential palace, Tan Son Nhut airport and even the newly constructed U.S. embassy.

Saigon received the most coverage although other cities were hit harder. Reporting on the embassy attack became controversial when Associated Press and the *New York Times* said the building was entered by the soldiers. UPI's report, which proved to be correct, was that there was gunfire at the embassy but that the enemy soldiers did not get inside the new structure.

When UPI's David Lamb quoted the commander of the Third Marine Division at Da Nang, Major General Raymond Davis, he was accused of revealing an "off the record" interview. The general had told Lamb: "It makes no sense to watch 400 trucks a day moving through Laos with ammunition to kill Americans. The quickest way to shorten this war is to destroy these sanctuaries."

Two days later, UPI reporter Robert Kaylor revealed that U.S. Special Forces units had been conducting secret forays into Laos and Cambodia for a year. A second dispatch, from Walter Whitehead, kept UPI ahead on the story by establishing that Cambodian Prince Norodom Sihanouk had given tacit approval for the operations.[6]

In the spring of 1970, veteran war correspondent Robert C. Miller and UPI photographer Kyoichi Sawada experienced what Miller called "a most curious capture" by Viet Cong guerillas.

"They giggled and smiled and bowed throughout the incident," Miller recalled. He said he and Sawada, who was to win a Pulitzer and later be killed in the war, were about five miles past a checkpoint on the road to Phnom Penh with a Cambodian interpreter and driver. Their captors, brandishing automatic rifles, told them to walk down the road. Miller and Sawada saw black-trousered soldiers lurking along the tree-lined road and they were sure if they went ahead they would be shot.

UPI reporters Ted Marks (center, talking to interpreter) and Ken Englade (left) on a sweep with Cambodian soldiers near Phnom Penh, Cambodia, spring 1973. (UPI photo from Ken Englade files via Wieck Photo DataBase.)

So they sat down in front of a nearby house. After awhile, a guerilla officer escorted them to his office and talked to them for two hours. They were then walked back to the place of their capture. They left quickly for friendly territory, waving white handkerchiefs.

Richard Nixon was elected president largely on a promise to get the United States out of the war. When he took office in 1969, he said American involvement would continue but be reduced.

William M. Hammond, an army historian, said the war had become "a bottomless pit."[7]

Nixon ordered that B52 bombers attack the communist bases in Cambodian territory as well as the supply lines. Officers in Saigon were ordered not to let the media know. The first raid took place March 18. A week later UPI reporter Jack Walsh learned about "Operation Breakfast" and filed a dispatch.

When Saigon was falling to the North Vietnamese forces on April 29–30, 1975, Americans in the city were hastily lifted by helicopter from the roof of the U.S. Embassy to naval vessels offshore. The evacuation became chaotic.

The UPI staff in Saigon had been advised to leave earlier, but they didn't attempt to get out until the twenty-ninth. That day, they went to a street corner where they had been told they would be picked up. Buses arrived, but the street was in bedlam. Hundreds of panic-stricken South Vietnamese stormed the vehicles.

"WE HAVE RETURNED TO THE BUREAU AND RESUMED FILING," Leon Daniel advised New York. "NOTHING TO WORRY ABOUT. WE'LL GET OUT IN DUE TIME."

A few hours later, Paul Vogle, Bert Okuley and Ken Englade went by car to the embassy for another attempt to leave. Only Okuley and Englade were able to get inside the building. Vogle was stranded in the seething mob. The helicopters were lifting off anyone who could fight their way to the roof and climb aboard. UPI photographer Hugh Van Ess made some dramatic photos of the frantic crowd trying to board the copters.

Al Dawson, then UPI bureau chief in Saigon, knew the whereabouts of a senior official of the victorious Viet Cong and went to talk to him. He was told by this official that the UPI staff would be safe at the bureau at 19 Ngo Duc Ky.

At noon on April 30, Viet Cong tanks rolled into the city. Dawson was on the wire to New York, "DO NOT WORRY. ALL IS WELL. EVERYBODY IS WELL. THE THING IS GOING VERY SMOOTHLY."

Dawson was one of two American reporters who stayed in the city when the communists took over. The other was Francis Starner, a freelancer. Dawson later wrote a piece for *Editor & Publisher* in which he said they experienced "no harassment and surprisingly little hostility." The communists, he said, expressed pride on their victory over the Americans but did not "lord it over us."

Kyoichi Sawada (left) and Toshio Sakai, both Pulitzer Prize–winning UPI photographers, in a U.S. helicopter in South Vietnam, late 1960s. Sawada was killed in Cambodia on October 28, 1970. (Photo courtesy of Hideko Sakai.)

The American pullout, which had begun in 1972, left 50,000 dead.

Five UPI staffers were killed in the conflict and two stringers were missing and presumed dead. In all about seventy journalists were dead or missing in the war.

Kent Potter, of Philadelphia, was one of the adventure-seeking photographers who went to Vietnam. He was killed February 10, 1971, when two South Vietnamese helicopters were shot down during a raid into Cambodia. One of them carried four news photographers.

Hiromichi Mine, a photographer, was killed March 5, 1968; Charles Eggleston, photographer, May 6, 1968; Frank Frosch, reporter, October 28, 1970; and Kyoichi Sawada, photographer, October 28, 1970.

Freelancers killed while on assignment for UPI included Terry Reynolds, April 26, 1971, when he and UP jeep driver Chim Sarath were ambushed April 26, 1972 in Cambodia.

Eggleston, anticipating that he might not survive, willed all his possessions to Vietnamese charities. Others on the scene said he was carrying a machine gun and shooting at the enemy when he was killed.

Among those wounded in Southeast Asia was Tea Kim Heong, UPI photographer, in Cambodia on March 30, 1971.[8]

Some of the events of the Vietnam War were underreported even though there were more than 500 correspondents in Vietnam. Little was said about riots and racial unrest among the American troops. When Bob Hope performed for the GI's in Vietnam, he was hooted when he mentioned President Nixon favorably.

Also largely underreported were incidents in which American soldiers refused to fight. A UPI dispatch by Tom Tiede reported that a platoon from Company B, 2nd Battalion, 25th Infantry division refused to go on patrol in October 1969.

"I never did get those men to obey me," the company commander told Tiede, "I tried, but they just wouldn't go. I had to bring charges against all of them."

The My Lai massacre, in which American troops killed hundreds of civilian Vietnamese, was not reported until a year after it happened. It came to light in the United States, not in Vietnam. On September 5, 1969, in Fort Benning, Georgia, army news officials revealed that Lieutenant William Calley was up for charges in connection with deaths of up to 350 civilians in Vietnam in March 1968. The only reason it came to light at all was that a soldier, who had heard about it while in Vietnam, wrote a letter to General Westmoreland asking him if it was true.

Westmoreland himself did not learn about it until more than a year after it happened. Even with the disclosure at Fort Benning, American news media gave it slight attention for a month.

The Viet Cong radio had broadcast the story of the mass civilian killing a few days after it happened, and American news agencies monitoring the communist radio asked army spokesmen about it. The communists blamed the 82nd Airborne for the assault. army officials said the 82nd was nowhere near the area, so correspondents assumed the atrocity report was enemy propaganda.

Hiromichi Mine, shown here shortly after arriving in South Vietnam in January 1968. Mine was killed March 5, 1968, when a U.S. Marine armored personnel carrier he was on hit a booby-trapped bomb in Vietnam. (Photo courtesy of Mine's survivors).

UPI reporter Robert Kaylor earlier had reported an incident of excessive slaughter. The dispatch said 33,000 communists were slain through "indiscriminate use of mass firepower" during an engagement between the 9th Army Infantry Division and the Viet Cong near Dong tam in the Mekong Delta. The commander of the division, Major General Julian Ewell, had announced only 6,000 enemy casualties in the battle for fear of being criticized.

Kaylor said he learned from talking to troops in the area that Ewell had encouraged slaughter of the enemy by rewarding special privileges to units on the basis of body count.

A press issue arose over another somewhat similar story. Leon Daniel of UPI was with the American 11th Armored Cavalry in an attack on the Cambodian town of Snoul, a major transit point on the Ho Chi Minh trail. He reported that the American troops looted the town, seizing liquor and property.

The Associated Press did not use the story. Wes Gallagher, AP general manager, said he killed it on U.S. wires because it was "inflammatory." Katherine Graham, publisher of the *Washington Post*, also had reservations about the story, but her newspaper ran it on the editorial page.

As Vietnam became overloaded with correspondents and adventure-seeking freelancers, self-discipline deteriorated. One press center was shut down early in 1972 after a fight broke out between an NBC correspondent and a public affairs officer.

The routine in Vietnam for UPI correspondents was tougher than for other major media. The schedule was seven days a week, with ten days R&R outside of Vietnam every three months, according to Maggie Kilgore.[9]

The UPI and other agencies began using more stringers to cut down expenses. These freelancers lived day-to-day on whatever the agencies would pay for their stories. They were less reliable than staff reporters.

In order to be accredited, a stringer had to have a letter from a legitimate news agency. Bureau managers gave these letters freely to anyone who looked like they might get a story.

Some freelancers were actually political operatives, but their reports occasionally were informative. Don Luce, a correspondent for the U.S. Conference of the World Council of Churches, was known to be liaison between anti-war groups in the United States and the Viet Cong. He broke a story on the inhuman "tiger cages" used by South Vietnamese to imprison captured Viet Cong. He had seen the prison and told other newsmen about it. The South Vietnam government retaliated by lifting Luce's credentials, accusing him of being a representative of anti-war groups.

When Al Dawson of UPI reported that American helicopters were flying South Vietnamese reinforcements to a fighting zone, his credentials were lifted. He was told it was against the guidelines to disclose when American forces were being sent into a fighting area.[10]

In 1973, the U.S. Congress voted to cut off financing the war. Nixon signed a peace agreement on January 27, and the final session of Saigon's "five o'clock follies," American briefing for reporters, was held the same day.

Photographers David Kennerly, Kyoichi Sawada and Toshio Sakai won Pulitzer prizes during the war.

By the time U.S. forces fought their last battle in South Vietnam, the number of reporters in the country had diminished to about 200. When thousands of South Vietnamese fled to escape the communist takeover in 1975, Nguyen Anh Tuyet, a former UPI employee in Saigon, and his family were located in a crowded refugee camp but UPI arranged for Tuyet and his family to transfer to Los Angeles where he was given a job in the news bureau.

27

No Point of View

WHEN UNITED PRESS SELECTED AL KUETTNER TO HEAD ITS COVERAGE OF the South's civil rights conflicts in 1955, Atlanta radio station WSB invited the soft-spoken bureau manager to an interview show.

One of the first questions asked was, "What's your point of view on integration?"

Without hesitation, Kuettner answered, "I work for United Press. I have no point of view."

Kuettner had recited the philosophy of United Press from its birth in 1907 to that point in the middle of the 1950s

"No point of view."

United Press was born with and maintained a passion for objectivity. Employees sometimes boasted that they were "sexless." UP's independence gave the news service a huge edge over rival AP in covering the conflicts that grew from the 1954 U.S. Supreme Court decision striking down the South's long-held "separate but equal" laws.

The Associated Press was an association of its member newspapers and those publishers helped write the rules. AP also depended on those member newspapers to cover the news for AP's wires.

In the 1950s, many newspapers in the South were reluctant to cover the increasing civil rights demonstrations and blamed most of what was happening on "outside agitators." AP, by its ties to those papers, was colored by the same brush.

United Press was forced to cover the civil rights movement with its own staffers and stringers and the UP editors saw the story as it was—packed with the conflict and the significance of historic change.

Martin "Marty" Murphy, one of the key Atlanta editors in the 60s, believes UPI's independent resolve to cover racial unrest despite opposition from many southern publishers helped the cause of civil rights by putting the conflict on the world stage.

"Had it not been for UPI sending reporters to check on demonstrations in various towns, the momentum would have never built and MLK [Martin Luther King] would have been left preaching to the choir," he said.

In 1960, the KKK endorsed Spesard L. Holland in the Florida gubernatorial primary. A Klan spokesman said Holland was the best candidate because "he knows what to do with Jews and niggers." The UP used the quote, AP didn't.

Drew Pearson, the national columnist-commentator, said AP ignored the quote because "the AP, of course, is owned by publishers and caters to publishers."[1]

Many southern newspapers did not feel that United Press International operated without a "point of view." Some considered Kuettner, himself an "outside agitator."

Lawrence "Lonnie" Falk recalls an incident in 1963, when Dr. Martin Luther King came to Birmingham, Alabama, to take part in a civil rights march.

Falk said Kuettner had traveled to the Alabama steel town to help cover the march.

"MLK was leading the march," Falk said, "and it was a jostling kind of thing. Kuettner was near the front line and he moved next to King and put his arm around the civil rights leader to keep him from being knocked to the ground."

Falk said someone snapped a picture of Kuettner with his arm around King and the widely circulated picture touched off harsh criticism from southern newspapers. Several Alabama papers said Kuettner was "hugging" King.

Ku Klux Klan leader Bobbie Shelton ran the picture of Kuettner and King in the KKK magazine, *The Fiery Cross.*

Shelton apparently believed that Falk was more open-minded that Kuettner. The Alabama Klan leader sent Lonnie, the Birmingham bureau manager, a free copy of the

Al Kuettner, who directed UPI's civil rights coverage in the '60s, left, interviews white supremacist J.B. Stoner at a Birmingham, Alabama, school in September 1963.

Photographer Denny Kinsella, shooting pictures of National Guard tanks rolling down Detroit streets from under a car during 1960s racial rioting. UPI photographer Art Chernecki, who was partially under the same car, after barely escaping sniper shots, took the photo.

Klan magazine every month. He once called the UPI bureau manager and boasted: "You're the only person in the world who gets a free copy of *The Fiery Cross*—but that's okay because I'm sure you wouldn't pay for it anyway because you're Jewish."

Alabama was the stage for many of the signal events in the long quest for civil rights in the South.

Some historians mark "Bloody Sunday" at the Edmund Pettus bridge in Selma, Alabama, as the beginning of the end for southern states using their police powers to defy federal court orders.

It was March 7, 1965, and a group of civil rights activists led by John Lewis, who would later serve in Congress, had planned to march from Selma to the Alabama capitol at Montgomery.

Alvin Benn, who worked in the Birmingham bureau, recalled that nobody really expected the marchers who left the Brown Chapel in Selma to go all the way to Montgomery.

He said men in suits and women in dresses and high heels left after services and headed for the bridge to begin the march. When Lewis and the marchers reached the approach of the bridge, they stared into a sea of brown and blue—Alabama State troopers and the Dallas County Sheriff Department's mounted posse. Alabama Governor George Wallace had ordered Alabama State Police Major John Cloud to stop the marchers. But, he didn't say how to do it.

When Lewis and his followers refused an order to stop and return to Selma, the troopers and mounted police waded into the crowd.

John Lynch of the UPI bureau in Montgomery was on the bridge and recalled the chaos framed in a curtain of tear gas.

"A large woman was lying on the ground and she wasn't moving," Lynch said. "One of the troopers said she had been faking and suggested that they drop a tear gas canister near her head. The canister hit the ground and enveloped the woman in the gas, but still she did not move."

The grim television pictures along with graphic accounts by UPI and others of Alabama police beating peaceful marchers hit a nerve nationally. President Lyndon B. Johnson quickly nationalized the Alabama National Guard and ordered it to protect the marchers when they resumed their trek to the state capitol two weeks later.

Kuettner later said he believed the 50-mile march from Selma to Montgomery protected by federal troops and nationalized guardsmen broke the back of Alabama's strong-armed opponents to integration. "After its violent beginning at the Pettus Bridge in Selma," Kuettner said, "it was almost a celebration for the hundreds of blacks who made it."

Benn remembered he was sitting in his UPI office in Birmingham after the march had ended, "drinking coffee and smoking cigarettes and thinking how peaceful it had finally been."

Then the bells rang on the teletype. A UPI bulletin said the body of a white woman had been found in her car along the route the marchers had followed. Her name was Viola Liuzzo. The Detroit woman had been driving a black man back to Selma after the march when she was shot. Three Klansmen had killed her and were later brought to trial along with a fourth member of the KKK.

Another civil rights march along another Dixie highway would provide Associated Press one of its most agonizing moments and reward United Press International for its unyielding faith in its reporters.

It was June 6, 1966, and James Meredith, the young black who had broken the "color line" at the University of Mississippi, was leading a group of civil rights activists on a 225-mile march from Memphis, Tennessee to Jackson, Mississippi to encourage Negro voter registration.

It was the second day of the march and a typical Mississippi scorcher. Meredith was wearing a pith helmet and walking shorts as he led a small group about one mile south of Hernando, Mississippi.

United Press International reporter James K. Cazalas said Meredith was in a good mood and twirling a swagger stick as he came to a small patch of woods. Cazalas heard the first shot.

"Meredith hit the dusty shoulder of the blacktop immediately and started crawling across the highway toward some parked police cars. A second shot rang out and he was squirming like a snake. I could tell he was panic-stricken, his eyes were white and his mouth was wide open."

UPI staff photographer Sam Parrish had dropped to one knee and was shooting pictures as fast as he could. After a third gunshot, Meredith reached the cover of a police car and Cazalas rushed to his side.

Cazalas said Meredith was moaning and covered with blood, but his face looked peaceful just minutes later when he was loaded aboard an ambulance that headed for the John Gaston Hospital in Memphis, some thirty minutes away.

Cazalas hurried to a nearby farmhouse to call the Atlanta bureau and dictated the dramatic news to Al Kuettner, who was working the control desk. Kuettner knew that

UPI photographer F.W. "Bill" Lyon (white shirt with cameras draped around his neck), shown covering the funeral in Birmingham for three of the four girls killed in the September 15, 1963, bombing of an all black church.

AP had already filed a bulletin saying that Meredith had been shot and killed, but he trusted Cazalas. Kuettner took the time to call the hospital and he reached Dr. William T. Tyson, who was director of the emergency room. Tyson told Kuettner that Meredith had been admitted, but that doctors did not believe his gunshot wounds were too serious.

UPI's account of the shooting was thirty minutes behind the AP's bulletin that Meredith had been shot to death and it caused some concern for the editors at NBC, CBS and ABC who had all rushed to broadcast the faulty AP report.

AP later apologized to its subscribers for the error, which it took more than thirty minutes to correct. AP officials said that reporter Ron Alfred of its Memphis staff had left the march before the shooting and returned to Memphis. According to the AP, Alfred was allowed to listen in as a reporter from the *Memphis Commercial Appeal* dictated word of the shooting to his paper.

The AP apology said the newspaper's reporter said Meredith had been shot in the head and that Alfred had thought he said "shot dead."

Claude Sitton, a former INS and UP staffer, covered the civil rights movement for the *New York Times,* and he reported that UPI also got caught with its "pants down" on one occasion.

Sitton said UPI had a winning team to cover a failed civil rights campaign led by Dr. Martin Luther King, Jr., in Albany, Georgia. Robert Gordon was handling the reporting and Kuettner was on the desk in Atlanta. It was the summer of 1962.

The problem was, Sitton recalled, that Gordon had rushed to Albany from Atlanta and had only the pants he was wearing. After chasing civil rights marchers around Albany's city hall for about a week, his pants were dirty and Gordon decided to send them to a one-hour cleaner near his hotel.

"No sooner had he parted with his britches," Sitton said, "than King, [Ralph] Abernathy and company arrived across the street from the hotel, dropped to their knees in prayer in front of city hall and were scooped up quickly and carted off to jail by Albany cops. I remember seeing Bob flailing his arms in frustration from his hotel room window."

The civil rights battles of the South were an integral part of the new conscience of the 60s. However, the lines were drawn by the U.S. Supreme Court in 1954 and the opening battles were part of the 50s.

Billy Ferguson recalled a hot August night in the dingy Atlanta bureau in 1955 when he was trying to switch from handling sports to hard news.

Ferguson was on the night news desk, working on the two nights the regular night desker was off. Fortunately Ferguson was working for William Tucker, the model for Southern Division news hands and one of UP's top writers.

The story popped up on the wire that connected bureaus to the main Southern Division news desk in Atlanta. There was no urgency, no bells, nothing seemingly to distinguish it from the scores of other stories crowding the wire.

The 150-word item filed by the Jackson, Mississippi, bureau carried a Sumner, Mississippi, dateline and reported the details about a 14-year-old Negro boy who was missing from the small nearby community of Money, Mississippi.

He took scant notice of the story. The missing boy was from Chicago and had been visiting relatives in Mississippi. Ferguson dutifully relayed the item to the UPI bureau in Chicago then put the story on the dead spike used for items that had been handled.

He turned his attention to another story he was preparing for the "A" wire, the main circuit that served newspapers throughout the United States.

When Tucker came back from a long dinner, Ferguson anticipated the night manager's praise on the way he handled the A-wire story.

However, Tucker picked up the "dead" spike before he looked at the "live" spike that held A-wire copy. After he had thumbed through several stories, Tucker bit down hard on the wooden tip of his cigarillo and pulled the Sumner story from the spike.

"What are we doing on this Sumner story?," Tucker asked. "Have you got someone on the way there?"

Ferguson was dumbfounded.

Tucker was on the phone with the Jackson bureau before Ferguson could answer and he set into motion blanket coverage of a story that would win headlines around the world.

Alabama Governor Geoge Wallace in Tuscaloosa, Alabama, on June 11, 1963, the day of his famous stand in the door to block integration at the University of Alabama. Photo was taken by then freelancer Joe Chapman, later a UPI staffer. It shows Wallace walking through a crowd that includes Lonnie Falk (sunglasses, dark coat with lapel pin), then a student at Alabama and later a UPI staffer and UPI photographer Gary Haynes (left center, adjusting lens of his camera, just above another photographer with sunglasses).

The teenager was named Emmett Till and his brutal lynching inflamed the nation.

Ferguson, a native of Indiana, had missed sensing the impact of one of the biggest stories of the civil rights conflict in the 50s.

The Alabama-born Tucker had a keen understanding of what goes on in rural Dixie. He had realized immediately that a teen-aged boy from Chicago could easily get in serious trouble in that area of Mississippi. He was right.

Despite the gaffe, Ferguson was entrusted to a seat on the night desk and he worked the Sunday shift. Staffers are usually alone in the UPI office on Sundays with little news breaking and they need to call around their region for news. Some astute promotion people know Sunday is a good day to get on the wire. A young preacher in Montgomery, Alabama, often called Atlanta on Sunday.

Martin Luther King, Jr., knew the value of national exposure for his bus boycott in the Alabama capital and how to get it on Sunday. Ferguson learned quickly that this articulate Baptist preacher was winning national attention for his Montgomery bus boycott. His phone calls always led to A-wire stories that received wide use by northern newspapers.

The Atlanta bureau provided the foundation for United Press's solid coverage of the growing racial conflicts. In addition to the guidance of Kuettner and Southern Division news Editor Chiles C. Coleman, the bureau in the 50s and 60s was staffed with many superb editors and writers.

They included Tucker, who had written the main UP war leads for morning newspapers from New York during World War II; Dick West, a quiet Texan who became UPI's humor writer with a daily column, "The Lighter Side;" Edwin "Ed" Rogers, who was a legend in UP with bizarre tales of his hell-bent pursuit of news; Claude Sitton, an ex-INS staffer who later earned key editorial assignments with both UPI and the *New York Times*; Lowry Bowman, William O. Tome and Peter S. Willett.

A lot of the faces in the Atlanta bureau changed in the 60s, but UPI continued to dominate the story. H.L. Stevenson, who would become UPI's editor-in-chief, was Southern Division news editor and teamed with Kuettner in directing the coverage.

Southern Division Manager Rhea Eskew, a southern gentleman who kept a picture of General Robert E. Lee on his office wall, staunchly supported his reporters' aggressive coverage despite continual complaints from clients.

Staffers who manned the Atlanta general desk operation included three of UPI's finest writers: Jack Warner, Buddy Hendrick and Martin "Marty" Murphy.

However, the UPI staff in the South was badly outnumbered by the rival AP bureaus.

John N. Herbers recalled that the Emmett Till lynching brought reporters from all over the world to rural Mississippi, but UP covered the story with just the regular Jackson bureau staffers.

Herbers said it was several days after Till disappeared before the teen's badly mutilated body was found in the Tallahatchie River, weighted down with a heavy fan taken from a cotton gin. He had been beaten and shot before he was tossed into the muddy waters.

Herbers covered the trial of two men accused of the lynching, grocery store owner Roy Bryant and his half-brother, J.W. Milam. The two men admitted kidnapping Till because they said the young man had flirted with Bryant's wife at the grocery store. However, they denied the killing.

The young Jackson bureau manager, who later went on to work for UP in Washington and then the *New York Times*, said he never worked harder than covering that trial. The courtroom was packed with out-of-state reporters, including a major rival, James Kilgallen, of the International News Service.

Since he was working alone, Herbers had to call his copy to the Atlanta bureau, and the general desk handled the writing. This meant leaving the courtroom, running downstairs and dictating from a pay phone. Herbers said he was constantly running in and out of the courtroom since UP was transmitting five or six leads on both the A.M. and P.M. newspaper cycles.

Herbers was hardly surprised when the jury acquitted the two men of all charges. "I did not know anyone there who thought the verdict would be anything different," Herbers said.

"Exhausted and angry after the cleanup reporting, I drank a beer, got in my car and headed for Jackson," Herbers recalled. "A little ways out of Sumner, I had a terrible feeling in the pit of the my stomach. It wouldn't stop. All I could do was cry and I did for many miles."

UPI's efforts to be objective sometimes brought its reporters dangerously close to the leaders of the Ku Klux Klan.

Alvin Benn recalls a night in 1965 when he, Joe Chapman, a UPI freelance photographer, and *Life Magazine* photographer Vernon Merritt drove to a little park in Linden, Alabama, about 55 miles west of Selma, to cover a KKK rally. The rally was held in support of the four Klansmen who had been indicted for the murder of Viola Luizzo.

Benn said that when the fiery cross had burned out and the rally ended, they found that someone had slashed all four tires on Chapman's VW, probably because of its UPI decal. Benn knew the Klan leader, Bob Creel, and Creel knew that the Klan needed some national attention for its message.

Benn said Creel passed the pointed hat around to get donations and sent someone to nearby Tuscaloosa to buy four new tires. The Klansmen, including the four facing murder indictments, put the new tires on Chapman's car.

Some UP staffers in North Carolina also had tire trouble trying to cover a Klan rally in 1958. The KKK was stirring up trouble with the Lumbee Indians of Robeson County, North Carolina. The Lumbees are a mixed racial group without official recognition as an Indian tribe. A South Carolina KKK "Dragon," James "Catfish" Cole, announced a big Klan rally at Maxton, North Carolina, the heart of the Lumbee population.

Richard Hatch, who was the bureau manager in Charlotte, North Carolina, recalled that tensions were high in the area and hardware stores reported they had sold out of ammunition. Hatch said Alvin Webb came down from the Greensboro,

North Carolina, bureau to help him cover the KKK rally and the two drove to the rally site with two other newsmen, Loyd Jeffers from the UP Columbia, South Carolina bureau and George Thomas, a reporter for a UP-client radio station in Winston-Salem.

Hatch said the KKK rally never started because the Indians surrounded the site, shouting threats and waving guns. Law enforcement officers escorted the Klansmen from the field as the Indians, many of them drunk, beat on their cars with rifle butts.

The reporters phoned in from a nearby farmhouse that the Indians had routed the KKK, then they piled into their car for a drive to King Cole hotel in Maxton where they planned to get organized and file their stories for the following newspaper cycle.

On the way to the hotel, a couple of cars of drunken Indians forced the reporters off the road. Hatch recalled that the Indians were armed with rifles and pistols and twitching lengths of chain. They accused the reporters of being Klansmen because of the South Carolina license plates on the car, but finally agreed that maybe they were really newsmen.

"They told us to get the hell out of there," Hatch recalled. "As we drove away, volleys of pistol and rifle shots hit the back of the car. The back tires went flat but we made it to a lighted farmhouse that turned out to be the home of a deputy sheriff."

The deputy escorted the reporters to the hotel and the next day they counted ten bullet holes and numerous shotgun pellet marks on the car. Hatch said UP swept the newspaper play on the Indian-Klan battle, the main story. However, he and Webb decided they would wait until the Monday A.M. newspaper cycle to file the story about their own close call.

Unfortunately, they didn't know that the radio reporter, Thomas, was a stringer and had already called INS with his own account of the ambush and his story won wide play.

In the winter of 1964, unrest broke out at the University of California campus in Berkeley, the beginning of a movement that spread across the nation.

Richard Harnett of the San Francisco bureau was assigned to cover the promised "strike" against the university. He found the campus in chaos. Many classes were canceled, and those that met were disrupted by chanting demonstrators snaking through the classrooms.

After checking half a dozen classroom buildings Harnett phoned in a story saying "One quarter of the students launched a boisterous strike against the University of California today, parading noisily through classrooms and laboratories, vowing to 'shut this place down.'"

When he returned to the bureau in San Francisco later in the day he looked at the lead on the wire. It said "Seventy-five percent of the students at Berkeley ignored a strike call, etc."

The bureau manager, who had changed the story, explained "That's the way AP has it." He wanted the same news as AP only sooner.

Campus "free speech" turmoil spread across the country, from San Francisco State University to Harvard. It was a daily story on the wire for months.

Especially difficult was the task of providing number of participants in protest rallies and anti-Vietnam War marches. Those sponsoring the demonstrations frequently exaggerated attendance, while police seldom offered more than a guess.

UPI, on one occasion when it had a lower figure than the opposition for a rally at Berkeley, examined an enlargement of a photo taken at the scene and counted heads, then calculated that no more than 6,000 people could be crowded into the campus plaza.

Another time three reporters were sent to an anti-Vietnam War march in Oakland, California, to stand at a corner and count the marchers as they passed. They came up with a total of 10,000 in the march on that Saturday, far under the estimate of 60,000 given out by the organizers.

28

Watching the Birds

THE QUESTION CAME FROM THE MAIN DESK AT UPI'S SPECIAL SPACE FLIGHT bureau just outside Houston. None of the UPI space experts, editors or writers crowded into the small bureau had a quick answer.

Everyone was a little puzzled by the astronaut's words, words that had traveled a quarter-million miles and were destined for history.

Apollo 11 had landed on the moon and Neil Armstrong had stepped into the lunar dust with those words for a waiting world.

"That's one small step for man, one giant leap for mankind."

That was the way it was recorded by spacewriter Paul K. Harral who was on the "transcription desk" monitoring NASA's "Capcom" communications link that connected Houston to the space travelers. Several others watching the eerie, black and white TV pictures from the moon agreed with Harral.

It didn't quite make sense. "Man" and "mankind" would seem the same in Armstrong's quote.

Harral thought the quote should be "one small step for a man, one giant leap for mankind." But when he replayed the tape, despite some static, he came up with the same puzzler, "that's one small step for man, one giant leap for mankind."

Getting the quote right was vital, but getting the quote on UPI's newswires in a timely manner was paramount. All agreed to use the quote without the article "a."

For the UPI men and women in that bureau, this was the assignment of a lifetime, like getting to cover the voyage of Christopher Columbus.

Apollo 11 was the climax of the turbulent 1960s, and scores of newsmen and women, who had carried the UPI logo to great heights during those years, maneuvered for a chance to help with the coverage.

UPI had assembled its top talent—reporters, writers, science writers, broadcast writers, audio reporters, photographers and teletype operators.

The team was headed by UPI Editor Roger Tatarian and Managing Editor H.L. Stevenson and they pulled out all the stops, even on expense guidelines, to give the UPI staff a level playing field against AP.

They organized a strong newswire operation with Al Rossiter, Jr., the bureau manager at Cape Kennedy; Edward DeLong, manager of UPI's bureau at the NASA

Spaceflight Center; Lucien Carr, the top New York general desk editor: H. Jefferson Grigsby an assistant managing editor; Marty Murphy, a writer-editor from the Atlanta bureau; Ken Englade, reporter-writer from the Denver bureau and Paul Harral, a young spacewriter from the Dallas bureau.

Two veteran writers with familiar bylines, H.D. "Doc" Quigg from New York and Jack V. Fox from Los Angeles, handled the main color copy while Darrell Mack, the "one-man gang" bureau manager in Houston, did just about everything else.

Broadcast Editor Billy Ferguson set up operations at Cape Kennedy and Houston Spaceflight so that he could file directly to the national broadcast department a running account for broadcasters on the critical phases of the attempt to put a man on the moon.

Scott Peters, who had handled the Mercury and Gemini space shots as well as the earlier Apollo missions, headed UPI's Audio Network coverage team.

Along with the thrill of covering news of such magnitude came the pressure of UPI's mandate: "Get it first, but first, get it right."

Marty Murphy, a low-key writer-editor with a knack for leads that were always right on target, remembers the endless "committee" meetings in the crowded Spaceflight bureau to decide on how each and every major development should be handled.

Murphy, who was the chief writer for morning newspapers on UPI's report, said there was a long discussion on what the lead should say when the astronauts landed on the moon. Murphy said he felt the high drama needed no hype and recommended a straightforward lead beginning with "Man landed on the moon today." Roger Tatarian agreed, and that is the way it went.

Everything had to be perfect—no errors, not even a dropped article.

Any blunder, no matter how minor, could damage UPI's credibility.

Thick NASA technical manuals detailed every small step of the Apollo 11 mission flight plan, timed right down to the second, and provided guidelines for covering this Odyssey of twentieth century engineering.

UPI editors and reporters, prodded by the spacewriters, had studied the manuals and were prepared to handle the events.

UPI staffers knew that they could not "flash" the word of man standing on the moon when Armstrong's foot first hit the lunar surface. The exact procedure outlined by NASA called for Armstrong to test the moon's surface with his right foot while still holding firm to the ladder on the spindly leg of the lunar lander. Then, if the lunar surface was firm enough, Armstrong would step on the moon.

"FLASH
MAN ON THE MOON"

But the manual did not cover what Armstrong would say.

At first, NASA was non-committal about his historic words.

Because what he said would live forever, UPI managers decided to do the repugnant: go against history, tradition and human nature: they would check with their bitter rivals, the Associated Press reporters working just 100 feet down the hall.

Harral recalled that he was sent to meet with AP Space Editor Howard Benedict. They listened to the tape several times and then made a command decision. UPI and AP would stick with the quote as they heard it: "One small step for man; one giant leap for mankind."

NASA later made its decision on the missing article, reporting that Armstrong actually said, "One small step for 'a' man; one giant leap forward for mankind."

Thirty year later, at a news conference to commemorate the Apollo 11 flight, Armstrong said "the 'a' was intended. I thought I said it, but I don't hear it on the tapes. I'll be happy if you just put it in parentheses."

It did not sully UPI's performance. Flashes on both the newspaper A-wire and the broadcast wire cleared within one minute of the time that Armstrong first stood on a sun-drenched surface of the moon 250,000 miles from Houston.

The "play" logs that compared whether major dailies chose UPI or AP stories were just about even. Many papers had their own correspondents covering and other papers combined information from both wires.

One newspaper, the *Birmingham News*, ran a front page that was an actual copy of the UPI broadcast wire's running account of the dramatic descent and touchdown of the lunar landing.

UPI had gone all out to cover the Apollo space program. It wasn't always that way.

After the launch of Russia's "Sputnik-1" in October 1957, UP established a one-person bureau in Cocoa Beach, a few miles south of the Cape Canaveral launch site. Chiles Coleman, the soft-spoken Southern Division news editor, gave the new bureau the code letters BW for BirdWatch. Many staffers in the Atlanta bureau thought Coleman had passed up the obvious CC for Cape Canaveral because his modesty would not allow him to designate a new bureau with his own initials. Actually, it was because there was already a bureau with the CC code, Carson City, Nevada.

The BW bureau was set up in Cocoa Beach at 440 East Grant Avenue on the north side of a two-story duplex on the beach with windows overlooking the launch pads three miles away. Binoculars were needed.

Richard Roper was UP's first official birdwatcher, but he left in the summer of 1959 for the *Wall Street Journal*. Coleman offered the job to Alvin Webb, a high-strung young bureau manager in Charlotte, North Carolina. Webb was recommended by Peter S. Willett, regional executive for North Carolina. Willett felt Webb could handle the technical aspects—he had covered a conference on high science and returned with a readable story.

Webb, who had been offered a pay-your-own way transfer to London by always frugal UPI, chose the Cape Canaveral job, partly because his science was better than his geography. He said he thought Cape Canaveral was one of the Florida Keys and liked the idea of going there until he rented a U-Haul trailer and checked a map. He eventually did get to London, years later by the way of Vietnam.

There were no manuals or detailed flight plan for the media in 1959. Most launches were conducted by the military and were off-limits to the press. Webb, like other reporters at the Cape, had to develop his own sources.

He found a gas station attendant who seemed to know when most launches were scheduled, probably through customers who worked at the launch site.

On a day when he expected a launch, Webb focused his binoculars on a tall pole at the Cape that gave the public its only advance warning of a launch. Three minutes prior to takeoff, a red ball was hoisted to the top of the pole to alert boats in the area to stay clear.

During the highly secret testing of submarine-launched Polaris missiles, Webb realized that tracking vessels in the Atlantic Missile Range required radio contact with the blockhouse at the Cape. He dug out a short-wave radio he had brought to the Cape and soon found the frequency used for the countdowns. The "red ball watches" ended.

The radio almost got UPI into trouble. Webb got some dramatic quotes by monitoring the missile submarine USS *Theodore Roosevelt* when it launched a Polaris missile about twenty miles offshore.

The Polaris broke the surface of the Atlantic, then came back down, just missing the submarine. When it hit the ocean floor, the Polaris broke apart and the second stage ignited. The rocket shot toward the surface, again barely missing the sub, and once more broke the water's surface. Soon it exploded, either by accident or command.

Webb's story, complete with colorful quotes, got good play in the papers and, apparently, a lot of attention from the Navy.

A few weeks later, Webb was monitoring another secret countdown on the short-wave when he answered a knock on the bureau door. It was two men from the Office of Naval Intelligence and they wanted to know where Al got his information on the Polaris shot. When the visitors walked into the bureau, the short-wave radio was blaring out the new countdown. "T-minus 10 minutes and counting."

Webb gritted his teeth and told the agents he could not reveal his sources. They persisted with polite questioning until the countdown had almost reached zero. To Webb's great relief, they left just ahead of the new launch and he never heard from them again.

While America's seven original astronauts were preparing for their Mercury flights, NASA expanded its media accommodations. United Press International was allowed to set up at the Cape on an elevated, open-air platform. Staffers were also given access to the hangars where the astronauts prepped for their missions.

Webb spent hours poring over the developing Mercury flight plans, technical journals detailing the Mercury hardware, and the life stories of the seven young Americans destined to show the world they were made of "the right stuff."

However, American astronauts were temporarily consigned to a back seat in the escalating space race between the East and West.

On April 12, 1961, the Soviet Union launched cosmonaut Yuri Gagarin into orbit and padded its lead significantly in the race to space.

The Russian Air Force major, cramped inside his Vostok space capsule, flew around the world in one hour and 48 minutes, reaching an altitude of 203 miles at the top of the orbit.

As news of Gagarin's feat was flashed around the world, the U.S. astronauts were training at Langley Field, Virginia. UPI's Washington bureau chased the Mercury astronauts for reaction.

It was about 3 A.M. when a Washington overnight staffer got through to Lieutenant Colonel John N. "Shorty" Powers, Public Information Officer for NASA. Powers was miffed at being awakened and when he was asked for his reaction, he exploded, "You can tell them we're all asleep here."

Powers' angry quote gave UPI a highly newsworthy exclusive and fueled the frustration of many Americans afraid the United States was falling behind in the space race. Powers, an Air Force officer handling public relations for the Mercury program, was long haunted by that quote and was unable to forgive UPI for reporting his blurted response.

Alvin A. Spivak, a reporter in Washington, had a vivid memory of Powers.

While the Mercury astronauts were at Langley, they sold exclusive rights to their personal stories to *Life* magazine. Julius Fransden, a vice president in charge of UPI's Washington operations, filed a vigorous protest with the space agency and demanded that UPI be allowed to interview the men of Mercury. NASA agreed and Powers was forced to notify Frandsen that UPI could have the interviews.

Frandsen assigned Spivak. When he arrived at Langley, Spivak learned that Powers, still piqued at UPI, had granted similar interviews to an Associated Press reporter the day before.

Spivak realized that with a one-day beat, the AP reporter would be back in Washington writing his story, probably for Sunday morning newspapers, while Spivak still was conducting his interviews.

Nevertheless, Spivak interviewed Mercury astronauts Alan Shepard, John Glenn and Scott Carpenter, then wrote a piece for the Sunday papers that won him praise from his bosses in Washington. However, his story was not used in any of the Sunday papers that took both AP and UPI. The AP story already had been set in type before the editors ever saw Spivak's story.

At the Cape, NASA was relaxing restrictions on the media. Al Webb recalled that reporters were allowed within a few feet of the venting Redstone rocket just hours before astronaut Alan Shepard became the first American in space.

Webb recalled in sharp detail a vision of Shepard, clad in a bulky white space suit, walking by the towering rocket. Webb said Shepard stopped, shielded his eyes from the glare of the TV lights, looked straight up to the Freedom-7 capsule and nodded approvingly. The brash young Navy lieutenant then walked to the elevator at launch pad 5, the first 72 feet of a trip that would take him 115 miles into the heavens.

Webb no longer had to rely on his cat "Timothy" for company at the Cape. UPI relaxed its purse strings, and sent an impressive phalanx of reporters and editors for most of the Mercury missions.

Southern Division news editor Chiles Coleman led a UPI invasion of the suddenly bustling community of Cocoa Beach. The UPI Mercury team included Atlanta Bureau manager Al Kuettner; Washington staffers Charles Corddry, Joe Myler and Leon Burnett; Murray Moler from Salt Lake City; and Bill Sexton from the New York bureau. Southern Division picture manager Jack Young and UPI assistant manager Bill Lyons moved in to direct the news picture operations.

New York reporters Jack Fox and Ed McCarthy were assigned to Navy ships of the recovery fleet that would patrol the target area near the Bahamas and hopefully pluck Shepard from the Mercury capsule after splashdown.

The exclusive arrangement between the Mercury astronauts and *Life* magazine was a constant irritant for UPI, AP, the networks and anyone else covering the Mercury program. However, it did help UPI get hours ahead of the competition when NASA announced which of the seven astronauts would make the first flight to orbit the earth.

UPI photographer Russ Yoder was a close friend of a *Life* photographer who got advance warning on the astronaut assigned to the historic flight. Yoder called Webb at 3:30 on the morning of the launch and told him, "It's John Glenn."

Webb, whose bedroom was in the bureau duplex, rushed to the teletype and sent a bulletin that Glenn had been chosen. For the next three hours he worried he was too exclusive—no one else came up with the story. He relaxed when NASA trooped Glenn from hangar 5 to make the announcement later that morning.

His historic orbital flight on February 20, 1962, made John Glenn a national hero, but it was Glenn's role aboard a recovery vessel fourteen months later that made the former Marine pilot Webb's special hero.

Webb once again was tuned in to NASA's communications during the Faith-7 Mercury flight of Gordon Cooper when he heard the words "re-entry on emergency manual sequence." It was the voice of John Glenn aboard a recovery vessel in the Pacific. He was advising NASA that Cooper was having control problems and would have to fly the Mercury capsule to a splashdown.

Webb rolled out a bulletin, somewhat to the consternation of Managing Editor H.L. Stevenson, who had flown to the Cape to oversee the operation. Stevenson wanted to know how Webb was so sure that Cooper was going to an emergency re-entry based on the cryptic communications he heard over the Navy's radio communications.

Stevenson was a tough competitor, but he also felt a heavy responsibility for editorial credibility, and agonized when NASA spokesman "Shorty" Powers officially denied there was any problem aboard the orbiting capsule.

Webb was gathering remarkable detail from the radio communications between Glenn and NASA and was pouring it out on the wire. About 30 minutes before the scheduled splashdown, NASA confirmed that there was a problem and that Cooper had gone to a manual re-entry sequence.

Thanks to Webb's shortwave radio and his audacious confidence, UPI had scored an impressive, 90-minute beat over AP on one of the biggest stories of the year.

The fun-loving Cooper, known throughout NASA as "Gordo," made a successful bulls-eye splashdown befitting a former Air Force test pilot. The next day Stevenson gave Webb that rarest-of-all UPI prizes: a $30 weekly pay raise.

When NASA opened its sprawling Manned Spaceflight Center just south of Houston, UPI decided to open a new, space-age bureau there. Webb accepted a transfer from the Cape to the new space hub and coined the bureau's call letters: LX, for lunar exploration.

Webb also came up with a name for some ancillary accommodations. As one who appreciated the need for a handy spot where journalists could gather around low-priced beverages, Webb helped form a media club at the new NASA village. He named it "The Escape Velocity Press Club."

It was January 1964, and the nation was mourning the assassination of John F. Kennedy, the president who had promised that America would put a man on the moon before the end of the decade. The sandy hook that jutted into the Atlantic Ocean and provided a stepping-off point for America's voyages into space was renamed from Cape Canaveral to Cape Kennedy.

UPI's birdwatch (BW) bureau also had a new name on the door. Al Rossiter, Jr., son of a newspaper editor, was the new bureau manager. He brought a new order to UPI's presence in the burgeoning rocket community that hugged the banks of the Indian and Banana Rivers, just north of Melbourne, Florida.

Rossiter was as subdued and orderly as Webb was flamboyant and spontaneous. But he shared Webb's studied knowledge of the space program and the unrelenting drive to beat the bigger and better equipped AP crew at the Cape, a team headed by Howard Benedict, one of the most prominent space writers in America.

Rossiter covered the ten two-man Gemini launches from 1964 to 1966 working out of a small trailer at the Cape Kennedy Air Force Station. Rossiter sent his running reports on the Gemini launches on an internal wire to the Washington bureau where the newspaper leads were written by Science Editor Joe Myler and Norm Runnion, a veteran reporter.

After each Gemini launch, production of the story moved to the LX bureau at the Manned Spaceflight Center and Rossiter flew to Houston to join Webb, Houston bureau manager Darrell Mack and other UPI reporters.

UPI's dedication to the space race took a quantum leap forward in 1966 as NASA moved into the Apollo program designed to eventually launch three astronauts into space and land two of them on the moon.

UPI rented an office on the ninth floor of a 10-story office building in the heart of Cocoa Beach that provided an exceptional view of the Apollo launch pad to the north and the Atlantic Ocean. NASA's press center was one floor up.

Jack Warner, night editor in the Atlanta bureau, vividly recalled a chilly Friday night in January of 1967. He returned with a chocolate malted milk shake to the bureau overlooking the I-75 expressway that carved a never-ending path of traffic through the heart of the Georgia capital.

As he approached, Jimmy Mauldin, a teletype operator, came hurtling out of the door and yelled to Warner, "Something's happening down at the Cape." Warner rushed into the bureau and picked up a phone to hear the somewhat excited voice of Rossiter saying there had been a fire in the Apollo capsule during a ground test, and an astronaut was killed.

Warner and Rossiter crafted a bulletin that another teletype operator, Marty Locker, punched onto UPI's main A-wire. It read:

APOLLO 1/27
AJ BULLETIN
BY AL ROSSITER, JR.
UNITED PRESS INTERNATIONAL
CAPE KENNEDY (UPI)— U.S. SPACE AGENCY SAID FRIDAY
AN ASTRONAUT WAS KILLED IN A FIRE IN THE APOLLO 1
SPACE CRAFT DURING A TEST ON THE LAUNCHING PAD.
MORE MI804PES

Details were needed quickly and Rossiter was in a bind. UPI's Birdwatch bureau manager had made one of his rare rambles off the cape to attend a Sigma Delta Chi dinner meeting on the mainland. Fortunately, AP's Howard Benedict was also at the dinner.

Rossiter got the initial word of the tragedy by phone from his wife, Sylvia, who had fielded an emergency call from NASA spokesman Gordon Harris.

Rossiter sped back to the bureau and was quickly in touch with NASA and spacewriter Ed DeLong in the LX Houston bureau. Soon he had the grim information and was on the phone again with Warner.

The tall and gangly Warner was one of UPI's best writers and had a long history of deftly handling breaking news stories. But on this night, January 27, 1967, he was nervous. It had been more than thirty minutes since he sent the initial bulletin and more was unknown than was known about the tragedy at the Cape.

He felt relieved to finally hear from Rossiter again, but was immediately sobered by Rossiter's report that all three of the Apollo 1 astronauts had been killed by a fire in the space capsule during a test on the launch pad.

In all his years on the desk, Warner never had sent a news flash, the 10-bell alert that warned clients around the world of earthshaking news. But Warner knew, instinctively, that the Apollo tragedy was indeed a FLASH.

He yelled to Marty Locker, the teletype operator, to hit ten carriage returns and ten bells. Then, in a loud voice, he dictated the flash:

FLASH
CAPE KENNEDY AMERICA'S THREE APOLLO ASTRONAUTS
KILLED
AJ ML837PES 1/27

Locker signed off the flash with ten more carriage returns and ten more bells while Rossiter and Warner put together the bulletin:

APOLLO 1/27
AJ BULLETIN PRECEDE
CAPE KENNEDY (UPI) AMERICA'S FIRST THREE APOLLO
ASTRONAUTS VIRGIL GRISSOM, EDWARD WHITE AND
ROGER CHAFFEE WERE KILLED FRIDAY NIGHT WHEN FIRE
ENGULFED THE APOLLO MOONSHIP DURING A LAUNCH
PAD TEST.
ML840PES

UPI's Space flight bureau near Houston during Apollo-13 mission. From left, David Langford (striped shirt), Toni Frazier, Don Reed (leaning on table), unidentified woman with dark hair, Paul Harral (glasses and earphone leaning over typewriter), Ed DeLong (earphones and cigarette) and Tom McGann with glasses leaning over typewriter.

There was, that night, for Rossiter, Warner, DeLong, Locker and all the other UPI writers and editors who handled the tragic story, a nagging, almost embarrassing euphoria of a job well-done that seemed incongruous with the tragedy of death.

In the 70s, UPI was trying to win the confidence of America's newspaper editors by shedding its reputation for sensationalizing news copy. At the same time, AP seemed bent on becoming less stodgy.

The results were best seen, according to News Editor Ron Cohen, during the cliff-hanger Apollo-13 space flight.

When an explosion in the main section of the Apollo-13 spacecraft damaged the main power supply and cut off the chief source for oxygen, astronauts James Lovell, Fred Haise, Jr., and John Swigert, Jr., were forced to adopt emergency back-up measures that put the entire mission in jeopardy.

The moon landing was canceled, but night after night, Cohen recalled, AP's lead on the main story for morning newspapers warned that the mission appeared doomed

UPI's spacewriters and editors tried to keep the story in perspective by featuring the back-up systems NASA was using to bring the crew safely back to earth.

But, Cohen recalled, most of the morning newspaper editors seemed to prefer AP's "perils of Pauline" approach to a story that did not need any added drama. UPI tried to win the confidence of those newspaper editors with its measured approach to the Apollo-13 coverage, but AP apparently won their hearts with doomsday leads that swept the play each and every day until the Apollo-13 returned safely to earth.

It had been a close call, but still another success for NASA engineering, built on a foundation of numerous redundancies for all systems. During the nineteen years after the fatal Apollo-1 fire, NASA shepherded fifty-seven manned flights into space and brought them all home safely. The space shuttle flights to orbiting space stations became so routine that NASA decided to invite civilians to join the astronauts as passengers.

A school teacher, Christa McAuliffe of Concord, New Hampshire, joined six NASA astronauts aboard the Challenger space shuttle for its tenth trip January 28, 1986. It was a cold Tuesday morning on Florida's northeastern coast. UPI Cape Canaveral bureau manager William Harwood remembered that the baseboard heaters on UPI's 50-foot trailer, located just four-point-two miles from the launch pad, were barely adequate. Joining Harwood in the trailer were UPI Space Writer Ed DeLong, from Houston, and Rob Navias, covering the launch for the UPI Radio Network.

The one UPI space expert missing from the trailer that morning was UPI Science Editor Al Rossiter, Jr., who had covered every NASA manned launch since the beginning of the Gemini program in 1964. Rossiter was at the Jet Propulsion Laboratory in Pasadena, California covering the Voyager 2's flyby of the planet Uranus.

Harwood, who had covered eighteen Shuttle launches, had a firm routine. He arrived at the trailer Monday night to be on hand as they fuelled the rocket with one-half million gallons of liquid oxygen and hydrogen. He also put the finishing touches on brief profiles of the seven people who would fly on Challenger-10. While the profiles were rarely used, there was a hidden agenda. The profiles could also serve as instant obituaries.

Harwood had written a stock lead to the pre-launch Challenger copy and sent it to the Washington general desk to hold until after the blast-off. Three minutes before launch, he opened a telephone line to the Washington UPI bureau and was talking with general desker Bill Trott, who had Harwood's stock lead on his computer terminal.

Hartwood cautioned Trott not to release the launch lead until he had confirmed vertical motion by the big space package. Two previous launches had been scrubbed in the last seconds.

There were no such problems this time and NASA's twenty-fifth Shuttle mission rose from its launch pad over billowing fire and smoke at 11:38 A.M.

"Let it go," Harwood told Trott and immediately the story was moving on UPI's main newspaper circuit, the A-wire. Harwood watched through the trailer's big picture window as the Challenger rose gracefully over the Atlantic Ocean.

As the Challenger arched away, Harwood recalled, it was obscured by the heavy plume of smoke that marked its path. "Then, the exhaust plume seemed to balloon outward and I had a peripheral impression of debris sparkling in the sunlight…then a single booster emerged from the cloud, corkscrewing madly through the sky," Harwood said.

"Wait a minute, something's happened," Harwood shouted to Trott. "They're in trouble, let me dictate something."

"OK, OK, hang on," Trott said as he started writing the header codes for a bulletin precede. Confused and trying to sort out what he had seen, Harwood dictated the bulletin.

BULLETIN PRECEDE CHALLENGER
CAPE KENNEDY, FLA. (UPI) THE SPACE SHUTTLE CHAL-
LENGER APPARENTLY EXPLODED ABOUT TWO MINUTES
AFTER LAUNCH TODAY. THE FATE OF THE CREW WAS NOT
KNOWN.

In the windowless audio booth, Rob Navias was doing a running commentary on the launch, using the mission event clock and NASA's television feed, which had a much clearer picture of the Challenger explosion.

"Wait a minute," Navias told his listeners, "I believe the vehicle has exploded. Is that possible?"

UPI managing editor Ron Cohen, in Washington, and science editor Al Rossiter, in Pasadena, California, were also watching the NASA TV feed and they felt certain the Challenger had exploded.

As Harwood continued to add details to the story, Rossiter and Cohen conferred by phone and decided to re-lead the story to eliminate the "apparently" from the lead. Later, after reviewing the NASA close-up of the explosion, UPI 's story was led again to add that it was unlikely any of the seven people aboard survived. However, it was more than four hours later before NASA officially said the same thing.

Harwood had been a true eyewitness to history, but the technology of the 80s had brought Unipressers hundreds of miles away much closer to the story.

29

The Lure

TO BE THE FIRST TO KNOW AND ABLE TO TELL IT TO THE WORLD.

This was the irresistible lure of United Press International.

This was journalism's strongest narcotic and it was so readily available in just two places, UPI and the Associated Press.

There was a long, slow line at AP with just the grizzled veterans allowed to cover the big news or submit stories to its worldwide client wires. At UPI, it sometimes took just a day or two.

The "try harder" wire service was always battling long odds and short finances. There was no time and little money for training programs. The UPI mission was to match AP on news coverage but without its huge staff, its abundant resources and its cumbersome bureaucracy.

This called for a sink-or-swim approach to training and tempering

For years, UPI made it work by testing its staffers "under the gun."

Most former Unipressers have vivid memories of their early days at UPI, days often filled with daunting assignments. "First-day" stories are part of the ritual when UPI vets get together for reminiscing.

A newsman who truly became a legend in the Southern Division got his "first day" before he actually got his job with UP.

It was 1946 and Edwin Rogers, a World War II vet, wanted a job with United Press, but he was having trouble applying.

Rogers was an insomniac who usually needed to read a lot or drink a lot to get to sleep. Since his finances were running low and the Atlanta public library was close to his room at the downtown YMCA, Rogers usually read himself to sleep.

Unfortunately, it was often dawn before Rogers got to sleep and then it was early evening before he was awake. William Tucker, the Atlanta bureau (AJ) night manager, recalled that the tall, slender Rogers, hoping to apply for a job, appeared several times in the bureau hours after the top managers had left. Finally, Tucker found an application and gave it Rogers. Tucker told him to fill out the application and get back into the bureau before 5 P.M. on a weekday to apply with the people who did the hiring.

The insomnia persisted, however, and Rogers was still reading about 3 A.M. several days later when the shrill scream of sirens jolted him into reality. Rogers leaned out a window to see one fire truck after another racing by the Y. Rogers was quickly dressed and on the street.

He followed the trail of flashing lights several blocks and found them surrounding the huge Winecoff Hotel. When he got to a corner across from the hotel, he saw the sobering signs of tragedy. Flames were roaring out of the upper-story windows and terrified hotel guests were standing on window ledges far beyond the reach of the firemen's tallest ladders. Soon, many were jumping even though there were no nets below.

Rogers broke out of his initial shock and started looking for a pay phone. Soon he was on the line with Burns Beauregard Bennett, the UP overnight editor in Atlanta. Bennett was confused by the caller, who identified himself as a "United Press applicant." However, Rogers sketched a grim picture of the bedlam he had witnessed and told Bennett that people were still jumping from the hotel.

Bennett, alone in the bureau, was a little overwhelmed, but he told Rogers to get back to the fire and wait at a specified corner until he was contacted by a UP staffer. In the meantime, he suggested that Rogers should try to count the dead, or at least those jumping from the hotel.

Bennett confirmed the fire's location with the fire department, sent a bulletin, then started turning out the UP troops. The overnight chief called Tucker as well as Bernard Brenner, Herb Foster and Roland Dobson, who lived on Atlanta's northside.

Brenner, UP's Southern Division radio editor and later UP's agriculture editor, shared an apartment with Foster and recalled that he and Foster had a transportation problem since they did not have a car, and the Atlanta buses did not run that early in the morning. Brenner said the two managed to persuade a milk truck deliveryman to temporarily abandon his route and give them a lift about five miles to the downtown hotel. On the way, the trio spotted Dobson, who also crowded into the milk truck.

Tucker was the first on the scene, and it didn't take him long to spot Rogers, standing on a corner just across from the hotel, which by then was totally engulfed by flames. Tucker said Rogers was meticulously scanning the windows to spot the jumpers and then recording each one on a small pad.

Rogers and Tucker went to the UP bureau in Atlanta's Western Union Building as other arrived at the scene. The "United Press applicant" was able to provide some chilling eye witness testimony for the main story and he wanted to help more. Bennett gave him a list of the dead from the morgue to compare with hotel records that had been released.

When UPI's top managers arrived in the bureau, Rogers was hard at work compiling the list of the dead, but he had taken time to place his completed application of the desk before him. After checking around and conferring with division manager Stanley Whittaker, Atlanta bureau manager Brooks Smith told Tucker, "I guess we'll have to hire him."

Joseph L. Galloway, who distinguished himself as a war correspondent for UPI in Vietnam, vividly recalled his first day at the news service. It was in the winter of 1961 when he reported to the Kansas City bureau.

Bureau chief Dave Oestreicher gave him a quick welcome, then a question:

"Do you know anything about basketball?"

"Not really."

"Ever cover basketball?"

"No, never."

"Never mind," Oestreicher told the rookie, "here's a portable typewriter. You walk down the street two blocks and there's a large concrete building. They're having something called the NCAA finals. You cover the first two games and phone in your stories."

Galloway recalled that as he trudged down the street he figured his wire service career would be short.

At the arena, he set up the portable and admitted to others at the press table that he didn't know anything about basketball. They told him not to worry, but it was hardly comforting.

On the opening play of the first game, the referee fell dead in front of the press table with a heart attack.

"Saved by a tragedy," Galloway recalled. "Tragedies I can write. Basketball takes care of itself."

Some "first day" stories featured UPI wannabe's who failed to make it through the opening round. Ron Cohen, who ended a 25-year career as UPI's managing editor, believes he witnessed the shortest career in UPI's history.

Cohen recalled that in 1963 he was being transferred from the Hartford, Connecticut, bureau (HF) to Montpelier, Vermont , (VT) and was to report to the division headquarters bureau in Boston (BH) for a one-week fill-in on division news operations.

Cohen said he arrived at the bureau at 9 A.M., just ahead of a new BH hire, a young man who seemed taken aback by the informality and seeming confusion of the bureau.

Division New Editor Stan Berens was the next to arrive and he was hardly cordial. He nodded at Cohen and shot a hard glance at the newcomer, then disappeared into his office.

After a few minutes, Berens came out of his office, tossed a piece of wire copy at the kid and snarled, "Here, read this out."

"The kid sat frozen for a few minutes," Cohen recalled. "He turned to me and asked what it meant to 'read this out.'"

Cohen said he told the young man it meant he was to edit the copy.

"I remember he reached over to Berens empty newsroom desk near the slot, picked up Stan's pen and began writing on the copy.

"When Stan spotted his pen in the kid's hand, he grabbed it away and unleashed a stream of profanity. He then threw another pen on the desk that ricocheted and hit the young man's chest.

"By this time, the kid was frozen in fear like a deer about to be flattened by a 16-wheeler, tears of fright welling in his eyes. He sat there a minute, then turned to me and said, 'I need to feed my parking meter.'"

"He slinked out the door, never to return. I looked at the clock, it was 9:17 A.M."

UP's "sink or swim" philosophy went beyond the first days. Washington veterans of the pre-World War II era recalled the initiation of a young hot-shot who won a transfer from Atlanta to Washington.

Merriman Smith wasn't one to make friends quickly and would rarely ask for help. So it was no surprise that he wound up working all by himself on the Washington desk on New Year's Day.

Most Washington staffers got holidays off. When the New York general desk asked WA for a holiday story on the First Family, Smith was pretty much on his own. There were no UP reporters at the White House on the holiday and no easy way to get to the White House press office. "Smitty" read the previous day's White House story and learned that the president and his family were going to have a family dinner at the White House.

That was all this cocky young man needed. Georgia-born and raised, he knew what to do. His lead, as recalled by those pre-war staffers:

"WASHINGTON (UP) PRESIDENT FRANKLIN D. ROOSEVELT
AND HIS FAMILY TODAY SAT DOWN TO A TRADITIONAL
NEW YEAR'S DAY DINNER OF HOG JOWLS, BLACK-EYED
PEAS AND HOMONY GRITS."

Traditional for many Southerners, but hardly the bill of fare for the aristocratic FDR.

The real news junkies at UPI put "able to tell the world" ahead of the standard corporate perks, including titles, fame and even money.

Many of the real heroes at UPI were totally anonymous to the outside world. They were not the top executives or the high-visibility reporters. They rarely got big salaries, by-lines or even decent working hours.

They worked the "slots" on the general news desks: men and women who took the stories from UPI reporters around the world and polished, plugged the holes and perfected those reports until they were ready for UPI's clients.

These were the editors who got to "tell it to the world."

The "slot" was the editor in charge of the news desk. The name "slot" came from traditional newspaper offices where the main news desk was often U-shaped with the copy editors sitting around the rim and the editor-in-charge sitting inside the U, or in the "slot."

The central character in Reynolds Packard's novel *The Kansas City Milkman* captured the feel of working that key wire service job.

> "The slot: Christ, that was the brains of the bureau. I didn't give a bugger who was the bureau manager, the sales manager, the front man, the contact man. I just wanted to sit in the slot and slug it out with history as it whizzed by.
>
> "It was," he said, "the one place where I plunged into my work and forgot everything else; where my craftsmanship mattered more than my emotions."

The "slots" came in different sizes. They ranged from the state desks, where the slot editor was in charge of state and local copy, to the division headquarters, where the slot editor picked and preened the best of the regional copy. London's general desk and the New York cables desk handled foreign copy, and Washington had its own general desk to handle the news of the federal government.

All of this copy was funneled into the general desk at headquarters, first in New York and, during the '80s and '90s, in Washington. The slot on the headquarters general desk was UPI's Valhalla for the legions who yearned to tell it to the world.

A veteran editor who worked the general desk slot in New York and Washington for forty years was the role model for many Unipressers. While White House Correspondent Helen Thomas was the widely recognized face of UPI in the second half of the century, Lucien "Lou" Carr was, for many, the soul of the news service.

The tall, slim graduate of the "beat generation" rewrote, repaired, recast and revived more big stories on UPI's main newspaper circuit, the A-wire, than anyone before or after him.

Carr had few by-lines during his 47-year career, but he was the undisputed champion of getting copy with other by-lines onto the front pages of newspapers around the world.

Carr had great instincts for news. More importantly, he could squeeze the most from other UPI reporters and editors with gentle, persuasive leadership in a high-pressure job often peopled by lesser talents with bigger egos and quicker tempers.

A legend about Carr is that he was once called in by the editor of the *New York Daily News* who wanted to hire him. "You will be city editor of the entire New York," he said.

Carr is said to have responded: "Why should I want that? I am already city editor to the world."

During most of Carr's years on the night desk in New York, he was backed by Don Mullen, an often-caustic editor who shared Reynolds Packard's love for the "slot."

Mullen said one of the ways to survive on the general desk was to "get along" with the teletype operators who sat on the other side of the desk for many of those years.

"Teletype operators were true American characters. They followed in the footsteps of itinerant typesetters and telegraphers dating back to the 19th century," Mullen said.

"If the punchers liked you, they would correct your spelling, your syntax and your punctuation. If they didn't like you, God help you. They also offered advise about your politics, your wardrobe, your girlfriend and your future in the business. They usually knew where to find the closest bookie."

Every geographical division of UPI had its own stars in the key slot jobs.

In the Southwest Division, reporters and editors were spurred by division editor Jack Fallon, who always worked the slot and often worked some magic. His flawless desking of the John F. Kennedy assassination helped White House Correspondent Merriman Smith win a Pulitzer.

Ken Englade was a veteran of just four weeks with UPI when he was thrown onto the desk in the New Orleans (NE) bureau. Englade, working off of notes from a reporter covering a civil rights demonstration, filed a lead he was proud of.

"Bogalousa, La. (UPI) Two Negro men strolled into the Acme Cafe at mid-morning today, sat down at the counter and ordered pie and coffee, thus becoming the first members of their race to eat in a previously all-white establishment in this city in the last 75 years."

Before Englade could get the second paragraph of his story on the wire, Dallas broke into his transmission with an urgent message:

-95-
NE
WHAT KIND OF PIE?
FALLON/DA

Englade passed his rookie test when he re-punched his story and made the lead: "ordered apple pie and coffee, etc."

Most of UPI's top "slot editors" were little known to the outside world, but were heroes to the rank and file Unipressers. Men like Fallon, Mullen, Joe Morgan in San Francisco, Dave Smothers in Chicago, Bill Tucker, Martin Murphy and Jack Warner in Atlanta, Stan Berens in Boston, Bob Andrews and Mike Fiensilber in Washington.

Anonymity was the uniform for most of those who worked for the wire services. Few journalists who reported so much of the news of the world were as unknown as the men and women of UPI and AP.

Very few Unipressers won any fame outside of the industry. Helen Thomas, the dean of the White House press corps, was recognized because of her appearances on nationally televised presidential news conferences. But she was unique.

Even UPI's national columnists like Dick West, who wrote a daily humor column called "The Lighter Side," were little known to the general public and only a few of the familiar voices of the UPI Radio Network, such as Pye Chamberlayne, ever heard from their listeners.

Newspaper reporters, even in small towns, were generally known in their own communities, but wire service reporters were local strangers who got by-lines only in out-of-town newspapers

Few people were even aware of UPI or what it did. The usual retort to a staffer telling someone he worked for UPI was: "the parcel service?"

When a New York sportswriter sought to question boxer Mike Tyson, he identi-fied himself as Dave Raffo of UPI.

The heavyweight scowled at Raffo and told him angrily, "One of your mother-fucking trucks almost ran over my dog."

Hollywood believed that very few people had ever heard of United Press.

In 1931, UP correspondent Webb Miller flew to India to cover the unrest instigated by Mohandas Gandhi. While the British did their best to block his way, Miller got to the site of the salt mines where Gandhi was leading a group of his followers in a protest against the British-imposed tax on salt.

Miller was the lone correspondent at the remote area when hundreds of Gandhi's followers marched, unarmed and unresisting, and were mercilessly beaten by British troops. The British cable company refused to transmit Miller's story on the incident, but he managed to get it to New York by mail.

It was the first account of the protest to reach the outside world and the only eyewitness report on the bloody British response.

The "salt march" was the highlight of the classic film *Gandhi*, released in 1982. The movie sequence was taken from Miller's account of the incident. An American journalist at the scene does exactly what Miller did. The script was almost word-for-word identical to Miller's account in his book, *I Found No Peace*.

However, the American journalist in the movie was identified as a correspondent for the *New York Times*. Director Richard Attenborough apparently felt that United Press was too obscure for his critically-acclaimed film.

UPI's army of anonymous reporters provided one of the news agency's most important and popular services—the roundup.

With bureaus in all fifty states and around the world, UPI could, in a matter of hours, put a national, or world-wide, perspective to just about anything.

Staffers from Anchorage to Miami, and all points between, provided the drama of the blizzards, floods, tornadoes, draughts and hurricanes that unceasingly scour the nation. AP also offered national weather roundups, but UPI usually won the play with more spirited reporting and writing.

Eugene Patterson, a Unipressers who became publisher of the highly-respected *St. Petersburg Times*, recalled a day when New York City was paralyzed by a snowstorm and his UP boss, Arnold Dibble, assigned him to write the weather roundup.

Patterson felt the heavy weather news needed some lighter color. He called Gypsy Rose Lee and asked the famous fan-dancer how she was coping with the freezing weather. "Honey," she said, "I'm wearing my fur-lined G-string."

UPI also routinely produced a national roundup of accidental deaths during the major holidays. Bureaus in every state contacted authorities two or three times daily to get the details of fatal accidents, and messages were sent to New York or Chicago for roundups and tabulations of the holiday death toll. The UPI broadcast wire sent a table every hour showing national holiday death totals, broken into four categories: traffic; weather, including drowning; crime and other. The tabulations were made for Christmas, New Years, Memorial Day, Fourth of July and Labor Day.

Radio stations liked the holiday death toll tabulations. Programming was scarce on holidays and the stations could sell the hourly reports of carnage to advertisers. One UPI sales executive sent a message to the national broadcast department in Chicago that one radio station said it would sign a contract for the UPI broadcast wire if UPI would add the death count on the Easter weekend. Someone messages back, tongue-in-cheek, that UPI would he happy to add an Easter weekend death count and would even add a category for crucifixions.

The breath of UPI's national reach also provided a chance to compete head-on with AP on presidential elections. With political editors in every state, UPI could quickly analyze voting trends in those states and make early "calls," or predictions, on the winners.

The Washington bureau kept a running tabulation on the state-by-state victory calls. When one candidate had been declared the winner in enough states to collect the electoral votes needed to win, UPI sent a flash calling that candidate the president-elect.

The state political experts were also responsible for making those early calls on state races. UPI had many state political editors who were unrivaled in analyzing their state's voting trends, including Hortense Meyers in Indianapolis, Kurt King in Albany, New York, Barbara Frye in Tallahassee, Bessie Ford in Jackson, Mississippi, and Robert Kieckhefer in Chicago.

The ability to tell it to the world could sometimes vault UPI staffers into the strangest footnotes of history.

On the eve of Thanksgiving, November 24, 1971, a Northwest Airliner was hijacked on a flight to Portland, Oregon, and forced to land at the Seattle-Tacoma International Airport. The hijacker said he had a bomb and demanded $200,000 ransom money and four parachutes. The hijacker allowed the other passengers to leave the jet, which was refueled and ordered back into the air, heading for Mexico, via Reno, Nevada.

Soon after the plane took off and was flying, as ordered, at 10,000 feet with the landing gear down, the hijacker ordered the one remaining flight attendant into the cockpit. He then lowered the rear stairwell on the jet and apparently bailed out with the money, never to be seen again. The plane was over Lewis River in southwest Washington.

Veteran staffer Clyde Jabin was working alone in the Portland bureau when he got a tip of the first recorded skyjacking. He finally got in touch with law enforcement officials who had some details on the strange hijacking.

Jabin rolled out a colorful story of how the mysterious D.B. Cooper had pulled off this bizarre exploit and possibly escaped with $200,000. His story got wide play by newspapers and broadcasters. For days the media tracked the fruitless search for D.B Cooper and his loot.

However, some Northwest Airline and FBI agents were a little confused by the media accounts. These agents had the name of the skyjacker, taken from his ticket, as Dan Cooper and the FBI thought that was a fake name, as well.

The world continued to follow the search for D.B. Cooper without ever knowing they were partially duped by UPI's Clyde Jabin, who in his aggressive pursuit of the news copied the mystery man's name as D.B. Cooper instead of Dan Cooper. A small error, told to the world.

Like staffers in most UPI bureaus, Jabin had to serve as a "jack of all trades" with an ability to put anything, even something as brand-new as a skyjacking, into perspective for newspapers and broadcasters.

Most UPI bureau staffers covered and wrote stories of all descriptions: general news, politics, sports, financial, anything and everything.

Even some of the specialists, like sportswriters, often took great delight in winning play when they were pressed into duty covering straight news. And it didn't have to be a BIG story.

Mike Hughes, who was UPI's Editor in Chief when he ended a 30-year career in 1986, recalled a trip to the midwest when he was UPI's sports editor in New York. He had a seven-hour airline stopover in Omaha and decided to go by the bureau (WH). As he walked in the door and introduced himself, the lone Omaha staffer told him that the bureau manager had died that morning and that he had to go to the dentist. He asked Hughes to take care of the bureau.

As the staffer dashed out the door, he shouted back to Hughes, "Don't forget the hogs at 11 A.M." Hughes, a Brit who spent most of his career in Europe and doing sports, had no idea of what the man was talking about. He called the division control bureau in Chicago and found out that "doing the hogs" meant calling the USDA and reporting the 11 A.M. hog market prices. Hughes took care of that and the wheat prices as well and had the bureau humming when the staffer returned from the dentist and told the UPI veteran, "You're a pretty good Unipresser."

One of UPI's best known sportswriters, Oscar Fraley, proved that he could also win the play on straight news when he was pressed into service in Miami during America's abortive "Bay of Pigs" invasion of Cuba.

Fraley was in Florida to cover the major league baseball teams during spring training in 1961 when Cuban troops turned back an invasion force made up of anti-Castro militants supported by the Central Intelligence Agency (CIA).

The dapper New York sports writer rushed to Miami where he interviewed the dazed and battered survivors of the invasion force. These were the lucky ones who escaped capture and managed to make it back to Florida. Fraley, whose sports copy was sometimes on the florid side, used his flair for the dramatic to tell the story of a coup attempt against Fidel Castro that went terribly wrong. Fraley's survivor stories won front-pager play around the world.

When UPI staffers couldn't tell it to the world, they liked to tell it to each other. The message wire was the chosen venue, second only to the A-wire.

The UPI message wires sometimes were the internal scoreboards where editors sang the praises or, quite often, heaped the damnation on staffers who had done well or had stumbled with their news offerings.

It once worked both ways for Claude Sitton, who was on the Atlanta overnight general desk in the 1950s.

Sitton was "filling in" for the regular overnight editor, Dick West, and had sent what he thought was a nifty little kicker to the NX desk for use as a "light and bright" on the A-wire. NX overnight general desker Dave Whitney, who thought Dick West was working, fired a message to Atlanta:

> "DW/AJ
> THAT KICKER'S A STEM-WINDER, BUT YOU'VE MISSPELLED BACHELOR.
> DW/NX"

Sitton wrote a fast correction, but he was also anxious that New York's praise be properly directed to the real author. He sent a message to New York so that his sign-off would show Whitney, and the hundreds of other Unipressers reading the message wire, that he had written the attention-grabbing kicker.

> "DW/NX
> TNX RE KICKER. EYE MUST HAVE FORGOTTEN MY BLUE-BACK SPELLER.
> CS/AJ

Within a few minutes, NX responded.

> "CS/AJ
> YOU SURE AS HELL DID. IT'S SPELLED B-A-C-H-E-L-O-R.
> DW/NX"

Dumbfounded, Sitton checked the A-wire and found that bachelor had been corrected from "bachlor" to "bachleor."

Most of the men and women who worked for UP-UPI had favorite messages as well as favorite leads, favorite corrections and favorite gaffes.

The message most often recited was composed on the fly by a teletype operator in the Atlanta bureau (AJ) in the late 1940s.

Bernard Brenner recalled that he was working the desk on a Sunday afternoon and couldn't get the Raleigh, North Carolina, (RA) bureau to open the night news circuit. He messaged Jim Campbell in Raleigh and said to get with the program and put the wire through to Atlanta. Campbell responded that he was doing three other things and had only two hands.

Without hesitation and without consulting the young wire filer, chief operator Paul Butler, fired back:

> "RA
> FIRE THE CRIPPLED BASTARD.
> AJ"

A dapper, arrogant teletype operator had wrapped into a four-word message the spirit of United Press: the challenge to do more with less.

30

Jack of All

"THE BEAUTY OF WORKING FOR UPI WAS THAT HAVING ABSOLUTELY NO familiarity with the subject of a story was never a drawback."

The quote came from Janet Cawley, who worked as a reporter and editor for UPI in Canada, New York and Europe before joining the *Chicago Tribune*. It could have come from just about anyone who ever worked for the news service that boasted of having fewer but trying harder.

UPI staffers were expected to cover any type of news, politics, violence, science, entertainment, human interest, sports and business.

UPI had its experts in New York and Washington as well as separate departments for sports and financial news. However, the strength of UPI was the breadth of its coverage and the skill of its editors and reporters in the field.

When news broke anywhere, anytime, the UPI staffer nearest the story was expected to know how to cover the action and how to become an instant expert.

Sometimes they came up a little short. William Cotterell worked the night general desk in the Atlanta (AJ) bureau and spent a lot of his time in the fall editing and rewriting college football stories.

Cotterell said a young woman in the Memphis, Tennessee, bureau was forced to cover a National Football League exhibition game even though she said she had never seen a football game, even on TV.

Nonetheless, Cotterell said, she did a good job covering the game, got her facts straight and filed her story on time. Her writing, however, didn't look exactly like the standard game story, especially her third paragraph that began:

"The contest was played out on a broad, grassy field with white stripes every five yards."

Cotterell, a true southern gentleman, declined to identify the woman, whom he characterized as a "fine Unipresser."

Most of the news service's reporters were familiar with sports, particularly early in the twentieth century when the staff was overwhelmingly male. Roy Howard himself covered big sports events when he was head of the news service, including the World

Series and the Jack Johnson-Jim Jeffries championship fight in Reno, Nevada, July 4, 1910. Big-name writers like H. Allen Smith, Henry McLemore, James Kilgallen, Harry Ferguson and Westbrook Pegler all sharpened their prose in the United Press sports department.

Some big-name athletes also wrote sports for UP on a contract basis, including tennis star Helen Wills and baseball standouts Cy Young and Babe Ruth. None were paid better on a per-word basis than the Babe.

UP paid Ruth $100 each time he called to give a first-person account of each home run he hit.

James Kilgallen recalled in an interview many years later that when he worked for UP in Chicago, the Babe called in and would say, "low, inside," to describe the pitch he hit out of the park. That's all he said and it was up to Kilgallen and H. Allen Smith to turn that into a 500-word first-person story "by Babe Ruth."[1]

In 1914, United Press organized a specialized staff for sports coverage and appointed H. C. Hamilton as sports editor. In 1914, sports fans had to wait in the streets for the newspaper's "extra" to learn who won the World Series or Kentucky Derby. Radio and television, with instant results and live coverage, were still in the future.

Most large cities had more than one afternoon newspaper. The one hitting the streets five minutes ahead of its competition sold the most papers. On one World Series day, the Biddeford (Maine) *Record* boasted on the front page that its "breezy, snappy" United Press story was on the street before the competition.

Demands of World War I on Western Union—unable to handle requests for special wires to the ballparks—made it essential for newspapers to have a wire service. With their staffs depleted by the war, newspapers could not spare staff for out-of-town events.

After World War I, interest in college athletics, especially football, increased every year. Sports editor Henry Farrell, who replaced Hamilton in 1920, arranged in advance for coverage of upwards of 200 games on a Saturday afternoon. Thirty-two wires in the New York bureau were devoted on Saturday afternoon and evening to moving football scores, stories and statistics.

Farrell's full-time sports staff in New York included Frank Getty and Paul W. White. In the Middle West, sports was handled by Ed Derr and Clark B. Kelsey of Chicago. On the West Coast there was Lincoln Quarberg, H. E. Swisher and R. S. Moore.

Unlike other breaking news, sports events were scheduled in advance, giving the editors plenty of time to plan. Success depended on good planning. United Press sports editors learned to out-plan their opposition. Their advance work was the key to the sports wire's success.

Hamilton and Farrell carefully planned major events such as the Jess Willard-Jack Dempsey fight in Toledo, July 4, 1919; the 1920 Olympic Games in Antwerp; Wimbledon tennis; Epson Downs horse racing; track events; golf tournaments; regattas; and shooting competitions.

Leo H. Petersen, who ran the sports department for more than twenty years beginning in 1945, was known for his profanity and heavy drinking. However, it was his ability as an administrator and organizer that allowed UP to win wide acceptance by newspaper sports editors.

Speed meant more to the sports department than anywhere else. Newspaper deadlines were timed to catch the results of sport events. No morning newspaper could present itself on somebody's breakfast table without the scores of last night's games. Afternoon newspapers used to put out several editions. It was extremely important to have the latest scores and the latest horse racing results in a corner "fudge" box on page one.

Sports events usually occurred during daytime hours. This gave United Press an edge because it was primarily an afternoon service in the early years. Factory and office workers on the way home after work habitually gave a newsboy two cents or a nickel for the paper to glance at the scores. The details would be read later at home.

Partly because of sports, in those days many newspapers switched from morning to afternoon publishing, a trend that was reversed in later years when radio was available for instant scores and street traffic made the distribution of afternoon extras difficult and costly.

In 1917, UP introduced a precursor to "live" coverage of sports events. UP ordered Western Union leased wires directly from the press boxes of the World Series ballparks in Chicago and New York. Hamilton dictated play-by-play to a Teletype operator who flashed it immediately on the wire.

These play-by-play and blow-by-blow running stories on sports events were used by announcers in the early days of radio to "re-create" the action.

Western Union operators, using Morse keys, transmitted the play-by-play account to the radio station, where another operator converted the click-clack signals to brief descriptions of each pitch, hit, etc. The announcer could then present a dramatic account of the game, just as if he were in the press box. If a player hit a home run, the announcer might shout "Bye, bye, baby!" and then turn up the volume on the recorded crowd noise.

President Ronald Reagan and famous CBS anchor Walter Cronkite were among radio announcers who did sports re-creations in their early careers. The practice faded out when on-the-scene live broadcasting and television became routine for sports events.

However, as recently as 1971, the promoter of the Muhammad Ali-Joe Frazier heavyweight championship bout in Madison Square Garden was worried that re-creation by unauthorized stations would compete with broadcast rights sold to a closed-circuit television channel. The fight drew much attention because Ali had recently changed his name from Casius Clay and was accused of evading military service.[2]

Attorneys for the promoter sought an injunction against the UPI and Associated Press to prohibit the wires from carrying blow-by-blow reports during the fight.

"We do not sign contracts regarding our right to cover news events," Jack Griffin, UPI Sports Editor, told the promoter's lawyer.

The court rejected the request and UPI rejected the censorship. Associated Press signed an agreement promising to put no more than a 50-word, past-tense summary of each round's action on its wire, with an advisory to radio stations not to make a re-creation of it.

Early in 1923, Farrell interviewed former welterweight champion Jack Britton, who said he suffered from insomnia and would give a thousand dollars for a cure.

A day after the quote appeared on the wire, carriers began dragging sacks of mail to Britton's home from every state in the union and several foreign countries. Suggestions ranged from counting three billion sheep passing through a million gates to drinking 6,000 gallons of coffee, or holding his fingertips together over his head for seven years.

Kilgallen, who later spent much of his career with the Hearst newspapers, was a skilled sportswriter, covering such events as the "Black Sox" scandal in Chicago. In an interview he recalled his days with UP:

> "The UP was a jazzy organization. We shortened up the stuff, made it easier to read. Roy Howard was a stickler for that. The AP wasn't hitting features, it was strictly in the dignified style, straight-away....The thing that sticks with me more than anything else was the intense competition—very, very competitive. I liked it, myself."

For the 1929 World Series at Chicago and Philadelphia, UP engaged the celebrated Cy Young, then sixty-three, to write stories comparing the series with baseball when he was playing thirty years earlier.

UP also hired "Red" Solomon, a 13-year-old batboy for the Chicago Cubs, to write a sidebar after each game. Editors loved this material, although none of it was actually written by the people by-lined.

Henry McLemore, who worked the sports desk and produced a brilliant column, loved to cover tennis at Forest Hills. But when Harry Ferguson became sports editor he assigned McLemore to a PGA golf tournament in Philadelphia the same week as Forest Hills.

McLemore refused to miss the tennis event and ended up in Ferguson's doghouse. From then on McLemore's copy was frequently spiked. He was, in effect, forced out of UP.

For the 1930 British Open at St. Andrews, Virgil Pinkley of the London bureau used semaphore to get the outcome from the course to the press room in the clubhouse. A semaphore flag man accompanying Pinkley near the twelfth green, which turned out to be the final hole in the match play event, wig-wagged the outcome to a second semaphore man near the clubhouse, who flashed the outcome to the cable wire. Newspaper presses in the United States were rolling with the result while messengers for competing news agencies were still running to the clubhouse with the result.

Jack Guenther was assigned to cover the 1940 running of the Kentucky Derby in Knoxville, Tennessee along with Ed Sainsbury from Chicago. Jack arrived at the press box fully armed with twelve "canned" leads, one ready to slap on the wire for whichever horse won.

International sporting events were more important than national sports because client newspapers everywhere in the world had to have specialized coverage, particularly stories about participants from those countries. UP/UPI provided special stories for the foreign service, usually bringing to the event writers from all the participating countries.

At international events like the Olympics UP usually outstaffed AP because international clients in Latin America and Europe were more important to UP than to AP.

In 1962, UPI sent 10 sports staffers to cover a world football tournament in Chile. Communications were set up so that a picture taken at the opening of the final game in Santiago was transmitted across the Atlantic and was in print in a Frankfurt, Germany, newspaper before the game ended.

Two years later, a team of reporters was sent from Lima, Peru, 2,340 miles up the Amazon River to cover a women's basketball tournament in Iquitos. The Korean team's victory was sent around the world in forty languages.

"We got the Peruvian army to fly pictures down from Iquitos to Lima," International Vice President Joe Jones reported. Play-by-play accounts were flashed by cable to New York for transmission back to Latin America and to Asia and Europe on the teleprinter circuits. Pictures were relayed through New York to Europe and Asia and back to South American clients.

The UPI tried to cover as much local sports as it could. In the state of Indiana, the annual high school basketball tournament was a premier sporting event. The wire service managed to carry reports on each of 787 teams in the tournament.

Ed Fite, Southwest sports editor, developed a team rating system for high school sports in Texas.

For minor league games and all except the top collegiate games, UP hired reliable stringers, paying a few dollars each for the game results to be called or telegraphed from the stadium to the closest bureau.

For the 1960 Olympic winter games in Squaw Valley, California, UPI hired eight skiers as messengers to race down the slopes to the press headquarters with copy and film. Cliff McDonnell, managing the picture service, had six telephoto transmitters at the press center and was able to transmit photos to New York and Europe within a half hour of camera snap.

When the Pan-American Games were held in San Paulo in 1963, UPI planned to use the opportunity to bring a great deal of equipment into the country as baggage, including twenty teletype machines. This equipment was purportedly to be used to cover the games but UPI intended to leave it there for its needs in Brazil, avoiding import regulations.

Gray Neeleman accompanied sports editor Leo Petersen on the trip to Brazil. When they were about to go through customs he noticed that Petersen had an additional large box. "Pete" told Neeleman it was his liquor for the visit. Neeleman, more familiar with South America' customs, told Petersen he would not get it into the country unless he shared it with the inspection officers.

No way would Peterson share it. So they were stopped by police and Leo wound up in jail. Neeleman did not see him for two days.

Petersen pulled similar disappearances at the Rome Olympics and other big sports events. Nevertheless, he was praised as a first class sports manager because he knew how to hire excellent writers, and how to plan coverage. He always had plenty of manpower, equipment and communications to do the job.

"Somehow, he managed to put together what many outsiders viewed as the best sports staff in New York, including the big by-liners who worked for the *Daily News* and *Herald Tribune*," said Carl Lundquist, who was the UP baseball writer.[3] That staff included Lundquist, Oscar Fraley, Steve Snider, Milt Richman, Jack Cuddy, Fred Down, Jack Griffin and Stan Opotowsky.

The sports staff included Scott "Ace" Baillie, son of Hugh Baillie, president of the company. On Baillie's first day in sports, Leo Petersen took him across the street to Sellman's bar to get things clear between the sports editor and the president's son.

"Everyone else on the staff has proven ability," Pete told Baillie. "I don't know what you can do yet, and you obviously will be under some personal pressure and may have to take some guff. But we can work it out. I'll keep your old man out of our relationship and I expect you to do the same."

Scott didn't see eye-to-eye with his dad on a lot of things and assured Pete he would not be a pipeline to the front office.

The nattily-attired Oscar Fraley, on the New York sports staff, was one of UP's most familiar bylines. An old Philadelphia friend he had met on the boxing beat there, came to Fraley a number of times, pestering him about a "big story" he had. Fraley, like other wire service writers, knew that a friend coming in with a "big story" usually had nothing really worth writing about.

However, this particular friend came into the sports department in New York accompanied by another man. "This is Joe Grossman. He has a fantastic story," the friend told Fraley. They went out to lunch. When he returned to the office, Oscar sat down and wrote a week's worth of "The Sports Parade," his daily column. Then he went home and pounded out a book he called *The Untouchables*, the story of Eliot Ness, federal agent who invaded the criminal lairs in Chicago and convicted Al Capone.

The book sold nearly two million copies and was turned into a television series that was still having re-runs forty years later.

Major events like the World Series, Olympics, the Super Bowl and title fights often attracted several thousand sports writers. Even when newspapers sent their own staff writer, however, they depended on the wires for spot bulletins and the bread and butter facts. Newspapers also relied on the wire for agate box scores, team standings and other "stax" that involved tedious compilations.

Only the wire agencies could efficiently handle several events going on simultaneously at widespread locations, with hundreds of participants.

UP's staff at the Munich Olympics in 1972 was forced to switch instantly from covering sports to covering disaster that nearly set off a war.

Arab gunmen invaded the Olympic Village and killed two Israeli athletes. Fifteen people were killed in the raid and its aftermath, which shocked the world.

When it happened early on September 5, first a rumor swept through the press quarters. The athletes' residential "village" was off limits to reporters, but they raced to the scene and some managed to gain entry by unconventional means.

Pete Willett of UPI Audio put on a blue and white track suit and fell in step with two Australian girl runners. Attempting to look like an athlete he huffed and puffed past the security guards.

Willett was thrown out three times during that day. Other sports writers, including Darrell Mack, Stan Sabik and Milt Richman also sneaked into the off-limits village to gather details of the incident.[4]

Sometimes improvisation and slightly questionable tactics were employed in reporting sports. When a world tennis tournament was held in Australia, UPI did not have a reporter on the scene. Hal Wood, sports editor in San Francisco, listened to an overseas broadcast of the play and wrote stories for the wires under a Sidney dateline.

The Super Bowl was always a choice sports assignment. It had top fan interest. Super Bowl media were showered with lavish parties and "freebies" for a week before the event.

In 1973, the Super Bowl party for reporters was held aboard the *Queen Mary* ocean liner, docked in Long Beach, California. A year later, at the Astrodome in Houston, the press people walked over a red carpet to a feast of spitted steers and hogs.

In 1975, a press party in the New Orleans Convention Hall cost the National Football League $150,000. Sports writers were seen walking away from the event carrying bottles of champagne. At Super Bowl X in 1976 in Miami, nearly 2,000 accredited media representatives were furnished free Hertz rental cars, lavish food spreads and tokens including watches, wallets and briefcases.

NFL Commissioner Pete Rozelle, once a United Press stringer, knew how to nurture the media.

"We're not trying to buy anybody. We're just giving people a souvenir of the game. People need a press kit. We think it's a service to provide a briefcase. We're not going to buy anyone with a watch," Rozelle said through his spokesman, Don Weiss.

Very few sports reporters refused the freebies.

Generosity of sports promoters toward the fellow with the key to the sports page was so common it became an expected part of the journalist's income, but also an ethical dilemma. Free transportation, free food, free whiskey by the case, free clothing, free hotels, free "souvenirs," free tickets to give away to friends or sell, and sometimes a handful of $20 bills were the practice until it got through to newspaper editors and the writers themselves that this didn't look good.

Free air transportation and hotels for the writers were gradually eliminated. In the case of United Press International, the loss was felt deeply because the company had built the free ride into its sports budget, counting on the teams to pick up the writer's expenses at baseball training camps and golf tournaments.

Early in the 1960s, sports writers at newspapers were told by their employers they had to give up being the official scorers for major league baseball teams, a side job that paid about $60 a game at the time. For some UPI baseball writers, cutting out the extra income was a significant hit. A few defied the edict and kept scoring for money as long as the teams were willing to pay.

UPI Editor-in-Chief H. L. Stevenson had asked at an editors' meeting: "Are the reams of copy written prior to big time sports events and other spectacular's legitimate news? Or is it an orchestrated build-up to sell tickets?…Is the media being manipulated to help fill stadiums or closed circuit television theaters?"[5]

He cited the story of Evel Knievel, a Montana stunt man who promised to soar across the Snake River Gorge in Idaho on his steam-powered "skycycle."

Knievel went on a whirlwind trip around the country, stopping "wherever a few notebooks and a microphone or two could be found," Stevenson said. The event was a spectacular flop, ending with the daredevil stunt man landing by parachute in the river.

One of the more successful sports features was the coaches' poll, a survey of opinions from about forty college coaches ranking football teams. It was started by Stan Opotowsky who thought of it as a way to match the AP's poll of sports writers. Sports Editor Leo Petersen had to be persuaded that it would not involve overtime and that the various bureaus could collect the ballots of coaches in their area. The rankings became a leading sports story every week, anticipated by editors and fans.

At a meeting of UPI subscribers in San Francisco in October 1974, some editors from Oklahoma protested the wire service's refusal to list the Oklahoma football team in its weekly rankings.

The Sooners had been banned by the NCAA for player recruiting violations. Coaches were under NCAA rules and excluded the Sooners from their voting. However, AP, which polled sports writers, had Oklahoma high in its rating by sports writers.

A resolution, drawn up by editors of the Muskogee *Daily Phoenix* and several other newspapers was presented with some light heartedness at the UPI meeting.

H. L. Stevenson, executive editor, responded in the same vein, paraphrased Lincoln's Gettysburg address: "Two score and several Sooners ago, our coaches brought forth a rating board, conceived in liberty and dedicated to the proposition that all teams are created equal.…"[6]

A similar dispute arose in 1978 when the UPI coaches named USC as the nation's top team over Alabama. One newspaper, the *Raleigh Register*, put the question to its readers, who chose Alabama although that school was under sanction by the NCAA.

Horse racing, the "sport of kings," was of special interest to UP/UPI's clients, including the big South American customers.

Race results sometimes went through all the relays from London to Buenos Aires in less than 10 seconds.

The New York bureau's racing desk, which handled all the U.S. tracks, was in a corner far removed from the rest of the news operation. There, Ray Ayres assembled the entries, jockeys, scratches, results and other horse racing news from all the tracks for instant movement on a special racing wire.

Ayres was always swamped under a flood of tip sheets and handouts from the tracks. The actual race results came in on a Western Union ticker. The "off" time of each race was known, and if the result was not on the UPI wire within a minute there would be a call from a client.

Horse racing news was a tender, well-guarded part of the agency's business. In Nevada, bookmakers used racing information but could not buy it directly from UPI because a federal law forbade transfer of gambling information across state lines.

However, in a deal that was kept as quiet as possible, the race wire was sold to an intermediary in Reno. UPI did not ask how the information was used, but the client paid heavily and presumably passed the information to bookies.

San Francisco bureau staffers were sometimes told that this Nevada client paid all of their salaries. The Agua Caliente track in Tijuana, Mexico, was also an important client carefully cultivated by UPI's president, Frank Bartholomew.

Mental sports also came in for intense wire service coverage, though usually not on the sports wire. International chess tournaments were of particular interest. *La Prensa* of Buenos Aires posted chess move-by-move action for a crowd around the front of the newspaper's office.

In New York in the 1930s, UP sent feature writers Henry McLemore and H. Allen Smith to a Lenz-Culbertson bridge match. They turned out widely printed accounts of the play.

UP hired famous aviator Eddie Rickenbacker to write stories on the Cleveland air races.

31

Not All Business

"DOWN BACK."

Those were the hurried directions for visitors to the United Press news bureau in New York if they were looking for the financial department in the 1920s.

News of the business world was "down back" not only in its location at the UP headquarters, but also it was "down back" in the minds of most UP reporters and editors. Covering wars, crime and politics was far more appealing to most of the news hands in the 20s.

William H. Grimes, an early staffer in the New York bureau who liked to write stories about business, found a direct line from "down back" to the front office.

Grimes talked to UP president Karl Bickel about the importance of financial news and Bickel made him the first United Press financial editor.

In April 1922, a new Teletype circuit was launched, the business wire, to carry news, stock prices and market summaries of special interest to the Wall Street crowd.

Grimes left in 1923, moving over to the *Wall Street Journal* where he became one of its top editors. *Deadline Every Minute*, the UP history, says financial news coverage then became "haphazard."

Staffers Edward J. Condlin, William Johnson, Todd W. Wright and others took the market reports by telephone. Stock price lists from the tickers had to be assembled and sent in a certain format and no one really wanted the chore.

One day in 1925, no one was around the office who was experienced with the task. Bureau manager Morris DeHaven Tracy was trying to figure out what to do when Elmer Walzer, a new member on the news staff, offered to help. Soon Walzer was United Press financial editor. He became the real father of UP financial.

UP began carrying American Stock Exchange quotes and over-the-counter prices in 1926. About a year later it put the Big Board on its wires, hiring a team of fifteen tabulators to prepare the list. The tabulators were recruited away from *Consolidated News*, which had been supplying stock prices to newspapers. *Consolidated* continued for a time to supply quotes to the Associated Press, but, later, AP also began its own stock price list.

Walzer was financial editor until he retired in 1960. He added many market reports, developed the first special quote products such as a list of the top traded stocks.

He wrote a regular Wall Street column every day. The financial staff gradually increased, peaking at thirty-five staffers in 1960. Besides the tabulators there were reporters and editors to write and edit business news.

The stock market hit the front page in 1929 when millions of shares were being traded daily and the great crash tumbled the world into depression.

Walzer said the financial community "always dreaded the times when Wall Street news hit the front pages" because it usually was bad news.

United Press set up a special stock wire to carry the New York Stock Exchange closing prices as quickly as possible.

When the company moved from the *World* building to the *Daily News* building, the financial service was again expanded. Several wires used exclusively to move the closing market prices. A business writer position was transferred from New York to Washington to cover government agencies with specialized news for business, such as the Treasury Department, Commerce Department and others.

Then followed years of depression and slow economic recovery for the country. Stock trading fell as low as a few hundred shares a day.

Dorothea Brooks, who joined the financial department in 1945, recalled that on the first million-share day the tabulators had to work very late to get all the prices listed. She said the department always seemed to be treated like a stepchild. She said the front office didn't take much interest in what went on back in financial.

In the 1940s. stock lists moved on the same financial wire as news copy, taking up at least one-half the available space. Tabulators each worked ten or twelve long sheets of stocks, reading the ticker tapes, changing last prices and highs and lows as necessary with each transaction and figuring net changes.

Brooks recalled that Walzer, providentially, had cornered the market on No. 2 pencils with metal tops and replaceable erasers, all in short supply during the war years. She said tabulator clerks went through at least two a day changing prices on the stock lists.

The tabulators, working under S. Richard "Dick" Brown, worked the stock lists by hand until volume climbed to around the one-million share mark and UP was forced to develop a computer system in 1962.

At the end of World War II many women reporters hired by the wire service during the war, were let go to make room for returning male staffers. Brooks and Shirley Abell were the only two females in the financial department who were kept on. Brooks stayed until 1987 when she retired as financial editor and, typically, worked ten hours on her last day.

The daily list of stock market prices was without a doubt the most important thing the financial department produced, not exactly glamorous but of biblical importance to the business community. It was drudgery for the two dozen tabulators who put it together and was usually exactly the same as a list provided by the competing Associated Press. The only way to win was to get it on the wires faster than the opposition and to keep mistakes to a minimum. One day the tabulators turned out a perfect list, no mistakes, Walzer took them all to dinner at the Hollywood Restaurant in Manhattan.

In 1960, Frank Bartholomew, president of UPI, said he had broached an idea to the AP. To save money the news agencies could create a subsidiary to handle the stock lists and other tabular material that was the same in both services. There was no real competition on the content of this material and the duplication of costs was paid by the newspaper clients of both services. Bartholomew said the cost of duplicated stock wires went into the pocket of the telephone companies. A jointly-owned subsidiary corporation could handle non-competitive material and the saving would be passed back to publishers.

AP was not receptive to the idea, Bart said in an interview published in *Editor & Publisher*.[12]

At that time, both news services were seeking technical solutions to the problem of moving huge stock lists to their newspaper clients quickly every day. United Press foresaw an expenditure of two million dollars to inaugurate a computerized system. Among computer companies being consulted were IBM, Fairchild, Photon, Inc., RCA, Royal McBee and several other engineering laboratories.

The objective was a high-speed stock transmission system that would be appropriate to the needs of the wire service and its newspaper subscribers, one that would not become obsolete before it was paid for.

The system finally agreed on by UPI was developed by Scantlin Electronics, Inc., of Los Angeles. Quotes from the stock exchanges were fed into computers at a Scantlin facility and distributed by UPI at high speed in tape ready for typesetting machines.

Twelve wires could simultaneously spit out sections of the list in twelve tape streams at a speed, which matched the performance of twelve linotypes. Transmission of the entire New York Stock Exchange list would take twelve minutes. UP thought this twelve-channel system was better than a faster one-tape system which would leave the tape piled up at the newspaper office until it could be cut and fed to the linotypes.

The new UPI system was tested at the *Chicago Tribune*. It could be adapted for any size newspaper because the closing prices could be transmitted on two lines, four lines or six lines as well as twelve.

The company also launched a teletypesetter wire to run for two hours after the market close and carry a list of 500 selected stocks from the New York Exchange and certain other market tables for smaller newspapers that did not want the full list. In January 1963, UPI added the American Exchange to the high speed system.

Henry J. Bechtold was named financial editor in July 1960, succeeding Walzer. Less than a year later he left for a public relations job and Jesse Bogue, who had been manager of the Chicago bureau for fifteen years and was then Central Division news manager, moved to New York to run the financial department.

When Bogue moved up to be assistant managing editor for the whole news services in August 1965, William D. Laffler, from the New York overnight staff, took over the job of financial editor. In April 1968, Dean C. Miller was named business editor and S. Richard Brown was named financial editor.

Brown was put in charge of the stock lists and Brooks managed the coverage of business news.

Computers made the manipulation of financial data much easier. Tabulators were no longer needed, and various product innovations were introduced. In 1968, the UPI Stock Market Indicator was begun. This was a computer-produced average of 1,628 stocks on the New York Exchange. It calculated the average price change for those stocks compared with the previous day's closing prices.

Technical improvements continued to come at a rapid clip. A printer was developed which could pelt out 3,400 words, or 1,100 lines a minute. The entire New York Exchange closing prices could be moved in 90 seconds.

In April 1970, UPI started its Stock Pulse service, with the computer picking out and tabulating the ten most active stocks by volume and the ten with the greatest change from the previous close. These new products and improvements kept the UPI financial wires competitive.

An arrangement with the *Financial Times* of London gave UPI business wire clients the British financial newspaper's material at no extra cost.

In 1970, the company switched its computer stock operations from Scantlin, Inc. to its own new computers in New York, and the financial department got new, enlarged quarters in the *Daily News* building. At that time, UPI had 200 clients for Unistox, the name it gave its high-speed service.

The company then introduced Unistox DataTwo, which produced the same tabular material as Unistox but in a narrower version, two thirds of a column instead of a full column, to meet the requirements of some newspapers.

Bob Woodsum was named UPI director of stock market services in 1972, in charge of selling the various financial products.

In September 1975, the New York Stock Exchange decided it was going to charge the wire services for picking up its list. Up until then the wire services had paid only for the technical equipment of transmitting the prices into their computers. Now, through a subsidiary, the Consolidated Tape Association, the New York Stock Exchange wanted to impose a $1,500 per month charge on the wire services.

UPI and AP protested vigorously and the exchange cut the proposed fee to $750 per month. AP accepted and signed a contract. UPI continued to resist but eventually had to pay. The Stock Exchange said it was not "a charge for news" as alleged but was "a facilities charge to cover day-to-day operating costs."

Another innovation, in May 1976, was the "Modifier," which was nothing more than adding a small letter like "d" for Denver, or "h" for Midwest, to the stock symbol to indicate that the source was an exchange other than the Big Board or the American Stock Exchange.

In September 1976, UPI announced a partnership with Commodity News Services, owned by Knight-Ridder Co., to establish Unicom, an economic news wire serving the international business community everywhere except in the United States and Canada. Harald P. Bauer, a salesman in Los Angeles, was named general manager of the UPI/CNS service, which had headquarters in London and began to function in January 1977. Richard T. Service, of CNS, was named editor of the wire.

News on the business pages is extremely touchy—money is involved. Readers of that section of a newspaper are always sensitive to any news, which might affect the markets, corporations or personalities in the business world.

Brooks kept the business wire relevant by assigning two reporters to work the most important financial "beats." Roz Liston, who had worked in UP's Ocean Press News Service, was assigned the energy beat and Mary Tobin, a former Teletype operator, to banking. The geopolitics of oil was a front page story throughout much of the 1970s.

"They hired an unending parade of consultants and experts," Brooks said. One of these consultants met with her and said: "Now, tell me everything you know about financial." She said she told the consultant it might be hard to condense it into a half-hour interview everything she had learned in forty years.

Brooks resigned in 1987 and Liston was named to replace her. Liston moved to diversify UPI's financial product by hiring three veteran editors in New York: Ivan Zverina from the international desk; Lillian O'Connell, who had worked the teletypesetter wire, and David Dugas, who had handled UPI's archives.

Liston developed her skills as an editor in one of the wire service's most unique departments.

In 1932, UP developed a special service for luxury ocean liners that plied the high seas. UP's *Ocean Press* service published personalized newspapers for the *Queen Elizabeth* and her sister ship, the *Queen Mary*, and 150 other vessels. The service was a substantial operation and profitable, probably because it sold advertising, unlike other UPI products which were strictly objective news.

Different newspapers were produced for the various big passenger steamship companies. It was *Ocean Times* for the queens and other Cunard ships, *Ocean Press* for United States Lines vessels, *Sun-Lane News* for American Export Lines' SS *Constitution*, *Ocean Post* for Holland-American Lines' SS *Rotterdam*, *Good Neighbor* for Moore-McCormack Lines' vessels in the South American trade. Passengers aboard the French Line's *France* and *Flandre* received *L'Antique*. The Italian Lines' *Leonardo Da Vinci* and other liners had *Corrier del Mare*.

In 1960 it still went to 125 ships on the seven seas, but the day of passenger ocean liners was fading. *Ocean Press* folded when it began losing money early in the 1970s.

The seagoing newspapers were prepared in advance by a few editors in New York headed by Lillian O'Connell, a newslady who liked to race her Porsche 1600 Super on weekends. They were mainly tabloid size publications. There was a new issue, usually about twenty pages, for each day of the voyage.

Inside pages carried stories and pictures that were not spot news but usually had an angle related to the ship's itinerary. There were stories about attractions to see in England and for those going on to Paris, a story about Notre Dame Cathedral.

Ocean Press handled advertising for these publications from hotels, restaurants, fancy department stores like Harrods of London and Saks in New York, and services that might be of use to passengers. The advertising rate in 1969 was $18.75 per column inch per day.

Bundles of these pre-printed newspapers, one for each day of the voyage, were put aboard ship in New York or London. The front page of each was left blank. That was for the day's spot news, transmitted daily from New York, San Francisco or London by a commercial radio service, RCA or Mackay, Radio and picked up by the ship's radio room.

This file of news was carefully edited to include major world events that would be of interest to passengers, about twenty stories a day. All the resources of the wire service were available to the editors of Ocean Press.

When the first page was ready, the pre-printed newspaper was run off on a printing machine aboard. Large liners like the *Queen Mary* had fully-equipped printing plants with linotypes and presses.

UPI's Ocean Press operation was headed by William Manley. When he died of a heart attack, the division came under the direction of Ed Allen of the company's special services department.

Through its entire history United Press International saw business and industry as potential cash customers for specialized journalistic services. The special services division, which handled business clients, was enlarged in 1958 when UP merged with INS, which also served business clients.

The service ran into trouble, both domestically and internationally, because it created the potential for conflict of interest between the commercial purpose of a special service client and the strictly objective policy required for news subscribers.

INS special services had gathered news under a contract with the Dominican Republic Information Center on behalf of General Rafael Trujillo. Charges of $2,000 a month were paid directly by the Dominican government.

Special services, under Ed Allen, also operated a commercial photo business, separate from news pictures, with outside photographers for commercial assignments.

Some special service assignments were done for regular news clients. The *Paris Match* frequently hired the wire service to produce a dispatch, for example a 7,000-word story on the escape of three prisoners from Alcatraz.

Another tangential operation for the wire service was publishing news books.

After the death of President Kennedy, UPI, in cooperation with *American Heritage* magazine, published *Four Days*, a hard-cover letter size slick-paper book of text and news photographs made during the four days of mourning and the burial of Kennedy at Arlington Cemetery.

UPI editors worked feverishly to collect and edit the best pictures and text, including the stories of Merriman Smith, who won a Pulitzer Prize for his coverage of Kennedy's assassination. It was produced within a few days and was distributed through client newspapers, who used it as a promotion as well as a profit maker.

Ultimately several million copies of the book were distributed, putting it on the all-time best seller list.

Four Days was not the agency's first book project. In 1960 UPI had published *The Pilgrim Pope* about Paul VI's unprecedented visit to the United States. It was written by Jack Fallon of the New York desk, Lou Cassels, the religion editor, and Bill Sunderland of the Rome bureau.

The Pilgrim Pope was moderately successful, earning about $100,000 for the company. However, none of the other news books put out after *Four Days* were profitable, according to Wayne Sargent, sales manager.

The news book projects were an attempt by the wire service to diversify its product in hopes of getting into the black financially.

"I tried everything I could to diversify UPI's base," said Sargent. "I said we have to get into other ways of marketing that which we have now and get into new fields. One of them was the quickie books."

32

Getting Damn Mad

"I'M SO DAMN MAD," MARTHA MITCHELL FUMED IN A 3 A.M. PHONE call to the news desk at UPI's New York headquarters. The date was August 26, 1973.

"I asked them to let me speak to the president. They told me, 'tell it to UPI.'"

Martha Mitchell, the wife of Attorney General John Mitchell, did tell it to UPI; she often told it to UPI, usually in talks with Helen Thomas, the one White House reporter she felt she could trust. Mitchell's frequent talks with Thomas were a growing irritant to White House staffers trying to circle the wagons during the Watergate crisis.

While the *Washington Post* had the anonymous 'Deep Throat,' Helen Thomas and UPI had the very up-front Martha Mitchell.

Martha Mitchell told Thomas during one phone call that President Richard M. Nixon and his White House staff were trying to make a 'fall guy' out of her husband, who had resigned his cabinet post to head the Committee to Re-Elect the President (CREEP). She told Thomas that she would not allow John to be the scapegoat and Helen was surprised when John Mitchell picked up the phone and told her, "any attempt to make me do it isn't going to work. I've never stolen any money. The only thing I did was try to get the president re-elected. I never did anything mentally or morally wrong."

In another phone call to Thomas, Martha Mitchell said she had seen a two-inch thick booklet on campaign strategy written by Nixon and his chief of staff, H.R. Haldeman. She said the plans included a Watergate-style operation. The White House was quick to deny it and put it down as another reckless report from Martha Mitchell and UPI.

On September 16, 1973, Martha called Helen saying her husband had moved out. Then, about a year later, on August 25, 1974, she called Thomas again, disputing Nixon's claim that John Mitchell had not discussed Watergate with Martha.

However, the Watergate scandal was moving from the behind-the-scene sources to the main players when a select Senate committee headed by Senator Sam J. Ervin of North Carolina opened hearings.

The hearings were held in an ornate caucus room steeped in high drama. It was the same room where the Teapot Dome scandals were aired and where Tennessee's Senator Estes Kefauver put organized crime on public trial. It was also the same room where Wisconsin Senator Joseph R. McCarthy was found guilty of abusing his colleagues and the Senate processes.

UPI was assigned three seats in the caucus room and Grant Dillman, UPI vice president and Washington manager, was determined to make the most of those valuable chairs. They would be occupied by Mike Feinsilber and Ed Dooley of UPI's congressional staff. A third reporter would be assigned on a daily basis. Those three reporters would not be encumbered with the responsibility of writing and transmitting the breaking copy. Feinsilber, a superb writer, would get an overview of the Watergate story and he would write the overnight lead for afternoon newspapers. The other two reporters would be able to track down the participants for follow-up queries.

UPI's principal Watergate reporters, Wesley G. Pippert and Jane Dennison, wrote the running copy and the main story for morning newspapers. Since the hearings were televised live, Pippert and Dennison watched them at the UPI's National Press Building bureau. Bill Barrett, with help from several other Washington staffers, including Bill Clayton and Judy Frie, prepared condensed transcripts of the hearings.

The wire services received few "leaks" during the Watergate investigation. The *Washington Post, New York Times* and *Los Angeles Times* were the principal receptacles for leaks and trial balloons. Most of the revelations hitting the news were

Chicao bureau, 1974. News staffers (from left) Rob Gunnison, Dick Harnett, Carrick Leavitt, Gordon Sakamoto, Reeve Hennion, Bob Lurati, Walt Rehbein (teletype technician with phone). Operators, along teletype bank next to windows, from left, Vince Ferraro, Fred Watson, Herman Timmons, Dave Frizzell.

dug up by those newspapers. The *Washington Post* was the first to report high-level involvement in the illegal break-in at the Watergate Towers Democratic Party office.

Nevertheless, UPI was expected by its subscribers to have on the wire all developments in the case. It usually involved picking up, with credit, stories from the newspapers. The practice of pickups had previously been frowned on by UPI editors. But in Watergate the wire service did not have the means to put dozens of reporters on what became known as "investigative reporting."

Ex-Unipresser Ron Nessen, a GOP insider who became press secretary to President Gerald Ford in 1974, showed no particular interest in helping his old wire service on the cascading developments.

But UPI got at least one Watergate leak. On June 14, 1974, a Senate Watergate Committee staff member told UPI that the committee's report would accuse Nixon of masterminding "dirty tricks" during the 1972 election campaign.

When the question of whether Nixon's secret tapes could be made public was heard before the U.S. Supreme Court in 1974, UPI and AP each received two places in the courtroom. Thirty-three other news agencies and newspapers were chosen for one place each from among 120 that had asked for credentials.

The wire service had an inadvertent role in the aftermath of the Watergate scandal surrounding President Nixon. In September 1974, President Gerald Ford's press secretary, Jerald F. TerHorst, was asked by White House reporter Helen Thomas whether Ford was considering a pardon for Nixon.

TerHorst said it was not under consideration. But a short time later, Ford did pardon Nixon. TerHorst resigned as Ford's press secretary less than a month after he took the job, saying he had been imposed upon by the White House to lie about the matter to reporters.

UPI's coverage of Watergate was solid and won wide play by newspapers and broadcasters. It was the result of intelligent, long-range planning and a talented Washington pool of reporters and editors.

Later that year, as the Watergate scandal was moving toward the eventual resignation of the president, UPI was forced into some helter-skelter planning on another big story. The 1973 Middle East War caught the news media by surprise.

Richard H. Growald, UPI's tempestuous editor for Europe, Middle East and Africa, reported from Brussels, "In 1967, diplomatic noises gave the press a week to move its troops. This time we had an hour."

The tip, from a diplomatic source in Vienna, came barely sixty minutes before Israel announced that its troops had crossed the Suez Canal following attacks by Egyptian and Syrian forces. The scramble was on. Messages between Beirut, Tel Aviv, Cairo, Brussels, Rome, Paris, London, New York and a dozen other UPI bureaus wove the plan to move additional reporters and photographers into the war zone.

For the most part, it was up to individual correspondents to figure out how to get around closed airports and canceled flights to reach their assigned posts.

In Paris, Gerard Loughran, an old Mideast hand, was covering a bicycle race in Orly. He flew to Rome, then to Athens and, with photographer Arthur Grace from Brussels, scrambled aboard a jet headed for Cairo.

In Rome, Mike Ross phoned an Israeli Embassy contact and got newsman Wilborn Hampton and photographer Ray Paganelli priority aboard another flight to Cairo. Bonn's Wellington Long was in Vienna for diplomatic talks and got a flight to Damascus and another to Beirut, where the sun was too much for the suit he wore in Vienna. He put $4.00 on his expense account for a lightweight suit.

Roy Brightbill was told in Beirut there was no way to get to Amman other than flying via Ankara, Istanbul, Jedda and Mecca, then making a camel ride to the Jordanian border. Instead, Brightbill hailed a cab and, after a nine-hour ride, was in Amman.

On the Golan Heights, Mitchell Vinicor drove a back road past Israeli roadblocks to a hilltop bunker under fire. The Israelis inside told him to go away. However, as the shelling continued, an officer told Vinicor to come inside. "We wouldn't even make an Arab stand outside during a shelling."

Two hours later, Vinicor drove off, heading for a telephone. On the way down the hill, he saw a man wearing a black eye patch in a passing jeep. "My God, it's Dayan!," Vinicor shouted to himself. He spun his car around and headed back up the hill to get an exclusive interview with the Israeli defense minister. Moshe Dayan told him, "The road from Damascus to Tel Aviv is the same road that leads from Tel Aviv to Damascus."

Joseph W. Grigg, who had covered every European and Middle Eastern war since 1936, set up shop in the UPI Beirut bureau, and in Tel Aviv Peggy Polk went to report on Prime Minister Golda Meir in the command post at the defense ministry compound. Peggy said the prime minister's secretary asked Polk to please whisper lest their talk disturb the overnight guard sleeping on a mattress on the floor of the conference room.

Nearly everyone was in place. However, Richard C. Gross had a problem. In Syria, beyond the Golan Heights, Gross's Peugot 404 had a flat tire in a remote area in the middle of a shelling. When he checked, Gross found there was no spare. He managed to hitch a ride to a safe zone where he found a tire, then returned to change the tire and rescue his Peugot.

In just over one day, UPI had doubled its staff in the war zone from fourteen to twenty-eight photographers and reporters.

Back on the domestic news scene, Patricia Hearst, daughter of Randolph Hearst and granddaughter of W.R.H., who founded the newspaper empire, was kidnapped in Berkeley, California on February 4, 1974.

UPI, along with AP and most of the local news media, heard about the kidnap within two hours. They agreed not to put the story out because, according to police, "the safety of the victim was at stake."

The wire services kept a lid on the kidnap until several broadcast stations used it and the *Oakland Tribune* informed police it would carry the story in its noon edition. Hearst's *San Francisco Examiner* said it also planned to print the item. Then, AP and UPI put it on the wires for the rest of the world.

228A
HEARST 2-5
BULLETIN
BY ROBERT STRAND
BERKELEY, CALIF. (UPI) — THE 19-YEAR-OLD DAUGHTER OF
NEWSPAPER EXECUTIVE RANDOLPH A. HEARST WAS
KIDNAPPED FROM HER APARTMENT MONDAY NIGHT BY
TWO MEN WHO FIRED SHOTS AT NEIGHBORS AS THEY
DROVE AWAY, POLICE SAID.
UPI 02-05 01:51 PED

Withholding news from the wires was unusual in UPI. It happened only in circumstances like a kidnap when someone's life was at stake. In the case of Miss Hearst's
abduction, there was the added circumstance that her family was the principal owner
of more than a dozen newspapers, substantial clients of the wire service. A cautious
bureau manager sometimes wanted to be near the front of the parade but not at the
head of it.

The Hearst kidnap occasioned a wire service first—a UPI bureau on a tree.

Randolph Hearst lived in Hillsborough, California, a high tone suburb of San
Francisco. During Patricia's escapade as a fugitive with the "Symbionese Liberation
Army," reporters, sometimes as many as forty of them, were camped in front of the
publisher's home to get any news from the family. Vicki, Patricia's 16-year-old
sister, was a news target, as well as her father, when they went in or came out of
the house.

UPI had to be there 24-hours a day, so Reeve Hennion, San Francisco bureau
chief, ordered a telephone installed on a 200-year-old tree in front of the Hillsborough
residence for reporters to call in their stories.

Going into action on the Hearst kidnap, Hennion assigned staffers to locate her
former classmates and friends, the kind of exploratory digging that takes a lot of time
and often produces nothing worth the wire.

Other sidebars typical for a major news story include a chronology—date-by-date
of each important event—and closely related events such as the demand of the Hearst
kidnappers for a mass food distribution ransom (which Hearst complied with), and
the discovery that the young lady became herself a willing member of the Symbionese
Liberation Army and participant in a bank robbery and other crimes.

The search for Patty Hearst went on for a year, punctuated by numerous reported
sightings and a bloody firefight between the Symbionese Liberation Army and police
in Los Angeles. She was eventually captured in San Francisco and tried for the bank
robbery with F. Lee Bailey defending. She served a term in federal prison, then
married a policeman, moved to the East and resumed the life of the wealthy and
privileged, lending her name to do-good causes. She eventually won a pardon
from President Bill Clinton.

With an increase of terrorist activity throughout the world, UPI managing editor Paul G. Eberhart issued guidelines for covering acts of terrorism and kidnappings. He said every story should be judged on its own, and if it is newsworthy it will be reported despite the dangers. Other rules were very broad:

Coverage will be thoughtful, conscientious and show restraint.

Stories will not be sensationalized beyond the fact of their being sensational.

Demands of terrorists and kidnappers will be reported as an essential point of the story but not provide an excessive platform for their demands.

Nothing will be done to jeopardize lives.

Reporters photographers and editors will not become a part of the negotiations.

If there has been no mention of a deadline, kidnappers or terrorists will not be asked if there is one.

It all could be summed up in the final guideline: In all cases, apply the rule of common sense.

The Patty Hearst case was one which only a wire service with reporters throughout the world could cover adequately. There were sightings of the missing young woman in many places, and each place became a dateline requiring immediate local reporting.

The same was true of other stories that bounced from dateline to dateline. A women's air race, the "Powder Puff Derby," was an annual cross-country event. The wire service needed to report from each stop where any of the fliers in the race landed, many of them unplanned.

President Jimmy Carter at a July 4, 1980, softball game in Plains, Georgia. Two UPI spectators behind fence, Audio's Tom Foty (extreme left with UPI tee-shirt) and Helen Thomas, extreme right.

When President Jimmy Carter moved into the White House, the United Press International agreed not to flash the bright lights on his 9-year-old daughter Amy who was starting classes at Stevens, a public school.

In a directive to staffers, editor-in-chief H. L. Stevenson said UPI would cover the president's daughter "only when she is involved in official functions with her parents or as part of a legitimate news event." Washington news and newspicture editors were told to keep in mind that while normal life might not be possible for the president's daughter, she should be assured "some privacy in her most formative years."

In the mid-1970s, the era of herd journalism had arrived.

When the U.S. Apollo and Russian Soyez astronauts linked up in orbit high above the earth, more than 2,000 reporters from twenty-seven countries covered it from Moscow and the U.S. Space bases in Texas and Florida. UPI had fifteen people assigned, including four for broadcast, five photographers in Houston and four in Moscow.

About the same time, the UPI decided it would no longer try to buy stories from people celebrated in the news.

Ronald Adley was the only survivor of a mining disaster in Pennsylvania in 1977. The Associated Press paid him for a first person story about his 122 hours trapped in the mine. Stevenson said when he learned that "some sort of bidding" was to take place for Adley's account, he decided that UPI would not get involved. "We had sufficient coverage," he said. "UPI has gotten away from the old days of checkbook journalism."

On March 18, 1974, the Wire Service Guild called a strike against UPI. Nine hundred twenty-nine members of the union, walked off the job at 8 A.M. It was the first walkout of editorial employees against a wire service.

The Guild said it was seeking parity for UPI employees with AP in pay and other contract provisions.

Expecting support from the Commercial Telegraphers Union, whose members were threatened with the loss of their jobs to computers, the Guild made an issue of the increasing use of video terminals in place of typewriters. It wanted the contract to provide that editorial employees would not send news copy on "live" customer wires. But when the telegraphers failed to support the strike and crossed Guild picket lines, the issue of automation was dropped.

The company kept the wires moving with management people as editors and some employees in the Guild-represented group who crossed the picket lines. Sales and administrative employees worked long hours filing wires and getting news.

James Buckner, a West Coast salesman, happened to be in the East and enjoyed a chance to cover the Defense Department as a reporter. Most of the salesman had started out on the news side and often professed that they preferred it to sales.

There was no violence during the strike, but union members harassed management any way they could.

Where bureaus were located in newspaper buildings, picketing interfered with deliveries to the newspaper. However, at most bureaus in newspaper buildings, Guild members were persuaded to limit their pickets to side or back entrances, leaving the main entrances undisturbed for the newspaper's business. At the *New York Daily News* building, where UPI had its headquarters, the Guild picketed only at a side door.

Some strikers harried management with such tactics as telephoning in phony stories.

A hoax letter on Senator Edward Kennedy's letterhead was sent to the UPI bureau in Washington, saying the senator was reconsidering his position as a possible presidential candidate. A false dispatch moved on the wire but it was killed within an hour. Other bogus news included tips on plane crashes that did not happen and deaths of celebrities who had not died.

The company claimed that eighty-three of its ninety-eight bureaus continued to function during the strike, staffed by management personnel and about 160 employees in the Guild's jurisdiction who crossed the lines.

The walkout lasted 23 days. On April 9, Guild members voted 342 to 249 to reject a company contract proposal, but the union decided this vote did not represent enough strength to continue the strike. On their leaders' advice, union members then accepted a new two-year contract.

The pact brought UPI pay closer to AP scales but did not match them. Top pay for reporters, editors and photographers with at least six years experience was raised to $317 a week immediately and to $335 effective January 1, 1975.

UPI president Rod Beaton said later the strike was a mistake. He said he had told his negotiating team he did not want a walkout under any circumstances, but that something went amiss in negotiations that touched it off[1]

UPI staffers picketing the Chicago office during the Wire Service Guild strike in 1974. Identifiable, from left Wayne Hejka (white hat with feather), Barbara Hillebrand, Jordanka Lazarevic, Marcy Kreiter (background with sunglasses), Jay Gibianman with glasses and black coat, Rob Wishart (arm extended with placard), and Jim Pecora.

To cover the cost of the settlement, UPI assessed a 15 percent rate increase on its customers effective January 1, 1975. The increase was resisted by some clients and, as usual, compromises were made.

Early in 1975, Beaton told the Newpaper Advisory Board that an additional 10 percent rate increase was likely in 1976. He said there would be some changes in the rate structure as a result of board suggestions. A circulation element would be brought into the formula, which previously was based almost entirely on the size of the market where the client operated.

The Supreme Court ruled in 1977 that law enforcement agencies, armed with search warrants, had the right to search newsrooms, overruling a lower court that had decided in favor of the *Stanford Daily*, a college newspaper invaded by campus police with a warrant but without notice in 1971 during student disturbances.

UPI, along with most news media, was concerned about police tendency to seek information from news reporters. Some editors made it policy to destroy any material that might be sought or to keep it in a place away from the office.

"Neither of these suggestions is very satisfactory," said Editor H. L. Stevenson. He advised UPI reporters and editors that they should normally fully cooperate with the police carrying a search warrant. "Cooperation may be hard to swallow but it has its advantages," he said.

Warrants for media searches were relatively rare, only about five a year in the whole country.

The dominant international news story in 1977 was in the Mideast, which experienced a dirty civil war in Lebanon and a historic visit by Egypt's Premier Sadat to Israel.

UPI had a tough time covering Lebanon. Gun battles were going on throughout Beirut. At the bureau, the wires were down and the only lights were a few bulbs flickering from power of a gas generator. Bureau windows were taped to keep out gas. The walls were pock-marked by bullets. An ominous silence was broken only by the curses of staffers trying to find a working telephone. Several UPI correspondents were injured.

Mike Keats and Michael Ross were detained by guerrillas at one time or another. A UPI teletype operator, Tony Atallah, was kidnapped and murdered en route from the office to a nearby hotel.

Egyptian leader Anwar Sadat's historic visit to Israel was the top story of the year in UPI's poll of editors. The Associated Press said its editors picked the weather as the biggest news of 1977. UPI rated the year's extreme weather third in news value behind the death of Elvis Presley, which AP ranked fifth.

For the historic news conference with Sadat and Israel Prime Minister Menahem Begin, the government issued 2,178 press credentials. At the press center set up for the meeting the correspondents drank 10,071 cups of coffee and tea during the 44-hour visit, according to Allen Alter, a UPI correspondent who wrote about it for *Editor & Publisher*.

Alter was pleased to see the Israel government pick up the tab for free telephone service, thus saving his bureau budget from destruction. The regular rate for telephone service to the U.S. was $3 per minute.

The trip to Jerusalem was a particularly poignant one for UPI Cairo bureau manager Maurice Gunidi, his first visit to Jerusalem in twenty-five years. He and 335 other Cairo correspondents chartered a plane for the trip.

In 1978, correspondent Ned Temko went out with a couple of other newspeople to see how natives were getting along in the territory disputed by Israeli and Palestinian claims. Seven miles from the Israel border they came under fire from Israeli soldiers.

"For a half day we were target practice for the Israel Army, face down in a tiny garden in the southern village of Haddata," Temko recalled. "We shared the prayer, horror and despair of the neutral in a war."

When the FBI released documents on the assassination of President Kennedy in 1977, Grant Dillman assigned a dozen newspeople to flip through the thousands of pages and pick out anything wire worthy. They were told to toss the good stuff into three piles, one on the assassination itself, one on Ruby and one on Oswald. They quickly typed notes on the key parts and funneled them to Mike Feinsilber, who turned them into wire leads.

UPI paid more than $4,000 to get copies of the documents. Dillman wrote to the FBI saying the charge was unfair because a federal judge had given author-critic Harold Weisberg the documents free of charge under the Freedom of Information Act.

Stories appeared regularly in the press about congressmen taking perks from the federal treasury such as free haircuts. To turn the tables on reporters, Rep. David Obey of Wisconsin, disclosed that reporters were using free parking places worth $232 a month and free stationery and had discounts at the Capitol stationery room. He said if any news organizations felt awkward taking such perks, they could send a check to the Treasury.

UPI in 1975 re-centralized its operations. Division managers no longer would have control over personnel, hiring and firing or administration of bureaus. This was taken over by New York headquarters and put under the control of Robert Page, Beaton's "fair-haired boy."

Page was superintendent of bureaus, the first time that job had been filled since L. B. "Save a Nickel" Mickel had it. And his job was the same as Mickel's—to cut expenses. He gave every bureau a budget and enforced it with the authority to fire bureau managers as well as staffers if necessary.

In an interview in 1996, Page said: "The division managers would call up and squawk and scream. I'd tell them 'That's the way it's going to be. I have my orders from Beaton and he has his orders from the board.'"

Less than two years later, Beaton again changed structure, appointing Page general manager of the company and naming three senior vice presidents to supervise sales and administration on a regional basis. Donald J. Brydon would have the Eastern Seaboard, working out of New York. Robert E. Crennen in Chicago would have the Central zone, and Richard A. Litfin in San Francisco would be vice president for the West.

In a 70th anniversary story on June 21, 1977, UPI writer H. D. "Doc" Quigg said the agency was then turning out seven million words a day, on all the earth's continents, around-the-clock, seven days a week, in dozens of languages. The wire service had 6,972 subscribers overall, including 1,131 U.S. newspapers and 3,650 broadcast customers. UPI was devoting one third of its space to interpretative, color and analytical material.

The UPI had begun changing its news package in the '60s to a format with more analysis and feature material to satisfy a trend in newspapers. For a while it featured "Blue Ribbon" dispatches. Then "World Horizons" was launched in 1963. It was a weekly schedule of magazine-like stories that moved on the wire a week before the release date.

Most of this material was produced by regular news staffers, but some "team" and specialized writers were assigned. UPI president Mims Thomason said the times called for a "more analytical, interpretative and background" news product.

The new trend was best illustrated when editor-in-chief Roger Tatarian sent reporters Linda Franks and Tom Powers out on an unprecedented two-month assignment to do what was called a "blockbuster" about Diana Oughton, rich heiress who had joined the Weathermen revolutionary group and was killed when a home-made bomb exploded. The story won a Pulitzer Prize.

Even less extensive in-depth articles and features took staff hours and UPI was not adding more staffers. There was always some slack time in a news operation to work on features since the flow of news varies. However, UPI needed to have enough people free to send out on the breaking news events.

A squeeze came because the feature packages, "team reports" and special articles were advertised and promised to the customers on a weekly deadline. They, therefore, moved up in the work priority, which in United Press International was always overloaded anyway.

"Special" reporters with limited beats and "investigative" journalists looking for scandal became the darlings of the newspaper business in the 1970s.

In 1977, Richard Growald was named UPI's "national reporter." He traveled the country, from Hog Shooter, Oklahoma, to Romance, Arkansas, Cow Creek Valley, West Virginia, Dilles Bottom, Ohio, Zap, North Dakota, and other obscure places, filing dispatches packed with local color. He reported that residents of Hog Shooter Creek feel guilty unless they've gone to church on Sunday.

"I now think I have the best job in American journalism," said Growald, who had previously covered dozens of major news events in cities around the world for UPI. "Every American has a story and tells something interesting about America. Everybody is a story."

Growald was a reporter who was also an extremely gifted artist, drawing quick, humorous sketches on napkins, postcards and anywhere he had pencil and writing surface. His sketches enlivened his company correspondence and usually carried a subtle message about the UPI or the people he met. A natural wit, he sometimes boasted that at the age of six in 1931 he was the youngest person to fly on an airliner. "Since then, life has been downhill," he said.

UPI also named nine "senior editors" who were expected to lend prestige writing to the wire. Among them were Mike Feinsilber and David Langford who were to do "in depth" feature articles.

The company boasted that it was producing a package of features covering leisure, travel, entertainment, music, movie, books, citizen band radio and consumer news. The package of magazine-style stories was sold to 500 newspapers. Two hundred customers also bought 10 pages of "lifestyle" features provided in camera ready format for smaller newspapers.

In an effort to strengthen relations with clients in the 1960s and 1970s, UPI developed editors' organizations for newspapers and broadcasters. These groups, including state and regional organizations, held at least one meeting each year at which the editors were encouraged to vent their criticism and suggestions for the service. The associations also conducted awards programs and some had newsletters.

Management regarded the meetings as customer "shmoozing" affairs. They were held at places like Rickey's Spa in Palo Alto, California. Company representatives and client editors could lounge around the pool with drinks and become acquainted.

In 1960, UPI held its first national editors meeting in Washington, D.C., in conjunction with the annual meeting of the American Newspaper Publishers Association (ANPA).

Several hundred editors from around the country heard Merriman Smith talk about covering the White House. Various government officials were guest speakers, including Secretary of State Christian A. Herter and Secretary of Agriculture Ezra Taft Benson.

In 1961, UPI was host to President Kennedy, who delivered a speech at the conference.

The company's annual breakfast for editors and publishers, held in connection with the ANPA convention, reached a peak in 1965 when it drew 700 newspaper executives to the grand ballroom of the Waldorf-Astoria.[2]

In April 1974, UPI established a national Newspaper Advisory Board of fifteen members chosen from among executives of its clients. President Rod Beaton hoped the move would give publishers the kind of covenant in UPI that they had in AP, which always had nurtured a club spirit among its members.

The first meeting of the UPI Advisory Board was held July 11, 1974, in Chicago. Peter M. MacDonald, president of Harris Enterprises Inc., was chosen chairman.

"Our board was not formed to run UPI in the sense that the Associated Press board runs AP," MacDonald said. "Nor has the board been formed to 'rescue' UPI. We must make the UPI a wire service for the 70s, tailored to adapt to the last quarter of the 20th and the first quarter of the 21st century," said Harris.

The advisory board's first advice to UPI dealt with, of course, money. It asked management not to assess subscribers to pay for coverage of the 1974 political conventions. A "quadrennial" fee every fourth year was the usual way of covering the extra cost for political conventions, elections and Olympics. But because of the advisory board's request, it was not imposed in 1974.

Beaton, reacting to a growing preponderance of revenue from radio and television stations, formed a Broadcast Advisory Board in 1977.

Some of the nation's top broadcasters agreed to serve on the UPI board, including Arch Madsen, president of Boneville Broadcast, Al Shottlekotte of the Scripps Howard

TV station in Cincinnati and Norm Knight, president of the Knight Quality stations in New England.

Broadcast editor Billy Ferguson and Broadcast sales vice-president Gordon Rice were encouraged that UPI's top management, steeped in newspaper marketing, was rolling out the red carpet for the broadcasters. Beaton personally attended each and every meeting of the broadcast board.

But his sincerity was brought into question in 1978 when the UPI Broadcast Advisory Board held its meeting in Las Vegas. It had become a custom for the UPI executives to take the board members to dinner following their final meeting. This time, Beaton asked Ferguson and Rice to entertain the broadcast industry heavyweights. Beaton, as well as Broadcast Services Vice President Frank Beatty, hosted a dinner for Hank Greenspun, publisher of the Las Vegas *Sun*.

Beaton was trying to get his head into broadcast, but his heart still belonged to the publishers.

33

Getting It First and Getting It Right

UPI MORPHED IN THE 1970S, BUOYED BY ITS SUCCESSES OF THE '60S and a responsibility to a growing client base.

In the formative years of the wire service, Roy Howard, knowing he could not match the AP thoroughness, tried to make UP different by better writing and more excitement. In the 1970s, UPI began more and more to make itself like AP, extremely cautious, emphasizing accuracy and avoiding haste to get on the wire.

In 1970 Roger Tatarian, editor-in-chief, sent a memo to all bureaus and company executives:

New York
February 13, 1970
ALL BUREAUS, DOMESTIC AND FOREIGN
PLEASE POST
cc: NX and Divisional Executives

Gentlemen:

This is to express thanks to all who helped UPI establish a particularly important record in the 1960s in an area which demands unrelenting attention in the 1970s and beyond.

It concerns accuracy.

The stresses of our profession present many hazards to accuracy. And it is clear, in studying the record of the past 10 years, that we have been more alert in avoiding them than has the AP.

Failure by one journalistic organization rubs off on the entire profession. It is thus folly to chortle at the other man's discomfiture.

But because some people cling to the myth that the AP is particularly immune to error, it does not seem improper to note that we would be less embarrassed than the AP on any roll call of major blunders in the 1960s.

For example, it was NOT the UPI that circulated any of the following:

- The false report that Dag Hammarskjold arrived at Ndola, Northern Rhodesia, on September 18, 1961, drove to Kitwe, 30 miles away, and met there in a crucial session with Moise Tshombe of Katanga. The fact is that Hammarskjold was killed when his plane crashed en route; he never reached Ndola.

- The false report that both a Secret Service agent and a Dallas policeman were shot and killed near the area where President Kennedy was assassinated November 22, 1963. Neither did the UPI circulate the false rumors that Vice President Lyndon Johnson (1) had been slightly wounded or (2) had suffered a heart attack.

- The false report on September 13, 1965, that the death toll in Hurricane Betsy was 400 in the New Orleans area alone. The actual death toll in four states was 75.

- The false report on June 6, 1966, that James H. Meredith had been shot and killed near Hernando, Mississippi.

- The false report on November 22, 1968, that "France was forced to devalue the franc today." Devaluation talk was very much in the air (the corresponding UPI lead said it was awaited), it did not in fact happen until August 10, 1969.

This recital does not mean that we were error-free. But it does make clear that a very hoary myth in our business is precisely that.

To say it is tempting fate to discuss this subject is to say it is all a matter of luck. Sure, there have been rare occasions when a peculiarly unhappy combination of circumstances has conspired to produce an unfortunate result. But even these could have been minimized and possibly avoided with an extra ounce of care. So accuracy is not accident; it is the result of taking care, of reading copy back, of challenging the improbable, and of remembering, always, that if you must choose between being fast and being accurate, accuracy must always take first place.

I have mentioned only big stories here. Accuracy is just as important in lesser stories. The Unipresser in a one-man bureau who files only on a state split can help or harm our reputation and our record just as surely as the editor reading out copy for the A wire.

Perhaps even more so. When he writes a story concerning the mayor or district attorney or lieutenant governor, every subscriber in the area will know at a glance if he has so much as given the wrong middle initial. And the inevitable reaction is: if a service is wrong about things I can check, how about things I can't? This fosters a negative image that cannot be offset by even perfect records from Moscow, Paris, Washington or other distant places.

Every staffer in every bureau takes our reputation into his own hands every time he puts a story on the wire. If you make sure yours is beyond reproach, you will help preserve our most vital asset.

The old slogan—get it first, but first get it right—is still valid.

HRT

UPI policy discouraged use of anonymous sources. If a reporter did not want to name a source in a dispatch, he or she was required to share the name with a supervising editor, who would make a ruling. The use of a fictitious name was sometimes permitted, provided the dispatch made clear that the false name was being used to protect an innocent person. Editors insisted strongly that correspondents "strive for direct attribution on all interviews and briefings."

In 1974, UPI had a total of 6,622 customers, down from 6,972 in 1971. They included 1,140 newspapers, the rest were broadcasters and a few special clients. The next year it increased the number of clients to 6,911, including 1,146 newspapers and 3,680 broadcasters. But then, with changes in the industry, the newspaper base began diminishing, down to 1,131 in 1977.

Meanwhile, UPI's operating budget was increasing, from $67.5 million in 1976 to $73 million the next year. Savings from satellite transmission were still several years off, although computerization had reduced the Teletype staff to fifty-seven employees.

UPI executives cringed whenever the news agency itself became "part of the story." On September 6, 1970, an audio tape was delivered to the agency's office in Uruguay. It carried the impassioned voice of Dan Mitrione, an American member of AID (Agency for International Development) in that country, who had been kidnapped two months earlier by rebels.

U.S. officials pleaded with the Uruguay government, but President Jorge Pacheco Areco refused to ransom Mitrione by releasing 180 prisoners belonging to the Tuparmero rebels. Mitrione's body was later found, and the guerrillas continued terrorist raids.

In another Tupameros kidnapping, the rebels delivered to UPI photographs of Claude Fly, also an American AID representative, who had been kidnapped. Fry had better luck and was freed February 21, 1971, four months after being seized.

The UPI manager for Uruguay, Hector Menoni, was himself kidnapped on July 28, 1972, by a different revolutionary group but was released unharmed the next day.

Dr. Josef Gregor, describing himself as head of a distinguished scientific institute, spent $3,000 to rent an office for a New York press conference May 22, 1981. He sent UPI and other media a news release and invited them to attend a detailed presentation on the discovery of a remarkable new remedy for allergies and other ailments that he called "cockroach pills."

Ed Lion of UPI was sent to the press conference, along with a photographer. At the "news" conference a number of people were introduced by Gregor and gave testimonials about their experiences of relief from the "cockroach pills." Lion wrote a lengthy story for weekend use on the new discovery.

The story was a total hoax. "Dr. Gregor" was, in fact, Joseph Skaggs, a journalism instructor at the New York School of Visual Arts. With the help of his students as testimony givers, he had successfully made UPI look foolish.

Editors at the wire service cringed and went out for a drink when they learned they had been taken in by Skaggs, whose motive apparently was to demonstrate that news media are susceptible to such antics.

Associated Press did not attend the news conference. UPI tried to put the incident in its past without moving any correction. But weeks later when the *Wall Street Journal* reported that the wire service had refused to correct the story an advisory was issued on the wire notifying subscribers that the "cockroach pill" dispatch was based on false information.

Wire services were often targets of hoaxes, and most desk staffers quickly learned to be on the lookout for them. That's how wire service newspeople became cynics.

In the summer of 1976, all four major news agencies, UPI, AP, Reuters and AFP, transmitted stories saying singer Elvis Presley was to be married July 12 in Las Vegas to Alexis Skylar.

The story was a hoax meticulously planned. It defied checking. The perpetrators had made hotel reservations for the popular singer's entourage in New York. They had rented a wedding chapel and hotel rooms in Las Vegas. They provided reporters with telephone numbers at which the story could be confirmed—people answering the phone identified themselves as friends or relatives of Presley. The Clark County clerk had received a call requesting information on the procedure for Presley to get a marriage license.

All four news agencies killed their dispatches upon learning they were victims of a hoax, but the kill did not come quickly enough to prevent publication of the forthcoming marriage in many newspapers. This success, no doubt, touched off a celebration by the hoaxers, who obviously knew quite a bit about how wire services work.

Incidents like that were not uncommon. Accounts are legendary of college students or patrons at a bar calling wire services and newspapers with fictitious scores of college sports events, sometimes creating fictitious teams and even fictitious leagues.

After a moderate earthquake in San Francisco, the bureau received a call from someone identifying himself as a geologist at the University of California and giving lengthy quotes about "earthquake weather"—which, as far as real scientists know, has no validity in fact.

Experience with hoaxes made wire editors sometimes too cautious.

On Monday, June 8, 1981, the U.S. Supreme Court came down with a very important sex discrimination decision that had been eagerly awaited.

The court, in a 5-4 decision, ruled that women may not be paid less than men for the same job.

On the Sunday before the ruling, the *Washington Post* published a dispatch telling about the decision and attributing its information to Elizabeth Olson, UPI's court reporter. The wire service itself did not have the story on the wire.

It developed that Olson had found on her desk during the previous week a copy of the court decision. It was apparently, and in fact, authentic, but Washington editors knew that the court never released its decisions in advance. Olson could not account for how it happened to be on her desk.

Olson wrote the story on Friday and turned it in to her editors, who called her back insisting that she verify the authenticity of the document. She called five court experts who told her the form was correct and everything seemed to be consistent with a court document. The ruling was consistent with what many expected.

The UPI Washington desk spiked the story after scrupulous soul-searching that went as high as the president of the company, Rod Beaton, and Barrett McGurn, a high official of the court who had heard about it. Grant Dillman, Washington bureau manager, came into the bureau on Saturday.

One of the experts Olson had contacted told Fred Barbash, the *Washington Post* court reporter, that UPI had the decision. Barbash called Olson and she said yes, she had found the document, written a story for Sunday release and turned it over to her editors.

Later Dillman explained, "We had no way of confirming it was an accurate document." He said a justice may have planted a false document to test the water, or the paper may have been a hoax intended to embarrass the UPI.

Another Washington newspaper, the *Star*, said UPI had "caved in" to pressure from the court officials to withhold the story. It was a "lose lose" situation for UPI, which was frequently accused of slapping something on the wire without enough checking.

In January 1970, an inquest was being held into the death of Mary Jo Kopechne. Sen. Edward Kennedy, youngest brother of President Kennedy and a strong candidate for nomination to the White House, was the central figure. He had been driving Miss Kopechne home after a party at the Kennedy compound at Martha's Vineyard, Massachusetts. The car had gone off a bridge and Miss Kopechne was drowned.

At the inquest, held behind closed doors at the Dukes County Courthouse in Edgartown, Massachusetts, about seventy reporters and photographers waited outside. "Doc" Quigg of UPI was there.

For the trade journal *Editor & Publisher* Quigg wrote a light-hearted account about the army of reporters, calling it "The Dread Vigil—or How to Report No News in Front of a Courthouse." He told about the phalanx of newspeople whose attention was focused on "two Christmas wreaths with red ribbon gracing the front door of the Dukes County Courthouse."

The only news coming from inside the session was provided by an attorney who informed the press that witnesses "have been reading papers and books and playing gin rummy," while "all the lawyers do is talk to each other and tell each other lies."

UPI picked up one of the few newsworthy tidbits from the hearing. Phil Balboni of the Boston bureau knew someone in the hearing and learned that Senator Kennedy testified he drank only two rum-and-cokes at the Chappaquiddick cookout, which preceded the accident.

Another leak, which UPI had first, was a report that Kennedy's companions thought the senator was going immediately to the police when he swam away from the scene of the drowning. He actually waited nine hours before reporting to the police department.

There was never mention in news reports of outright sexual activity at that party, but in the 1970s the press still avoided exploiting that part of a politician's life. When Kennedy's brother, John F. Kennedy, was president, he reportedly had numerous trysts with women, even in the White House, but they did not get into the news until after his death.

In *The Dark Side of Camelot*, by Seymour M. Hersh, dalliances between J.F.K. and actress Marilyn Monroe were reported to have taken place at the Santa Monica, California, home of Patricia Lawford, Kennedy's sister, among other places.

UPI Hollywood writer Vernon Scott and AP's Jim Bacon knew about the goings on but did not make a news story of it. "Before Watergate, reporters just didn't go into that sort of thing," Bacon told Hersh.[1]

As a diversion for editors selecting the top ten news stories for 1975, the UPI asked them to select the ten "most forgettable" events of the year as well. Leading that list of forgettables was the story about a feast in Paris held by Craig Clairborn that cost $4,000 per person. Also rating highly forgettable was the disclosure that reporters went rooting into Secretary of State Henry Kissinger's garbage looking for something to write about.

In August 1976, New York City Hall reporter Tom Hillstrom picked up an astonishing rumor. A prostitution ring was operating in the city morgue. Call girls were being dispatched around the city and action was even taking place right down among the bodies in the morgue. Hillstrom saw the evidence—used condoms and liquor glasses.

The UPI reporter wrote a dispatch about the lively goings on amid the bodies at the morgue.

Associated Press put out a dispatch that implied the UPI story was a hoax. Then Hillstrom gave his information to the New York Police Department. Commissioner Nicholas Scoppetta assigned three undercover female officers to check it out. They infiltrated the operation and three weeks later two morgue employees and another man were arrested for running a vice ring.

The bizarre incident inspired two off-Broadway plays and the motion picture *Night Shift*.[2]

In a celebrated hoax of 1972, UPI was not the victim, but the whistle blower. *Life* magazine and McGraw-Hill were set to publish what they called the autobiography of Howard Hughes, a reclusive billionaire who had built a huge empire in the aircraft, electronics and entertainment industries.

Hughes had burrowed himself into deep seclusion, never being seen in public.

The affair of the Hughes "autobiography," written by Clifford Irving, was front page news for weeks when it was disclosed that Irving, a well-known author, had faked the entire story. *Time* magazine called Irving the "con man of the year" and conceded that editors of its sister publication, *Life*, had pulled a costly boner in arranging to buy serial rights to the book from McGraw-Hill.

High point of the incident was a bizarre news conference with seven carefully selected reporters in Hollywood, conducted by telephone from Hughes' hideaway somewhere in the Bahamas.

The strange press conference was masterminded by Carl Byoir, a public relations counselor working for Hughes. Among the select newsmen invited was Vernon Scott, UPI Hollywood writer. Others were from the AP, *Los Angeles Times*, *New York Times*, Hearst Newspapers, *Chicago Tribune* and NBC News.

Scott had personally known Hughes fifteen years earlier, before he went into hiding. Some of the other reporters also had heard Hughes' voice before.

The Hughes public relations people spent three weeks setting up the news conference. They summoned the reporters to an advance briefing at the Sheraton Universal Hotel in Burbank. Ground rules were laid down, including a ban on asking Hughes anything about his marital affairs.

Richard Hannah, a Hughes contact man from Carl Byoir, and Perry Lieber, another public relations man, gave the reporters written questions which he suggested they ask. However, the newsmen rejected that and agreed each would ask his own questions of the whoever was on the other end of the line.

The next day, on Friday, at 2 P.M., they assembled at the hotel in a room with a loudspeaker telephone. The air conditioning was shut off in order to keep the room as quiet as possible. Although the person to be interviewed was not there—only the reporters—television cameras were on the scene and heat from their lights made the writers sweat.

The interview stories were to be held for release precisely at 6:30 P.M. Saturday, the usual hour for Sunday embargoed stories.

Hannah dialed the secret number and the voice came on. Each reporter asked a question which he thought only the real Howard Hughes would be able to answer. Everyone was satisfied afterward that they had, indeed, talked to the recluse. The voice sounded like his, they said, and the answers and manner of speaking was as they remembered Hughes. In writing their dispatches the reporters identified the speaker as "a man introduced as Howard Hughes."

The "voice" called the Clifford Irving book "totally fantastic fiction" and a "fairy tale."

After the disclosure of the hoax, Irving and his wife, Edith, pleaded guilty to swindling the publishers, McGraw-Hill, of $750,000 and making up the story out of whole cloth.

Like most other news media, UPI was the target of occasional libel suits. The company's policy was that any demand for a correction or threat of action should be passed immediately to headquarters for advice.

Scripps-Howard was a privately owned company and it did not like to disclose its finances. If a suit against UPI went to court, the parent company might be asked to disclose its finances. Therefore, rather than risk having to open any books, UPI was told to settle claims out of court.

Synanon, a California drug rehabilitation organization, harassed newspapers throughout the country during the 1970s by filing numerous libel suits. When UPI carried a dispatch printed widely, Synanon lawyers filed suit against each of the newspapers printing the story and against UPI itself.

H. L. Stevenson, UPI news chief, decided the agency should take a stand against the unfounded harassment suits. He told clients they need not publish corrections because there was no error. But some timid newspapers did publish retractions, blaming UPI for the asserted libel.[3]

UPI said the Synanon Foundation was engaged in a systematic effort "to threaten UPI's reputation and relationships with subscribers and, generally, object to any news coverage, which reflects unfavorably upon Synanon."

In 1979, the National News Council, a self-discipline organization for newspapers, made an investigation of the Synanon matter. It found that Synanon's "retraction project" created an atmosphere of apprehension among many news executives and reporters.

"It is clear that Synanon is using a law presumably passed to protect publishers and broadcasters—Section 48A of the California Civil Code—as a weapon for coercing the press into silence about Synanon and its affairs. It is also clear that as a result of this legal harassment many editors and news directors, especially those associated with small news organizations of limited resources, are refraining from publishing or broadcasting news they deem legitimate affecting Synanon."[4]

This intimidation of the media occurred despite a court ruling that newspapers could not be sued for libel if the report they printed came from one of the wire services. The court said four newspapers accused of reporting that the Merritt-Chapman & Scott Corporation was bankrupt were blameless because they relied on the Associated Press wire.

The most important advantage AP had over UPI in news coverage was the access to all the content of its members. James O. Clifford, who worked for UPI before going to AP in 1984, said he immediately noticed that "AP didn't have to wait for a copy of a newspaper in order to pinch stories. It had access almost as soon as they were written." A newspaper staffer was customarily assigned to telephone everything to AP immediately. Later, the stories were sent to AP as electronic carbons.

During the 1960s wire service competition was at its fiercest. Associated Press, according to the conventional belief of UPI executives, was using its guaranteed solvency to kill UPI which had been gaining new business through the usually disastrous business sin of selling cheap and trying to make up losses by volume. It was worse because the total market was shrinking.

Smaller customers of either service could buy a worldwide comprehensive news report for less than the cost of hiring a single reporter. Sometimes the wire service customer paid less than the cost of the wire transmission, teletype lease and paper. The cost of collecting the news was usually ignored. The product was assumed to be already available—"We're just adding one more customer to the wire."

The Wire Service Guild, during an arbitration on wages at the AP, brought in figures illustrating the problem.

The union cited a drive by Associated Press for new customers in Oklahoma, where it had only twenty-four exclusive newspaper subscribers, compared to forty-one who received only UPI. Fifteen dailies took both.

AP had offered one newspaper a rate of $51.50 a week for a complete report, more than $20 under what the newspaper was paying UPI.

Sidney A. Wolff, the arbitrator, said he had been shown another case in which a customer was paying UPI $51.10 a week and the Associated Press offered its service for $48. For both agencies a rate like that was far below costs.

AP denied it was engaging in a rate war.

"The Associated Press has been making membership gains in Oklahoma and other states but there is no rate war," an AP official asserted, "The Associated Press' basic membership rates are fixed according to a formula established by the board of directors and apply equally everywhere across the country."

Such price competition was unheard of elsewhere in the news industry. Competing newspapers in a city almost always raised or reduced their subscription and advertising rates in unison.

Charges to the news retailers for both services were much lower than they needed to be. The typical newspaper's budget for all its wire services was less than one-tenth of one percent of its overall expense, and less than one percent of editorial costs.

A Wire Service Guild study in 1962 showed that the rate for a six days per week news wire for small newspapers in various parts of the country was:

West	UPI $44.28	AP $47.80
Midwest	UPI $64.50	AP $71.20
South	UPI $66.00	AP $62.35
North	UPI $54.00	AP $61.90
East	UPI $85.55	AP $90.40

These rates were charged in cities of 12,000 to 50,000 population where there was no direct newspaper competition. They provided a complete news report including international, national, state news, sports and some financial market information.

The situation for broadcasters was even better. Radio stations had lower rates than newspapers although their newscasts brought in more profit than any other programming. Seventy percent of their news came from the wires.

Roger Tatarian, UPI's highly respected editor-vice president, once explained the economics of competing with Associated Press. He said larger clients paid the freight for the news production and distribution. Profit from those big clients was used to compete among radio stations and smaller newspapers.

At the time, Tatarian said, the *San Francisco Chronicle* was paying the full cost to bring the UPI news report to San Francisco, about $2,500 a week. The wire could then be sold to smaller customers in the area, including radio stations, with little additional cost.

"The problem," Tatarian said, "is that the AP gets about $5,000 a week from the *Chronicle* and so they have a lot more money to throw around to the smaller radio stations, and they are doing it."[5]

Wayne Sargent, vice president for sales in UPI, said he approached Associated Press executives more than once in an effort to establish a minimum rate structure. He said he told them that if they would set a minimum of $50 for broadcast subscribers, the UPI would "go five dollars higher" and never offer a rate below $55.

Sargent said the AP representatives agreed to the concept but wanted to limit it to one geographical region, the Washington, D.C., area where UPI happened to be exclusive with its Capital News Service wire that was going to dozens of government offices at $35 a week. Thus it would mean in that market UPI would have to raise the charges substantially, giving AP an opportunity to come in at a lower rate.

Sargent said he unilaterally established $55 as the minimum contract for new UPI service. However, a few influential representatives of the company's sales side did not want to be restricted. They persuaded president Mims Thomason to overrule the minimum. This led to Sargent's resignation. He left and become a publisher for the Gannett Company.

"Thomason conceded, and correctly, that price fixing was illegal. We did it for about a year. I thought maybe we could start a structure which will allow the guys to sell the product on its merit and not have to wrestle over 50 cents a week," Sargent recalled. "AP really wasn't interested in having it in effect in any place except where they were clearly the minority."[6]

UPI's highly respected editorial chief, Earl J. Johnson, extolled the existence of competition in the news business in a February 10, 1965, William Allen White memorial lecture at the University of Kansas.

"One of the most important developments in my time has been the emergence of two highly responsible and intensely competitive worldwide news services, the Associated Press and the United Press International. It is my conviction that their toe-to-toe competition and the balance of power that exists now in this area of news communicating have become the public's best guarantee of being accurately and promptly informed about world and national events," said Johnson.

He said even one-service newspapers could be sure of their news because an opposition service was out there ready to challenge any poor reporting.

In 1960, Alan Hathway, managing editor of *Newsday*, told a meeting of publishers that his newspaper paid about three percent of its editorial budget for its wires, including AP, UPI and Reuters, and that the editorial budget was less than 10 percent of the overall newspaper budget. He told the executives they should "up the ante" to keep the two agencies competing strongly.[7]

Some people concerned about the economics of the wire services observed that AP and UPI, by including transmission costs as an important part in their rates, were, in effect, not selling news but selling American Telephone and Telegraph services.

Roy A. Schafer, national president of the Young Democratic Clubs of America, surprised everyone in both the United Press International and the Associated Press on June 13, 1960, by asserting that the two wire agencies were talking merger. His statement was made to Senator John O. Pastore, who was then holding hearings on newspaper mergers.

When asked about the rumor, a UPI spokesman said such an unlikely deal had never been discussed. "Competition between the two news services is a mainstay of press freedom," the UPI statement said. Frank Starzel, AP general manager, also denied there had been any talks and added, "None is contemplated."

Drew Pearson, a popular national commentator, predicted on his radio broadcast February 11, 1962, that the two major wire services would be consolidated, with UPI merging into AP. On December 29, 1963, the syndicated columnist again predicted a consolidation but this time said AP would be taken over by UPI.[8] In neither case was he given credibility.

At the same time an attempt was being made by some broadcasters to get the Federal Communications Commission to supervise wire service contracts. Some stations objected to having to sign five year contracts. They said it restricted their news options. Both AP and UPI opposed any FCC control. They said long-term contracts were needed to establish stability of revenue to maintain their operations.

The relationship between wholesalers and retailers in the news business was always complicated. Exclusive franchises dealt out in the early years of the twentieth century disappeared, but newspaper clients remained protective of their markets and did not hesitate to let the wire services know it. They expected UPI to stand by the old customer even at the cost of losing a new one.

In 1964, newspaper unions went on strike against the Detroit newspapers. The unions began publishing a strike paper they called the *Detroit Daily Press*. The walkout continued for weeks and the union sheet began getting substantial amounts of advertising, but it lacked a wire service.

The strike newspaper wanted to sign up with UPI. The agency, however, felt it could not antagonize its long-time customers who were shut down by the strike, in spite of the Supreme Court ruling against exclusive contracts.

To avoid selling to the strike newspaper, UPI presented it with an offer for service that it knew was insurmountable. UPI would deliver news to the *Daily Press* for $2,480 a week. The contract would have to be for the full service, including pictures, sports and financial. And it would have a five-year term, with the total fee for the entire fifth year paid in advance of signing.

The unions took UPI to court, saying it was deliberately restraining competition. They asked for $7.5 million in damages. The case dragged on, and the strike ended. In 1969 a federal judge dismissed the suit.

The wire services for many years also avoided servicing free circulation throwaways that were called "controlled circulation" publications. However, in the early 1970s, the Associated Press began serving such newspapers and UPI followed. UPI began with service to the four-times a week *Valley News* of Van Nuys, California in May 1973.

UPI also served college newspapers with special rates at cost or near-cost.

The Scripps-Howard Company had a little secret that cost it quite a lot of money but could have cost much more had it been known more widely. The company had immoderate fear of disclosing its financial condition. As a privately-owned corporation it did not have to publish information about revenue and profit and did not want to.

In January 1965, E.W. Scripps Company. refused to disclose to the Department of Justice its revenue figures. The case involved the *Cincinnati Post,* which had merged with the *Cincinnati Times-Star* in 1958. The government sought to force the company to relinquish controlling interest in a third local newspaper, the *Enquirer,* of which Scripps-Howard was majority stockholder.

Company lawyers said the financial information was irrelevant to the case and successfully kept it from the record.

There had been suggestions that Scripps-Howard juggled figures between its wire service and newspapers for best tax benefits.

Another motive was disclosed in 1977 when the Scripps-owned *Cincinnati Post* and the *Cincinnati Enquirer* wanted to merge operations. Scripps argued that the *Post* was losing money, which under the newspaper anti-trust law would permit merger.

At a U.S. Justice Department hearing in Cincinnati, opponents of the merger said the newspaper was losing money because it overpaid UPI for service and all the money was going into the same Scripps-Howard pot. They said that in 1975 the *Post* paid UPI $409,000 when similar service was available to the *Enquirer* from AP for only about $200,000.

Post editor William Burleigh testified that the newspaper was then paying about $4,500 a week to UPI and that comparable AP services had been quoted at $5,000 a week.

It was disclosed that payments by the *Post* to UPI were cut by more than 50 percent in 1976 when UPI went to a new rate system. Eventually, the joint agreement was approved by administrative law judge, Donald Moore.

In many civil actions involving the UPI and other Scripps entities, such as libel cases, the lawyers fought to withhold requests by the courts for financial data. If pressed sufficiently, Scripps-Howard, tightly controlled by its sixteen common shareholders, was more likely to make a costly out-of-court settlement rather than disclose financial information.

34

Opportunity Lost, Television

THE PULITZER PRIZE–WINNING COVERAGE OF THE ASSASSINATION OF President Kennedy was a watershed for UPI.

During that memorable Friday afternoon, the world was figuratively hanging on the wires of UPI and AP for information on the shooting.

A study by the University of Chicago's NORC (National Opinion Research Center) estimated that in the first hour after the assassination, more than seventy-five million adult Americans heard about the shooting and the death of John F. Kennedy from news outlets reading from the wires of United Press International and the Associated Press.

News editors at the radio and television networks and at such influential newspapers as the *New York Times* and *Washington Post* could only crowd around their UPI and AP Teletypes to keep up with the breaking story.

But never again would the news agencies so dominate the news.

Sunday, November 24, 1963, just two days after the young president was killed, the unflinching eye of television took over the story in Dallas with incredible live coverage of another assassination.

The Dallas police department was thinking about television and not security when it announced that Lee Harvey Oswald would be transferred from a cell at police headquarters to the county jail at 11 A.M. Sunday.

At UPI's Dallas bureau, Jack Fallon was sure the announcement was a smoke screen and that Oswald's transfer would be made earlier. He assigned reporters to around-the-clock vigils at both the police department's lockup and the county jail. UPI could have saved the overtime.

Dallas was wrestling with a civic dilemma, a feeling that the city must somehow make amends for allowing a sniper to kill the president of the United States on its streets. The transfer of Oswald was to take place right on schedule. Officials wanted television cameras, microphones and reporters to witness the skill of law enforcement in Dallas at work.

When detectives led Oswald through a door into the garage, UPI was well protected. Dave Moffit, a young, energetic reporter, was inside the garage, now crowded with reporters, police and just about anyone who wanted to be there.

Moffit was backed by two veteran UPI reporters. Terry McGarry was just outside the garage near a pay phone and Phil Newman was also near a phone at the county jail.

Moffit had a communications link to the office. At least a dozen times, since his 6 A.M. arrival, he had trudged from the garage to a bank of pay phones to give the Dallas bureau a status report. Moffit recalled that after several trips, the policeman guarding the doorway quit asking for his press credentials and just waved him in and out of the garage.

By 11 A.M. the garage was jammed. Everyone pressed forward as two detectives wearing the traditional Stetson hats pushed through the swinging doors with Oswald between them.

Moffit recalled that he was struggling to get a better view of the accused assassin when he spotted a "brown blur," then heard the pop of a single gunshot. The blur was Jack Ruby wearing a brown suit. He had surged to within a yard of Oswald to fire the fatal shot.

Oswald was handcuffed to one of the two detectives and they went down on the concrete floor together as other policemen wrestled Ruby to the floor and pried the revolver from his hand. Moffit vividly recalled one police officer running around the garage with his gun drawn, ready to deal with anyone else in a murdering mood. It was part of the incredible, confused panorama playing out in the glare of TV lights.

The young reporter moved instinctively toward the double doors and the telephones but the way was blocked by Oswald and Ruby, both on the floor and surrounded by policemen. When he found a way to the doors, police had already sealed off the entire garage so they could check out each person inside.

Moffit said it seemed like an eternity before an ambulance arrived. Oswald was losing a lot of blood. He recalled the numbing picture of Oswald's head wobbling from side to side as his stretcher was slammed into the ambulance.

When his ID was checked and he was finally allowed to leave the garage, Moffit found that McGarry was on the phone with the office. McGarry handed him the phone and Moffit was relieved to learn that the editors at the bureau had witnessed the shooting live on television. His job was to dictate an eyewitness account.

Just before Ruby fired those fatal shots, Don Smith was going to bed. He had not been home since early Friday morning when he drove to Fort Worth to help cover President Kennedy's breakfast speech to Dallas and Fort Worth business and community leaders.

When Smith returned to the Dallas bureau Friday he was trapped on the news desk with Fallon for the next forty hours. Fallon told Smith to go home early Sunday morning and get some sleep. However, Fallon was on the phone just two hours later telling Smith that Oswald had been shot and that Smith had better get back to the office.

Live TV would put UPI editors, along with most of the world, on the scene of many of the biggest stories that broke in the days, months and years that followed.

UPI's success in covering the assassinations in Dallas was dangerously euphoric for the wire service born of the marriage of Scripps-Howard's United Press and William Randolph Hearst's International News Service.

The feeling by staffers, and the management as well, that UPI could compete across the board with AP grew steadily through the 1960s as one earth-shattering event after another tested the mettle of those who gathered the news.

AP had more clients, more staffers and more money. But UPI was catching up.

Before the merger, UP and INS used guerrilla tactics to win some small battles with the Associated Press. The two smaller news services were not able to match AP on total coverage but concentrated instead on carefully picking their targets, then out-hustling and out-writing the staid and often complacent Associated Press.

But UPI in the '60s was flexing its new muscles and had visions of competing with AP on all fronts: "Around the World, Around The Clock," was the way UPI promoted its news service.

Unipressers were having fun battling Goliath. They barely noticed that they were also battling a new competitor. Television was leading a new order in the collection and distribution of news.

While United Press International bylines thrived in the '60s and '70s, UPI's bottom line was sinking into an endless sea of red ink.

Television and later cable television opened promising new markets for UPI but these news distribution systems also presented growing problems.

The impact of television on UPI's bottom line was subtle but just as devastating as an undetected cancer.

Television had become the dominant force in news, and newspapers, many struggling to survive, were looking for ways to cut their costs in the new age of instant news, live, in every living room.

One easy way for newspaper to cut costs was to eliminate "redundant" wire services. For the most part, UPI and AP covered the same stories. One of the wires would do it better or faster and that was important in the old newspaper glory days of "stop the presses" and youngsters hawking "extras" on the street corners. But TV preempted those days.

Newspapers learned they could serve their new role in the "Information Age" with a single news service and most editors and publishers were loathe to eliminate the bigger and older Associated Press, their "club."

There also was new competition for UPI in the newspaper markets. Some of the larger newspapers like the *New York Times*, the *Washington Post* and the *Los Angeles Times*, even the Scripps-Howard papers, started selling their news on so-called supplemental wire services. Other newspapers could buy these supplemental wire services for a fraction of UPI's weekly charges. It cost newspaper supplements very little to serve subscribers since the news they sold was a by-product of news covered for their own papers. Many editors of the big city dailies felt comfortable subscribing to AP and one of the supplemental services.

Getting bigger with an even bigger agenda was costly. The fledgling United Press had made a $500,000 profit with 1,200 clients in 1932. Yet, UPI realized its last profit in 1961 and lost over $300,000 in 1962 when its news wires served nearly 6,000 newspapers, radio and television stations. The losses mounted steadily and reached $2 million by 1972. Scripps-Howard was forced to cover UPI's annual losses.

Since television was depressing UPI's newspaper revenues, it seemed logical that UPI should concentrate on increasing its services to the lucrative television markets.

UPI did not have a news service designed for television. Television stations were sold news wires designed for radio stations or newspapers. Even UPI's picture service, formerly Acme Pictures, shot only black-and-white "stills" and sent TV stations news photos edited for newspapers, stressing the horizontal photographs and not the vertical.

Just after World War II in September of 1947, UP and Acme pictures created a TV news program using still photographs and a script of the top news. Phil Newsom, UP's national radio manager and a pioneer of the agency's service for broadcasters, was in charge of the project.

The idea was that selected photos would be sent to the TV studio where two easels would be set up, one on each side of the anchor desk. The cumbersome TV camera would zero in on one of the easels and the anchor would read the part of the script covering the first picture. Then the camera would switch to the other easel. While the newsman read the story of the picture on the second easel, someone out of the camera's view would put a new photo on the first easel. And so on.

The first test of the service was scheduled, not coincidentally, on a September Sunday when the Miss America Pageant was underway in Atlantic City, New Jersey.

Acme sent a package of its top news photos from its New York bureau near Penn Station to the radio department in UP's headquarters in the *Daily News* Building on 42nd Street.

Thomas L. McGann, then a copy boy, recalled the spectacle of UP's brand-new TV news team gathered in an executive's office with glossy 8-by-10 prints covering the plush carpeting. The kneeling editors seemed to take the most time examining the pictures of Miss America contestants parading in their bathing suits.

Eventually, the editors selected twenty pictures and wrote a script to fit the photos. The pictures and scripts were bundled and rushed by an Acme motorcycle messenger to a television station that had agreed to test the service.

The test went well and, as the service was developed, broadcast writer Johnny Zischang, aided by copy boy Wally Martin, took over the job of selecting the prints and writing the scripts.

UP, however, had bigger ideas for television.

On July 13, 1948, United Press announced an agreement with Twentieth Century-Fox Movietone to shoot news film for television stations. UP-Movietone would send TV stations film from Movietone's library and current newsfilm on a weekly basis. In the 1930s and 40s, Fox Movietone produced news films that were shown in movie theaters, between the cartoons and the featured movie. Millions of Americans got their most graphic glimpses of World War II watching Fox Movietone newsreels.

UP-Movietone tried to compete with the three big television network. However, CBS, NBC and ABC could all afford the bill for leasing coaxial cable from coast to coast. UP-Movietone couldn't.

Major news events were covered with Movietone film crews, most of them independent agents, and United Press news staffers, who tried to learn the art of television reporting on the fly. It didn't measure up to the standards of the networks. It wasn't the quality of the newsfilm that sank the service: it was the delivery problem.

UP-Movietone used airlines, trains and sometimes chartered planes to move its newsfilm. Film shot in the field would be hurried to an airport and put aboard the first plane headed for New York. In New York, the film would be edited and multiple copies rushed to subscribing television stations by other trains and airliners.

UP and Acme photo staffers often had to pick up the reels of film from airports and rush them to anxious television news producers battling deadlines. As often as not they didn't make it on time due to bad weather that grounded the planes, other airline delays or heavy street traffic between the airport and the TV station.

Without the immediacy of live coaxial cable delivery, the UPI-Movietone service couldn't compete with the networks.

Although UPI-Movietone was succeeding and making a profit for UPI, with sales in Europe and South America as well as the United States, Fox executives wanted to get out of the deal because they felt they were not making enough from it. UPI Vice President LeRoy Keller and Scripps attorney Ezra Bryan went to London in 1967 and negotiated a new 50-50 deal with ITN (Independent Television News). Later, the whole thing was sold to ABC.

Keller said Rod Beaton, UPI president, "had no love for this service."[1] Beaton himself said the powers at Scripps refused to put up the money for the cable for UPI because they had other television plans.

The addition of ITN's foreign news coverage enticed some of the independent TV stations in the larger markets to stick with the service for several years.

Burt Reinhardt,who had directed the Fox-Movietone newsreel operation, was named editor of UPITN. He soon brought aboard Reece Schonfeld, a reporter-producer who had helped in the early days of UP-Movietone. Schonfeld had joined UP in New York as a copyboy and worked his way into the fledgling newsfilm operation.

The TV film service continued to rely on airline freight to deliver its news clips and it failed to attract many U.S. television stations other than a few big-city independents like WOR-TV in New York and WGN-TV in Chicago. Most network affiliates were not interested in UPITN.

UPI became a minority holder in UPITN in 1975 when Paramount Pictures bought 50 percent of the service. UPI and ITN each held 25 percent. UPI's editorial participation in UPITN dissipated in the 1970's and finally, in 1982, the new owners of the company got out of the television business entirely. UPITN by then included ABC as a 30 percent partner and was serving 120 subscribers in seventy nations.

Frank Bartholomew, president of UP/UPI from 1955 until 1962 and long-time member of the UPI board, said UPITN's failure to blossom was the signal event in what became Scripps-Howard's increasing dissatisfaction with the news service.

Never short of ideas but usually short of resources, UPI tried some oblique approaches to television by developing services for cable television, the 1970's manifestation of the "Information Age."

When cable television was growing, channels were looking for content. UPI, in September 1971, began producing a wire exclusively for cable television.

Broadcast editor Billy Ferguson and broadcast bureau manager Thomas L. McGann in Chicago developed a prototype of a new UPI cable news service with a crawling text printout of the top news of the world that could be displayed on television screens.

Running at ten words a minute, the printed news scrolled slowly on the screen. The printer preparing the service had to be set at thirty-two characters per line instead of the usual forty-two so that the copy would fit television screens.

Fifteen-minute news shows were updated around the clock and repeated constantly to give cable systems continuous news programming.

The UPI scrolling screen text service was used by more than 300 cable systems. But cable television was growing and operators wanted a better system for presenting news than the Teletype-like printout; they wanted it to include pictures and sound.

UPI reacted with a second cable television service called "UPI Newstime," a multimedia service that combined an off-camera anchor reading a script of the world's top news matching selected pictures, voice reports and "actualities" from the UPI Audio Network.

Newstime was UPI's first satellite-delivered service and it was transmitted on the satellite system of Ted Turner's cable superstation WTCG-TV.

Newstime relied on a transmission system called slow-scan that required electronic scrambling as it was uplinked to the satellite and other electronics that unscrambled the pictures and sound at each cable system's downlink dish.

To minimize communications costs, UPI first located Newstime's editorial and sales headquarters in an office building in Smyrna, Georgia, near the RCA satellite dish that uplinked Turner's WTCG-TV signal. It began programming July 4, 1978, serving just three CATV systems.

Later, Newstime's operations moved to the site of the Southern Satellite System's uplink dish in a bucolic suburb west of Atlanta, actually on the edge of a large cow pasture.

The original concept for Newstime was the brainchild of Frank W. Beatty, a UPI sales executive and a former UP photographer. He put together a Rube Goldberg-style carousel of 8-by-10 frames that could be loaded with UPI pictures and rotated like a Ferris wheel before a camera.

A script was written to match the photos and played onto the audio track of the film. Bill Reilly, an audio reporter who had covered the war in Vietnam, worked with Beatty on the project in the Chicago bureau.

Veteran executive Roy Mehlman and Tom Hawley of UPI's Special Services refined the process and persuaded general manager Robert E. Page to open a Newstime bureau in Georgia. Mehlman, along with Jack Klinge of the Dallas bureau, handled the marketing for both UPI's alphanumeric and Newstime services and established close ties in the burgeoning cable industry.

Mehlman and Hawley picked Richard Boggs, a bright, hard-working reporter and editor from the Southwest Division, to run the new operation. Boggs, who had worked for International Television News, was uniquely qualified to handle the myriad technical as well as editorial complexities of the new-age news service.

Boggs found the technical problems sometimes got in the way of overseeing the editorial operations. It was several days before he discovered that Newstime was illegally running *New York Times* copy. He had hired two young Columbia University journalism grads, Jonathan Witt and Leslie Goldwater, the granddaughter of presidential candidate Barry Goldwater. The two rookies felt the *New York Times* was the final word on news so they used text from the daily to write Newstime copy.

Boggs turned over the day-day editorial responsibilities to news editor Jordanka Lazarevic, formerly a supervising editor of the National Broadcast Department in Chicago. She tightened the editorial parameters and taught the staff to write in the short, concise style that distinguished the UPI broadcast wire.

Early in 1980, Newstime was serving 130 CATV systems and seemed on the edge of profitability.

UPI audio staffers (from left) Bill Reilly, Tom Foty, Bill Wilson, Pete Willett and Roger Norum hold up the bar at a reunion of "Downholders" in New York.

But that summer Ted Turner, who earlier had toured the Newstime operations, inaugurated CNN (Cable News Network). The days were numbered for both of UPI's suddenly archaic cable services.

UPI had a good chance to beat Ted Turner to the punch in 1978. A long line of UPI broadcast executives including Pete Willett, Burt Reinhardt, Roy Mehlman and Frank Beatty, had applied constant pressure on UPI President Rod Beaton to expand services for television and cable.

Beaton recalled that they finally persuaded him to call an exploratory meeting with all the news directors of Scripps-Howard's television stations to discuss the possibility of a television news network.

The meeting, held in New York, was positive. The TV news directors, led by Al Shottlekotte of WCOP-TV in Cincinnati, saw the potential of a plan that would use their satellite uplinks to collect TV newsfilm from around the nation. UPI would act as a clearing house and would produce a network, complete with anchored newscasts.

Beaton recalled that he was initially leery of the idea because UPI had been financially burned on UPITN. However, UPI's first venture in TV newsfilm had been hampered by its horse and buggy delivery system. The newly-proposed TV network would operate on a satellite distribution system.

Beaton made a trip to Chicago to look into WGN-TV's satellite network operations. He also sent Communications Vice President James Darr to Atlanta to investigate the satellite delivery system of Ted Turner's superstation. Beaton was then encouraged enough to pitch the idea to Don Perris, who was president of Scripps-Howard Broadcasting. Beaton recalled that Perris was ambivalent, but did not oppose the plan.

However, Beaton said, the meeting with Perris was the calm before the storm.

"Jack Howard went off like a rocket when he got wind of it," Beaton said. The UPI president was summoned to a meeting with Howard, president of Scripps-Howard, in his Park Avenue office. Beaton recalled much of Howard's stern lecture.

"What the hell are you doing?" Howard asked Beaton, "Scripps-Howard Broadcasting is a highly-successful company, but it is linked to the tender mercies of network affiliations and relationships, not to mention the F-C-C.

"The UPI record is that of a not-so-successful news agency with no network experience," Howard continued. "We suffered flack on the start-up of UPI's audio network and so we might well understand the reaction if we were so much as thinking TV news network, even a half-assed one."

Beaton said he still felt the idea was sound, but he could understand Jack Howard's concern. Beaton tabled the idea for a more opportune time.[2]

After Ted Turner opened his cable new network in 1980, the hopes of a TV network at UPI evaporated.

Richard Boggs went into UPI broadcast sales and later was named vice president in charge of the audio network.

Tom McGann, Wally Martin and Bill Reilly were absorbed into other UPI operations.

Roy Mehlman joined CNN and found it looked familiar, staffed by key UPI television people. Reece Schonfeld, was president and Schonfeld's old boss at UPITN, Burt Reinhardt, was a CNN vice president for editorial. Frank Beatty, who had conceived Newstime, was a CNN sales executive.

Despite AP's best efforts, UPI's broadcast services remained strong. Audio sales ballooned when it became the UPI Radio Network, complete with newscasts on the hour and half-hour and sports and business shows that stations could use to sell advertising.

In October of 1981, UPI served more than 3,600 radio and television stations as well as 900 newspapers.

When continuing financial problems led Scripps-Howard to abandon UPI in 1982, many broadcasters bailed out and AP became the dominant broadcast news service. Still, UPI's broadcast wire and Radio Network pumped out competitive news shows around the clock every day until July of 1999. That's when UPI gave up as a wire service and sold its broadcast operations and broadcast clients to the Associated Press.

35

Sailing on the Titanic

AMERICA'S PUBLISHERS GOT AN EARLY WARNING.

"UPI is not, nor has it been, a profit center for some time," said Edward W. Estlow, who had succeeded Jack Howard as president of the Scripps-Howard organization. "There are some things the nation's editors and publishers may not be fully aware of."

Estlow's remarks came at a United Press International breakfast meeting during the annual convention of the American Newspaper Publishers Association April 24, 1979, at the Waldorf-Astoria Hotel in New York

Estlow was serving notice that the Scripps-Howard Trust, the family trust that owned UPI, would some day terminate.

He said, as an employee of the trust, he had to consider his fiduciary duty to the heirs, who were subsidizing a wire service that was no longer necessary to their newspapers and was losing money every year.

"America should have two major wire services," Estlow said, "and Scripps-Howard wants UPI to survive, but not at the cost of subsidizing it indefinitely."

Estlow had come up through the Scripps-Howard newspapers and had no wire service experience.

Editor & Publisher, the newspaper industry's leading journal, ran an editorial October 6, 1979, pleading UPI's case. It said:

> "The free press needs UPI, particularly in this country, just as it needs the Associated Press. It needs both. Their services are better because of the competition between them and their employees to exceed and excel. The combined service of newspapers and broadcasters to their subscribers would be poorer without UPI, without each news service pushing the other. It is in the interest of American journalism and the American people for major newspapers to find a way to perpetuate two, not just one, aggressive and responsible news services."

UPI General Manager Robert Page made sure UPI's staffers got the message that the straits were dire. He asked them to accept a one-year wage freeze in 1979. The Wire

Service Guild went along in exchange for promise of a $35 a week boost for its top-scale employees in 1980.

However, even the wage freeze, tied to a 21 percent hike in UPI's rates for its subscribers the previous year, failed to slow the bottom-line bleeding.

UPI lost $5.5 million in 1978 and was facing the heavy "quadrennial" expenses in 1980 to cover the summer and winter Olympics as well as the Democratic and Republican nominating conventions and the general elections.

Facing these grim realities, UPI decided to try for support from the industry. It would ask big newspaper and broadcast clients to buy equity in the company. In September of 1979, top executives fanned out to forty-five of the top-paying customers in the United States and asked each of them to buy two percent of UPI for $345,000.

UPI executives figured that such a partnership plan would develop loyalty among its customers and improve the bottom line. The partnership investments would provide $15.525 million. Scripps-Howard and the Hearst Corporation would kick-in $5 million to give the new partnership $20 million at the onset. Hearst owned five percent of UPI, but told Estlow that it would go along with whatever was needed.

Estlow and Larry Lesar of Scripps-Howard, along with Rod Beaton and Bob Page, would identify possible partners then try to sell them on the plan.

According to Page, Scripps-Howard planned to use its $5 million contribution to pay any outstanding debts at the time of the ownership change.

Scripps-Howard put a December 31, 1979, deadline on the offer. It was extended thirty days, but by the end of January 1980, only about 60 percent of the needed partners had signed on and the plan was called off.

Page said the plan failed mainly because the minority partners would have no say in managing the company. He recalled a meeting in Houston with Dick Johnson, the publisher of the *Houston Chronicle* at the time. Page said Johnson wanted to support the plan and had even volunteered to go to the *Houston Post* with Page in an effort to sell *Post* owner Oveda Culp Hobby on the idea.

However, Page recalled, Johnson later said he couldn't really join the partnership, not because of the money involved, but because the shares would have no management powers.

Page said Beaton and Estlow had several heated exchanges over the partnership plan. Estlow wanted the salaries of UPI's top executives listed in the information packet for possible minority partners.

Beaton was embarrassed that the top salaries were so low. At a time when many of the top managers in the news industry were breaking into six figures, Beaton was making $75,000, Page was at $60,000 and Editor and Chief H.L. Stevenson was paid only $55,000.

Even Estlow had to agree. He later gave all three $5,000 raises, but the limited partership plan had failed.[1]

UPI staffers had a healthy skepticism about the partnership plan, but most were genuinely surprised at how little support there was in the news industry for a second major news service.

Most Unipressers still felt the name of the game was to beat the Associated Press with better reporting, brighter writing, faster distribution and valuable new services. Given that, they felt, UPI would surely survive.

There was plenty of news to keep UPI's reporters, editors and writers at their competitive best in 1980. In addition to the political conventions, election and the Olympics, there was a continuing crisis in Tehran where Iranian militants were holding 53 American diplomats hostage after storming the U.S. Embassy in November of 1979.

UPI had seven correspondents in Tehran, including bureau manager Sajid Rizvi, three other newsmen, two photographers and an audio reporter. However, on January 14, 1980, about two months after the embassy take-over, Iran's ruling Revolutionary Council expelled the 100 American journalists covering the hostage crisis.

Rizvi, a native of Pakistan who had been in Iran for three years, was allowed to stay in Tehran for an additional ten days, but he could not file news reports back to New York. UPI sent him to a nearby post, outside Iran, where he could monitor Iranian radio reports.

The hostage crisis in Tehran dragged on month after month. Occasional glimpses of shackled and blindfolded American hostages imprisoned in the shattered U.S. Embassy became a constant irritation for President Jimmy Carter. When numerous diplomatic attempts failed to win the freedom of the prisoners, the president approved a Pentagon plan to rescue the hostages with a surprise, airborne raid.

The rescue mission was launched in April 24, 1981, but was aborted at a staging area 200 miles from Tehran. Officers called off the planned surprise landing in Tehran when mechanical problems grounded three of the eight carrier-launched helicopters. As the Americans flew out of the Great Salt Desert, a Sea Stallion helicopter and a C-130 Hercules transport plane collided, killing eight American servicemen and wounded five other.

The first word for UPI came in a phone call to the home of UPI correspondent Wes Pippert at 1 A.M. It was a conference call for the wire services from White House Press Secretary Jody Powell, who gave only sketchy information.

Pippert immediately called the Washington bureau and dictated a bulletin to general desker Pat Killen, who felt that Powell's 200-word announcement "was not a very precise statement."

Killen and Pippert got on the phones to gather information.

"We got some of our best early details from Senator Charles Percy, (R-Illinois)," Killen recalled. "He was the second ranking member of the Senate Foreign Relations Committee and had been notified of the mission by Deputy Secretary of State Warren Christopher."

Pippert, a former aide to the Illinois senator, said Percy called UPI and volunteered the information he had, including the fact that the operation involved C-130 transport planes as well as helicopters.

"We could get nothing from the Pentagon or the White House beyond Powell's statement," Killen said. "We were told the president would go on air later in the morning to make a statement."

Killen said President Carter's statement was also vague and it was twenty-four hours before the details were known. Still, with the help of a U.S. senator who had warm feelings towards UPI, Pippert and Killen had managed to get a solid story of the aborted raid well ahead of the competition.

UPI was a little too far ahead on the next big development in the hostage story.

The militant Iranian students, backed by Ayatollah Ruhollah Khomeini, were ready to release the hostages that they held for more than one year, but there seemed to be a caveat. It was widely felt that they would not release the imprisoned diplomats while President Jimmy Carter, now a lame-duck, was still in office. The speculation seemed to have been on target when they scheduled the release for January 20, 1981, the day Ronald Reagan was to be sworn in as the fortieth president of the United States at noon EST.

UPI sent a flash, its highest-priority news item, at 11:33 A.M. (EST) that the hostages had taken off aboard an Algerian airliner. It seemed illogical that the diplomats were released in the final minutes of President Carter's four-year term.

Unfortunately UPI's flash was nearly one-hour premature.

The official Iranian news agency PARS reported that the hostages' plane took off at 12:30 P.M.

Reuters had two correspondents in Tehran who reported that the hostages were aboard two planes and that one took off at 12:28 P.M. (EST), the other at 12:33 P.M. (EST).

Unfortunately, Iran had expelled all AP and UPI reporters and UPI was relying on a stringer in Tehran.

The stringer couldn't get into the airport, but UPI had hired a man at the airport to protect UPI.

Managing editor Don Reed said, "We had a source in the airport manager's office. Our Farsi speaker (translator) in London had talked to him many times and said he was reliable."

Reed said the mix-up on departure time occurred because the source was looking at his timetable. The hostages were aboard the plane by 11:30 and ready to go, but the plane had not taken off. The source hung up before the New York editors could question him.

Reed, a level-headed editor long accustomed to making snap news judgments, faced the toughest call of his career.

It was widely believed that the Iranians were delaying the hostage release until Reagan had taken the oath of office. However, no such plan had ever been announced by either the Iranian government or the so-called radical students who held the fifty-two American diplomats.

Reed said that since the source was reliable and well placed, he decided to go with the flash. He said speed was vital at that time of day because of newspaper deadlines.

Reed also rationalized that the hostages were really in Algerian custody when they got aboard the plane.

Fortunately for UPI, unfortunately for many newspaper editors, AP also reported the hostage release before Reagan was sworn in.

During 1981, UPI's message wires were devoting about as much space to tracking the wire service's fate as they were to planning and chasing the news of the world. The agency itself had become a continuing story and all of them used an unhappy qualification, describing the agency as the "financially-troubled UPI."

At the company's annual Edicon meeting for publishers, Scripps-Howard president Ed Estlow said that talks had been going on with several organizations interested in buying UPI. He did not identify them.

Estlow believed the limited partnership offering had failed because most news organizations were reluctant to invest without having a vote on UPI's operations. Estlow offered some of the biggest news organizations a revised partnership plan that would allow them to share control of UPI as well as its liabilities. There were no takers.

Reuters was next. UPI had, in years past, refused several overtures from the British news agency. But, things were different now and it was up to UPI president Rod Beaton to work out a deal with the rival news agency that carried the code name "Rand" in UPI messages.

Reuters expressed an initial interest and Beaton agreed to give the Brits carte blanche in their investigation of UPI. Beaton hoped Reuters would absorb UPI and use UPI's extensive American coverage, network and customer base, to create the world's leading news agency.

Reuters launched an exhaustive, six-month investigation of UPI, dispatching teams across America to talk with employees and customers of the UPI. All of its books were opened for Reuters and managers were instructed to offer Reuters every courtesy.

While Reuters had its rival targeted under the microscope, UPI's hard-pressed editorial staff dealt with a story that gave a glaring lesson on the need for two major news agencies on March 30, 1981.

Correspondent Dean Reynolds was just a few steps behind President Ronald Reagan as he left the Washington Hilton Hotel following an appearance and headed for his limousine.

Reynolds recoiled in shock when a young man, later identified as John W. Hinkley, pulled out a gun and opened fire on the presidential party, hitting Reagan and critically wounding White House Press Secretary James Brady and Secret Service Agent Timothy McCarthy.

The athletic Reynolds raced back into the hotel, ran up a down escalator and called Washington editor David Wiessler, whose bulletin gave UPI another beat on an assassination attempt. But there was more.

Associated Press distributed a false report that Brady had died, and the three major television networks followed AP's lead. UPI was besieged with calls from angry clients who wanted to know why UPI wasn't matching the networks with Brady's death.

Brady survived and became the inspiration for new federal gun legislation.

Reuters apparently wasn't keeping score on UPI's editorial muscle. The British news agency was more concerned with the company's financial reports than its fast and accurate coverage of banner news.

On November 30, Reuters pulled out of the negotiations and headed home with tons of valuable information about UPI, its people and its customers.

UPI staffers were keeping score on the efforts to sell UPI and Reuters' decision to end negotiations was an emotional setback. But, always hopeful for their jobs as well as UPI, most were heartened again when it was learned that NPR (National Public Radio) was interested in acquiring UPI.

It sounded a bit ridiculous to many, but a top NPR executive had suggested that Scripps donate UPI to the non-profit radio network and claim a healthy tax deduction. Scripps-Howard president Ed Estlow felt the idea was a good one. NPR was highly respected and a tax write-off could go as high as $100 million. NPR president Frank Mankiewicz, a former adviser to President Kennedy, wanted to expand his empire and felt UPI would be a perfect acquisition. But the NPR money experts, already facing their own financial problems, decided taking on the wire service was too big of a risk and vetoed the plan.

The rumor mill continued grinding out new names and new hopes. However, there was never a hint that two mystery men, Ruhe and Geissler, were also talking to Scripps-Howard's top executives at the Scripps-Howard New York offices on the 43rd floor of the Pan Am Building and the S-H executive offices in the Central Trust Tower in Cincinnati, Ohio.

Tom Quinn, who operated the Los Angeles City News Service and Colorado radio station owner Doug Faigan were among those who met with Estlow and UPI comptroller Fred Green, UPI's head financial officer. Estlow also met with Thomas Wise, founder of the PR (Public Relations) Newswire.

A rescue plan was proposed within the Scripps family. Ted Scripps, one of E.W.'s six grandchildren, had a deep affection for UPI and, in April of 1982, asked his brother, Charles Scripps, and Estlow to hold onto UPI. Ted volunteered to take-over as chief executive officer of the struggling news agency. Still no deal.

In mid-May, as UPI's West Coast editorial team struggled to cover a devastating volcanic explosion on Mount St. Helens, the powers at Scripps-Howard decided to give UPI to the suitors with the fewest credentials and the least money, Doug Ruhe and Bill Geissler.

Following a meeting with Estlow and Leser in Cincinnati, a jubilant Ruhe called Tom Haughney, a Nashville friend and accountant who had helped put together the offer to buy UPI.

"Tom, they've drawn the line," Ruhe exclaimed happily. "They'll give us seven and a half million dollars to take it off their hands—and not one penny more."[2]

36

Going, Going!

THE COMPANY THAT E.W. SCRIPPS STARTED IN 1907 WITH "$500 AND a bag of wind" was sold for one dollar seventy-five years later.

On June 3, 1982, Scripps-Howard finally waved the white flag and paid two brash entrepreneurs millions to take United Press International off its hands.

Doug Ruhe and Bill Geissler, who stepped from obscurity to journalism's center-stage, had to pay the dollar to make the sale official, just as E.W. Scripps had to put up $500 in capital when he incorporated United Press.

That one-dollar bill bought a lot. In addition to taking over the men, women, machines and customers of the worldwide news service, Ruhe, 38, and Geissler, 36, heading a newly formed acquisition group, were promised capital and interest-free loans from Scripps-Howard of more than $7 million.

What had happened? UPI was the world's second largest source of news and it was the dawn of the information age. The venerable news agency had more than 200 bureaus around the world and more than 1,500 employees reporting, writing and distributing more than 12-million words of fresh information every day.

Scripps Howard's costly give-away puzzled the news industry and the UPI staff as well. Even though it was known that Scripps wanted to unload the wire service and its perennial, multi-million dollar losses, it was believed that UPI still had value.

The UPI staff got the official word on June 4, 1982, when the deal was announced. The new owners were Ruhe and Geissler, along with Bill Ahlhauser, their financial manager, Cordell Overgaard, a Chicago attorney, and Rob Small, whose family operated several newspapers in Illinois.

The five men were introduced to and answered questions for a group of stunned UPI managers and staffers assembled in a meeting room at New York's Harley Hotel, next door to the wire service headquarters at 220 East 42nd Street.

Anxious staffers came away with more questions than answers. Ruhe and Geissler were the owners of a Nashville, Tennessee, television company, but they were virtually unknown, even in Nashville. The tall and handsome young men said they were entrepreneurs who would keep UPI afloat, intact, and turn it around with its own revenues. The 39-year-old Small, the only familiar face on the stage, would be UPI's new chairman.

Ruhe and Geissler controlled the company with 60 percent of the stock while Ahlhauser, Small and Overgaard were minority shareowners.

In New York, Nashville and Chicago, reporters started digging to learn more about the new owners. One common thread, quickly found, alarmed newshands for whom independence was the life blood of the wire service. Ruhe, Geissler and Ahlhauser were all members of the Baha'i faith. Many feared they might bring a religious agenda to the agency.

Ruhe and Geissler worked together at the Baha'i National Center in Wilmette, Illinois. They operated a small public relations firm in nearby Evanston, and it was through this venture that they met Chicago attorney, Cordell Overgaard.

Overgaard had represented holdings of Illinois publisher Len Small, including the successful "Family Weekly." The lawyer felt that Ruhe and Geissler needed someone in the news industry on their team. He led them to Rob Small. Like his father, Len Small, he was a big supporter of UPI and was anxious to see it survive.

The Baha'i connection also led Ruhe and Geissler to Bill Ahlhauser, a young Harvard Business School graduate who became UPI's treasurer.

Barely had Ruhe and Geissler quelled the fears over their Baha'i background when an investigative reporter at the *Nashville Tennessean* disclosed that both Ruhe and Geissler had arrest records and that Geissler had served time in a federal penitentiary.

This, too, was smoothed over with the UPI staff when it was learned that the arrests came because of civil rights demonstrations and Geissler had voluntarily surrendered for federal prison time rather than register for military service during the Vietnam war.

There were even some hopeful signs. The new owners promised that UPI would continue as a full-service news agency. They talked convincingly about opening new markets for the 75-year-old agency and curing its financial ills by increasing revenues. For years, Scripps-Howard had tried to fix UPI's problems mainly by cutting expenses with the endless "downholds."

The man responsible for maintaining the "downhold" philosophy at UPI knew his days as president were numbered. Roderick W. Beaton, his husky six-foot four-inch frame bent by years of trying to make UPI profitable, was appalled by the naiveté of Ruhe and Geissler and was anxious to leave.

Ruhe and Geissler were also anxious for Beaton to leave. They wanted a big-name president who could bring to UPI the credibility and visibility they lacked. Walter Cronkite, the veteran CBS television news anchor and former UP correspondent, turned down the job, but another network news executive didn't.

In mid-September 1982, it was announced that Bill Small, a TV news executive with both NBC and CBS, would succeed Beaton as president of UPI. Small, with some powerful friends at CBS and a lot of enemies at NBC, came with a big price tag: $250,000 a year.

The hiring of Small was seen as a positive step, but there were other, bigger problems at the top. Ruhe and Geissler stubbornly insisted on unfettered control of UPI and they ran roughshod over minority partners Rob Small and Cordelle Overgaard.

Early in 1983, Small and Overgaard resigned, just a step ahead of the arrival of a flamboyant new player who joined the Ruhe and Geissler team. John Jay Hooker, a Nashville, Tennessee entrepreneur who had failed in political campaigns for governor and U.S. senator, had so dazzled Ruhe and Geissler that they named him chairman of UPI to replace Rob Small.

The turnstile to the top was starting to spin and it would not stop until the end of the century. During the next eighteen years, twelve different men served as presidents of UPI and they answered to four different chairmen.

On April 14, 1983, changes were felt at lower levels around the world. The staff remembered it as their St. Valentine Day massacre when 100 UPI veterans were fired. That day's pink slips went to employees not protected by the Wire Service Guild— lower level managers, secretaries and non-editorial support personnel. It was the first in a series of mass layoffs that trimmed the employee ranks from more than 1,500 to less than 300 by the end of the century.

UPI International Editor Bobby Ray Miller, the news agency's guru on style, was part of a committee to plan the staff cuts. Miller, who later became personnel director, said the cuts, at the time, actually trimmed UPI's expenses to a little less than the company's income. But UPI's bookkeepers did not need to stock up on black ink.

Ruhe and Geissler, buoyed by modest successes in sales, were ready to expand in hopes of finding new revenues. Soon the 13th floor of the *Daily News* Building in New York was crowded with consultants who took home big fees while spending most of their time picking the brains of weary managers who had kept UPI somewhat competitive.

A communications specialist who had provided TV program guides to newspapers, Jim West, was retained at a salary equal to nearly $100,000 a year. Economist John Nasbitt and Michael Evans got $350,000 for a regional economic service championed by John J. Hooker. It fizzled quickly.

Steven Pruett, who had helped Ruhe and Geissler with a pay television venture, was hired as a consultant on broadcast sales and service. Pruett's wife, Paula Baird, was hired as a vice president and put in charge of the broadcast sales force. She came from a job in Chicago selling advertising for television station WMAQ.

A Baha'i friend, Seward Rist, was hired to form a new subsidiary, UPI Real Estate, Inc., intended to seek equity in buildings where UPI bureaus were housed.

Ruhe and Geissler "spent money as if they had it," Greg Gordon and Ron Cohen said in their book *Down to the Wire*, which chronicled the company's perils following the Scripps-Howard surrender.

UPI comptroller Fred Green was appalled that expenses were once again far ahead of income, but he could not convince Ruhe that UPI was running out of money. Ruhe and Geissler publicly disparaged Green, as well as their own friend and financial adviser Tom Haughney, as "bean counters." UPI Treasurer Bill Ahlhauser seemed oblivious to the problems or not willing to confront Ruhe and Geissler about money.

Without leaving his desk, Green could gauge the severity of the financial problems. Every drawer was jammed with checks written by the accounting office computer to vendors who served UPI's far-flung bureaus. The computer program automatically wrote checks when invoices were approved.

Green had to hold back checks that would result in an overdrawn bank account. He mailed them when funds were available, on the basis of priority needs such as rent and telephone service. At one time there was nearly $1,000,000 worth of checks in his desk.

Even the optimistic John Jay Hooker was worried about UPI's finances. Hooker lined up several interested investors, but he was unable to persuade Ruhe and Geissler to share any control of the company. They wanted investors, but they insisted on maintaining total control.

Hooker finally gave up in May, relinquishing his role as chairman, and headed home to Nashville. Ruhe was quickly on the phone to Luis Nogales, a bright, young Californian who had made a mark with Gene Autry's Golden West Broadcasting Corporation.

The tall, handsome Nogales, who picked fruit with migrant workers as a teen, had earlier expressed an interest in joining Ruhe and Geissler. He enthusiastically signed on as executive vice president.

Nogales had no idea of the financial problems that awaited him. The man who could have and would have told him how bad things were, Comptroller Fred Green, had resigned in May and taken a position at Reuters.

Right after calling Nogales, Ruhe and Geissler were busy looking for a new editor-in-chief. The boss of UPI's editorial operations was H. L. Stevenson, a tough veteran of thirty years in UPI newsrooms in Mississippi, Atlanta and New York. Steve and the new owners did not agree on what was needed to salvage the news operation. Geissler thought Stevenson was arbitrary and locked into old school journalism.

The search for a new editor led Geissler and Bill Small to the *Chicago Tribune* and its vice president for news, Maxwell McCrohon. McCrohon had led the *Tribune* to several Pulitzer Prizes but he had been kicked upstairs to make room for *Orlando Sentinel* editor James Squires. McCrohon, a native of Australia, was out of the news mainstream at the *Tribune* and saw UPI as a way to get back in its excitement. He agreed to join UPI for a hefty salary that would approach $200,000 in his third year.

Stevenson had been active in the ASNE (American Society for Newspaper Editors) for years and was close friends with many of the men who called the shots at major newspapers. He also had a strong following among UPI's editors and reporters. To put the best possible spin on the change, Small announced that Stevenson had been bumped upstairs to executive vice president for editorial, with the assignment of developing new products. McCrohon was named editor-in-chief.

Overseas correspondents were still having problems in the 1980s. Steven M. Hagey, in Beirut in December 1984, was seized by revolutionaries who demanded $100,000 ransom from UPI.

His captors knocked him around and played Russian roulette with a 9mm pistol against his head, laughing among themselves because, unknown to Hagey, the bullets had been removed.

Hagey said afterward he pondered the reaction of the London UPI bookkeeper if he put the ransom on his expense account. He tried unsuccessfully to get the amount reduced. The gang demanded "sex," which befuddled Hagey until he realized they were asking for six checks, one for each of them.

He wrote two $16,000 checks on UPI but then told his captors that it was unlikely any bank would cash them. The bandits argued loudly among themselves. They then asked him how much he had in his personal account. He said "about $1,500." They told him to write a $1,400 personal check, leaving him with $100.

"We shook hands, exchanged kisses, and they prepared to let me go," said Hagey. "But first, they said, I must meet them the next day with $10,000 in cash. They would hold my passport as collateral.

"Little did the gunmen know I had a second passport."

The UP Beirut bureau managed to get him out to Paris, with the help of Terry Anderson of AP, who was taken prisoner several months later and held for six years.

When they learned he was gone, the bandits called the Bierut UPI bureau saying, "Tell Mr. Hagey he is no gentleman."

On the night of April 26, 1986, Soviet scientists were performing an experiment at the Chernobyl nuclear power plant 80 miles north of Kiev in what is now Ukraine.

Through a disastrous series of human errors a reaction was touched off which blew the top off one of the plant's four reactors, spewing deadly radiation like a roman candle. It spread over a vast area, contaminating fields, animals and people. Thirty people were killed immediately by the blast.

For United Press International, then in precarious standing with its customers, the Chernobyl story was also a disaster, the worst since Roy Howard's premature end of World War I.

The Russians did not disclose the Chernobyl nuclear disaster until the next day when mysterious radioactivity showed up on instruments in Norway.

G. Luther Whittington, recently arrived in the Moscow bureau, frustrated at being unable to get an official report, telephoned a hospital at Kiev. A nurse told him 2,000 persons were dead.

Whittington filed a bulletin to the desk in Washington. Editors, who had been drilled to be extremely cautious about casualty figures were jolted. They didn't know what to do. Whittington was inexperienced, and he did not have an official source for his figure. As far as the desk knew, no news agency had gone out with any number near that.

The Washington desk finally called Max McCrohon, editor-in-chief, at home. After being told the situation, McCrohon instructed the desk to go with it. The UPI story hit headlines around the world.

When Soviet official sources became available the next day, they denied the huge loss of life. Thirty workers at the plant had been killed. The extent of the radiation release was minimized.

It was years later before Russia disclosed the full consequences of the disaster. Thousands of square miles of the "breadbasket" of the Soviet Union were permanently contaminated. More than 100,000 people were evacuated from the region. Several villages near Chernobyl were permanently evacuated.

UPI had taken a severe blow. Clients, already concerned because of the company's known troubles, demanded an explanation. Luther Whittington was targeted and the implication went out that he had been fired. In fact, Whittington was transferred from Moscow to Los Angeles and "hidden" on the local staff there. He was not to have any bylines.

Ironically, although the figure of 2,000 casualties at Chernobyl was very premature, the nuclear accident was eventually blamed for the deaths 55,000 people from cancer and other effects of radiation exposure. On the anniversary of the accident in 2000, Interfax, a Russian news service, quoted a Russian official with the huge death figure.

Ruhe and Geissler thought they had put a happy face on UPI's public image. Every week, rosy press releases trumpeted new sales successes or announced new product rollouts.[2]

Geissler, born in Venezuela and fluent in Spanish, forged a joint-venture in the fall of 1983 with EFE, the Spanish News Agency, for a Spanish-language radio network. The network, "Nuestras Noticias," or "Our News" was an immediate hit with the burgeoning Latin American market. "Nuestras Noticias" shared the UPI Audio Network's satellite feeds and eventually became profitable.

Within months, UPI also rolled out its custom news products, which had been in the works for several years. "CustomData" for newspapers and "CustomNews" for broadcasters were 1,200 word-a-minute, newswires that used special codes that allowed clients to tailor their own UPI news and information services. Electronic selectors, which could be downloaded with new menus in an instant, filtered the news subjects and datelines customers wanted to receive and eliminated all the unwanted copy.

McCrohon hired a long-time associate, Andrea Hermann, to bring UPI's feature report up to date. While Andrea couldn't quite figure out the logistics of a word-wide wire service or even how to use the UPI computer system, she did use her connection to McCrohon to build a top-flight lifestyles department. She drafted two excellent women editors, Judy Dugan, a former editor in the national broadcast department in Chicago, and Michelle Mundth, one of the top general desk editors in Washington. She also brought aboard the free-spirited Frank Cook, a former Texas State editor with a flair for the contemporary.

Unfortunately, while UPI was cranking up new services, it was selling off old ones. Cash was needed to cover payroll, new product start-up costs and finance the growing army of consultants.

Ruhe rushed through deals to sell UPI's cable television service to Denver businessman Clint Ober, a friend of UPI consultant Jim West, for $1.1 million and UPI's database operations to Comtex Scientific Corporation for $1.2 million. The Comtex deal, necessary to meet another payroll crisis, was so one-sided that UPI marketing director James Buckner, who handled the negotiations, quit UPI and joined Comtex.

Ken Braddick, a hot-headed Aussie who had been fired from UPI in the final days of Scripps-Howard ownership, rejoined the news agency as a key adviser to Ruhe and Geissler. He was assigned two major projects—one, to help sell off "non-essential" services; and two, to plan and implement a move of company headquarters out of high-rent Manhattan. The administrative offices relocated to Nashville, Tennessee and editorial headquarters to Washington, D.C.

Braddick negotiated a deal that gave Bettman photo archive 10-year exclusive control of and marketing rights to UPI's picture library, which included more than eleven million photo negatives dating back to the Civil War.

The Bettman deal, strenuously opposed by the editorial staff, gave UPI $1.1 million up front and 25 percent of gross revenue from picture sales. However, it was no bargain because the photo library itself grossed about $1 million per year.

Braddick also helped raise another $1 million by selling UPI's 50 percent share in a European financial news service called UNICOM to its partner in the venture, Knight Ridder.

There was still another plum for Jim West, the consultant who seemed to be everywhere and usually somewhere close to Doug Ruhe. West was charged with upgrading UPI's stock quote service. To make things work, the consultant persuaded Ruhe to buy a new $680,000 computer and turn it over to a new company, Fintex, a joint venture with West and UPI each owning 50 percent. Fintex promised newspapers updated stock quotes twenty-five times a day. It never really got off the ground. The only winner was West, who pulled in a $96,000 annual salary as president of Fintex and a share of all UPI revenue from its stock quote services.

All the consultants and their joint ventures cost UPI far more than the revenue realized from new sales to newspapers and broadcasters. Each payroll brought a new crisis.

Undaunted, Ruhe and Geissler assigned Braddick and Tom Haughney, who owned five percent of UPI's stock, to find an angel, someone willing to put up $12 million as a minority stockholder. Braddick and Haughney weren't able to find an angel, but they did open the door for a few more expensive consultants.

Rinaldo Brutoco, a West Coast attorney interjected himself into UPI's efforts to get a loan from the Foothill Capital Corporation in Los Angeles. While Brutoco didn't help get the loan, he did get next to Doug Ruhe and the two soon were fast friends.

Early in 1984, Brutoco persuaded Ruhe to hire Jerry Hillman as a consultant. Hillman, who came from a wealthy Boston family, was hired at $20,000 per month and he paved the way for still another consultant, Ray Wechsler, a former chief financial official for AT&T International.

Foothill finally agreed to loan UPI up to $4 million, but that was not nearly enough. Ruhe decided it was time for another sale and he handled this deal himself, secretly. Ruhe stunned his key editorial and international executives by agreeing to sell UPI's foreign newspicture operations to Reuters for a total of $5.7 million.

Reuters got all of the UPI foreign photo staff and all of its overseas customers. UPI agreed to provide Reuters with pictures from America and Reuters would provide foreign pictures for the company's customers in the United States.

When Nogales finally caught up with the UPI numbers, he was thunderstruck. He told Ruhe and Geissler that expenses had to be drastically reduced. He recommended cutting the staff by 200 people and seeking concessions from the Wire Service Guild.

UPI had lost $14 million in 1983, faced debts of $15 million, and 1984 losses were running at $1 million a month. The move of the company headquarters, budgeted at $1.5 million had ballooned to an estimated $5 million and Ruhe's plan for a satellite system using 10-foot Harris dishes had failed.

Aware that the agency was facing bankruptcy, the Guild reluctantly agreed to accept steep pay cuts in exchange for 6.5 percent of the stock of Media News Corporation, the Ruhe and Geissler holding company that owned UPI. Top scale editors and reporters who would have been making $580 a week would get only $420.

The 200 employees cut from the payroll eventually included company president Bill Small. With Nogales now running UPI, Small had little to do. The former network TV newsman refused an initial UPI settlement offer and kept returning to his office until the locks were changed. Later, he sued the company, Ruhe and Geissler for breach of contract. His claim was settled out of court.

Nogales was named president. He assembled a team of executives he thought could save UPI; Ray Wechsler, consultant Jerry Hillman and Jack Kenney, another financial adviser.

Nogales' team succeeded in keeping the tap open for emergency loans from Foothill. But bigger problems remained. UPI was losing $1.5 million per month, according to Wechsler. Ruhe and Geissler adamantly refused to surrender any control to attract investors. They also refused to consider chapter 11 bankruptcy protection for fear they would lose control.

The solution seemed simple to the Nogales team: get rid of Ruhe and Geissler.

Ruhe and Geissler were also taking a hard stand. They had hired their own money man, Rinaldo Brutoco, as president of their Media News Corporation at $50,000 per month and instructed him to raise money by selling the corporation's three small television stations.

Two teams fighting for control of United Press International: Nogales-Wechsler-Hillman-Kenny versus Ruhe-Geissler-Brutoco. Oddly, not one of the seven had ever been a Unipresser, not one had battled AP to be first with a bulletin, or pulled up to a Teletype at 5 A.M. to write an early morning newscast for broadcasters.

Those two warring factions carried their battle all the way to bankruptcy court where the only truce was a bitter agreement to sell UPI to the highest bidder. The only bidder who had the money to get it out of bankruptcy was Mexican publisher Mario Vasquez-Rana.

37

Gone!

MARIO VAZQUEZ-RANA SPENT MILLIONS OF DOLLARS TO PROVE THAT UPI'S problems were much deeper than just financial.

The feisty Mexican businessman was certain he could make a success of UPI, just as he had with a string of furniture stores and newspapers in Mexico. He was willing to bet his considerable fortune that he could.

Aides to the new owner had scrutinized the financial records of UPI from the Scripps-Howard days to the bankruptcy. And Vazquez had a personal ace in the hole: his UPI translator and confidant, Pieter VanBennekom.

Austrian-born Pieter VanBennekom was a battle-tested veteran of seventeen years with UPI who had scoured the capitals of Europe. Africa and Latin America, working as a reporter, an editor, a salesman and a manager.

Fluent in six languages and schooled in UPI politics, VanBennekom was invaluable to Vazquez-Rana and always at his side, seemingly the only English-speaking UPI executive trusted by the new owner. Even with VanBennekom's experience and his own bare-knuckle knack for making money, Vazquez-Rana didn't see what UPI needed most at the time: stability and credibility.

The revolving door at the top, the power struggles during the Ruhe and Geissler years, the disruption of constant staff cuts and the resulting service reductions had shattered the reputation UPI built during the seventy-five years tenure of Scripps-Howard.

Stability seemed to be the last thing on Vazquez-Rana's mind, control was uppermost. Within two years, he fired three presidents, two editors-in-chief and four managing editors.

Short and stocky, the mustachioed Vazquez-Rana was a hands-on boss who could not read, write or speak English. This handicap made the Mexican publisher suspicious of most of UPI's existing top managers. Luis Nogales had a good idea of what UPI needed, over and above Vazquez-Rana's money, but he became the first top-level casualty when he tried to steer his stubborn new boss.

When Vazquez-Rana first came aboard, Nogales organized a coast-to-coast tour so that the new owner of UPI could meet its most important clients.

Nogales, Editor Max McCrohon, sales executives John Mantle and Tom Beatty joined Vazquez-Rana in his sleek private jet, a three-engine Falcon 50, on a one-week, hop-scotch journey from Boston to California.

The trip was a disaster. Rather than sit back and let the experienced UPI executives handle these vital meetings with publishers and broadcast executives, Vazquez took center stage with clumsy bravado. Speaking only Spanish through an interpreter, Vazquez boasted unrealistically of a rosy future for the struggling wire service.

Donald Graham of the *Washington Post* refused the new owner's gift of a bottle of expensive Tequila. In Chicago, *Sun-Times* publisher Robert Page, a former UPI general manager, took several of the UPI executives aside and told them that Vazquez need not come back until he could speak some English.

Vazquez even struck out when he tried to impress his UPI guests with his jet's luxurious accommodations. As the Falcom 50 was climbing out of Chicago's O'Hare airport on a flight to Los Angeles, Vazquez decided to showcase the entertainment center and shoved a video into a hidden VCR. The picture popped up on several television screens, and, behold, it was a porno film. Mantle, an unflappable Brit, laughed uproariously and slapped his thigh as Vazquez dove to eject the movie.

Nogales had several times pulled UPI operations from the brink. He saw the signs of trouble when Vazquez-Rana was slow to provide a promised $1.5 million in operating capital. When Nogales realized that without the money payroll checks could bounce once more, he threatened to sue the new owner and call a news conference to tell the world why. Vazquez sent the money,

In June 1986, right after a champagne party on the ninth floor of the UPI building in Washington to mark the arrival of the new owner, Vazquez-Rana told Nogales that he could not work with him.[1]

The charismatic Nogales threatened to sue for the balance of his contract and finally settled for a $350,000 buyout. Nogales announced his departure on July 8, 1986, without mention of his dispute with UPI's new owner.

Vazquez-Rana also moved to minimize the role of minority partner Joe Russo. Vazquez-Rana had named the Houston real estate mogul head of UPI's sales operations, but he told two top UPI sales executives, William Adler and Arthur Bushnell, that they would report directly to him.

Adler, a vice president in charge of public information, had the job of trying to make all the departures and changes look positive. He also had an eye for sound bytes.

Adler recorded for posterity the parting shots of four UPI Presidents who left during his watch:

Rod Beaton to Adler: "Don't let the bastards screw the place up."

Bill Small to the New York phone operator: "Catherine, I'm going to lunch, and I'll never be back."

Ray Wecshler to no one in particular at the elevator: "I only wanted to help."

Luis Nogales at his goodbye party: "Don't forget what the whole thing is about."

Vazquez-Rana's "one-man rule" had also spread into UPI's editorial operation. The new owner, aided by VanBennekom, had blocked the appointment of cables desker Louis Toscano to replace Mexico City bureau manager Fred Keil, even though the move had been approved by foreign editor Sylvana Foa and editor Max McCrohon. Toscano had already moved to Mexico City when he was met by VanBennekom who told him he had to return to Washington because he didn't speak Spanish.

McCrohon, who had long straddled the executive fences at UPI, was miffed that he had been overruled, but he was unable to change Mario's mind, mainly because Vazquez-Rana had already decided that McCrohon was part of the problem and not part of the solution.

To solve the problem, McCrohon was "kicked upstairs," just as he had been at the *Chicago Tribune*. He was named president, replacing Nogales. Sylvana Foa was fired soon after International vce president Mike Hughes was named Editor.

The fingerprints of Vazquez-Rana, a workaholic who routinely was in his office eighteen hours a day, were everywhere.

Just weeks after naming Hughes editor, Vazquez-Rana approved a sweeping editorial re-organization without once consulting his new top editorial aide. Vazquez approved a plan to replace UPI's six domestic editorial divisions with twelve smaller regions in an effort to bring editorial direction closer to its clients. Hughes was furious and angrily confronted Vazquez-Rana, which succeeded only in putting Hughes in the new owner's doghouse.

Hughes brought UPI's London news editor, Barry James, to Washington to replace Sylvana Foa as foreign editor. During a meeting with Vazquez-Rana, James said he was offered Ron Cohen's job as managing editor. James said that at a later meeting, after Vazquez-Rana had another falling out with Hughes, he offered him Mike's job as editor.

Hughes was discouraged with Vazquez-Rana but he had put together his own plan to replace Cohen and appoint three executive editors. Mike's plan called for naming James as executive editor for foreign operations; Billy Ferguson, editor of UPI's Broadcast Service, would become executive editor for national operations, and Mike Freedman, editor of UPI's radio network, would be appointed executive editor for broadcast.

Ron Cohen told this story of his meeting with Hughes in *Down to the Wire*, the book Cohen wrote with Greg Gordon.

Cohen said Hughes called him into his office at 4 P.M. and closed the door.

"Sorry, mate, I'm not going to make you one of the new executive editors. You can stay through the elections, do some writing, have some fun while you're looking for something else. I won't insult you by offering you something below your stature. The one thing I want to do is make sure you walk out of here with honor and dignity."

Vazquez-Rana was preoccupied with his chess game of staff changes and not paying enough attention to UPI's fading relationship with its biggest and most influential newspaper subscriber, *The New York Times*.

Nogales and McCrohon had persuaded the *Times* to continue its UPI service through 1986 with a promise that UPI would beef up its foreign coverage by adding six new staffers overseas.

Inexplicably' Vazquez-Rana stalled on approving the six new jobs and, on October 27, the *Times* ran a story announcing that it would drop its UPI service at the end of the year. The *Times*, which operated its own syndicated new service, said it had better things to do with its money.

In addition to the revenue loss of more than $800,000 a year, the *Times* cancellation caused a broadening ripple effect among newspaper publishers looking for excuses to drop UPI and improve their bottom lines.

McCrohon had had it. The chain-smoking UPI president had been isolated and cut out of most of UPI's decisions. The last straw came when Vazquez-Rana broke the promise McCrohon made to the *Times*. He told the UPI owner he wanted out and wanted the $350,000 that his contract provided for such an eventuality.

Mario didn't try to talk McCrohon into reconsidering. The CEO-turned-personnel-player had already started the search for McCrohon's replacement and had hired consultant Milt Benjamin to help.

Benjamin was a former *Washington Post* foreign editor who had worked for UPI as a reporter in Boston and Washington. Vazquez-Rana originally hired Benjamin to conduct a secret search for a new president. However, when McCrohon opened the door, Vazquez-Rana persuaded the well-connected Benjamin to personally come aboard as president.

On November 6, 1986, UPI ran a story announcing McCrohon's departure and Benjamin's appointment. One the same day, Ron Cohen revealed on UPI's message wire that he had been fired.

Five months into his watch, Vazquez-Rana had obliterated any hope of stability and his new president had plans for even more disruption.

Benjamin, a towering man at six-foot eight-inches, had also served as an assistant to *Washington Post* Chairman Katherine Graham, and he felt that he could lure from the *Post* the talent UPI needed.

Mike Hughes resigned as editor after a meeting with Benjamin. Hughes said the new UPI president told him he felt UPI needed a "big name" editor.

The top three editors of UPI—McCrohon, Cohen and Hughes—were all gone in a matter of weeks. Benjamin appointed Billy Ferguson acting managing editor to hold the editorial helm until recruits could be found at the *Washington Post*.

Early in the new year, 1987, Benjamin introduced his new editorial team. There were no "big name" editors, but all three had solid credentials from the *Washington Post* and the Post-owned *Newsweek* magazine.

Benjamin introduced the new editors at a cocktail party. Two of three were mid-level editors at the *Washington Post*; Barry Sussman, who had directed the Watergate coverage of Bob Woodward and Carl Bernstein; and Ben Cason, an assistant managing editor. The third editor was Kim Willenson, who had helped cover the Vietnam War for UPI and most recently was a reporter-writer at *Newsweek*. Benjamin said the three, along with Billy Ferguson, would serve as managing editors until one proved himself the man to serve as UPI's editor.

Benjamin was beaming. His plan to make UPI look like the *Washington Post* was off and running. Vazquez-Rana was smiling, but he wasn't happy. The three editors had signed iron-clad contracts that totaled nearly $2 million over five years.

Ferguson, at the time a 36-year veteran with UPI, told radio network manager Mike Freedman, "I feel like a bastard at a family reunion."

Benjamin felt he had carte blanche when he offered generous contracts, complete with "golden parachutes," to lure the three men from the comfort of the *Post* to the uncertainty that was UPI. Vazquez-Rana didn't think he had offered Benjamin such a blank check.

To temporarily ease the void at the top, Benjamin named himself as editor as well as president of UPI. Cason would continue as executive editor for regional news, Sussman as executive editor for national; Willensen as executive editor for foreign news and Ferguson as executive editor for broadcast.

Benjamin had to divert his attention from the simmering contract dispute between Vaquez-Rana and his three new editors to concentrate on a flood of newspaper cancellations. Traveling with sales chief Charles Hollingsworth, another *Washington Post* recruit, Benjamin hit the road to put out the spreading fires. Determined to head-off any more defections, Benjamin offered drastic rate cuts to UPI's highest-paying customers, the *Chicago Tribune* and *Chicago Sun-Times;* the *Detroit Free-Press;* the *Atlanta Constitution;* the *Houston Post;* the *Philadelphia Inquirer;* the *Seattle Post-Intelligencer* and the *Portland Oregonian.*

Vazquez was furious with his hand-picked president and editor. In addition to the generous contracts he had given the three new editors, Benjamin's "deals" to save newspaper cancellations were taking a toll on UPI's bottom line. Cutting rates succeeded in winning UPI some contract extensions, but the lower rates went into effect immediately and significantly reduced UPI's current newspaper revenues. The final straw probably was added just a few blocks from the UPI building in Washington. Benjamin was so anxious to keep UPI's newswires at the *Washington Post,* he gave Editor Ben Bradlee a year of free service.

UPI's losses were piling up at the rate of $2 million per month and Vazquez-Rana was frustrated.

Half-joking, Vazquez-Rana told the Broadcast Advisory Board, "UPI made me a millionaire. Before I bought UPI, I was a multi-millionaire."

Benjamin knew that Vazquez-Rana was only half-joking. The consultant who became president and editor in just one month decided to leave UPI even though he was still one month short of the six-month period considered probationary for most Unipressers. Nevertheless, the crafty Benjamin left with a smile that cost Vazquez-Rana another quarter of a million dollars.

With Benjamin gone, Vazquez-Rana set his sights on his new editor, Ben Cason, along with Barry Sussman and Kim Willenson. The trio had contracts that assured them unfettered editorial control and Mario had lawyers trying to break those contracts.

When the new top editors proposed hiring a number of editors and reporters at salaries far above the top union scale, Vazquez-Rana countered by setting up a screening committee to approve all hires. Editorial had a seat on the committee, but Mario controlled it.

UPI's client services sagged as its top three editors and Vazquez-Rana, who had now assumed the title of president as well as chief executive officer, waged a destructive war of wills.

Vazquez had taken over the negotiations with the Wire Service Guild and was trying to win a new contract that would clear the way for layoffs in exchange for a very modest pay increase. At the beginning of November, Vazquez-Rana gave Cason two weeks to come up with a plan to cut 250 editorial jobs.

Cason, Sussman, Willinsen and their attorney launched a vigorous protest and the three editors let it be known that if Vazquez-Rana did not grant their demands for editorial control, they would leave UPI.

With contract negotiations deadlocked and UPI's top bosses at each other's throats once again, weary UPI staffers updated their resumes and crossed their fingers. A group of mid-level editorial managers came to Washington to try to mediate in the battle between Mario and his editors. The group included division news editors Jim Weick, from Dallas and Jaques Clafin from Los Angeles; sports editor David Tucker, New York; and Lou Carr, the veteran chief of UPI's general news desk in Washington.

The managers ran into a communications lapse that was aggravating all of UPI's current problems. Vazquez-Rana was spending his 18-hour days in Mexico City to avoid logging more than six months in the United States and paying U.S taxes. Unable to meet with Mario face to face, the group faxed its plea for a truce to Mexico City.

On November 1, Vazquez-Rana' representatives declared an impasse in the union negotiation and two days later, the three top editors, Cason, Sussman and Willenson, announced they were resigning. Many UPI staffers were furious when the three announced that they could "no longer assure the quality and integrity of the UPI report." Most Unipressers were unhappy with what had happened to the company in the last six years, but they felt they had somehow upheld the quality and integrity of the news reports and that the three men they had nicknamed "The Post Toasties" had little to do with it.

The imports from the *Post* were being paid twice as much as veteran UPI editors who had been around for their entire careers and were still doing the "nuts and bolts" of the news operation.

Cason, Sussman and Willenson sued UPI for a total of one-million dollars for breach of contract. Vazquez-Rana counter sued, claiming the three had breached the contract by defaming UPI.

With Mario marooned in Mexico, Pieter VanBennekom was pulling UPI's strings in Washington. He decided that UPI needed to get back some of its old image and he turned to veteran UPI managers to fill the editorial void. Science editor Al Rossiter was appointed executive editor; Billy Ferguson was named managing editor national; Leon Daniel, one of UPI's top reporters who had distinguished himself in Vietnam, was appointed managing editor foreign and UPI radio boss Mike Freedman was named managing editor broadcast.

VanBennekom had a bigger problem to solve. Vazquez-Raana wanted him to find a buyer for UPI. Mario wanted to go home to Mexico City, somehow save face and maybe get back some of the reported $50 million he had poured into UPI.

While UPI's new editors wrestled with the impossible task of cutting another 100 jobs without trimming UPI services, VanBennekom was looking at a way to cut just one job, that of president and chief executive officer Mario Vazquez-Rana, without endangering his own position of power.

The answer was the runner-up in the chapter-11 sweepstakes that Vazquez had won, Dr. Earl Bryan and the Financial News Network. Few negotiators other than VanBennekom could have brought the two enemies, Vazquez-Rana and Bryan, together. Bryan didn't want to spend any money to buy UPI and Vazquez-Rana didn't want to pour any more of his millions into the wire service. The Wire Service Guild offered a third obstacle since Mario contractually had given the union first refusal rights on any sale.

The solution was that Vazquez-Rana didn't sell UPI to FNN, instead he sold his "proxy" to Bryan for ten years. Vazquez-Rana remained the owner but Bryan had total operating control of UPI until 1997. Bryan and Vazquez-Rana were happy, the guild was shutout and VanBennekom remained in the driver's seat as executive vice president.

On paper, Earl Bryan looked great. In addition to the highly successful Financial News Network, Bryan's Infotechnology Inc., operated or was involved with more than two dozen high-tech companies. He was well-connected, bright and had left a promising medical career to jump into the information age.

The 45-year-old Bryan, who had served as a surgeon in Vietnam, seemed to have what Vazquez-Rana didn't, a keen understanding of corporate America.

As it turned out, Vazquez-Rana also had something that Dr. Earl Bryan didn't, a lot of money. Bryan's "Infotechnology" turned out to be a house of cards built on a maze of financial dealing that finally landed Bryan in a federal penitentiary for fraud.

As 1987 drew to a close, however, UPI was somehow still alive and Bryan was promising better days, just as Ruhe, Geissler and Vazquez-Rana had before him.

The UPI handed to Bryan was less than half of what Ruhe and Geissler got in 1982. The UPI staff had been cut from nearly 1,800 to less than 900. The client base of 4,500 newspaper and broadcast subscribers had shrunk to less than 2,400.

Bryan's right-hand man, Paul Steinle, became UPI's seventh president in seven years. Steinle had good credentials. A former journalist with an MBA, Steinle had served as a reporter in Southeast Asia for Group-W Broadcasting and was a news director for TV station KING in Seattle before he became news director of FNN.

Bryan and Steinle planned to make UPI healthy by serving emerging markets as well as newspapers and broadcasters, and by making UPI as efficient as possible with improved computer and communication systems. New computers and programs, along with improved microprocessors on the communication system, would enable reporters and editors to write their news stories in a manner that would serve newspapers, broadcasters, databases and other emerging markets with a single transmission.

But doing more with less meant new, demoralizing staff cuts and a resulting loss of confidence in the broadcast and newspaper markets. With very few full-service newspaper clients still under contract, UPI announced that it would "unbundle" its wire service and sell separate parts, like sports, business, lifestyles, etc. at reduced rates.

UPI reporters became multi-media, reporting for print and broadcast, doing voice and actuality cuts for the Radio Network and even shooting pictures in some instances. Instead of assigning four staffers to campaign with the presidential hopefuls as in the past, just one UPI staffer, responsible for everything, covered each candidate during the 1988 political campaign. Photographers did aid in the coverage when they were available. Most campaign reporters gave it their best shots, but obviously they weren't able to do the quality work that four had done in the past.

Bryan was a big man, loud and intense; his orders were usually high-tech, laced with profanity. Many UPI executives found the North Carolina native hard to work for. However, Bryan knew that UPI needed to show some stability. He initially kept his editorial team intact and named Pieter VanBennekom UPI's chief executive officer, a move that led to Steinle's resignation as president 11 months later.

I.J. Vidacovich, a former reporter and sales executive, was the keeper of the keys to the executive offices at UPI. As vice president for client relations, Vidacovich headed the Newspaper and Broadcast Advisory Boards and kept the news agency's top clients up to date. It was his job to introduce the new players at UPI and explain, as credibly as possible, who they were and why they could help UPI.

Vidacovich, known as "Pinky" throughout UPI, had paraded eight UPI presidents before the boards and countless other top executives. With Bryan in charge, "Pinky" had more new executives to introduce. Most of new faces were from Bryan's past and lacking experience in journalism.

A square-jawed former Navy fighter pilot named Joe Taussig was hired as UPI's general manager. Taussig decided, like many before him, that UPI needed someone with more newspaper background and he hired Jim White as a vice president and executive editor. White had retired as publisher of the Florida *Times-Union* in Jacksonville. White lasted less than six months at UPI.

In the summer of 1990, Brian was dismayed that nothing seemed to be working. UPI losses were mounting and none of his high-tech projects had made it to the marketplace. Brian ordered VanBennekom to drastically cut UPI's expenses and told him Infotech would no longer cover UPI's losses. VanBennekom and his closest confidant, personnel director Ann Kott, whom he later married, hurriedly drew up plans for closing bureaus, pay cuts and a round of firings that included managing editor Billy Ferguson and division news editors Jim Wieck in Dallas and Jaques Clafin in Los Angeles.

It was too little and too late. In 1991, the *New York Times* ran a story quoting VanBennekom that UPI would seek protection under a Chapter 11 bankruptcy petition. UPI editors were shocked that UPI didn't have the story. Inexplicably, VanBennekom had given the *Times* an exclusive on the wire service's plans for a second trip into bankruptcy.

Editor Al Rossiter was temporarily diverted from the internal developments by Iraq's invasion of oil-rich Kuwait. He needed to quickly arrange coverage of the U.S. "Desert Storm" incursion into the Middle East. His new Washington bureau chief, Beryl Schwartz, had taken a six-month leave of absence. Rossiter appointed Steve Geimann, the assistant managing editor for regional, as the new Washington news manager and told him to put together a team of reporters to travel to the desert with U.S. armed forces.

Rossiter, who had also been saddled with the job of UPI's director of public relations, resigned early in 1992 and Van Bennekom appointed Geimann vice president and executive editor. Bob Kieckhefer, who was running UPI's operations in Chicago, was brought to Washington and named managing editor.

UPI's bankruptcy was moving toward a final assets sale in May of 1992 and the major bidder was Pat Robertson, owner of the Christian Broadcast Network, who had offered $6 million. But Robertson wanted 30 days for "due diligence" since UPI was unable to share any financial or operational details before the asset sale.

UPI editorial leadership 1987: Editor Al Rossiter, Jr., (seated); from left standing, Mike Freedman, managing editor broadcast; Leon Daniel, managing editor foreign; Billy Ferguson, managing editor national.

Robertson's people weren't thrilled with what they found during their extensive investigation of UPI. Robertson dropped his bid from $6 million to a reported $500,000.

The company rejected Robertson's bid and put itself in a hole since the well-known television preacher had been providing operating funds for UPI on a week-to-week basis.

UPI staffers were generally pleased because they felt that Robertson had a religious agenda. However, they weren't much happier when the next bidder appeared. The Middle East Broadcast Centre Ltd. of London announced that it was interested in buying UPI. The company was less than one-year old, but it apparently had money and had operated a television station for the Middle East and Africa.

UPI had broken the will, the hearts and the bank accounts of many would-be owners, but still they lined up. A New York real estate broker, Leon Charney, said he would bid on UPI. Charney, who also hosted a public television show on the Middle East, put up $180,000 to keep UPI operating for ten days so that a new asset sale could be arranged.

At the second auction, there were three bidders. Robertson opened at $900,000; Middle East Broadcast raised it to $3.5 million, then, in succession, Middle East and Charney pushed the price up to $3.95 million. Charney couldn't match the $3.95 million and asked for additional time to raise more money. After five hours, the judge closed the auction and declared that Middle East Broadcast was the new owner of UPI.

VanBennekom, who had survived longer than anyone on the 9th floor at 1400 Eye street, would leave. Even though he had steered the company through still another bankruptcy, the new owners told the durable Austrian that they wanted an America in charge and would bring in a new CEO. After guaranteeing his "golden parachute," VanBennekom resigned.

The new owners, now called Worldwide News, Inc., took over on June 28, 1992. They bought UPI out of bankruptcy and were free of any of UPI's liabilities. They immediately voided the Wire Service Guild contract and asked all employees to agree to new working terms to keep their jobs. The terms included two weeks vacation, some holidays off and overtime for work above forty hours. Bob McNeill, a longtime Washington desker and style expert, refused to sign and left the company.

It took the new owners nearly one year to find a new chief executive officer. During that time, Robert Kennedy, a London-based consultant to the Arabs, established a CEO office in Washington with Geimann, Anne Kott and chief financial officer David Noir. The three would make decisions as needed and consult Kennedy when it was essential.

Worldwide News hired the consulting firm of Booz, Allen and Hamilton for $1 million to come up with an operating plan. Their agents met with many UPI staffers and UPI clients, but came up with very little in the way of a rescue plan.

UPI did finally hire a new CEO. L. Brewster Jackson, a former top executive with Reuters, was brought aboard in 1995 with a three-year contract worth a reported $1 million.

Steve Geimann, who was eased out of his job as executive vice president and editor, said that Jackson seemed to concentrate on appearances at UPI and never did come up with a viable operating plan. He said the haughty CEO spent days consulting on questions of office decor and seemed to revel in adding a jumbo world map to the ninth floor conference room.

With Geimann gone, UPI's editorial direction shifted to two other veterans, national editor Tobin Beck and international editor Bob Martin directed UPI's news coverage even though they worked with different titles as more changes were made on the 9th floor.

Beck, a solid, low-key news manager, had worked as a state editor in Nebraska, as a regional editor and then as a managing editor in Washington. Martin was a Los Angeles bureau manager who also became a regional editor and managing editor in Washington.

By the time former Worldwide advisor Jack Hayes replaced Jackson as CEO in 1996, UPI was basically a broadcast news service with only a few small newspaper clients. The national broadcast department had moved from Chicago to Washington where it could work closely with the UPI Radio Network. Howard Dicus, the Network Director, was named general manager of all broadcast services. UPI's broadcast services were having major distribution problems since there were no newspaper services to share the satellite communications costs.

James Adams, who replaced Hayes as CEO in the summer of 1997, felt that the internet was the solution to UPI's fading customer base and high communications costs. He not only worked to move UPI services onto the internet but boasted that UPI was at the cutting edge of new internet services; including data security as well as focused, analytical items on significant news.

UPI's news reports were displayed on a number of worldwide web pages, but the push into these emerging markets apparently produced little revenue. UPI's traditional revenue base, now almost exclusively broadcast, continued to wither and Worldwide News was forced to cover growing losses.

Adams' watch at the helm of UPI lasted only fourteen months. Next to move into the CEO's office was Arnaud de Borchgrave, a former editor of the *Washington Times*, who eventually would ring down the curtain on UPI as a traditional wire service.

The new CEO said he wanted to transform UPI from a news service that was a "mile wide and an inch deep" to one that is "an inch wide and a mile deep."

In 1998, UPI had very little national recognition beyond Helen Thomas, the longtime dean of the White House press corps. However, de Borchgrave, who had won wide respect as a foreign correspondent, just about scored a major triumph with an exclusive interview with Yugoslavian President Slobadon Milosevic. It was UPI's last big beat, but since UPI no longer served any major newspaper, the story got scant attention. And through a strange quirk, AP also got de Borchgrave's interview. Even though he was CEO at UPI, de Borchgrave remained an editorial advisor at the *Washington Times*. When the *Times* ran the story, AP was able to pick it up under the terms of its contract with the *Times*.

UPI had not found a formula for profitability by the middle of 1999 and on August 6, de Borchgrave ended UPI's 92-year run as a traditional wire service.

In a joint announcement with the Associated Press, de Borchgrave said UPI was selling all of its broadcast services, along with their clients to AP and would switch exclusively to internet delivery of its news.

The sale involved more than 400 broadcast stations, all in the United States. De Borchgrave said forty-seven people at UPI would be fired.

"It is time to move on," he said, "The world does not need another traditional wire service."

The day had finally arrived. Associated Press reporters no longer needed to hurry to the phone.

Endnotes

Chapter 1

1. The third man in the press pool, Sid Davis of Westinghouse Broadcasting, got off *Air Force One* before it took off to remain in Dallas and brief the reporters left behind.
2. *Kennedy Assassinated* by William Bradford Hampton.
3. Lorenz recalled that Darr lifted Guenther from her chair. Roberts believes Darr pushed Guenther aside in her chair and leaned over to reach the Teletype and transmit the flash.
4. *American Journalism Review.*

Chapter 2

1. *AP, the Story of News*, Oliver Gramling, J. J. Little, New York, 1940, p. 19.
2. *Nation's Newsbrokers Vol. 1*, Richard A. Schwarzlose, Northwestern University Press, 1990. Schwarzlose said "newsbrokers" was more fitting than "wire service" for what UP and AP did. He defined this as "the daily collection and distribution of general news dispatches via communication systems among journalists in several communities, a process controlled by an agent or agency."
3. *American Mercury.*

Chapter 3

1. *Lusty Scripps, the Life of E. W. Scripps 1854–1926*, Gilson Gardner, Vanguard Press, New York City, 1932, p. 10.
2. Ibid.
3. *Great Companions*, Max Eastman, Farrar, Straus and Cudahy, New York, 1951, Chapter "Old Man Scripps," p. 8.
4. In 1979 when a UP story referred to E.W. there was the following exchange of messages on the interbureau wire between the New York desk editor, Hy Heller, and John D. Lowry, bureau manager in Los Angeles: (Lowry to Heller) "When the middle name of E.W. Scripps comes up, I usually spell it WYLLIS, the way he himself did in a letter." (Heller to Lowry) "Called Scripps people and they say they have statues with name spelled WYLLIS. But the board chairman of Scripps says the birth certificate spells it WILLIS and that's the way they want it in any story."
5. *I Protest*, p. 453.
6. *Astonishing Mr. Scripps*, p. 486, a memo from Robert E. Winkler to Vance H. Trimble on September 21, 1981.

7. Ibid, p. 183.
8. *Lusty Scripps*, p. 112.
9. *I Protest*, p. 486.
10. *Journalism History*, 21:2, summer, 1995.
11. *National Cyclopedia of American Biography*, E.W. Scripps.
12. *Great Companions*, Max Eastman, Farrar Straus and Cudahy, New York, 1949, "Old Man Scripps."
13. *New Yorker*, August 9, 1941, by A. J. Liebling.
14. *I Protest*, p. 486.
15. Ibid, p. 415.
16. Ibid, p. 414–415.
17. Ibid, p. 599.
18. Ibid, p. 237.
19. Ibid, p. 238.
20. *Damned Old Crank*, p. 198.

Chapter 4

1. *Deadline Every Minute*, Joe Alex Morris, Doubleday, 1957, p. 27.
2. *I Protest*, E.W. Scripps, University of Wisconsin Press, 1966, p. 3.
3. Ibid, p. 203.
4. *San Francisco Chronicle*.
5. President Theodore Roosevelt wished to "show the flag" in the Pacific. He sent the U.S. fleet over from the Atlantic under Admiral "Fighting Bob" Evans. UP hired Norman Rose, a Navy crewman aboard Adams' flagship, to provide stories. Rose filed a couple of items by radio through the Navy station at Pensacola. The only significant news that came through from him was a report on the illness of Admiral Evans. It really wasn't a great scoop but UP was seeking some attention as the new fellow in the news business.

Chapter 5

1. *Covering the Far East*, Miles Vaughn, Covici Friede Publishers, New York, 1936, p. 375.
2. Ibid, p. 377–78.
3. Ibid, p. 378.
4. Ibid, p. 388.
5. *I Protest*, Oliver Knight, University of Wisconsin Press, Madison, Wis., 1966, p. 312.
6. Ibid, p. 308.
7. Ibid, p. 49.
8. Ibid, p. 310.
9. *Astonishing*, p. 476.
10. *Press Lord* by Forrest Davis, *Saturday Evening Post*, vol. 210, no. 37, March 12, 1938, p. 32. When he was asked about this later, he said it was untrue and that he slept "in the raw."

11. *Divided Dynasty*, Jack Casserly, p. 1.
12. *Toronto Evening Telegram*, March 6, 1917.
13. Ibid, March 6, 1917.
14. Ibid, March 6, 1917, p. 4.
15. *Editor & Publisher,* November 11, 1916.
16. Letter to Howard, September 10, 1960. RWH Archives. quoted by Wieten p. 36.
17. The comparisons with Napoleon resulted because "both men were energetic and restless careerists, who disposed or were assumed to dispose, enormous, unprecedented power, and the will to use that power. The comparison was also easily made in view of the stature of both men," p. 32.
18. *World Press News*, April 18, 1929.

Chapter 6
1. "The Associated Press and Journalist Jazz," the "Independent," vol. 120, no. 4066, p. 425.
2. *Power of News: A History of Reuters*, gives 1911. *Deadline Every Minute* gives 1912.
3. See Scripps Family Tree, *Editor & Publisher*, May 9, 1936, p. 8.
4. *Kent Cooper and the Associated Press*, autobiography, Random House, 1959, p. 34.
5. Oswald Garrison Villard, *The Nation*, May 17, 1930, p. 540.
6. *New York Times* , January 25, 1918, p. 3.
7. *New York Times*, June 22, 1917, "Citizen Hearst," p. 306.
8. Ibid, June 23, 1917, p. 8:3.
9. Ibid, June 23, 1917, p. 8:3.
10. *Harper's*, October 9, 1915. "Citizen Hearst," p. 299.
11. Minutes of General Editorial Conference, January 11, 1911.

Chapter 7
1. *I Found No Peace*, Webb Miller.
2. Ibid, Webb Miller.
3. Ibid, Webb Miller.
4. *Deadline. Every Minute.*
5. *The Chief,* David Nasaw, Chapter 14.
6. Ibid, David Nasaw, Chapter 14.
7. *I Found No Peace*, Webb Miller.
8. *Witness to a* Century, George Seldes, p. 85–86.
9. Reuters History, p. 145.

Chapter 8
1. *Mr. Howard Goes to South America*, Terhi Rantanen, Roy Howard Monographs, Indiana University, no. 2, May 15, 1992.
2. Fenby, p. 49.
3. *New York Times*, March–April 1944.

4. Ibid, p. 92.

5. The International News Services, p. 7.

6. R.A. Litfin conversation with R. Harnett.

7. Ibid, p. 71.

8. Fenby, p. 206.

9. Executives of all three American services, in their memoirs, claim credit for ending the cartel, Kent Cooper of AP, Karl Bickel and Hugh Baillie of United Press, and Koenisberg of International News Service.

10. Letter to R. M. Harnett.

Chapter 9

1. *New York Times*, June 21, 1946, 10:6.

2. John F. Barton, in letter to authors.

3. Interview by author with John Hlavacek.

Chapter 10

1. Howard to his mother on June 13, 1918, Howard Archive, cited by Rantanen.

2. *New York Times*, September 22, 1946, 32:2.

3. The radio-teletype circuit was named for a New York teletype operator named "Chester."

4. Letter to Harnett, 1997.

5. Buckingham said Lloyd confirmed this to him later but bore no grudge against Bradford for it.

6. *Editor & Publisher*, September 22, 1973.

7. Ibid, August 5, 1972.

8. Account by Jules Dubois, Overseas Press Club collection.

Chapter 11

1. *Deadline*, p. 196.

2. *New York Times*, March 13, 1926, p. 16.

3. Ibid.

Chapter 12

1. A letter from Hugh Baillie to broadcaster Paul White, August 1, 1947.

2. A letter from General Manager Frank Tremaine to President Mims Thomason, April 3, 1972.

Chapter 13

1. Baillie's interview with Chamberlain never moved on the wire. It was submitted to the British official to check and Chamberlain had his aides completely re-write it. UP declined to publish the version prepared by the British.

2. Letter from Joe Grigg to Harnett, January 12, 1995.

3. *High Tension.*

4. Letter to Bradford, January 24, 1950.

5. Letter from Hugh Scott Baillie, Jr.

6. Musel letter to Harnett.

7. Interview with Joe Morgan.

8. Interview with Joan Younger Dickinson, 1997.

Chapter 14

1. *Editor & Publisher*, April 30, 1927.

2. Oswald Garrison Villard, a press observer, said United Press was the first service to transmit news on the Teletype, but both the other services, AP and INS, claimed in promotional material that they had it first.

3. *The Brass Check*, Upton Sinclair, p. 406.

4. *The American Mercury*, vol. 10, no. 40, April 1927.

Chapter 15

1. *New Yorker*, December 12, 1936, p. 38.

2. *High Tension*.

3. Ibid, p. 118.

4. *I Found No Peace*, p. 132–33.

5. Morgan letter in Harnett files.

6. *On My Own*, Mary Knight, p. 84.

7. Ibid, Mary Knight, p. 157.

8. Wallace Carroll tape.

9. Leonard Mosley, *Lindbergh*, Doubleday New York, p. 114, quoting Waverly Root of the Paris *Chicago Tribune* bureau.

10. *Lindbergh*, p. 315.

11. Ibid, p. 232.

12. Ibid, p. 319.

13. Ibid, p. 58.

Chapter 16

1. *I Found No Peace*, p. 242.

2. *Balcony Empire*, p. 31.

3. Ibid.

4. *Deadline*, p. 205.

5. *Boot*, p. 90.

6. *High Tension*, p. 91.

7. *I Found No Peace*, p. 235.

8. *First Casualty*, p. 185.

9. *Rome Was My Beat*, Reynolds Packard, Lyle Stuart, p. 4.

10. *New York Times*, August 1, 2:39 3:2

11. Ibid, p. 9–12. In another Reynolds Packard memoir, *Balcony Empire*, published by Oxford University Press in 1942, the correspondent gave a somewhat different

account. He said Ciano was seated alone at a table with two bodyguards, when the Packards arrived at the club, and called them over to his table (p. 99).

12. *New York Times*, August 1 2/39 3:2 and 8/1 5/39 8:2.

Chapter 17

1. *Freely to Pass*, Edward W. Beattie, p. 157–58.
2. *Berlin Diary*, p. 221.
3. *Freely to Pass*, Edward W. Beattie, p. 204.
4. *Tides of War*, Robert W. Desmond.
5. *Freely to Pass*, Edward Beattie, Jr., p. 204.
6. Ibid, Edward Beattie, Jr., p. 205.
7. Dickinson papers at American Heritage Archive, Laramie, Wyoming.
8. William L. Shirer.
9. Letter from Richard McMillan to Richard Harnett, January 8, 1995.
10. *Twentieth Century Journey*, William L. Shirer.
11. Logan's unpublished memoir.
12. *A Reporter's Life*, Walter Cronkite, p. 106.
13. *Deadline Every Minute*, p. 276.
14. *A Reporter's Life*, p. 98–99.
15. *Editor & Publisher*, May 5, 1945.
16. *Deadline*, p. 284–85. Boyd Lewis in his book says this happened on river Mulder April 16.
17. *Editor & Publisher*, May 5, 1945.
18. This anecdote is from a telephone interview by Richard M. Harnett, with William Mandel, of Berkeley, California, on March 21, 1998.

Chapter 18

1. *Rape of Nanking*, or *In the Name of the Emperor*.
2. *New York Times*, September 28, 1939, p. 3.
3. *Editor & Publisher*.
4. Ibid, March 1935.
5. *More than Meets the Eye*, Fram Carl Mydans and from an interview by Hugh Crumpler with Hal Stewart September 5, 1996, published in CBIQF, a newsletter for veterans of the China Burma India theater.
6. *Editor & Publisher*, March 3, 1945.
7. Unpublished memoir *Logan's War*, p. 60.
8. *Editor & Publisher*, March 1945, p. 13–58.
9. Ibid, March 1945, p. 58.
10. *Can Tell It Now*, Robert Sherrod, published by the Overseas Press Club and E.P. Dutton, 1964.
11. British journalist Alistaire Cooke.

Chapter 19

1. *Los Angeles Times*, Sunday, October 10, 1982.
2. Letter to Downhold Club, R. W. Hefty, a former Unipresser.
3. *New York Times*, November 10, 1957.
4. Ibid, August 17, 1957, 2:7.

Chapter 20

1. Interview with R. M. Harnett, 1999.
2. *Editor & Publisher*, February 26, 1972.
3. *New York Times*, February 3, 1957, 21:6.
4. Ibid, January 6, 1957, 16:1, May 23, 1957, 5:5.
5. Ibid, February 22, 1958, 2:7.
6. Ibid, October 4, 1957, 3:3.
7. Ibid, February 3, 1958, 15:1.
8. Ibid, May 14, 1992.
9. Letter from Wilbur Landrey to R. Harnett, September 2000.
10. *New York Times* May 9, 1957, 14:6, May 11, 1957, 11:1.

Chapter 21

1. Letter to author, 1996.
2. *Once Upon a Distant War.*
3. Letter to author, 1996.
4. Memo to "All Unipressers," August 2, 1950.
5. *Asia Is My Beat.*

Chapter 22

1. Ken Smith, promotion manager of INS, in interview with R. Schwarzlose, September 1, 1970 (notes from Schwarzlose).
2. Koenigsberg memoir, *King News*, p. 464–65.
3. *Bart*, p. 213.
4. Ibid, p. 211.
5. Interview with R. Harnett, 1997.
6. *Bart*, p. 216.
7. Ibid, Memoirs of Frank Bartholomew.
8. *Editor & Publisher*, June 21, 1958.
9. Interview with R. Harnett, 1997.

Chapter 23

1. Bill Snead's reflections in the Lawrence *Journal-World.*
2. UPI Reporter, 1971.
3. *Editor &Publisher*, April 21, 1973.
4. *New York Times*, February 5, 1986, 28:6.

Chapter 24

1. The UPI Havana bureau remained open until 1969, with a Cuban citizen, Pedro Bonetti, providing limited news. He left Cuba voluntarily after an Associated Press representative was expelled and both AP and UPI bureaus were forced to close.

Chapter 25

1. Joe Morgan, interview with Harnett, July 1998.

Chapter 26

1. *First Casualty*, p. 419.
2. Letter to Charles Bernard of UP in Hawaii.
3. *Reporting Vietnam*, p. 67.
4. Ibid, p. 55.
5. Ibid, p. 35.
6. Ibid, p. 147.
7. Ibid, p. 219.
8. *New York Times*, April 1971.
9. *Editor & Publisher*, December 4, 1971.
10. *Reporting Vietnam*, p. 269.

Chapter 27

1. *Drew Pearson's Diaries*, Holt Rinehart, 1973, p. 474.

Chapter 30

1. *Editor & Publisher*, August 18, 1973.
2. *Editor & Publisher*, March 13, 1971.
3. Letter to Harnett.
4. *Editor & Publisher*, September 16, 1972, p. 11.
5. *Editor & Publisher*, October 5, 1974.
6. *Editor & Publisher*, October 19, 1974.

Chapter 31

1. *Editor & Publisher*, April 1, 1960.

Chapter 32

1. Beaton interview with Harnett.
2. *New York Times*, April 20, 1965, 50:4.

Chapter 33

1. *Dark Side of Camelot*, p. 105.
2. *Editor & Publisher*, April 1, 1972.
3. Ibid, June 9, 1959.
4. Ibid, March 15, 1980.

5. Conversation with Dick Harnett.
6. Interview with Dick Harnett.
7. *Wireport*, a Wire Service Guild newspaper, July 1961.
8. *Editor & Publisher*, March 21, 1964.

Chapter 34

1. Interview with author.
2. Beaton interview with Billy Ferguson.

Chapter 35

1. Page interview with Ferguson.
2. *Down to the Wire.*

Chapter 37

1. *Down to the Wire.*

Bibliography

Agee, Warren, Phil Ault and Ed Emery. *Introduction to Mass Communications.* New York, New York: Harper & Row, 1994.

American Correspondents and Journalists in Moscow 1917–1952, a bibliography of their books on the USSR, Department of State Bibliography No. 73 Washington, D.C.: December 1953.

Arnett, Peter. *Flash! The Associated Press Covers the World.* New York, New York: Harry N. Abrams, Inc., 1998.

Association for Education in Journalism. *Freedom vs. Control: The United States and World News Flow, a Plenary Session of the Association for Education* in *Journalism.* International Communication Division, 1979.

Baillie, Hugh. *High Tension.* New York, New York: Harper & Brothers, 1959.

———. *Two Battle Fronts.* New York, New York: United Press Association, 1943.

Baker, Russell. *Good Times.* New York, New York: William Morrow & Company, 1989.

Bartholomew, Frank H. *Bart.* Sonoma, California: Vine Brook Press, 1983.

Bassow, Whitman. *Moscow Correspondents Reporting on Russia from the Revolution to Glasnost.* New York, New York: William Morrow and Company, 1988.

Beattie, Edward W., Jr. *Diary of a Kriegie.* New York, New York: Thomas Crowell Company, 1946.

———. *Freely to Pass.* New York, New York: Thomas Y. Crowell Company, 1942.

Behr, Edward. *Good Frenchman: The True Story of the Life and Times of Maurice Chevalier.* New York, New York: Villard Books, 1993.

———. *Hirohito, Behind the Myth.* New York, New York: Villard Books, 1989.

Behrens, John. *Typewriter Guerillas.* Chicago, Illinois: Nelson Hall Company, 1977.

Bent, Silas. *Ballyhoo, the Voice of the Press.* New York, New York: Boni & Liveright, 1927.

Bickel, Karl A. *New Empires.* Philadelphia, Pennsylvania: J. B. Lippincott, 1930.

———. *First Twenty Years.* 1927.

Blondheim, Menahem. *News Over the Wires.* Cambridge, Massachusetts: Harvard University Press, 1994.

Boyd-Barrett, Oliver. *International News Agencies.* Beverly Hills, California: Saga Publications, 1980.

Brackman, Arnold C. *Last Emperor.* New York, New York: Charles Scribner's Sons, 1975.

Braestrup Peter. *Big Story.* Garden City, New York: Doubleday, Anchor Books, 1978.

Brayman, Harold. *The President Speaks Off the Record.* Dow Jones Books, 1976.

Brinkley, David. *David Brinkley*. New York, New York: Alfred A. Knopf, 1995.

Brown, David and N. Richard Bruner, eds. *I Can Tell It Now*. Overseas Press Club. New York, New York: E. P. Dutton & Co., Inc., 1964.

Butler, David. *Fall of Saigon*. New York, New York: Simon and Schuster, 1985.

Canham, Erwin D. *Commitment to Freedom*. Cambridge, Massachusetts: Riverside Press, 1958.

Carroll, Wallace. *Persuade or Perish*. Boston, Massachusetts: Houghton Mifflin, 1948.

———. *We're in This with Russia*. Boston, Massachusetts: Houghton Mifflin, 1942.

Casey, Robert J. *I Can't Forget*. New York, New York: Bobbs-Merrill Co., 1941.

Casserly, Jack. *Divided Dynasty, a History of the First Family of American Journalism*. New York, New York: Donald I. Fine, Inc., 1993.

———. *Scripps, the Divided Dynasty*. New York, New York: Donald I. Fine, Inc., 1993.

Chaney, Lindsay, and Michael Cieply. *Hearst Family & Empire, the Later Years*. New York, New York: Simon & Schuster, 1981.

Chang, Iris, and William Kirby. *The Rape of Nankin*. New York, New York: Viking-Penguin, 1998.

Cheshire, Maxine with John Greenya. *Maxine Cheshire, Reporter*. Boston, Massachusetts: Houghton Mifflin Company, 1976.

Clapper, Olive. *One Lucky Woman*. Garden City, New York: Doubleday, 1961.

———. *Washington Tapestry*. New York, New York: Whittlesey House, 1946.

Clapper, Raymond. *Watching the World*. New York, New York: Whittlesey House, 1944.

Cloud, Stanley, and Lynne Olson. *Murrow's Boys*. Boston, Massachusetts: Houghton Mifflin Company, 1996.

Coblentz, Edmond D., ed. *William Randolph Hearst, A Portrait in His Own Words*. New York, New York: Simon and Schuster, 1943.

Cohen, Ronald E., and Gregory Gordon. *Down to the Wire UPI's Fight for Survival*. New York, New York: McGraw-Hill Publishing Company, 1990.

Cook, Philip, ed. *The Future of News: Television-Newspaper-Wire Services-News magazines*. Baltimore, Maryland: John Hopkins University Press, 1992.

Cooper, Kent. *Barriers Down*. New York, New York: Farrar & Rinehart, 1942.

———. *Kent Cooper and the Associated Press*. New York, New York: Random House, 1959.

Coughlin, William J. *Conquered Press: The MacArthur Era in Japanese Journalism*. Palo Alto, California: Pacific Books, 1952.

Cray, Ed. *General of the Army, George C. Marshall*. New York, New York: W. W. Norton, 1990.

Cronkite, Walter. *A Reporter's Life*. New York, New York: Random House, 1997.

Crozier, Emmett. *American Reporters on the Western Front 1914–1918*. New York, New York: Oxford University Press, 1959.

Custer, Joe James. *Through the Perilous Night: the Astoria's Last Battle*. New York, New York: Macmillan, 1944.

Daniliff, Nicholas. *Two Lives, One Russia*. Boston, Massachusetts: Houghton Mifflin, 1988.

Dennis, Charles H. *Victor Lawson*. Chicago, Illinois: University of Chicago Press, 1935.

Desmond, Robert W. *Tides of War.* Iowa City, Iowa: University of Iowa Press, 1984.

———. *Windows on the World: The Information Process in a Changing Society 1900–1920.* Iowa City, Iowa: University of Iowa Press, 1980.

———. *Information Process-World News Reporting to the Twentieth Century.* Iowa City, Iowa: University of Iowa Press, 1978.

Desmond, William. *Crisis and Conflict: World News Reporting Between Two Wars 1920–1940.* Iowa City, Iowa: University of Iowa Press, 1982.

Diamond, Edwin. *Behind the Times,* New York, New York: Villard Books, 1994.

Diehl, Charles Sanford. *Staff Correspondent: How the News of the World Is Collected and Dispatched by a Body of Trained Press Writers.* San Antonio, Texas: Clegg Company, 1931.

Dunn, William J. *Pacific Microphone.* College Station, Texas: Texas A&M University Press, 1988.

Duranty, Walter. *I Write as I Please.* New York, New York: Simon and Schuster, 1955.

Eastman, Max. *Great Companions.* New York, New York: Farrar, Straus and Cudahy, 1959.

Ebener, Charlotte. *No Facilities for Women.* New York, New York: Alfred A. Knopf, 1955.

Edwards, Julia. *Women of the World.* Boston, Massachusetts: Houghton Mifflin Company, 1988.

Ellis, Edward Robb. *Diary of the Century: Tales from America's Greatest Diarist, 1927–1995.* New York, Tokyo, London: Kodansha International, 1995.

Emery, Edwin. *History of American Newspaper Publishers Association.* Minneapolis, Minnesota: University of Minnesota Press, 1950.

Emery, Michael. *On the Front Lines.* Washington, D.C.: American University Press, 1995.

Epstein, Edward Jay. *Legend: The Secret World of Lee Harvey Oswald.* New York, New York: McGraw-Hill Book Company, 1978.

Ernery, Edwin and Michael. *The Press and America: An Interpretive History of the Mass Media.* Englewood Cliffs, New Jersey: Prentice Hall, 1978.

Farr, Finis. *Fair Enough: The Life of Westbrook Pegler.* New Rochelle, New York: Arlington House, 1975.

Fenby, John. *International News Service.* New York, New York: Schocken Books, 1986.

Friedrich, Otto. *Grave of Alice B. Toklas.* New York, New York: Henry Holt and Company, 1989.

Gardner, Gilson. *Lusty Scripps, the Life of E.W. Scripps, 1854–1926.* New York, New York: Vanguard Press, 1932.

Gates, Gary. *Air Time, the Inside Story of CBS News.* New York, New York: Harper & Row, 1978.

Glasser, Theodor. *Language of News.*

Gohlke, Mary with Max Jennings. *I'll Take Tomorrow.* New York, New York: M. Evans & Company, 1985.

Gould, Randall. *China in the Sun.* Garden City, New York: Doubleday, 1946.

Government Press Services. United Nations, Geneva, 1935.

Graham, Katherine. *Personal History.* New York, New York: Alfred A. Knopf, 1997.

Gramling, Oliver. *AP: The Story of News,* New York: J. J. Little, 1940.

Hachten, William A. *World News Prism.* Ames, Iowa: Iowa State University Press, 1981.

Halberstam, David. *Making of a Quagmire.* New York, New York: Random House, 1965.

Hammond, William M. *Reporting Vietnam.* Lawrence, Kansas: University Press of Kansas, 1998.

Hasokawa, Bill. *Thunder in the Rockies.* New York, New York: William Morrow, 1976.

Healy, George W., Jr. *Lifetime on Deadline.* Gretna, Louisiana: Pelican Publishing Company, 1976.

Herr, Michael. *Dispatches.* New York, New York: Alfred Knopf, 1978.

Hersh, Seymour M. *Dark Side of Camelot.* New York, New York: Little Brown and Company, 1997.

Hertsgaard, Mark. *On Bended Knee, the Press and the Reagan Presidency.* New York, New York: Farrar Straus Giroux, 1988.

Hess, Stephen. *International News & Foreign Correspondents.* Washington, D.C.: Brookings Institution Press, 1996.

Hoberecht, Earnest. *Asia Is My Beat.* Tokyo, Japan: Tuttle, 1961.

Hohenberg, John. *Foreign Correspondence: The Great Reporters and Their Times.* New York, New York: Columbia University Press, 1964.

———. *Pulitzer Prize Story II, 1959–1980.* New York, New York: Columbia University Press, 1980.

———. *The Pursuit of Excellence.* Gainesville, Florida: University Press of Florida, 1995.

Hoyt, Ken, and Frances S. Leighton. *Drunk Before Noon: the Behind-the-Scenes Story of the Washington Press Corps.* Prentice-Hall International, Inc., 1979.

Hoyt, Kendall K. *Ink & Avgas.* Aviation Writers Association, 1936.

Hunt, Frazier. *One American and His Attempt at Education.* New York, New York: Simon & Schuster, 1938.

Iwanagal, S. *Story of Japanese News Agencies.* 1980.

Jim Fallows. *Breaking the News.* New York, New York: Random House, 1996.

Kent, Ruth Kimball. *Language of Journalism.* Kent, Ohio: Kent State University Press, 1970.

Kilgallen, James L. *It's a Great Life, My 50 Years as a Newspaperman.* New York, New York: International News Service, 1956.

Kluger, Richard. *The Paper: The Life and Death of the New York Herald Tribune.* New York, New York: Alfred Knopf, 1986.

Knight, Mary. *On My Own.* New York, New York: MacMillan, 1938.

Knightley, Phillip. *First Casualty.* New York, New Yoprk: Harcourt Brace & Jovanovich, 1975.

Koenigsberg, M. *King News.* Philadelphia, PA, New York, New York: F. A. Stokes Company, 1941.

Krulak, Theodore E. *Two Faces of Tass.* Minneapolis, Minnesota: University of Minnesota Press, 1962.

Lande, Nathaniel. *Dispatches from the Front.* New York, New York: Henry Holt, 1995.

Lee, Alfred McClung. *Daily Newspaper in America.* New York, New York: MacMillan Company.

Lee, James M. *A History of American Journalism.* Boston, Massachusetts: Houghton Mifflin, 1923.

Liebling, A. J. *Press.* New York, New York: Ballantine Books, 1961.

Lippman, Walter. *Public Opinion.* New York, New York: Simon & Schuster, 1922.

Lorenz, Larry, and John Vivian. *News: Reporting and Writing.* Needham Heights, Massachusetts: Allyn & Bacon, 1996.

Lundberg, Ferdinand. *Imperial Hearst: A Social Biography.* New York, New York: Modern Library, 1936.

Lutz, William W. *News of Detroit.* Boston, Massachusetts: Little, Brown and Company, 1973.

Lyons, Eugene. *Assignment in Utopia,* New York, New York: Harcourt, Brace and Company, 1937.

Lyons, Louis M., ed. *Reporting the News. Selections from Nieman Reports.* Cambridge, Massachusetts: Belknap Press of Harvard University Press, 1965.

Macvane, John. *On the Air in World War II.* New York, New York: William Morrow and Company, 1979.

Manchester, William. *Death of a President.* New York, New York: Harper & Row, 1963.

Matthews, Joseph J. *Reporting the Wars.* Minneapolis, Minnesota: University of Minnesota Press, 1957.

Mayer, Martin. *Making News.* Boston, Massachusetts: Harvard Business School Press, 1993.

McCabe, Charles R., ed. *Damned Old Crank.* New York, New York: Harper & Brothers, 1951.

McDougall, William H., Jr. *By Eastern Windows.* New York, New York: Charles Scribner's Sons, 1949.

McDougall, William. *Six Bells Off Java.* New York, New York: Charles Scribner's Sons, 1948.

McRae, Milton. *Forty Years in Newspaperdom.* New York, New York: Brentano's, 1924.

Means, Gaston B., and May Dixon Thacker. *Strange Death of President Harding.* New York, New York: Guild Press Ltd., 1930.

Melnik, Stefan R. *Eurovision News and the International Flow of Information: History, Problems and Perspectives 1960–1980.* Bochum, West Germany: N. Brockmeyer, 1981.

Merrill, John C. *Global Journalism.* New York, New York: Longman, 1990.

Merriman Smith's Book of Presidents, A White House Memoir. Edited by Timothy G. Smith, forward by Robert J. Donovan, New York, New York: W.W. Norton & Co., 1972.

Miller, Lee G. *The Story of Ernie Pyle.* New York, New York: Viking Press, 1960.

Miller, Webb. *I Found No Peace: The Journal of a Foreign Correspondent.* Garden City Press, 1938.

Misselwitz, Henry. *The Dragon Stirs.* New York, New York: Harbinger House, 1941.

Mitchell, Dave, Cathy Mitchell and Richard Ofshe. *Light on Synanon.* New York, New York: Seaview Books, 1980.

Moore, Harold G. and Joseph L. Galloway. *We Were Soldiers Once...and Young.* New York, New York: Random House, 1992.

Moore, Herbert. *More News After This....* Warrenton, Virginia: Sun Dial Press, 1983.

Morris, Joe Alex. *Deadline Every Minute.* Garden City, New York: Doubleday & Company, 1957. Republished by Greenwood, 1968.

Mosby, Aline. *View from No. 13 People's Street.* New York, New York: Random House, 1962.

Mott, Frank Luther. *American Journalism, A History 1690–1960.* New York, New York: Macmillan Co., 1962.

———. *News in America.* Cambridge, Massachusetts: Harvard University Press, 1962.

Nasaw, David. *Chief, The Life of William Randolph Hearst.* New York, New York: Houghton Mifflin Co., 2000.

Negley, C. *E. W. Scripps.* New York, New York: D. Cochrane, 1933.

Newman, Edwin. *Strictly Speaking.* New York, New York: Bobbs-Merrill Company, 1974.

News Agencies, Their Structure and Operation, UNESCO 1953, reprint by Greenwood Press, 1969.

Newsom, Phil. *United Press Radio News Style Book.* New York, New York: United Press Association, 1943.

Oechsner, Frederick. *This Is the Enemy.* Boston, Massachusetts: Little, Brown and Company, 1942.

Oestreicher, J. C. *The World Is Their Beat.* New York, New York: Essential Books, 1945.

Othman, Fred. *Man on the Half Shell.* New York, New York: McGraw Hill, 1947.

Overseas Press Club of America. *Deadline Delayed.* New York, New York: E. P. Dutton & Co., 1947.

Packard, Reynolds and Eleanor. *Balcony Empire.* New York, New York: Oxford University Press, 1942.

Packard, Reynolds. *Dateline Paris.* New York, New York: Berkley Publishing Corp., 1959. (This is a reprint of *Kansas City Milkman.*)

Page, Tim. *NAM.* New York, New York: Alfred A. Knopf, 1983.

Parris, John A., and Ned Russell. *Springboard to Berlin: The Story of the African Invasion.* New York, New York, Crowell, 1943.

Payne, George Henry. *History of Journalism in the United States.* New York, New York: D. Appleton, 1920.

Pegler, Westbrook. *Taint Right.* New York, New York: Doubleday, 1936.

———. *The Dissenting Opinions of Mr. Pegler.* New York, New York: Scribners, 1938.

Persico, Joseph E. *Edward R. Murrow.* New York, New York: McGraw Hill, 1988.

Phillips, Cabell, ed. *Dateline Washington.* Garden City, New York: Doubleday, 1949.

Phillips, Walter Polk. *My Debut in Journalism and Other Odd Happenings.* New York, New York: International Telegram Company, 1882.

Pilat, Oliver R. *Pegler: Angry Man of the Press.* Boston, Massachusetts: Beacon Press, 1963.

———. *Drew Pearson, an Unauthorized Biography.* New York: Harper's Magazine Press, 1973.

Poats, Rutherford M. *Decision in Korea, an Authentic History of the Korean War.* New York, New York: McBride, 1954.

Powers, Thomas, *Man Who Kept the Secrets, Richard Helms and the CIA*. New York, New York: Alfred A. Knopf, 1979.

Prochnau, William. *Once Upon a Distant War*. New York, New York: Random House, 1995.

Pyle, Ernie. *Brave Men*. New York, New York: Grosset & Dunlap, 1944. (Copyright Scripps-Howard Newspaper Alliance.)

———. *Here Is Your War*. New York, New York: Henry Holt & Co., 1943.

Ramsey, Guy. *One Continent Redeemed*. London, England: George G. Harper & Co., 1943.

Rantanen, Terhi. *Mr. Howard Goes to South America, the United Press Associations and Foreign Expansion*. Bloomington, Indiana: Indiana University Press, 1992.

———. "Howard, Roy and Stalin." Monographs in Journalism and Mass Communications, 1994.

Read, Donald. *Power of News: A History of Reuters*. New York, New York: Oxford University Press, 1992.

Reed, John. *Ten Days that Shook the World*. New York, New York: Mentor/New American, 1967.

Reston, James. *Sketches in the Sand*. New York, New York: Alfred A. Knopf, 1967.

Reynolds, Quentin, and Robert Leckie, eds. *With Fire and Sword*. New York, New York: Dial Press, 1963.

Richard McMillan. *Mediterranean Assignment*. New York, New York: Doubleday, 1943.

Righter, Rosemary. *Whose News: Politics, the Press and the Third World*. New York, New York: Times Books, 1978.

Rivers, William L. *Other Government, Power and the Washington Media*. New York, New York: Universe Books, 1982.

———. *Mass Media (2nd edition)*. New York, New York: Harper & Row, 1975.

Robertson, Pat. *Plan*. Nashville, Tennessee: T. Nelson Publishers, 1989.

Robinson, Michael J., and Margaret A. Sheehan. *Over the Wire and on TV: CBS and UPI in Campaign '80*. New York, New York: Russell Sage Foundation, 1980.

Rooney, Andy. *My War*. New York, New York: Random House, 1995.

Rosenblum, Mort. *Coups and Earthquakes*. New York, New York: Harper and Row, 1979.

———. *Who Stole the News?: Why We Can't Keep Up with What Happens in the World and What We Can Do About It*. New York, New York: John Wiley & Sons, 1993.

Rosewater, Victor. *History of Cooperative News-Gathering in the United States*. New York, New York: A. Appleton, 1930.

Ross, Ishbel. *Ladies of the Press: The Story of Women in Journalism by an Insider*. New York, New York: Harper & Brothers, 1936.

Rosten, Leo C. *Washington Correspondents*. New York, New York: Harcourt Brace Co., 1957.

Rubens, Doris. *Bread and Rice*. New York, New York: Thurston Macauley Associates, 1947.

Rutland, Robert A. *Newsmongers, Journalism in the Life of the Nation, 1690–1972*. New York, New York: Dial Press, 1973.

Salinger, Pierre. *With Kennedy*. Garden City, New York: Doubleday & Company, Inc., 1966.

Salisbury, Harrison. *Journey for Our Times*. New York, New York: Harper & Row, 1983.

———. *Russia on the Way*. New York, New York: Macmillan Company, 1946.

———. *Without Fear or Favor*. New York, New York: Times Books, 1980.

Salmon, Lucy Maynard. *The Newspaper and the Historian.* New York, New York: Oxford University Press, 1923.

Scharff, Edward E. *Wordly Power: The Making of the Wall Street Journal.* New York, New York: Beaufort Books, 1986.

Schwarzlose, Richard Allen. *Nation's Newsbrokers.* Evanston, Illinois: Northwestern University Press, 1990.

Scripps, E. W. *I Protest.* Edited by Oliver Knight. Madison, Wisconsin: University of Wisconsin Press, 1966.

Scripps-Howard Handbook, 1983, Update of Third Revised Edition 1981. The E. W. Scripps Company, Cincinnati, Ohio

Seldes, George. *Facts Are…: A Guide to Falsehood and Propaganda in the Press and Radio.* New York, New York: In Fact, 1942.

———. *Freedom of the Press.* DeCapo Press, 1935.

———. *Tell the Truth and Run: My 44 Years Fighting for a Free Press.* New York, New York: Greenberg, 1953.

———. *Witness to a Century: Encounters with the Noted, the Notorious and the Three S.O.B.'s.* New York, New York: Ballantine Books, 1988.

Sevareid, Eric. *Not So Wild a Dream.* New York, New York: Alfred A. Knopf, 1946.

Sevy, Grace, ed. *American Experience in Vietnam.* Norman, Oklahoma: University of Oklahoma Press, 1989.

Shenkman, Richard. *Legends, Lies & Cherished Myths of American History.* New York, New York: William Morrow & Co., 1988.

Sheehan, Neil. *Bright Shining Lie.* New York, New York: Random House, 1988.

Shirer, William L. *Berlin Diary,* New York, New York: Knopf, 1941.

———. *Twentieth Century Journey.* New York, New York: Simon & Schuster, 1976.

———. *Native's Return.* Boston, Massachusetts: Little, Brown and Company, 1990.

Smith, H. Allen. *Low Man on a Totem Pole.* New York, New York: Doubleday, 1941.

———. *To Hell in a Handbasket: The Education of a Humorist.* Garden City, New York: Doubleday, 1962.

Smith, Howard K. *Events Leading Up to My Death.* New York, New York: St. Martin's Press, 1996.

Smith, Merriman. *Good News Days.* New York, New York: Bobbs-Merrill, 1962.

———. *Meet Mr. Eisenhower.* New York, New York: Harper's, 1955.

———. *Thank You, Mr. President.* New York, New York: Harper & Brothers, 1946.

Snyder, Louis L., and Richard B. Morris, eds. *Treasury of Great Reporting.* New York, New York: Simon & Schuster, 1949.

Sore, Nancy Caldwell. *Women Who Wrote the War.* New York, New York: Arcade Publishing, 1999.

Squires, James. *Read All About It: The Corporate Takeover of American Newspapers.* New York, New York: Times Books, 1994.

St. John, Robert. *Foreign Correspondent.* Garden City, New York: Doubleday & Company, 1957.

Stealey, O. O. *Twenty Years in the Press Gallery.* Published by author, 1906.

Stein, M. L. *Under Fire: The Story of American War Correspondents.* New York, New York: Julian Messner div. of Simon & Schuster, 1968.

Steinbeck, John. *Once There Was a War.* New York, New York: Viking Press, 1958.

Stenbuck, Jack, ed. *Typewriter Battalions.* New York, New York: William Morrow and Company, 1995

Stevenson, Robert L., and Donald Lewis Shaw, eds. *Foreign News and the New World Information Order.* Ames, Iowa: Iowa State University Press, 1984.

Stone, Melville. *"M.E.S." His Book, A Tribute and a Souvenir of the Twenty-Five Years 1893-1918 of the Services of Melville E. Stone as the General Manager of the Associated Press.* New York, New York, Harper & Bros., 1918.

———. *Fifty Years a Journalist.* New York, New York: Doubleday, 1923.

Stringer, Ann. *German Faces.* New York, New York: William Sloan Associates, 1950.

Swanburg, W. A. *Citizen Hearst,* New York, New York: Scribner's Sons, 1961.

Swing, Raymond. *Good Evening.* New York, New York: Harcourt, Brace & World, 1964.

Talese, Gay. *Kingdom and Power.* New York, New York: New American Library, 1966.

Taylor, S. J. *Stalin's Apologist.* New York, New York: Oxford University Press, 1990.

Thomas, Helen. *Dateline White House.* New York, New York: Macmillan Publishing Co., Inc., 1975.

Toland,, John. *In Mortal Combat.* New York, New York: William Morrow and Co., 1991.

Tregaskis, Richard. *Guadalcanal Diary.* New York, New York: Random House, 1943.

Trimble, Vance H. *Astonishing Mr. Scripps: The Turbulent Life of America's Penny Press Lord.* Ames, Iowa: Iowa State University Press, 1992.

Truman, Margaret. *Harry S. Truman.* New York, New York: William Morrow and Company, 1973.

Tuohy, William. *Dangerous Company: Inside the World's Hottest Trouble Spots with a Pulitzer Prize-winning War Correspondent.* New York, New York: William Morrow and Company, Inc., 1987.

United Press Manual, 1929.

United States vs Associated Press. 52 Federal Supplement 362 (New York 1943) affirmed in 326, United States Reports (1945).

UPI and American Heritage Magazine. *Four Days.* American Heritage Publishing Company, 1964.

UPI Stylebook, 3rd Edition. NTC. Lindenwood, Illinois: United Press International, 1977.

Vaughn, Miles. *Covering the Far East.* New York, New York: Covici Friede, 1936.

Villard, Oswald Garrison. *Disappearing Daily.* New York, New York: Knopf, 1940.

von Kaltenborn, Hans. *It Seems Like Yesterday.* New York, New York: G. P. Putnam's Sons, 1956.

Voss, Frederick. *Reporting the War: The Journalistic Coverage of World War II.* Washington, D.C.: Smithsonian Institute Press, 1994.

———. *Reporting World War II: American Journalism 1938–1946.* New York, New York: Library of America, 1995.

Waugh, Evelyn. *Scoop*. Boston, Massachusetts: Little, Brown and Company, 1937.

Whipple, Sidney B. *Scandalous Princess: The Exquisite Teresia Cabarrus*. New York, New York: Century Company, 1932.

———. *The Lindbergh Crime*. New York, New York: Blue Ribbons Books, 1935.

White, Graham J. *FDR and the Press*. Chicago, Illinois: University of Chicago Press, 1979.

White, Theodore H. *In Search of History*. New York, New York: Warner Books, 1979.

Whittemore, Hank. *CNN, the Inside Story*. New York, New York: Little Brown, 1990.

Wicker, Tom. *On Press*. New York, New York: Berkeley Publishing Group, 1979.

Willard, Jack. *Wire God*. New York, New York: Doubleday & Company, 1953.

Willenson, Kim. *Bad Wars: An Oral History of the Vietnam War*. New York, New York: New American Library, 1987.

Winchell, Walter. *Winchell Exclusive: "Things That Happened to Me—and Me to Them."* Englewood, New Jersey: Prentice-Hall, 1975.

Wren, Christopher, *Hacks*. New York, New York: Simon & Schuster, 1996.

Wyatt, Clarence R. *Paper Soldiers: The American Press and the Vietnam War*. Chicago, Illinois: University of Chicago Press, 1993.

Zelizer, Barabie. *JFK Press*. Chicago, Illinois: Chicago University Press, 1992.

Index

About
the Authors

RICHARD M. HARNETT joined United Press in San Francisco in 1951 and spent thirty-six years with the company, all in the San Francisco bureau. A veteran of World War II, Harnett served as UP's Asian editor during the Korean War and was later named California state editor and San Francisco bureau manager. He left UPI in 1987 to help Market News International establish an information network. A native of Devils Lake, North Dakota, Harnett earned his journalism degree from Marquette University after a stint in the public information office of the Army of occupation in Japan. Shortly after retiring, Harnett published *Wirespeak*, a book about wire service codes and jargon. He also published a newsletter for and about UP-UPI veterans called "-95-" and later established an internet chat-wire linking Unipressers around the world via the web. Harnett died at the age of seventy-four in a Virginia hospital on February 24, 2001, in Palo Alto, California, shortly after completing the manuscript for *Unipress* in collaboration with Billy Ferguson. He was survived by his wife of fifty-one years, Joyce, and seven children.

BILLY G. FERGUSON spent forty years with UP and UPI. A veteran of World War II, he went to work for UP as a sports writer in Atlanta after two years with the Jacksonville (Florida) *Journal* and wound up as UPI's managing editor in Washington in 1990. In between, Ferguson sampled just about everything a wire service could offer. He covered state legislatures, racial unrest in the South, the Apollo-11 landing on the moon and the development of UPI's broadcast services. He was heavily involved in UPI's technological changes, including computerization of UPI's news wires. Ferguson worked in the Atlanta, Chicago and Washington bureaus. He now is a part-time journalism instructor at Columbia College in Chicago and lives with his wife, Betty, in Evanston, Illinois.